FREDERIC SEEBOHM

TRIBAL CUSTOM IN ANGLO-SAXON LAW

Elibron Classics
www.elibron.com

Elibron Classics series.

ISBN 1-4021-0311-5 (paperback)
ISBN 1-4021-0310-7 (hardcover)

This Elibron Classics Replica Edition is an unabridged facsimile of the edition published in 1902 by Longmans, Green, and Co., London, New York and Bombay.

TRIBAL CUSTOM
IN ANGLO-SAXON LAW

TRIBAL CUSTOM
IN ANGLO-SAXON LAW

BEING AN ESSAY SUPPLEMENTAL TO

(1) 'THE ENGLISH VILLAGE COMMUNITY'

(2) 'THE TRIBAL SYSTEM IN WALES'

BY

FREDERIC SEEBOHM, LL.D., F.S.A.

LONGMANS, GREEN, AND CO.

39 PATERNOSTER ROW, LONDON

NEW YORK AND BOMBAY

1902

PREFACE

To the two former Essays, on 'The English Village Community' and 'The Tribal System in Wales,' is now at last added in this volume a third on 'Tribal Custom in Anglo-Saxon Law.'

In the first Essay an attempt was made to approach the early Anglo-Saxon evidence from the point of view of the Manorial system, and mainly by tracing back its connection with the open field system of agriculture—the shell, so to speak, in which it had all along apparently lived.

The object of this third Essay in the trilogy is to approach the Anglo-Saxon laws from the point of view of tribal custom.

As a preliminary to this attempt, a detailed study of Cymric tribal custom was made in the intermediate Essay in the belief that the knowledge so gained might be used as a clue to the understanding of survivals of tribal custom in the laws of the tribes most nearly allied to the invaders of Britain, and lastly in the Anglo-Saxon laws themselves.

The interval which has elapsed between the publication of the three Essays has made it necessary to make each of them, to some extent, independent and complete in itself.

It thus becomes necessary in this volume briefly to repeat, as well as further to develop, what was learned of Cymric tribal custom in the previous volume, especially as regards the 'gwely,' or family unit of tribal society, and as regards the methods of payment of the galanas, or death-fine for homicide in lieu of the blood-feud between kindreds.

The death-fine or wergeld of the Continental tribes forms so important a test of the position of classes in tribal society that it became necessary to ascertain at the outset what were the currencies in which the wergelds were stated and paid. A brief explanation of these will be found in the first chapter.

Then follows the summary of the Cymric evidence. And as some of the points connected with the payment of wergelds can only be rightly understood when regarded from the point of view of the blood-feud for which the wergeld was a substitute, the Cymric evidence is followed by a brief examination of the rules of the feud incidentally revealed in 'Beowulf.'

A chapter on Irish or Goidelic tribal custom completes the preliminary evidence.

The inquiry into the tribal custom of the Continental tribes as revealed in their laws is proceeded with in the following order :—

First the Burgundian and Wisigothic laws are briefly examined, as showing most clearly the disintegration of tribal custom caused by early contact with Roman and Christian influences.

Next are examined the traces of tribal custom in the laws of the Salic and Ripuarian Franks and of the tribes conquered by the Merovingian Kings. Separate consideration is then given to the laws of the tribes conquered by Charlemagne.

The earliest Norse and Scanian laws next claim a full share of attention; for, although much later in date than the others, they exhibit earlier conditions of tribal custom.

Lastly, after a short chapter on tribal custom in the ancient laws of Scotland and the 'leges inter Brettos et Scotos,' attention is turned to the Anglo-Saxon laws, and they are approached from the tribal point of view and the vantage-ground afforded by the previous study of the tribal customs of the Continental tribes.

That by this method of study some fresh light may have been thrown on the conditions of early Anglo-Saxon society I think the reader will admit. And imperfectly as the work has been done, the bringing of Anglo-Saxon evidence more into line with the Continental evidence will, I think, be accepted as a permanent gain.

After all, we are but trying to advance a step or two further, as regards some particular points, the general intention of the masterly contributions of Dr. Konrad von Maurer, made nearly half a century ago to the *Kritische Ueberschau*, which I think have hardly been sufficiently kept in view by English historical students.

How far the evidence contained in this Essay may be found on full consideration to modify previous views of others or my own the reader will be left to judge. I have tried throughout to bring an open mind to the inquiry from a fresh point of view, with but little regard to foregone conclusions. Any new facts elicited will find their proper place without displacing those already known, however much they may ultimately modify the conclusions provisionally drawn from the latter.

The method of inquiry from the known to the unknown is essentially a tentative method. It necessarily leads to results which, if isolated, easily mislead and may be still more easily misapprehended. But correction comes with perseverance in the same method from other points of view, whilst in the intermediate stages of such an inquiry the student has to learn to be content sometimes with a provisional restatement of a problem rather than a premature solution.

It would be absurd to pretend that, were it necessary to rewrite the Essay on 'The English Village Community' after an interval of nearly twenty years, modification of many points might not be needful. But as further editions were called for, it seemed best to leave it as it was, a link in a chain of inquiry which has not yet come to an end. Other links have been added by far more competent inquirers, and these have generously given it a place in the chain from which it would indeed be ungrateful in me to wish to unlink it. But I venture to hope that the addition of this third Essay will be accepted not only as a further contribution to the understanding of a difficult subject, but also as evidence that kindly criticism of the former volumes has not been thrown away.

For constant help in the preparation of this volume I am indebted to my son, whose essay on 'The Structure of Greek Tribal Society' really ought to form one of this series. My thanks are due to Dr. ATKINSON and Prof. RHYS for help as regards the Irish and Welsh chapters; and to Mr. CRAIGIE for careful revision of the text and translations of the passages quoted from the early Norse laws. To Prof. LIEBERMANN and Mr. W. H. STEVENSON, for help in the reading of some difficult passages in the Kentish laws, I am especially indebted. I regret very much that I have not had the help which Prof. LIEBERMANN'S notes to his text of the Anglo-Saxon laws would have been. To Mr. F. G. HILL, of the British Museum, I owe very much in connection with the study of the currencies used in the various laws. Finally, I cannot too warmly express my gratitude especially to Prof. VINOGRADOFF, Prof. MAITLAND, and Mr. W. J. CORBETT, amongst others, for the help and encouragement which only fellow-workers can give to the otherwise solitary student.

THE HERMITAGE, HITCHIN:
January 1, 1902.

CONTENTS

CHAPTER I.

THE CURRENCY IN WHICH WERGELDS WERE RECKONED AND PAID.

CHAPTER II.

SUMMARY OF THE CYMRIC EVIDENCE.

CHAPTER III.

CHAPTER IV.

TRIBAL CUSTOM OF THE IRISH TRIBES

CHAPTER V.

THE WERGELDS OF THE BURGUNDIAN AND WISIGOTHIC LAWS

CHAPTER VI.

TRIBAL CUSTOMS OF FRANKS AND OF THE TRIBES CONQUERED BY THE MEROVINGIAN KINGS.

CHAPTER VII.

TRIBAL CUSTOMS OF THE TRIBES CONQUERED BY CHARLEMAGNE.

CHAPTER VIII.

THE TRIBAL CUSTOMS OF THE OLDEST SCANDINAVIAN LAWS.

CHAPTER IX.

TRIBAL CUSTOM IN SCOTLAND.

CHAPTER X.

ANGLO-SAXON CUSTOM FROM THE NORMAN POINT OF VIEW.

CHAPTER XI.

DANISH VIEW OF ANGLO-SAXON CUSTOM

CHAPTER XII.

ANGLO-SAXON CUSTOM FROM THE VIKING OR NORTHMEN'S POINT OF VIEW.

CHAPTER XIII.

EARLY ANGLO-SAXON CUSTOM.

CHAPTER XIV.

THE LAWS OF THE KENTISH KINGS.

CHAPTER I.

THE CURRENCY IN WHICH WERGELDS WERE RECKONED AND PAID.

I. CONNECTION BETWEEN THE WERGELD OF 100 HEAD OF CATTLE AND THE MINA OF 100 GOLD STATERS.

The currencies in which wergelds were paid

THE inquiry pursued in this volume partakes so much of the character of a study of the wergelds of the various tribes of North-western Europe that it becomes necessary as briefly as possible to call attention at the outset to the currencies in which they were reckoned and paid.

Cows.

The Cymric galanas or death fine was reckoned in cows, and the cows were equated with silver.

Female slaves.

The Irish 'eric' of the Brehon laws was stated in *cumhals* or female slaves, and lesser payments in cows and heifers, and these were all equated with silver.

Silver.

The Anglo-Saxon wergelds were stated, with perhaps one exception, in silver scillings.

The wergelds of the Scandinavian tribes were generally stated in their laws in silver marks, ores, and ortugs, with the equivalent in gold at a ratio of 1 : 8, and also in cows.

Gold solidi.

Those of the Continental German tribes were generally stated in gold solidi, but the statements were sometimes supplemented by clauses describing the value of the animals, whether oxen or cows, in which the payments were, in practice, still evidently made, at the date of the laws.

Early equation between cattle and gold.

Professor Ridgeway[1] has shown that the equation between cattle and gold may go back a long way into the past of Eastern tradition. The result of his careful inquiry was the brilliant suggestion that the ox—the most usual unit of payment in agricultural countries—was very early and very generally equated in Assyrian, Babylonian, Persian, and Greek usage with the gold stater or didrachma.

Greek stater the ox-unit.

The stater was reckoned in Greek usage as of 192 wheat-grains.[2] It was divided into 6 diobols of 32 wheat-grains. And throughout the East the usual multiples of the stater were the *light mina* of 50 staters and the *heavy mina* of 100 staters or 19,200 wheat-grains.[3]

---

[1] *Origin of Currency and Weight Standards*, Camb. U. Press, 1892.

[2] For convenience I adhere throughout to reckoning in *wheat-grains*. Professor Ridgeway informs me that three barleycorns were equated with four wheat-grains, and that a passage in Theophrastus shows that in the fourth century B.C. 12 barleycorns = obol and 12 obols = the stater. The Greek diobol = therefore 24 barleycorns, *i.e.* 32 wheat-grains, and the stater = 144 barleycorns, *i.e.* 192 wheat-grains. The reader will understand that as Romans, Celts, Anglo-Saxons, and Normans reckoned in wheat-grains, there will be great convenience in adhering throughout to wheat-grains in this inquiry. And further the theoretic building up of weights in wheat-grains was preserved traditionally more easily than the actual standards of weight.

[3] The range of the variation in the actual weight of the stater as a coin (without necessarily implying variation in the theoretic weight in wheat-grains) is given by metrologists as follows:

	Grammes
Babylonian . . .	8·18
Crœsus . . .	8·18
Darius . . .	8·36 to 8·41
Attic . . .	8·64 to 8·73
Philip of Macedon and Alexander the Great . . .	8·73
The Greek cities on the Black Sea .	9·06.

Now if the gold stater of 192 wheat-grains is to be recognised as the ox-unit in traditional equations between cattle and gold, another very important recognition suggests itself.

Normal wergelds of 100 head of cattle

Wergelds being first paid in cattle, it was natural that a round number of cattle should be chosen, and instances are not wanting in the Eastern world suggesting that 'a hundred head of cattle' was a customary normal wergeld of wide prevalence.

Among the Arabs to this day Professor Robertson Smith states [1] that the camel is the unit of payment, and that, in a feud between two Meccan tribes, the manslayer has the alternative of paying 100 camels or bringing 50 of his kin to take oath of purgation, or lastly of abiding the blood-feud.

According to the laws of Manu, if one of the highest of the twice-born Brahman class slew one of the Warrior class involuntarily, he might cleanse himself by paying to the Brahmans or priests 1000 cows and a bull. If he slew one of the agricultural or trading class, the payment was 100 cows and a bull. If he slew one of the servile class, the payment was 10 cows and a bull.[2]

In this case 100 cows seem to have been the normal wergeld, and the wergelds of those of higher or lower caste or rank seem to have been multiples or fractions of it.

In Homer there are indications of the same thing. Lycaon was sold as a captive for 100 oxen and

[1] *Kinship &c. in Arabia*, p. 53.

[2] *Ordinances of Manu*, xi. pp. 128–131.

redeemed as a chieftain's son for 300 oxen—being apparently valued at a threefold wergeld on account of his recognised princely rank.

Iliad, XXI. 39. 'And at that time he sold him into well-peopled Lemnos, sending him on shipboard, and the son of Jason gave a price for him and thence a guest-friend freed him with a great ransom, Eetion of Imbros, and sent him to goodly Arisbe; whence flying secretly he came to his father's house (at Troy). Eleven days he rejoiced among his friends after he was come from Lemnos, but on the twelfth once more God brought him into the hands of Achilles again.'

71. 'Then Lykaon besought him . . . . At thy table first I tasted meal of Demeter on the day when thou didst take me captive in the well-ordered orchard, and didst sell me away from my father (Priam) and my friends unto goodly Lemnos, and *I fetched thee the price of an hundred oxen.* And now I have been ransomed *for thrice that*, and this is my twelfth morn since I came to Ilios after much pain.'

The normal wergeld equated with the gold mina of 100 staters.

Now if a herd of 100 head of cattle had come to be a common normal wergeld in the Eastern world, and if the gold stater had come to be regarded as the ox-unit, it follows that the heavy gold mina of 100 staters would easily come to be adopted as a common equivalent for the wergeld of 100 head of cattle.

Nor are we without examples which show that this connection of the wergeld with the gold mina was not altogether foreign to traditional modes of thought.

In the laws of Gortyn[1] a man whose life was forfeit for crime might be redeemed by his kindred for 100 staters, *i.e.* the heavy gold mina.

The ransom of prisoners between certain Greek

[1] Sections 8 and 11.

tribes or states according to Herodotus was two minas, *i.e.* one heavy mina.[1]

There is a curious instance in the Mosaic law of the connection of something like a wergeld with the mina of silver. In the last chapter of Leviticus the price to be paid for the redemption of a man dedicated by a vow to the service of the Sanctuary was 50 shekels of silver: that is, the light mina of silver.

II. THE SAME EQUATION REPEATED BETWEEN THE WERGELDS OF WESTERN TRIBES AND 200 GOLD SOLIDI OF CONSTANTINE.

The gold solidus of Constantine a half-stater.

Following the same thread of suggestion and turning from the Eastern to the Western world, we pass at a leap from the Eastern gold stater of 192 wheat-grains to the gold solidus of Constantine, of exactly half that number.

Up to the time of Constantine there had been confusion in the currency of the Roman Empire. It had been mainly a silver currency. Few gold coins were in general circulation, and these were of various standards. But at last the gold solidus of Constantine placed the world in possession of a fixed gold standard acknowledged all over Europe and remaining unchanged till the fall of the Eastern Empire.

The importance of this fact is obvious. For our knowledge of most of the wergelds of the tribes conquered by the Merovingian Franks and later on by Charlemagne is dependent upon it, inasmuch as the laws in which the customs of these tribes were in

[1] Herod. v. c. 77 and vi. c. 79.

some sense codified, almost always describe the wergelds in gold solidi.

The gold solidus of Constantine was fixed by him at $\frac{1}{72}$ of the Roman pound or $\frac{1}{6}$ of the Roman ounce.

The Roman pound (originally used for copper) was built up from the scripulum according to the duodecimal system of the *As*, thus :

Scripulum	24	wheat-grains	= 1·135	grammes
Uncia (of 24)	576	"	= 27·25	"
Libra (of 288)	6912	"	= 327·	"

Gold tremisses of 32 wheat-grains.

The solidus of Constantine therefore contained 96 wheat-grains of gold, exactly the same number as the Eastern drachma, and half that of the stater or didrachma. At the same time smaller coins—thirds of the solidus, called *trientes* or *tremisses*—were issued in great numbers, and these tremisses contained 32 wheat-grains of gold, exactly the same number as the Greek *diobol.*

The normal wergeld of 200 gold solidi = gold mina.

So that, in wheat-grains, the very prevalent statement of the wergeld of the full freeman in the laws of various tribes as 200 gold solidi was in fact the same thing as a statement that the wergeld was a *heavy gold mina*, for 200 solidi of 96 wheat-grains contained exactly the same number of wheat-grains as did the heavy mina of ancient Eastern usage—viz. 19,200. In other words, so persistent seems to have been the traditional connection of the wergeld with the gold *mina* that Roman monetary usage was overruled, and instead of reckoning in Roman drachmas, ounces, and pounds, the wergelds were reckoned once more, or perhaps we should say continued to be reckoned, in what was really the heavy gold *mina* of 200 solidi.

And was often the equivalent of 100 oxen.

Further than this, in the laws of some of the tribes, as we shall find, the double solidus or stater still retained its position as the gold equivalent of the ox, so that the typical wergeld of 200 gold solidi in these cases was actually, like the *mina*, the gold equivalent of 100 oxen.

Even where variations are found from this prevalent equation we shall still sometimes find the principle preserved, some other animal being substituted for the ox, and sometimes the long hundred of 120 being substituted for the decimal hundred.

The standard weight of the wheat-grain varied.

If this had been the whole truth the matter would be simple. But the fact is that, although the wergeld of 200 solidi of Constantine was the exact equivalent of the heavy gold mina reckoned in *wheat-grains*, there were differences in the standard weight of the wheat-grain. As already mentioned, the actual weights of Eastern and Greek staters were not exactly alike, and the Roman standard, in actual weight, was higher than the Eastern and Greek standards.

The latest authorities, Hultsch and Lehmann,[1] on the evidence of inscribed weights, describe what may for convenience be called the Eastern gold mina —*i.e.* the *heavy* gold mina of Assyrian and Babylonian metrology—as weighing 818 grammes, or 100 staters of 8·18 grammes. They tell us also that there was a *commercial* mina of 120 of the same staters. This commercial mina therefore weighed 982 grammes, and

[1] The latest results of metrological research are most conveniently stated by Hultsch in his *Die Gewichte des Alterthums nach ihrem Zusammenhange dargestellt*, Leipzig, 1898. And Mr. F. G. Hill, of the British Museum, has recently issued an excellent hand-book of the Greek and Roman coins containing information on these points.

metrologists have inferred that the Roman pound was derived from this commercial mina being in fact exactly one third of its weight, or 327 grammes.

Now, as the commercial mina contained 120 staters of 8·18 grammes, it is obvious that the Roman pound, being one third of it, ought to have been divided, had Eastern reckoning been followed, not, as Constantine divided it, into 36 staters of 9·08 grammes, but rather into 40 staters of 8·18 grammes.

In other words, had Constantine, instead of following the Roman system of division, followed the Eastern system and divided the Roman pound into 40 staters of 8·18 grammes in weight, his double solidus, whilst containing 192 Eastern wheat-grains, would have contained only 172·8 Roman wheat-grains. As a matter of fact the Eastern stater of 8·18 grammes, if put in the Roman scales of Constantine, would have weighed only 172·8 wheat-grains of Roman standard, and the tremisses 28·8 wheat-grains. The Roman pound would have contained 240 of such tremisses, and the ounce 20 of them.

The Roman lb. divided into 240 smaller tremisses of 28·8 wheat-grains.

This is not the place to enter more deeply into the metrological question, but its interest in this inquiry lies in the fact that in Western Europe, in spite of Roman conquests and Roman influence, and in spite of the general knowledge and prevalence of the gold solidi and tremisses of the Empire, there seems to have been a remarkable tendency, consciously or unconsciously, to revert to the Eastern standard by dividing the Roman pound into 40 staters, 80 solidi, and 240 tremisses.

The ancient Gallic gold coinage, extending from the valley of the Danube across Gaul into Britain, was apparently of this ancient Eastern standard. And Cæsar himself, after his conquest of Gaul, reverted to it when he issued gold staters of one fortieth of the Roman pound.[1] Finally we shall find, in our next section, the Merovingian Franks, consciously or unconsciously, doing the same.

III. THE FRANKISH CURRENCY.

Most of the laws of the Continental tribes seem to have had their origin in the necessity to commit into writing what remained of local custom after Frankish conquest. The early currency of the Franks mostly gold.

Broadly speaking they belong to two periods—the earlier one that of the conquests of the Merovingian Franks, and the later one that of the conquests of Charlemagne.

It becomes necessary, therefore, to distinguish between the coinage and currency of the two periods.[2]

When we turn from the Imperial currency of gold solidi and tremisses to that of the Frankish princes, we find them using a peculiar system of monetary reckoning, founded upon the metrical system already alluded to, of 20 tremisses or pence to the ounce and 240 to the pound.

At first the Merovingian kings seem to have used or copied the Imperial solidi and tremisses. But before long they issued an abundant gold currency At first of Roman solidi and tremisses;

---

[1] The relation of the ancient Gallic gold currency to the subject of wergelds is interesting and important, but cannot be enlarged upon here.

[2] For the authorities for the following short statement see *infra*, Chap. VII. s. 1.

of their own, consisting almost entirely of tremisses. And these tremisses were reduced in weight by the division of the Roman pound of 6912 wheat-grains into 240 tremisses of $\frac{1}{20}$ of the ounce, *i.e.* 28·8 instead of 32 wheat-grains. The abundant currency of these lighter gold tremisses continued till nearly the close of the Merovingian period. And how abundant this gold currency was, is shown by the fact that nearly 10,000 examples are recorded in the catalogues of Merovingian coins in public and private collections.

afterwards of the smaller tremisses of 28·8 wheat-grains;

But towards the close of the Merovingian period came one of those strange monetary changes, so difficult to account for, which before long put an end altogether to the issue of these gold tremisses.

then of silver tremisses or pence of the same weight.

All through the Merovingian period payments had no doubt been made in silver as well as in gold, by weight, and during the later part of the period silver tremisses were issued of the same weight as the gold. And thus gradually, at first concurrently with the gold tremisses and at last driving them out, came into use a silver currency of 20 pence to the ounce and 240 to the Roman pound.

With this silver currency and the following of this weight system came in apparently the method of silver monetary reckoning, so familiar to us, of dividing the pound of 240 pence into 20 solidi or shillings of 12 pence—the pound being still the Roman pound of 6912 wheat-grains. This silver solidus was, however, only one of account and was never issued as a coin.

The *nova moneta* of Charlemagne.

Finally, just before Charlemagne assumed the title of Emperor another change was made by the issue of his *nova moneta.*

The silver currency had by this time become predominant, and in the capitularies the silver solidus of 12 pence had already come into use. Charlemagne, in issuing the *nova moneta*, made no alteration in the method of reckoning, except that he brought the weight of the silver tremissis or penny back again to the Imperial standard of 32 wheat-grains, thus making his pound of 240 of the new pence 7680 wheat-grains instead of 6912 and the ounce 640 instead of 576.

His pound of 240 silver tremisses of 32 wheat-grains, and silver solidus of account of 12 pence.

At the same time we shall find that he tried, by making his *nova moneta* legal tender, to force the new silver solidus of 12 pence into use as equivalent, in payments, for the gold solidus of three gold tremisses, which up to that time had been the solidus of the Salic laws.

This involved the altogether impossible ratio of 1 : 4 between the two metals instead of the Imperial ratio of 1 : 12.

Made legal tender at a ratio of 1 : 4 with gold.

In considering the wergelds of the laws belonging to this period, we shall find plenty of evidence of the confusion resulting from this remarkable experiment, made more apparent by the fact that the ratio of 1 : 12 was restored by one of Charlemagne's successors.

It has been necessary to trouble the reader with this brief statement of somewhat complicated facts, because it would be impossible to understand the wergelds of the various Continental tribes if they were not borne in mind.

For the understanding of these wergelds the points to be considered will be :—

(1) As regards the laws, the recensions of which date from Merovingian times, it will be necessary to

ask whether the solidi and tremisses were of Imperial or of Merovingian standard.

(2) As regards the later laws, the recensions of which date from the conquests of Charlemagne, we shall have to consider whether the wergelds are stated in gold solidi and tremisses, or in the silver solidi and pence of the *nova moneta* of Charlemagne.

IV. THE NORMAN AND ANGLO-SAXON CURRENCY.

Working back from the known to the unknown, the facts relating to the Norman and Anglo-Saxon currency, speaking generally, confirm what has already been said of the Frankish currency, and become intelligible when the two currencies are considered together.

The Norman and later Anglo-Saxon pound of 240 pence of 32 wheat-grains.

In the first place, the Norman and Anglo-Saxon pound at the time of the Norman conquest was the pound of 7680 wheat-grains of silver or 240 silver pence of 32 wheat-grains, like that of the *nova moneta* of Charlemagne, and the Normans, like the Franks, divided it for monetary purposes into 20 shillings of 12 pence.

At the same time the Normans recognised that the Mercians had all along reckoned in silver scillings of 4 pence, and the men of Wessex in scillings of 5 pence.

The earlier pound of 240 sceatts or silver tremisses of 28·8 wheat-grains.

If we examine the actual coinage of the Anglo-Saxons we find that, like that of the Franks, it may be divided into two periods. The earlier one corresponded to the Merovingian period during which the penny or sceatt of Mercia and Wessex was of 28·8 wheat-grains, like the silver tremisses or pence across the Channel.[1] The later period commenced when Offa in Mercia, followed by Alfred in Wessex, abandoned the 'sceatt' and issued pence like those of the *nova moneta* of Charlemagne of 32 wheat-grains.

So marked is the distinction between the silver pence of the two periods in type and weight that they are known by numismatists as the 'Sceatt series' and the 'Penny series.'

Finally, just as, in the case of the Frankish currency, the pound of 240 sceatts was the Roman pound of 6912 wheat-grains, so the pound of 240 of the later pence was the pound of the *nova moneta* of 7680 wheat-grains, which in England after the Conquest became the standard or Tower pound.

At the same time it must be remembered that the identity or difference in these cases is in the reckoning in wheat-grains, and that there was room for some variation in the actual weight of the coins.

V. THE MINAS WHICH SURVIVED IN USE SIDE BY SIDE WITH THE ROMAN POUND.

According to the writers of the Merovingian and later period collected by Hultsch,[2] the Roman pound was not the only standard of weight which was in customary use in Europe.

The gold mina of 200 gold solidi.

We have seen that the commonly prevalent wergeld of 200 gold solidi was in fact the same thing,

---

[1] Besides these silver *tremisses* some silver *scripula* were issued, but it is with the sceatts mainly that we have to do. In connection with the next section, however, the fact that the scripulum was current as a coin is worth notice.

[2] *Metrologicorum Scriptorum Reliquiae* (Lipsiae, 1866).

in wheat-grains, as the heavy Eastern and Greek gold mina of 19,200 wheat-grains. But besides this, there were two other minas of interest to this inquiry which seem to have been more or less locally in use, and more or less connected with the wergelds.

The *mina Italica* of 240 scripula of 24 wheat-grains or 20 Roman ounces.

It seems that the Roman pound of 12 ounces was not the only pound in use in Italy. A still older Roman pound of 10 Roman ounces or 5760 wheat-grains seems to have existed,[1] which was in fact a pound of 240 scripula of 24 wheat-grains. And two of these pounds made what was called the *mina Italica* of 20 Roman ounces. This mina Italica survived into Merovingian times. It contained 480 Roman scripula, and according to authorities quoted by Hultsch [2] the *scripulum* was so far a common unit in Gaul as to have earned the name of the *denarius Gallicus*. The number of Roman wheat-grains in the mina Italica was 11,520. Its weight was 545 grammes.

In the Merovingian formulæ and in the early charters of St. Gall there are constant references to fines of so many *libræ* of gold and so many *pondera* of silver, from which the inference may be drawn that the pondus of silver was a different weight from the libra of gold. Whether the older Roman pound or half-mina-Italica was the 'pondus' or not, the fact that it consisted of 240 scripula may possibly have made it a precedent for the monetary mode of reckoning of 240 pence to the pound, adopted by the Franks and Anglo-Saxons.

---

[1] Hultsch, *Die Gewichte des Alterthums*, pp. 53 and 203.
[2] *Metr. Script.* ii. 131–139.

This mina Italica has also a Celtic interest. It is curious to note that whilst so late as the tenth century the Cymric galanas or wergeld was paid in cows, the cow was equated with a monetary reckoning in scores of pence, or *unciæ argenti*, of which twelve made a pound of 240 pence. At the same time in the Cymric Codes there are mentioned, as we shall find, two kinds of pence: the *legal* pence, probably those current at the time in England of 32 w.g., and the *curt* pence or scripula of one third less, viz. 24 w.g. Now, whilst 240 of the former would equal the pound of the *nova moneta* of Charlemagne, and of later Anglo-Saxon reckoning, 240 of the *curt* pence or scripula would equal the older Roman pound or half-mina-Italica.

Turning from the Cymric monetary system to that of the early Irish manuscripts and Brehon laws, we shall find that it was based on the Roman scripulum of 24 wheat-grains, and not, like the Anglo-Saxon and Frankish system, on the tremissis. And we shall find that though thus based upon the scripulum and the ounce, when payments were made in gold and silver, the reckoning, instead of making use of the Roman or any other pound, counted rather in *scores of ounces*; *i.e.* consciously or unconsciously, in so many of the mina Italica.

So much for the *mina Italica* and its possible Anglo-Saxon and Celtic connections.

The *mina Attica* of 16 Roman ounces or 2 marks.

The other mina, the mention of which is important, formed the probable basis of Scandinavian reckoning in *marks* instead of in pounds.

The authorities collected by Hultsch describe this

mina as of 16 Roman ounces, and as the '*mina Attica*.'[1] It is a fact that 16 Roman ounces did exactly equal in weight (though not in wheat-grains) the light mina of 50 Attic staters or 100 drachmas. But under Roman influence this Attic mina no longer was divided like a mina into 100 drachmas, but had become twisted, as it were, into 16 Roman ounces and into 96 solidi of Constantine.

In Northern Europe, in nearly all the systems of reckoning which survived from mediæval times, the pound of 12 ounces was ignored. A pound of 16 ounces had taken its place. And this pound or mina of 16 ounces lay, as we shall find, at the root of the system of the earliest Scandinavian laws, with its monetary marks, ores, and ortugs, for it was the double of the *mark* of 8 ounces. The Russian zolotnic (or 'gold piece'), on which the weight system of Russia is based, was theoretically identical in wheat-grains with the Roman solidus, and the Scandinavian ortug with the double solidus or stater.

The mark, ore, and ortug of Scandinavia.

It is not needful to dwell further upon these points at this moment; but it will become important to recognise the Byzantine or Eastern origin of the mina of 16 Roman ounces when we come to consider the wergelds of Northern Europe, and particularly the equation between the Danish wergeld of 8 half-marks of gold and the silver wergelds of Wessex and Mercia as described in the compact between Alfred and Guthrum.

In that compact we shall have to recognise not only the contact of two methods of monetary reckoning widely separated in origin, the one of gold and

[1] Hultsch, *Metr. Script.* i. pp. 66 and 87.

the other of silver, but also the clashing of two traditional ratios between the two metals, viz. the Scandinavian ratio of 1:8, and the restored Imperial ratio of 1:12 followed by the Anglo-Saxons.

VI. THE USE OF GOLD TORQUES AND ARMLETS, &C., INSTEAD OF COINS.

Wergelds paid in cattle or gold or silver by weight.

Although the amounts of the wergelds are generally stated in the laws in gold or silver currency, more or less directly equated with the cattle in which they were originally paid, it would be a great mistake to imagine that the wergelds were often paid actually in coin.

A moment's consideration makes it clear that a wergeld of a hundred head of cattle, whether paid as of old in cattle or in gold or silver, was a payment too large to be paid in *coin*. It was a payment that no ordinary individual could pay without the aid of his kindred, and it is hardly likely that so large an amount in actual coin could be collected even from the kindred of the murderer.

Gold torques &c. made of a certain weight and used in payments.

There is plenty of evidence to show that large payments in gold and silver were mostly made by weight, and very often in gold articles—torques, armlets, and bracelets—made to a certain weight.

In the Scald's tale is the well-known passage:—

> He to me a beag gave
> On which six hundred was
> Of beaten gold
> Scored of sceatts
> In scillings reckoned.

Whether the true meaning be six hundred sceatts or

six hundred scillings, we have here a beag with its weight marked upon it.

The museums of Scandinavia and of Ireland—the two poles of German and Celtic culture—are full of these gold objects, and very frequently little coils of fine gold wire are wound round them to raise their weight to the required standard.

Gold and silver objects weighing so many mancuses.

It may be mentioned, further, in passing, that in many early Anglo-Saxon charters payments and donations are made in gold and silver objects, and that the weights of these are sometimes stated in so many *mancuses*—the mancus being apparently a weight of gold or silver of 30 pence, and equated in the later laws, in its silver value, with the value of the ox.[1]

An historical example.

It may be worth while before concluding this chapter to refer to an historic example of the use of gold objects of definite weight, and the adjustment of their value in differing currencies. The incident deserves to be noticed, and may be of use in helping to fix upon the memory the difference, so often alluded to, between the Roman pound of 6912 wheat-grains and Charlemagne's pound of 7680 wheat-grains. It belongs to the precise moment when Charlemagne, having issued his *nova moneta*, was contemplating his visit to Rome and the assumption of the Imperial title, and it has an historical interest as showing that the *nova moneta* was issued before the Imperial title was assumed.

Alcuin, who had long resided at the Court of

---

[1] Athelstan, vi. 6, s. 2 and vi. 3; and see Schmid's Glossary under *Geldrechnung*.

Charlemagne, was now lying ill at Tours. In order to consult him, probably respecting the Imperial title, Charlemagne, with his queen Liutgarda, proceeded to visit him at Tours. Liutgarda was apparently taken ill while there, and died June 4 A.D. 800.

Alcuin weighs gold bracelets in the scales of the *nova moneta.*

During her illness Alcuin sent a messenger to Paulinus, the Patriarch of Aquileia, with two *armillæ* of fine gold from Liutgarda,[1] so that he and his priests might pray for her. He stated in his letter to Paulinus that these armillæ weighed 'xxiv. denarii less than a full pound of the *nova moneta* of the king.'

Alcuin thus weighed the bracelets in the scales of the *nova moneta,* and they weighed twenty-four pence less than Charlemagne's pound of 7680 wheat-grains. The interesting point is that 24 pence of the *nova moneta* ($24 \times 32 = 768$) deducted from the pound of Charlemagne left exactly 6912 wheat-grains. So that when Paulinus weighed the gold bracelets in his Roman scales he would find they weighed exactly a Roman pound.[2]

But in correspondence with Ireland uses Roman weights.

And yet, though writing from Charlemagne's Court, Alcuin, when addressing his ecclesiastical friends in Ireland, no longer used the terms of the Frankish currency. It was after all a local one. Charlemagne's Empire had its limits, and Ireland was beyond them. The area of ecclesiastical rule was wider than both Empires put together. Alcuin writes that he and his Imperial master had distributed among the Irish monasteries so many *sicli* of silver.

[1] There can hardly have been at Tours at this moment any other Liutgarda than the queen under Alcuin's spiritual charge.

[2] For this incident see *Alcuini Epist.* xxv.

The *siclus*, according to the authorities collected by Hultsch,[1] was equal to two Roman *argentei* or drachmas of silver. So that Alcuin used the di-drachma or stater of Roman reckoning as fixed in the time of Nero, when corresponding with churches outside the Empire of his Frankish master.

Arch-bishop Egbert also uses Roman weights instead of local ones.

As we proceed in our inquiries we shall find another great ecclesiastic (Egbert, archbishop of York and brother of the Northumbrian king) using the same Roman monetary terms in replying to the question of his clergy respecting the wergelds to be claimed in taking their proper position and rank in the Northumbrian kingdom. The answer was given in Roman *argentei* and *sicli*, and not in Frankish solidi, or Anglo-Saxon scillings, or any other local currency.

In conclusion, the various currencies in which wergelds were paid may at first sight be perplexing, but the relevance of the facts stated in this chapter to a right understanding of the wergelds of various tribes under tribal custom, and of the amount of the wergelds to a right understanding of the constitution of tribal society, will become more and more apparent as the inquiry proceeds.

[1] *Metr. Script.* ii. 31, 99, 114, &c.

CHAPTER II.

SUMMARY OF THE CYMRIC EVIDENCE.

I. THE UNIT OF CYMRIC TRIBAL SOCIETY.

THE next step in this inquiry will be to give a brief summary of the results of the evidence contained in the volume on the 'Tribal System in Wales,' adding at the same time such further details as may be useful in helping us to realise the methods by which tribal custom worked itself out in practice.[1]

The Cymric unit of landholding was the gwely.

The chief fact revealed by the examination of the Extents and Surveys of different parts of Wales made after the English conquest, taken together with the Cymric Codes, was that the unit of society and of land-occupation under Cymric tribal custom was not the individual, and not the immediate family, but the group of kindred known as the '*Wele*' or '*Gwely*.'

Such and such a Villata or District is described in the surveys as in the occupation of the gwelys of so and so, the Latin word used for gwely being 'lectus' or bed.

---

[1] For the references to the Codes and Extents, and authorities for the statements in this summary, the reader must be referred to the former volume. But for additional statements full references will be given. Where not otherwise stated, the figures refer to the two volumes of *Ancient Laws of Wales*.

The gwely was a family group of a great-grandfather and his descendants.

The form of society thus revealed was *patriarchal* in the sense that the common ancestor (generally conceived to be the great-grandfather) during his life, and even after his death, was regarded as the head of the *gwely* or group of his descendants for three generations. In his name as its head this family group occupied land and had grazing rights over certain districts, sometimes alone, more often in common with other family groups.

As to what is meant by land ownership in the full modern sense, the question may not have arisen, or it might have come in gradually sooner or later, as agriculture came more and more into prominence. What property, strictly speaking, the tribesmen owned consisted mainly of herds of cattle.

Naturally, therefore, what rights over land they may have had were mainly rights of occupation and grazing in certain districts for their herds. Their agriculture was secondary, and consisted of the right to plough up such portions of the waste or common pasture as year by year might be required for their corn crop. All that need be said at this moment about their agriculture is that it was an open field husbandry, the result of the co-ploughing of a common plough-team normally of 8 oxen, the joint contribution of several tribesmen.

The tribesmen recover their *da* or cattle from him as their chief for their maintenance.

Returning to the gwely, we find that when a child was born into it, whether boy or girl, it was formally acknowledged by the kindred. It remained 'at the father's platter' to a certain age (generally 14), and then the father ceased to be responsible. The boy at 14 became the 'man and kin' of the chieftain of the family group, or it might be of the higher kindred embracing several of the gwelys. From that moment the boy obtained by 'kin and descent' a tribesman's right of maintenance. That is to say, he received from the chieftain his *da*, probably in the form of an allotment of cattle,[1] and with it the right to join in the co-ploughing of the waste. He became thus a tribesman on his own hook, apart from his father. So that the unit of society was not simply the family in the modern sense of a parent and his children, but the wider kindred of the gwely or the group of related gwelys headed by the chieftain who provided the *da*.

The young tribesman is dependent on the chief, not on his father.

II. THE CONSTITUTION AND WORKING OF THE GWELY.

Now, as the gwely was the unit of land-occupation, it is worth while to try to realise a little further what it was and how it worked.

Viewed in its simplest, and perhaps original form,

---

[1] Prof. Rhys informs me that *da* in Carnarvonshire local dialect still means 'cattle,' while in other parts of Wales it has the wider meaning of 'goods.'

The allotment of cattle involved grazing rights, and often separate homesteads. Accordingly in the Denbigh Extent we find that so and so 'habet domum' or 'non habet domum.'

This dependence for maintenance of the boy upon the higher chieftain is indirectly confirmed by the Extents, which mention among the chieftain's rights the 'fosterage of youths' &c. See *Tribal System in Wales*, p. 169.

That the chieftain who gives the *da* was the 'chief of kindred' and not a mere territorial lord is shown by the fact that when a stranger family have lived in the land till they have formed a kindred by intermarriage with Cymraes, all the members of the family become 'man and kin' to the chief of kindred of the new kindred. *Tribal System in Wales*, p. 132.

The simplest form of the gwely. The landed rights vested in the chief, and he gives cattle out of the common herd to tribesmen for their maintenance.

it was a family group of four generations, the landed rights of which were vested in the great-grandfather as its chieftain.

The tribesmen, his descendants, had only rights of maintenance. By right of 'kin and descent' they had received their *da* from the chieftain. The flocks and herds of the chieftain were the common stock out of which the *da* had been given, and there is reason to believe that under earlier custom, on the death of a tribesman, his *da* went back into the common stock of the chieftain.

Probably at first no succession by representation on a tribesman's death. But in the codes a *peculium* admitted which went to children.

At the date of the codes it did so when the tribesman died *without issue*. But in the codes a *peculium* of private property of which the *da* was the kernel is recognised and allowed to descend to a tribesman's children instead of falling into the common stock.

When the great-grandfather died, the chieftainship, with the landed rights and the herds, was divided between his sons, who as brothers thus became chiefs of sub-gwelys. But the original gwely did not then break up, because there would be a right of division *per capita* when the brothers were dead between first cousins, and when the first cousins were dead between second cousins.

A redivision takes place *per capita* as each generation dies off.

The division between brothers was probably originally made only between those sons of the parent who were living at his death. Like the sons of the surviving brothers, the sons of a deceased brother must be content with their *da* till all the brothers were dead, and in the division between first cousins they would take their share *per capita* along with the rest.

But at the time of the codes, by what Continental examples lead us to regard as an innovation, the orphaned nephews were allowed in the division to succeed at once, side by side with their uncles, to the share and position which their father would have taken had he survived.

Even after this innovation, if a brother had died *without issue*, his brothers as brothers did not at once succeed as co-heirs. The share fell into the common stock till a division, and then went to all the co-inheritors *per capita*, so that cousins, and it might be even second cousins, took their shares in it.

The rights and property of a tribesman dying without issue fall into the common stock.

The introduction of succession by representation to a deceased father's property and privilege was, as we shall see in Continental cases, a step taken in the direction of individual ownership. It complicated the matter of the division or devolution of the chieftainship in the gwely, but it is a point of interest in connection with the Continental evidence.

A clear understanding of the constitution and working of the gwely, as a typical family group, is so important to this inquiry that it is worth while to place before the reader the passages in codes upon which, taken together with the surveys, the foregoing description of it rests.

The following is the clause in the Venedotian Code describing what took place in the gwely, under the heading 'The Law of Brothers for Land:'

Clauses in the Venedotian Code.

Thus, brothers are to share land between them: four erws to every tyddyn [homestead]. Bleddyn, son of Cynvyn, altered it to twelve erws to the uchelwr, and eight to the aillt, and four to the godaeog; yet, nevertheless, it is most usual that four erws be in the tyddyn. . . .

If there be no buildings on the land, the youngest son is to divide all the patrimony (trew y tat), and the eldest is to choose, and each in seniority choose unto the youngest.

If there be buildings the youngest brother but one is to divide the tyddyns, for in that case he is the meter; and the youngest to have his choice of the tyddyns; and after that he is to divide all the patrimony; and by seniority they are to choose unto the youngest; and that division is to continue during the lives of the brothers.

And after the brothers are dead, the first cousins are to equalise if they will it; and thus they are to do: the heir of the youngest brother is to equalise, and the heir of the eldest brother is to choose, and so by seniority unto the youngest; and that distribution is to continue between them during their lives.

And if second cousins should dislike the distribution which took place between their parents, they also may co-equate in the same manner as the first cousins; and after that division no one is either to distribute or to co-equate. Tir gwelyauc is to be treated as we have above stated.[1]

Clauses in the Dimetian Code.

In the Dimetian Code the same rules of division are stated as follows:

When brothers share their patrimony (tref-eu-tat) between them, the youngest is to have the principal tyddyn, and all the buildings of his father, and eight erws of land, his boiler, his fuel hatchet, and his coulter, because a father cannot give those three to any but the youngest son, and though they should be pledged they never become forfeited. Then let every brother take a homestead (eissydyn) with eight erws of land, and the youngest son is to share, and they are to choose in succession from the eldest to the youngest.

Three times shall the same patrimony be shared between three grades of a kindred, first between brothers, the second time between cousins, the third time between second cousins, after that there is no propriate share of land.[2]

. . . .

---

[1] i. pp. 167–169. [2] p. 543.

After there shall have been a sharing of land acquiesced in by co-inheritors, no one of them has a claim on the share of the other, he having issue, except for a sub-share *when the time for that shall arrive.* Yet whosoever shall not have any issue of his body, *his co-inheritors, within the three degrees of kin from the stock, are to be his heirs.*[1]

Only by adhering very closely to these texts can the gwely be understood. They seem at first sight to refer to the tyddyns or homesteads, but, as we have seen, the landed rights of grazing in the villatæ in which the gwelys were located were included also.

How the divisions worked out in practice.

It would obviously be a fair critical question to ask, what happened when the second cousins at last broke up the gwely of their grandfather and divided the land, or let us say the homesteads and the tribal rights of grazing on the land, for the last time equally *per capita*? There might be twenty or thirty of such second cousins. Did the original gwely split up into twenty or thirty new gwelys? Let us try to realise what happened by carefully following the text, in the light of the Denbigh Survey.

Let us take a hypothetical case in which the gwely of X is described by the surveyor as holding an undivided share of the rights of pasture, &c., in a particular villata or in several villatæ; and assume that, according to the record, the internal divisions of the gwely followed the family division of the descendants of X, as in the following table. Then, applying the rules of the clauses as to *tir gwelyauc*, let us see how it would work out in the hypothetical case stated.

[1] p. 549, s. 19.

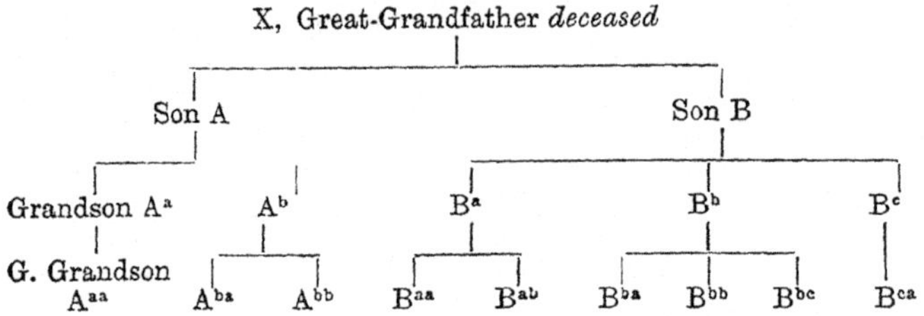

Now let us suppose that X (the great-grandfather, from whom the gwely is called the gwely of X) is dead. While his sons A and B are alive they share equally in the grazing and other rights. When A is dead and so long as B is alive no change is made except that A's two sons share equally their father's right to which, in the phrase of the codes, they have 'ascended.' B at length dies. There are five grandsons, first cousins, who have a right to share in the rights of the gwely of X *per capita*. There is now therefore a rearrangement after which A's sons share and hold jointly only 2-5ths, while B's three sons hold jointly 3-5ths. Equality *per capita* among grandsons has now been effected. But the gwely goes on. It cannot be broken up because in another generation the great-grandsons may require a fresh division.

The process is a continuous one.

Next let us see what happens when all the grandsons are dead and the final division *per capita* takes place. There are nine great-grandsons. Is the gwely of X now to be divided into nine new gwelys? Certainly not. The grandsons of A are entitled to 3-9ths only, and this they divide *per capita*, being first cousins; one family takes 1-3rd and the other 2-3rds. The portion which has fallen to them of family rights in the gwely of X has become a separate gwely, called either the gwely of A or, as we sometimes find in the Denbigh Survey, the 'gwely of the grandsons of A'—'*gwely weiryon A.*' The other portion has become either the gwely of B or the gwely of the grandsons of B—'*gwely weiryon B.*'

The grandsons of B, being first cousins, have of course redivided their 6-9ths equally *per capita*, and the internal rights of the gwely of the grandsons of B are

B[a]'s two children have $\frac{2}{6}$ths.
B[b]'s three children have $\frac{3}{6}$ths. } of $\frac{6}{9}$ths.
B[c]'s one son has $\frac{1}{6}$th.

They cannot break up the gwely of 'the grandsons of B' because they are not second cousins. But when all of them are dead, their children will be second cousins and may do so, and then three new gwelys will be formed in the same way as above, and so on for ever. The process is continuous and always within the same rules of 'tir gwelyauc.'

This seems to be the state of things as regards succession within the gwely resulting from the rules laid down in the Codes and found at work by the surveyors of the Lordship of the Honour of Denbigh. But we must remember that, apart from these rights of succession, each tribesman on becoming a tribesman had been the recipient of his *da*, and so had had cattle of his own all along in the common herd.

The rights of females in the gwely.

Finally, the position of females in the gwely should not pass without recognition. They are not mentioned in the statements of landed rights because, provision having been made for their maintenance independently of their father, they were assumed, whilst claiming their 'gwaddol' or portion, to take this with them, on marriage, out of the gwely. They ought to be married into another gwely, within which their sons in due course would receive inheritance and landed rights by paternity. Only on failure of this could their sons claim landed rights by maternity in their mother's original gwely.[1]

III. THE LIABILITY OF THE WIDER KINDRED FOR *GALANAS* IN CASE OF HOMICIDE.

Such being the *gwely*, we pass on to the wider kindred, embracing the descendants of seven (and for some purposes nine) generations from a common ancestor.

The galanas in lieu of blood feud between kindreds for homicide, but none within the kindred.

We find from the Cymric Codes that the members of the wider kindred had common responsibilities in case of a homicide causing a blood feud between kindreds. A murder *within* this wider kindred was regarded as a family matter. The murderer was too near of blood to be slain. No atonement could be made for so unnatural a crime. There was no blood fine or 'galanas' within the kindred. The murderer must be exiled. But a murder of a member of one kindred by the member of another, inasmuch as, if unatoned for, it would under tribal custom have produced a blood feud between the two kindreds, was the proper subject for the substituted payment of the blood fine or 'galanas.' The galanas was thus a payment from one kindred to another in lieu of the blood feud. But its amount was divided in payment on one side and in distribution on the other, in

[1] i. 96 and 545.

varying proportion according to nearness of relationship to the murderer or the murdered person as the case might be. And in these payments and receipts all the individual tribesmen within the kindred who had received their *da* must take their share if needful.

Payment and receipt by maternal as well as by paternal relations.

The question who had to pay and who had to receive was moreover complicated further by the fact that it involved maternal relations as well as paternal relations. It has been very properly pointed out that, however it might be as regards money payments, it is difficult to conceive how the liability of maternal relations could be worked in the case of actual blood feud and fighting. A man might have to fight for his maternal relations against his paternal relations, or the reverse. In such a case what must he do? How should he act? He might be in an impossible position.

Light upon this point and others may be obtained, perhaps, when the evidence of 'Beowulf' is analysed. This evidence will show that a man may have good cause under tribal custom not to join in some feuds. And further it will remind us that feuds often arose in contravention of tribal usage, breaking the peace which in theory the link of marriage ought to have secured.

In the meantime it would seem possible that the custom of a tribe might, for anything we know, forbid marriage *within* the near relationships of the gwely, and *beyond* the limits of the wider kindred. In such a case, paternal and maternal relations might all be within the kindred, so that properly speaking a quarrel between them could not become the subject of a feud.

Marriage a link between two gwelys. But as regards galanas the wife remained in her own kindred.

In such matters it is obvious that a good deal must depend upon the view taken of marriage itself at the particular stage of evolution in which the society might be. And it may as well be said at once that we should be quite wrong were we to regard marriage from the Roman point of view, *i.e.* as a transfer of the woman out of the *potestas* of her parents into the *potestas* of the husband. The Cymric example, to begin with, was quite different. The marriage of sisters to tribesmen from whom their sons could inherit tribal rights was a duty cast upon the kinsmen of the gwely.[1] It was thus an arrangement between two gwelys—a link between them—but no transfer. If a wife were slain, her galanas or death fine did not go to the husband and his family; it went to her kindred.[2] If a wife should commit murder, it was the wife's family and not the husband's on which rested the payment of galanas for her crime.[3] If the husband were killed the wife took one third of the saraad or fine for insult and wounding, but she took no part of the galanas of her husband.[4]

These points are in a sense unexpected. They belong to a stage of social life as far removed from

---

[1] If the sister was married to an alltud and her son killed a person, ⅔ of the galanas fell on the mother's kindred (i. p. 209), but there was no liability beyond the gwely or second cousins (ii. p. 657).

[2] 'The galanas of every female shall always be to the kindred,' i. p. 241.

[3] 'Three cases wherein a wife is to answer without her husband. The first is for homicide,' i. p. 463. But for accessories to murder she and her husband pay her camlwrw and derwy, i. p. 105; and she can claim *spearpenny*, i. pp. 103, 705; ii. p. 65.

[4] i. pp. 231–3, 409, 517, 747; ii. p. 695. On separation husband and wife divided the cattle and most other things equally.

Roman rules, or modern ones, as they are from the stage in which a wife was either purchased outright or stolen. And yet we shall find them in principle more or less clearly repeated in the varying customs of some of the tribes whose laws we are about to examine.

IV. THE FISCAL UNIT FOR THE PURPOSE OF FOOD-RENTS TO THE CHIEFTAINS.

The geographical unit for food rents

The structure of tribal society in Wales is one thing. The practical working of its rules is another. Until we can to some extent realise its methods and see how its results could be worked out in everyday life, it must remain to some extent vague and mysterious. The nearer we get to its core, the greater its value as an instrument in further research.

We cannot, therefore, afford to disregard any hints that the Codes and surveys may give us, attention to which would help us to realise its methods or ways of working.

Districts called *villatæ*.

The Denbigh Extent, as already said, enables us to realise that, on the English conquest, the lordship of Denbigh was divided into grazing districts which had become the units of tribal food-rents, and which were adopted for purposes of future taxation. These districts were called by the scribes *villatæ*, and were occupied by gwelys of tribesmen and sometimes also by gwelys of non-tribesmen. Their homesteads or huts were occupied in severalty. Their grazing rights were undivided common rights, and within each gwely the rights of families and individuals were also undivided common rights.

Further, the Denbigh Extent shows how easy it

was to shift the whole body of tribesmen of this or that gwely, with its herds, from one district to another, according to convenience or the needs of population, without disturbing the complex rights within the gwely. The families and individuals carried their rights, *inter se*, with them wherever they and their herds might go, and were liable to pay the dues required from whatever villata for the time being might be occupied by them.

Even the homesteads of the tribesmen seem to have been temporary, in the light of the description given by Giraldus Cambrensis. They could carry their hearth-stones with them wherever they went, so that the result seems to be that the groups of kindreds could always have been easily shifted about, as they were in fact after the English conquest, from one district or 'villata' to another. The geographical divisions thus became the permanent fiscal units in tribal arrangements. Both in the surveys and in the Codes we find the villata or district, and not the family group, the fixed unit for tribal food-rents to the chieftain, and for taxation after the English conquest.

The 'tref' or 'maenol' paying the 'tunc pound.'

The surveys so far agree with the Codes. The *villata* of the surveys was the taxable unit, and in some cases still paid the tunc pound (or 20*s.*) in lieu of the chieftain's food-rents. In other cases escheats and other causes had varied the amount. In the Codes of South Wales the unit for the tunc pound was the *tref*, and in the Venedotian Code of North Wales the *maenol* of four trefs.

Now, as in the surveys the family groups or gwelys were located so as to occupy sometimes several villatæ, and sometimes undivided shares in villatæ along with others, so, if we may take the villata of the surveys as equivalent to the tref or maenol of the Codes, we must expect to find that the kindreds of tribesmen at the period of the Codes were scattered in the same way over the trefs and maenols. And, as the maenol was a group of trefs, the *tref* is the unit of tribal occupation as to which a clear understanding is most necessary. In this, however, we may be, after all, only partly successful.

The word *tref*, though generally used for a homestead or hamlet, seems from its other meanings to involve the idea of a *group*.

The tref and its 'randirs.'

There were cases in which a disputed matter of fact had to be established upon the evidence of men of the *gorvotref*, *i.e.* by men of the groups outside the tref in which the question in dispute arose.[1] And this *gorvotref* was not merely the next adjoining tref or trefs, but it consisted of those *randirs* or divisions of neighbouring trefs of uchelwrs, or tribesmen, whose boundaries touched the tref in which the disputed facts arose. Neighbouring randirs of taeog trefs, *i.e.* the trefs of non-tribesmen, were excluded, presumably because the testimony of taeogs in matters relating to tribesmen was not relied on. But this compound of the word tref implies that its general sense was a group of homesteads. That, in general, trefs had defined boundaries, is clear from the fact that it was an offence to break them, and this applied also to the randirs or divisions of the tref.[2]

---

[1] ii. pp. 281–2, 740.

[2] i. p. 765; ii. p. 269.

The trefgordd of one herd and one plough.

Speaking, then, of the group generally known as a tref, we must regard it, not only as a taxable area, but also as the natural group known everywhere as a *trefgordd, i.e.* the natural group of the homesteads of relatives or neighbours acting together as a single community as regards their cattle and their ploughing.

The typical lawful *trefgordd* is thus described :—

> This is the complement of a lawful *trefgordd* : nine houses and one plough and one oven (odyn) and one churn (*gordd*) and one cat and one cock and one bull and one herdsman.[1]

There is another passage which mentions the nine buildings in the tref.

> These persons do not forfeit life . . .
> The necessitous for the theft of food after he has traversed three trevs, and nine houses in each trev, without obtaining a gift though asked for.[2]

So, in case of fire from negligence in a tref, the holder of the house in which it arose was to pay for the damage to the next houses on each side if they took fire.[3] And again no indemnity was to be paid to the owners in a trefgordd for damages from the fire of a smithy if covered with shingles or tiles or sods, nor from the fire of a bath, provided always that the smithy and the bath were at least seven fathoms from the other houses in the trefgordd.[4]

Not always of one gwely only.

The description above quoted of the normal trefgordd suggests that the herd under the one herdsman did not belong to one person or homestead, but to many; and so far it seems to be consistent with the surveys which represent the

[1] ii. p. 693.
[2] ii. p. 531.
[3] i. p. 415.
[4] i. pp. 259, 447.

villatæ as occupied by the cattle of several family groups who had grazing rights therein.

And this, too, accords with what the Denbigh Extent tells us of the individual tribesmen, viz. that only some of them had homesteads. So-and-so 'habet domum' or 'non habet domum.'[1] The young tribesman with his *da* thus may have joined in a common homestead with some one else—probably with his parents or near relatives.

Distinguishing, then, the tref as a taxable area from the trefgordd, and still confining attention to the trefgordd as a cluster of homesteads united for the practical purpose of occupation, let us recur to the things which bound the trefgordd into one group, viz. the one plough, the one oven, the one churn, the one bull, and the one herdsman.

Here are the two elements combined of pastoral and agricultural co-operation, and the trefgordd is the local and physical unit of this co-operation.

The unit of co-operative dairy farming.

Taking first the pastoral element, the trefgordd was a working unit of co-operative dairy-farming. The cattle of several households or individuals were put together in a common herd with a common bull and under the care of a common herdsman (bugeil) and his dog. It may be regarded as a group of the homesteads of the persons in charge of such a herd, and the tribesmen of a gwely may have cattle in the herds of more than one trefgordd.

The common herdsman and his dog.

Three things were 'ornamental' to a trefgordd, 'a book, a teacher versed in song, and a smith (gov) in his smithy;' but a trefgordd herdsman was an

---

[1] *Tribal System in Wales*, App. p. 59, &c

'indispensable' of the *hendrev*,[1] and, when engaged with his herd in summer on the mountain, *his* 'three 'indispensables' were 'a bothy, his herdsman's dog, and a knife;' and the three indispensables of his bothy were a roof-tree, roof-supporting forks, and wattling, and he was at liberty to cut them in any wild wood he pleased.[2]

So far, then, as the pastoral element was concerned, the trefgordd was occupied by a little group of tribesmen engaged in dairy-farming having charge of cattle in a common herd, with a common bull, and under the care of a common herdsman and his dog.

The herd of 24 kine.

Custom, grown out of traditional experience of what a single herdsman and his dog could manage, had determined, it seems, the size of the normal herd. Thus in the Gwentian Code[3] we are told that 'a legal herd of cattle is 24 kine.' And custom tenaciously adhered to tribal rules in such matters.

Thus in the Denbigh Extent it is mentioned that the whole villata of Arquedelok was *in manu domini* by reason of escheats and exchanges, and that a portion of it was let *ad firmam* to nine firmarii, each of whom held for a term of years 31 acres, with one bull and 24 cows, paying per annum 73*s*. 4*d*., and rendering to the lord at the end of his term the said bull and cows or their price, together with the land and a house built thereon.[4] Here, even in a case in which Henry de Lacy was introducing into Wales holdings and herds in severalty, and very possibly introducing English tenants, he adhered to the Welsh

[1] The principal tref as contrasted with summer bothy on the mountains.

[2] ii. p. 563.

[3] i. p. 795.

[4] Fol. 280.

tribal rule of the one bull and 24 cows to the herd. So also in the survey of St. David's, under the head *Glaston* in Breconshire, the number 24 of *grossa animalia* is spoken of as the usual number *ab antiqua consuetudine*, and in the arrangement of common pasture one great animal is said to count as equal to twelve sheep.

The normal herd of the trefgordd was then 24 cows, or their equivalent in bullocks and sheep.

During the summer months the herdsman living out on the mountains was responsible with his dog for the cattle of the trefgordd. And his dog was worth as much as a cow or an ox, if it was one that 'will go *before* the herd in the morning and *behind* them in the evening, and make three turns *round* them in the night.'[1]

Having no cattle of his own in the herd, the herdsman's testimony as to whose cattle were injured, and as to whose cattle had done the injury, was held, when such cases arose, to be sufficient to make the owner responsible, while as regards injuries done by the cattle of one trefgordd to those of another there was joint responsibility.[2] There is common sense in such rules to begin with, and then, having grown into custom, they become perpetuated when custom is codified.

The trefgordd possessed further a common churn. This implies that the milk of the cows was thrown altogether into this one churn as in Swiss mountain communes now. One of the dues from a taeog trev, *i.e.* a group of *non*-tribesmen, was a cheese made from

The common churn.

[1] i. pp. 283, 499. [2] i. pp. 111, 459 745; ii. p. 257.

a day's milking of all the cows in the herd. So that we note in passing that the taeog-tref, *i.e.* of non-tribesmen, also had its herd and was in fact a tref-gordd.[1]

In winter the cattle came down into the lowlands and grazed on the pastures near the tyddyns or homesteads of the tref, and as each of these had its corn and cattle-yard,[2] we may conclude that each owner penned in his own cattle at night during the winter months or joined with some other tribesmen who had a homestead in doing so. The rules as to the divisions of the tyddyns probably referred to these winter homesteads so held in quasi-severalty.

We need not dwell upon the common *oven.* Every hamlet in Brittany possesses its common oven to this day, often in the middle of the village green. Nor need we more than mention the common plough, to the team of which the tribesmen contributed oxen for the *cyvar* or common ploughing of the portion of the waste agreed upon for each year's corn crop.

The trefgordd the unit for food rents. The tribesmen could be shifted about.

The attempt to realise what this practical unit—the trefgordd—was, will not be thrown away if it should help us to understand how easily it lent itself to the arrangement of the chieftain's food-rents or tribute in after-times of taxation. Granted that some such system of trefgordds or clusters of trefgordds pretty generally prevailed, having grown up as a matter of convenience in a grazing community, it is obvious how easily it might become the unit of tribute or taxation. Just as in the Domes-

[1] i. pp. 201, 535. [2] ii. p. 493.

day Survey the number of ploughs affords such a unit, so in a tribal community a district might easily be fiscally estimated at so many herds, or so many churns, or so many ploughs. All these would mean so many trefgordds. And whatever the relations of the trefgordd to the villata of the surveys might be, and however much or often the actual residents, with their herds, might be shifted from one district to another, the district, as in the Denbigh Extent, would remain the permanent unit for payments.

The *firma unius noctis.* Afterwards commuted into money payments.

In the early stages of tribal life, when the chieftain of the tribe moved from one district to another and received his food-rents in the actual form of 'the night's entertainment,' each customary place of encampment in his annual progress would become the centre at which the food-rents would be paid and services rendered for as many nights' entertainment as his accustomed stay in the place. In later stages, when the chieftain's dues were commuted into money, the 'tunc pound' in lieu of food-rents easily became, as we find it in the surveys, a charge on the district rather than on the shifting tribesmen and their herds.

And when the power of the chieftain had grown with time, and instead of 'nights' entertainments' obtained in the primitive way by the actual movement of himself and his retinue from place to place, the food-rents or the tunc pounds in lieu of them were delivered at his palace, he would become the recipient of a regular revenue. And out of this revenue it would become easy for him to reward a follower or endow a church by the transfer of so many food-rents or tunc pounds in lieu of them, or the revenue from such and such a district, or of so many of its tref-gordds, without disturbing the internal working of the system or the daily life of the tribesmen and their herds. When Beowulf returns to his chieftain after his exploit and is rewarded by the gift of a palace and so many 'thousands,' we naturally ask of what, and how it could be done. We may not be able to say off-hand what the unit was, but we get from the Welsh example some rough idea of what tribal tribute and income were, and how these could be readily gathered and transferred.

V. THE METHOD OF PAYMENT OF GALANAS BETWEEN KINDREDS.

Postponing for a while the consideration of the position of the various classes of non-tribesmen, but still keeping in view the fact that in considerable numbers they were practically sharers with the tribesmen in the rights of grazing and occupation of land, we are now in the position to realise to some extent what happened when a murder had taken place.

No galanas for murder within the kindred.

If it was of some one within the kindred, there was, as we have said, no slaying of the murderer. Whether it were a parricide or a fratricide, or the murder of a near kinsman, under Cymric custom there was no galanas, nothing but execration and ignominious exile.

The blood feud and therefore blood fine between kindreds.

But if a tribesman of one kindred were killed by a tribesman of another kindred, then it was a serious matter of blood feud between the kindreds, or of the payment of the blood fine. The tribal conscience demanded vengeance or composition.

It sometimes happened that the murderer had fled to a church for safety, taking his cattle with him. For the clergy or monks at the place of refuge had a herd of cattle of their own, and with them the murderer's cattle were allowed to wander and graze so long as they returned nightly to the refuge.[1]

The slayer flees to a church with his cattle.

There he remained presumably till the kindred of the murdered tribesman, through negotiation and arrangement of the chiefs of the kindreds, had agreed to accept the payment of the galanas, if it were the case of an uchelwr or full tribesman, of 126 cows. Six cows, as we shall see hereafter, were *saraad* for the insult, and 120 cows galanas for the murder. The saraad was paid first—six cows or other cattle to the same value belonging to the murderer were driven from the herd in payment.

Six cows for the saraad or insult.

The murderer's life was then safe, and presumably he might return with his cattle to his place.

Within a fortnight, the tribesmen of the murderer's kindred met to apportion the payment of the rest. They came from trefgordds far and near, from the territories sometimes of various higher territorial chieftains within whose districts they had grazing rights.

The collected tribesmen having apportioned the payment, fortnight after fortnight instalments must be paid till the whole number in value of 120 cows was completed.[2]

120 cows by fortnightly instalments for galanas.

But by whom was the payment to be made?[3]

---

[1] i. p. 141.

[2] i. p. 229.

[3] For the following statements see *Venedotian Code*, i. p. 223, &c.; and *Dimetian Code*, i. p. 407, &c.

The slayer's near family pay 40 cows.

Forty cows must first be found by the *murderer*, his *father*, *mother*, *brothers*, and *sisters* with him. They doubtless helped one another, but theoretically, in one or other of the common herds, there must have been cattle belonging to the murderer, his father, mother, brothers, and sisters, or how could they have paid their shares? There was nothing unreal in this liability of each to pay a share, for had the murderer been slain each one of them would have received, instead of having to pay, a share in 40 cows.

The murderer himself had to pay a third of the 40 cows if he had them. His father and mother between them paid the next third, and the brothers and sisters the remaining third, the sisters paying half what the brothers did.[1] The herds of many a trefgordd must be thinned before this could be done.

The other 80 fall on the kindred.

The remainder of the galanas, viz. 80 cows, fell on the kindred, to the seventh degree or fifth cousins. The paternal relations had to find two thirds of it and the maternal one third, and these kindreds embraced the descendants from the great-grandparents of the great-grandparents on both sides.

In the first fortnight the kindred on the father's side had to find half what was due from them. In the second fortnight they had to find the other half,

[1] Sisters paid for their possible children, and if these children were of age they paid instead of their mothers. After the age at which they could not have children, the sisters did not pay (i. p. 99). That the daughter after twelve was independent of her father with *da* of her own, see i. p. 205.

and in the third fortnight the maternal kindred had to find their share, till so at last the full tale of the 120 cows was paid. The oath of peace from the kindreds of the murdered man could then be given, and the murderer and his kinsmen be at peace.[1]

The slayer's right of 'spear penny.'

But what happened if the murderer could not find the cattle for his third of the 40 cows which he and his immediate family had to find? He had yet a right, as a member of the greater kindred, to claim in aid a 'spear penny' from all those male kinsmen descended from a common ancestor on his father's side two steps further back, *i.e.* still more distantly related to him than those included in the kindred to the seventh degree who had already paid their share. Even if the slayer were a woman, she had the same right of spear penny from the men of her kindred to help her to make her payment.[2]

The solidarity of the kindred and individual liability within it.

So this attempt to realise what was involved in the payment of an ordinary case of galanas brings us back to the recognition of the double aspect of the kindred in the structure of tribal society—its solidarity and joint responsibility, on the one hand, as against outsiders, the whole kindred being responsible in the last resort; on the other hand the individual responsibility of its members, graduated according to nearness of relationship, for the crimes of their relative.

In Cymric tribal society this was made possible by the broad fact that both males and females in the group of kindred, on both paternal and maternal sides, liable to pay, had cattle of their own in the common

[1] i. p. 229. [2] i. pp. 77, 103.

Each had his *da* or cattle for maintenance and so could contribute to the payment.

herd, each having received his or her *da* for maintenance by right of kin and descent from the common ancestor or chieftain of the kindred. The two things surely hang together. And therefore, if we find in the laws of other tribes somewhat similar rules regarding the payment of wergelds, it probably will be worth while to inquire further whether the corresponding structure of tribal society, or something more or less equivalent to it, may not be present also.

VI. THE AMOUNT OF THE CYMRIC GALANAS.

The galanas and the saraad distinct things.

In all the Welsh Codes the galanas, as already mentioned, is described in a peculiar form. It is a combination of two items, viz. the saraad, or payment for insult, and the galanas proper.

Thus the galanas of the innate boneddig, or young tribesman, accepted by the kindred as a tribesman of nine descents of Cymric blood, is described as 'three kine and three score kine,' that of the *uchelwr* or *breyr* as 'six kine and six score kine.'

The explanation of this is obtained from the following passage:—

> What is the galanas of the breyr without office? Six kine and six score kine. The six score kine is the galanas and the six kine is for saraad of the corpse.[1]

So also in the Gwentian Code:—

> When a married man shall be murdered his saraad is first paid and then his galanas, for the wife has the third of the saraad, and she has no part of the galanas.[2]

---

[1] ii. p. 693. [2] i. p. 747.

So also in the Venedotian Code:—

No one is killed without being first subjected to saraad. If a man be married, let a third of the man's saraad be given to his wife and let the two shares be placed with the galanas, and after that let the galanas be divided into three shares and let the third share go to the lord as exacting third.[1]

The wife shared in the saraad of her husband, not in the galanas.

The reason why the wife has a share in the saraad and not in the galanas has already been explained. She suffers from the personal affront or insult to her slain husband and shares in the saraad. But she has no blood relationship with her husband, and only the husband's kindred are therefore entitled to share in the galanas, as her husband's kindred alone would have been concerned in the feud.

The saraad and the galanas were therefore separate things and subject to separate rules, though both payable on the murder of a tribesman. The galanas proper is what must be regarded in any comparison with Continental wergelds.

That of the 'uchelwr' 120 cows; of the young tribesman 60 cows.

The real galanas of the uchelwr or breyr, apart from the saraad, was 120 cows, and that of the young innate boneddig who had received his *da* but had no family was 60 cows. In one of the Codes his galanas when *married* is said to be 80 cows.

Now in what currency was the galanas paid? Formerly, according to the Codes, all payments were made in cattle, and the galanas proper was reckoned in scores of cows.

But of what cow? How was the normal cow for practical purposes to be defined? It is a question worth answering, because we may probably take the Cymric method, of valuing the cow as a unit of

[1] i. p. 231.

currency in cattle, as at any rate suggestive of the methods generally adopted by other tribes.

Description of the normal cow.

According to the Venedotian Code the cow was of full normal value when in full milk and until her fifth calf.

And if there be any dispute concerning her milk, she is to be taken on the 9th day of May to a luxuriant place wherein no animal has been before her, and the owner is to milk her without leaving any for the calf, and put the milk in the measure vessel, and if it be full twice a day that is sufficient; and if it be not, the deficiency is to be compensated by oatmeal until the feast of St. Curic, thence until the feast of St. Michael by barley meal, and from thence until the calendar of winter by rye meal.

Others say that the worth of the milk deficient in the measure is to be returned to the possessor of the cow; if half the milk be deficient, half the worth; if a third of the milk, a third of the worth; and that is the best mode.[1]

Then the *milk measure* is described thus:—

The measure for her milk is, three thumbs at the bottom, six in the middle of the vessel, and nine at the top, and nine in its height diagonally (*enyhyd en amrescoeu*), and the thumb whereby the vessel is to be measured (in case of dispute) is the breadth of the judge's thumb.

In the Dimetian Code substantially the same rules are given, except that the measure of the cow's milking is smaller.

The measure of a vessel for a cow's milk is nine thumbs at its edge, and three at the bottom, and seven diagonally from the off-side groove to the near-side edge in height.[2]

The only difference is between the seven and the nine thumbs of diagonal measurement. Possibly there may be some error in the figures, and the measure may have been the same in both Codes.

Returning to the galanas; although it was reckoned in the Codes in scores of cows, a fixed

---

[1] i. p. 271. [2] i. p. 565.

equation had already been made between cows and silver.

The normal cow was equated in the Codes with 'three scores of silver.' And in the Latin version of the Dimetian Code the 'score of silver' is translated by 'uncia argenti.' The score of silver at the date of the Code was therefore an ounce of silver. So that the reckoning is the Frankish or Anglo-Saxon one of tweuty pence to the ounce.

The cow reckoned as three 'scores' or ounces of silver.

The score of pence of 32 wheat-grains would make the ounce of 640 wheat-grains: that is, the ounce of the pound of 240d., or 7680 wheat-grains—the pound in use in England after the time of Kings Offa and Alfred, and at the date of the Codes.

The galanas of the uchelwr or breyr being 120 cows, and the cow being reckoned at three scores or ounces of silver, the galanas would equal 360 scores or ounces, or thirty pounds of silver.

The galanas of the 'uchelwr' 30 lbs. of silver. At a ratio of 1:12 equal to the gold mina of 200 solidi.

The ratio of gold to silver after the temporary disturbance under Charlemagne had, as we have seen, settled down again to the Imperial ratio of 1:12.

Now thirty pounds of 7680 wheat-grains equal 230,400 wheat-grains, and this number of silver wheat-grains divided by twelve equalled exactly 19,200 wheat-grains of gold. So that this Celtic galanas of the Cymric uchelwr or breyr of 120 cows, like so many Continental wergelds, was apparently exactly equal to 200 *gold solidi* of ninety-six wheat-grains, *i.e.* the heavy gold mina of Imperial standard.

VII. THE METHODS OF TREATMENT OF STRANGERS OR NON-TRIBESMEN.

Strangers in blood how treated.

Another point upon which special inquiry is made in this volume regards tribal methods of treating strangers in blood and slaves.

There is no subject requiring more careful investigation than the combination of circumstances out of which arose what is roughly called serfdom, *i.e.* the attachment of tenants to the land rendering services to a lord. I shall not be suspected of suggesting that tribal customs and methods were the *sole* factors which produced serfdom and of ignoring the influences which came from Roman methods of managing landed estates, and from Roman law modified by ecclesiastical usage.

Indeed, I have insisted from the first that while, in the 'Germania' of Tacitus, the germs may be found of an 'embryo manor,' both Roman and German elements probably combined in producing the later manorial system and serfdom which grew up in what were once the Roman provinces of Gaul and the two Germanies, and even also in Britain.[1] But I think that in Cymric tribal custom we may find a fresh clue worth following in the attempt to gather from Continental evidence the methods likely to be used by conquering German or Anglo-Saxon tribes in the treatment of strangers in blood.[2]

In Welsh tribal custom *alltuds* or strangers and

[1] *English Village Community*, c. ix.

[2] For details and references to the Codes I must refer the reader to Chap. V. of *The Tribal System in Wales*.

their descendants (not necessarily otherwise unfree persons) having some special circumstances in their favour, being allowed to settle within the district of a greater or lesser chieftain upon land which, in a sense, may have been his demesne land, were free to remove and settle under another chieftain, unless and until they had remained on the same land or under the same lordship for four generations. But thereafter the great-grandchildren of the original settlers became *adscripti glebæ*. And this fixture to the land, or rather to the lordship, was apparently not looked upon as in any way a degradation in rank, but on the contrary a step in advance towards the recognition of tribal rights. The great-grandson of the stranger did not indeed become a Cymric tribesman, but he gained the recognition of his status as the founder of a kindred of his own, the members of which in after-generations would, as kinsmen, be able to swear for and defend one another.

After four generations on the land they become *adscripti glebæ* and obtain recognition of kindred.

This being so in the case of free strangers coming into the country, the next question is what was the position of the semi-servile class, the *aillts* and *taeogs* of the Codes, who and whose ancestors for many generations had been born upon the land in a semi-servile condition?

The fixture to the land of the aillt or taeog was not the special mark so much of a semi-servile condition as of his *want of recognised kindred*, and under the local custom of South Wales it seems that he too, like the alltud, could sometimes arrive at the recognition of kindred, without indeed becoming a Cymric tribesman, at the end of four generations of residence under the chieftain of the land; and even

Their rights increase with growth of kindred.

to further recognition of it, involving a still better position as to rights, at the ninth generation. The ninth man in South Wales seems according to local custom in some districts to have, at last, climbed the highest rung of the ladder, and to have attained the right to claim the status of a Cymric tribesman.

This curious rise under Cymric custom, by steps of four generations, up the ladder towards the recognition of tribal rights, seems to have a suggestive correspondence with the reverse process under manorial usage of proving the serfdom of a *nativus* by showing that the great-grandfather was a *nativus* on the lord's land, the manorial rule being that settlement on servile land for four generations made the posterity of an original settler into *nativi*.[1]

Want of kindred the key to their position.

Once more let us try to realise what this meant, and what was the position of these Cymric non-tribesmen in regard to their settlement on land.

If under the guidance of the Codes we turn to the extents and surveys, we find them living, in some cases, not mixed up with the tribesmen, but in separate groups, or trefs, or trefgordds. There may be here and there exceptional alltuds or strangers of a higher class growing up, by the gradual process of intermarriage for four generations with tribeswomen, into the status of tribesmen. But the mass of the stranger class were aillts and taeogs living in separate *taeog trefs*, though, according to the surveys, sharing, often in common, certain rights of grazing over certain districts with gwelys of tribesmen. Now these groups of taeogs and aillts were, according to the Codes, as we have seen, of two classes, and we

[1] See *infra*, p. 319.

recognise the same two classes when we find in the surveys not only groups of taeogs in taeog-trefs but also gwelys of non-tribesmen.

The normal group of the taeog-tref differed from the free tref in the fact that in it no family rights were recognised. All the members of it shared in its rights and payments equally *per capita*, and not *per stirpes*. They were all liable as a body, few or many, for the whole amount of the dues to the chieftains. During their fathers' lifetime sons shared *pari passu* and equally with their parents, and other members of the group, in the pasture and common ploughing, except youngest sons, who remained with their fathers.

In the gwelys, on the other hand, as in the gwelys of tribesmen, there was recognition of family or blood relationships, and a patriarchal element.

There were thus under Cymric tribal custom various subordinate grades or classes. Beginning at the bottom of the ladder were :—

(1) The slaves who could be bought and sold, and who were reckoned as worth one pound of silver.

(2) The taeogs and aillts or permanent *nativi*, born non-tribesmen, without recognised family rights.

(3) Non-tribesmen growing or having grown in four generations into gwelys of non-tribesmen with recognised family rights.

(4) Strangers of exceptional position who, having married into the tribe, had become tribesmen in the fourth generation by repeated intermarriage.

And once more the fact should never be lost sight of, that the gradual growth into tribal or quasi-tribal rights was not a growth into exactly what in a modern sense would be called individual freedom. It was accompanied by the growth of ties which bound the family to the chieftain, till at the moment that at the fourth generation the recognition of rights of kindred was attained, the family found itself, as we have seen, so closely tied to the chieftain and the land that the newly recognised gwely had become *adscriptus glebæ.*

Finally, the tribal logic of the case was probably something like this :—

The stranger a kinless man who has no protection but from his lord till a kindred has grown up around him.

The free tribesman is the man who belongs to a kindred who can protect him by oath and by sword. Until a stranger has kinsmen who can do this he is an odd or kinless man, protected only by his lord. If he be killed his galanas goes to his lord ; he has no recognised kin to receive it. If, on the other hand, he is charged with slaying another, he has no kin to swear to his innocence, the oath of a non-tribesman not being held good as against a tribesman. If guilty, he has no kin bound to fight in the feud for him, or to help him to pay a galanas for his crime. So that even when at the fourth generation the descendant of the alltud becomes the founder of a gwely he has gained only half the status of a tribesman. It is not till the fourth generation of descendants in the gwely, *i.e.* the seventh generation from the original settler, that a complete kindred has grown up. It is not till then that the descendant of the original alltud is surrounded by a full group of relatives, born in his great-grandfather's gwely, whose oaths can be taken and who can protect him by oath and sword or in payment of galanas. All this time the alltud family have been more or less dependent on the protection of the chieftain, and rights and obligations are apt to be correlative.

The object of this essay is to inquire how far, in the case of other tribes, evidence may be found of the working of somewhat similar tribal instincts, resulting in customary rules more or less like those of the Cymry, so that at last, turning attention to the Anglo-Saxon laws, we may be able all the more fully to recognise and appreciate in them the traits of tribal custom, which among other factors went to the making of Anglo-Saxon England.

In the meantime, for future reference, the following list of the galanas of various classes will be found convenient :—

The chief of kindred	180	cows	In Gwent and Dimetia 540, and his family 180
The uchelwr	120	,,	
Man with family without office	80	,,	
The innate boneddig unmarried	60	,,	
The alltud of the brenhin or chief	60	,,	
The alltud of uchelwrs	30	,,	
Bondman . 1lb. of silver or	4	,,	
Bondman from beyond sea	6	,,	

CHAPTER III.

THE EVIDENCE OF BEOWULF ON TRIBAL CUSTOM REGULATING FEUDS &c.

What were the laws of the blood feud?

THE object of the short study, in this chapter, of *Beowulf*, is to learn what incidental information it may give of tribal usage regarding the *blood feud*, especially on points which, in the case of the substituted wergeld, present doubt and difficulty.[1]

Allusion has already been made to some of these points. Did the rule excluding galanas or blood-fine within the kindred extend beyond the gwely to the greater kindred? What happened to a tribesman in a feud between his paternal and maternal kindreds? Did he abstain from taking sides, or did a marriage so far unite two families or kindreds as to make them one for the purpose of blood-fine or feud, so as to prevent the feud or blood-fine from arising?

These are questions upon which we want light from the point of view of Welsh tribal custom, and upon which we approach Beowulf for light, with eyes open also to other matters of tribal usage as they may turn up.

Beowulf for the present purpose may be taken as

[1] In the quotation of passages from *Beowulf* I have mostly followed Professor Earle's translations.

an Anglian or Northumbrian recension of a story founded upon Scandinavian tradition, and designed for use or recital at some 8th century royal court—possibly, if Professor Earle's suggestion be correct, that of King Offa.

An 8th century story of blood feuds,

The western horizon of the story extends to the Frisian shores, but the scene seems chiefly to lie in the Baltic.

The plot involves tribal relations between a chieftain of the Danes possibly of Zealand, and two Swedish chieftains. The two latter concern us most, and they seem to be the chiefs of two kindreds—Geats and Swedes—Beowulf himself being the link between them, his mother having married from one into the other kindred. This marriage at any rate was one *between* two kindreds.

There is no apparent effort on the part of the poet to enlighten the reader or those who heard him either upon the pedigrees of the persons mentioned in his story or upon the rules of Scandinavian tribal custom. But it happens that, by incidental hints dropped in the telling of the tale, the pedigree of each of the kindreds involved can be fairly made out, and has already been made out by translators and critics.

And as the story involves a homicide within Beowulf's maternal kindred, and fighting and bloodshed between the kindreds in spite of the marriage link, and as it deals also with outside feuds, it happens to present remarkable opportunities for studying the action of tribal custom in various cases.

involving blood feuds between Beowulf's paternal and maternal kindred.

The evidence it gives is made all the more

valuable by its being an Anglian version of Scandinavian traditions, inasmuch as the poet, or his Anglian interpreter, assumes throughout that the laws of the game, under Scandinavian tribal custom, were too well known to need explanation to his Anglian audience. So that by inference it would seem that the customs of Baltic chieftains were familiar at the court of Offa, and not very far removed from those of Anglian tradition.

The Scyldings.

The poet introduces us first to a tribe of *Gar-Danes* and the clan or kindred of Scyldings. Scyld the son of Scef is the ancestor of the Scyldings. He is an Adeling who has torn their meadthrones from many tribes (mægdum) and in true tribal fashion compelled them to pay tribute. Surrounded in his old age by numerous descendants and other *gesiths* who have resorted to him, the chieftain has become a great hero in his tribe (mægdh).

The burial of Scyld by his 'gesiths.'

A graphic description of the burial of Scyld in his ships by his gesiths is a fitting introduction to the poem. Let us mark in passing that the word mægd evidently may mean a much wider kindred than the near family of a great-grandfather's descendants (the Welsh gwely). One mægd conquers another and makes it pay tribute.

Again the word gesith evidently includes, with members of the near kin, such others, not necessarily blood relations, as may have joined the warrior band of the hero. They may or may not have been adopted into his kindred in becoming his men, but this extension of comradeship or kinship, as the case may be, to these gesiths adds to the greatness and power of his mægd.

SCYLD The great-grandfather	BEOWULF (not of the story) The grandfather	HEALFDENE The father	HEOROGAR (61 and 467)	HEOROWEARD (2162)	
			HROTHGAR The Scylding m. Wealtheow (61 and 613)	HRETHRIC (1190. 1837) HROTHMUND FREAWARE (2023)	
			HALGA (youngest son) (61)	HRODULF (1018, 1165, 1182)	
			ELAN daughter presumably married to Ongentheow the Scylfing (62 63)	ONELA OTHERE 'sister's sons' to Hrothgar 2929	EANMUND 2929 EADGIL 239

The opening episode of the burial of Scyld is followed by a few lines which reveal something of the pedigree of his descendant Hrothgar the Scylding. The pedigree of Hrothgar, in true tribal fashion, makes Scyld his great-grandfather. He is 'Hrothgar the Scylding,' may we not say, *because* Scyld was his great-grandfather, just as Hengist and Horsa were *Oiscings* according to Bede, who in stating their pedigree makes *Oisc* their great-grandfather, and just as in the Welsh surveys the gwelys still bear the great-grandfather's name though he be long dead, because the gwely hangs together till the fourth generation.

Hrothgar the great-grandson of Scyld.

So far as it goes here is at least an indication that the nearer kindred (or gwely) might be much the same thing both in Celtic and Teutonic tribes.

But Hrothgar is not described only as chieftain of his nearer kindred. Success in arms had made him head of many *winemâgas* (blood friends) and he was surrounded by a mighty *mago-dright* (band of kin). He had built himself a famous *folk-stede*, or hall, called 'Heort,' and all had gone well with him till the monster Grendel came upon the scene.

The deliverer from the monster was Beowulf, the hero of the story. He comes from another kindred, that of the Scylfings, whose pedigree, not fully given, seems to have been something like the following.

Scylf was the common ancestor of the Swedes or Scylfings. The tribe was divided into two families in the elder of which descended the chieftainship of the Scylfings (2382).

(1) Links not stated	ONGENTHEOW who presumably married Elan, sister of Hrothgar the Scylding (62)	ONELA	
		OHTHERE	EANMUND EADGILS

Second family of WÆGMUNDINGS.

(2) WÆGMUND .	. . . .	ECGTHEOW who fled to Hrothgar	— BEOWULF
		WIHSTAN	— WIGLAF

Beowulf a great-grandson of Waeg-mund and so a Wæg-munding.

At any rate the Scylfings seem to be divided into two families whose common ancestor was Scylf. But both Beowulf and Wiglaf are spoken of as *Wægmundings* (2608 and 2815). The headship of the Scylfings had passed into the older of the two families (2384), and this probably is the reason why Beowulf is never called Beowulf the Scylfing.

The reason why Beowulf appeared as the natural helper of Hrothgar from the monster Grendel was that his father Ecgtheow owed a debt of gratitude to Hrothgar. 'Fighting out a mighty feud,' Ecgtheow had killed Heatholaf the Wylfing (460), thereby raising another feud. Wherefore his own people (463) fearing invasion, had caused him to flee over sea, thereby seemingly wiping their hands of him. He seems to have fled to Hrothgar just as the latter had become chieftain of the Scyldings on his brother Heorogar's death. Hrothgar compounded the feud with money (470), sending to the Wylfings over sea 'ancient treasures.' Whereupon Ecgtheow swore oath to Hrothgar and presumably became his 'man.' And Beowulf now, 'at honour's call,' had come to fight the monster, thereby confirming the friendship between Geats and Gar-Danes, requiting what Hrothgar had done for his father (459).

The details of the fight need not detain us. But the fact is important that Beowulf comes to the rescue not as a Scylfing or as representing his paternal kindred, but as the thane of his maternal uncle Hygelac, the chieftain of his mother's kindred.

Beowulf a thane of his maternal uncle Hygelac.

He approaches Hrothgar with a band of fifteen chosen warriors. When asked from whence they came they said they were Geats, Hygelac's *hearth-geneats* (260). And the meaning of the word is illustrated further when the warriors accustomed to sleep in Hrothgar's hall are spoken of as Hrothgar's *hearthgeneats* (1581, and see 260 and 2419). When brought into the hall Beowulf himself calls his band Hygelac's *beod-geneats* (344) (table geneats), and to Hrothgar he calls himself 'mæg and mago-thegn,' literally 'kin and son thane' of Hygelac (408).

The daring deed accomplished, Beowulf's success is rewarded by many golden and other gifts from Hrothgar, and it is significant that on his return he lays all these at the feet of his maternal uncle Hygelac, his *heofodmagus*—chief of kin—whose man and kin he owns himself to be. His position in Hygelac's kindred thus demands careful study.

This seems to be the pedigree.

HRETHEL who had three sons and one daughter thus:	(1) HEREBEALD killed by Hæthcyn	
	(2) HÆTHCYN	
	(3) HYGELAC m. Hygd.	(1) A DAUGHTER who married Eofor (2) HEARDRED Hygelac's only son.
	(4) A SISTER Beowulf's mother	BEOWULF Hygelac's sister's son.

Beowulf is made to say that, when seven winters

old, Hrethel had received him from his father Ecgtheow and had kept him as his own child (2420). 'Remembering kinship' (sippe gemunde), the old chieftain held him in no less regard than his own three sons, Herebeald, Hæthcyn, and Hygelac. But Hrethel's old age was full of trouble. The worst tragedy that came upon him was the death of his eldest son Herebeald, killed by his second son apparently by accident.

Homicide within the family unavenged.

> Hæthcyn by arrow from hornbow brought him (Herebeald) down, his near kinsman. He missed the target and shot his brother. (2440)

Here, then, was an apparently accidental homicide within the family. How was it regarded?

> One brother killed the other with bloody dart. That was a wrong past compensation. . . . Any way and every way it was inevitable that the Etheling must quit life unavenged. (2445).

The poet likens the father's grief to that of 'an old ceorle' who should see his young son ride on the gallows-tree and can do nothing but wait while his son thus hangs, food for the ravens, as he cannot bring him help (2450).

> So did the crowned chief of the Stormfolk, in memory of Herebeald, carry about a tumult of heart-sorrow. He could not possibly requite the feud upon the man-slayer, neverthemore could he pursue the warrior with hostile deeds though not beloved by him. He then, with the sorrow wherewith that wound had stricken him, let go life's joys and chose the light of God. (2464.)

Thus incidentally is revealed by the poet the depth of the tribal feeling that homicide can only be atoned for by avengement and feud, making it a hard struggle against nature for a father to withhold revenge upon a son for even accidental fratricide As with the Cymry, it seems that there could be no feud or composition within the family. Nor in the case of accidental homicide was there apparently in the poet's mind the necessity of flight or outlawry, however great the craving for avengement. It is also significant that Hæthcyn, the slayer, is made to join with his brother Hygelac in the next warfare after Hrethel's death (2474). The accidental slayer remains a tribesman.

Quarrel between Beowulf's paternal and maternal kindred. He takes no part in it.

This next warfare was a quarrel—'provocation and reprisal'—between Swedes and Geats, *i.e.* between the paternal and maternal kindreds of Beowulf. He himself, it is worth noting, did not engage in it. Onela and Ohthere, the sons of Ongentheow (Beowulf's paternal relation and chief of the Scylfings or Swedes), apparently began the quarrel. They recklessly broke the peace between the two families—Swedes and Geats. Hrethel was no longer living. Beowulf's maternal uncles, Hæthcyn and Hygelac, fought on one side, and Ongentheow and his two sons on the other (2485). Hæthcyn fell on one side and Ongentheow on the other: the latter by the hand of Eofor—a comrade rather than kinsman of Hygelac, for he was rewarded by the bestowal of Hygelac's daughter. The quarrel seems to have been open fighting, possibly from the revival of the old enmities and in breach of tribal custom. Be this as it may, Beowulf himself took no part in the quarrel between his maternal and paternal kindreds.

This disastrous and unnatural quarrel left Hygelac the only surviving son of Hrethel, and so the chieftain of Beowulf's maternal kindred.

All this irregular fighting, incidentally mentioned by the poet, was past before Beowulf's great enterprise against the monster Grendel. And, as we have seen, it was as the 'man and kin' of Hygelac that Beowulf appeared at Hrothgar's court. And it was at the feet of Hygelac as his chief of kin, and at the feet of Hygd his queen, that Beowulf laid down his treasures on his return in safety. This exploit ended, Hrothgar thenceforth disappears from the poem, and the poet confines himself to Beowulf's nearer belongings.

But in feud with Frisians Beowulf fights for Hygelac, who is killed.

The next event in order of date is a quarrel between Hygelac and the Frisians. This time Beowulf fights for his chieftain. But Hygelac is killed (2357), and again the result reveals interesting traits of tribal custom.

Beowulf returns from Friesland to Hygd the widowed queen of Hygelac. She 'offers him rings and throne, not daring to trust that her young son Heardred would be able to maintain the chieftainship against all stranger folk.' Beowulf, however, declines to become *hlaford* over Heardred, but supports him in his chieftainship till he should be older (2370).

Young Heardred, however, is not chieftain long (2380). The old lawless quarrel between Beowulf's maternal and paternal relations rises up again.

The facts, when unravelled, seem to be these:—Within Beowulf's paternal kindred trouble had arisen. For some cause not told, the grandsons of Ongentheow (sons of Ohthere) had been outlawed. They are described as wräc-mäegas (2380) and as having cast off allegiance to the chieftain of the Scylfings. These outlawed kinsmen of Beowulf's paternal family came to young Heardred's court, and whilst his guests ('on feorme') the young chieftain fell by the sword of one of them (2388).

Homicide within the kindred again is unavenged, though Beowulf is guardian of the slain.

It was Eanmund by whom this outrage was committed, and once more the crime remained apparently unavenged. The slayer was allowed to withdraw in safety, leaving Beowulf to succeed to the chieftainship of his maternal kindred (2390). Again we ask why? Here was a crime committed by an outlawed paternal kinsman of Beowulf against the chieftain of his maternal kindred, of whom he was himself the guardian, and yet Beowulf did not avenge it! Was it because of the kinship, or because of the outlawry? Whilst nursing the remembrance of his chieftain's death, Beowulf is made to act with kindness to the other outlawed brother in his desolation, waiting for such avengement as might come at last in the course of things—as it did, according to the poet, when 'with a band of warriors over sea Eadgils died in cold and painful marches' (2396).

An outlawed tribesman not protected by his kindred.

Avengement is made to follow too in the same way upon Eanmund the murderer. It came from Beowulf's paternal uncle, Weohstan. But here again the poet is careful to record that it came not in a blood feud, but 'in fair fight' with weapon's edge (2612). And, as if to emphasise the fact that the outlawed kinsman had forfeited all tribal rights, the poet adds that 'Weohstan from his kindred carried off the armour and sword of Eanmund, Onela (Eanmund's uncle) yielding them up to him *without a word about a feud*, although he (Weohstan) had slain his brother's son' (2620).

Evidently the poet means to make it clear that Onela's passive attitude was due to the fact that his nephew was a lawless exile, and so no longer entitled to protection from his kin (2612 and 2380).

The old sword known among men as the relic of Eanmund (son of Ohthere), whom, when a lawless exile, Weohstan had slain in fair fight with weapon's edge; and from his kindred (magum) had carried off the brown mottled helmet, ringed byrnie, and old mysterious sword: which Onela yielded up to him, his nephew's war-harness, accoutrement complete. Not a word spake he (Onela) about the feud, although he (Weohstan) had killed his brother's son. He (Weohstan) retained the spoils for many a year, bill and byrnie, until when his own boy (Wiglaf) was able to claim Eorlscip rank, like his father before him, then gave he to him, before the Geats, armour untold of every sort, after which he gave up life, ripe for the parting journey.

Thus the restrained desire of avengement incidentally is made to find satisfaction at last as regards both the outlawed sons of Ohthere.

After these events the elder branch of the Scyldings passes out of the poet's interest. The only remaining heroes of the tale are the two Wægmundings—Beowulf and Wiglaf.

A long interval had elapsed between Beowulf's accession to the chieftainship of his maternal kindred and the final feat of daring which cost him his life. And it was Wiglaf, his nearest paternal kinsman, who in the last tragedy came to his aid bearing the sword of the outlawed Eanmund. Beowulf's dying words to Wiglaf were: 'Thou art the last left of our kindred (cynnes) the Wægmundings. Fate has swept into eternity all my kinsmen (mâgas)—eorls among men! I must after them!' As he comes to the rescue, Wiglaf remembers the honour done to him by Beowulf, who had already passed on to him the hereditary right of the chieftainship of the Wægmundings (2608).

Why had he done this? If we might tentatively

use the clue given by ancient Greek tribal custom to elucidate a Scandinavian case, we should say that on failure of male succession the 'sister's son' of Hygelac had been called back into his mother's kindred to become its chieftain, leaving Wiglaf, his next of kin on his father's side, to sustain the chieftainship of his paternal kindred. The right of the maternal uncle, known to have existed under early Greek law, to claim his 'sister's son' if need arose, to perpetuate the mother's paternal kindred, suggests a similar explanation in Beowulf's case. Such a right, found as well in the Laws of Manu, may possibly have been inherent in Scandinavian tribal custom also. Such a suggestion would be at least consistent with the fact of Beowulf's having been brought up from seven years old in the household of his maternal grandfather, and treated by him as a son. It would be in harmony, too, with what Tacitus describes to have been the relation of the 'sister's son' to the *avunculus* amongst the German tribes, and the peculiar value of the 'sister's son' as a hostage.[1]

Beowulf as 'sister's son' becomes chief of his maternal kindred.

Some indirect confirmation of the probable truth of such a suggestion may perhaps be also drawn from the fact that in Beowulf, when a man's father is no longer living, the poet sometimes seems to describe him as his maternal uncle's nephew instead of as his father's son.

Heardred, the young son of Hygelac and Hygd his queen, after his father's death is spoken of no longer as Hygelac's son, but as the *nephew of Hereric*, 'nefan Hererices' (2207). Now his paternal uncles were Herebeald and Hæthcyn, and it becomes an

---

[1] See *Structure of Greek Tribal Society*, by H. E. Seebohm, chap. ii.

almost necessary inference that Hereric was a maternal uncle. Thus:

HÆRETH (1929)
father of Hygd

(HERERIC ?)
uncle of Heardred (2207)

HYGD, m. Hygelac

HEARDRED
nephew of Hereric[1]
(2207)

So also in the case of Hygelac himself. He was the son of Hrethel. The poet calls him son of Hrethel (1486), and again *Hygelac Hrethling* (1924). But after Hrethel's death he calls him 'Hygelac of the Geats, *nephew of Swerting* ('*Hygelac Geáta nefa Swertinges*') (1204). Here again it seems likely that Swerting was the maternal uncle, though the poet, as in the other case, does not think it needful to explain that it was so. Otherwise, why the change of epithet?

We are here recording tribal customs as revealed in Beowulf, and not seeking for their origin in earlier stages of tribal life. We pass on, therefore, to consider what light the story throws on the customs of the Northern tribes as to marriage.

Tribal custom as to marriage.

It is with the chieftains' grade of rank that we have mostly to do in Beowulf, and nothing is more strongly emphasised by the poet than the important place of marriage between two tribes or kindreds as a link, recognised, however, to be a very brittle one, binding them together so as to end or prevent the recurrence of a feud.

[1] *Nefan* cannot mean son or grandson, for Hygelac was his father and his grandfather was Hrethel.

When Beowulf, after his first exploit in aid of Hrothgar against Grendel, has returned to his maternal uncle and chief of kindred Hygelac, and is recounting his adventures, the poet at the first mention of Hrothgar's queen makes him call her the 'peace bond to the people.' And in the same breath, in telling how in Hrothgar's hall the daughter Freaware bore the ale-flagon, he stops to tell how that 'she, the young, the gold dight, was promised to the 'gay son of Froda; it having pleased the Friend of 'the Scylfings that he, through that woman, should 'compose deadly enmities and feuds.' And the poet makes Beowulf moralise to the effect:—'Often and 'not seldom anywhere after deadly strife, it is but a 'little while that the baneful spear reposes, good 'though the bride may be!'

Marriage a link between kindreds.

It would seem that Hrothgar had been formerly at feud with the Heathobeards, that Froda had been killed in the feud, and that the marriage of Freaware to Froda's son, Ingeld, was to close the feud. But Beowulf repeats aside to Hygelac that he does not think much of the chances of a long continuance of peace between Scyldings and Heathobeards (2030).

Well may it mislike the ruler of the Heathobeards and every thane of that people when the lady goeth into hall with a prince born of Danes, amidst the high company; upon him do glisten heirlooms of their ancestors, ringed harness, once Heathobeardic treasure, while they could keep the mastery of those weapons and until they in an unlucky moment led to that buckler play their dear comrades and their own lives. Then saith one over the beer, one who observes them both, an old lance fighter. . . . 'Canst thou, my friend, recognise the blade, the precious steel, which thy father carried into battle, wearing his helmet for the last time, where the Danes slew him? . . . and the masters of the battle-field were the fiery Scyldings! Now here a boy of one of those banesmen walketh our hall . . . wearing the treasure which by right should have been thine!' So urged and egged on at every turn with galling words, at last the moment comes that for his father's deeds the lady's thane sleepeth bloodspattered after the falchion's bite, life-doomed! The other escapes alive! By-and-by the sworn oaths of the warriors on either side will be broken, when in Ingeld's mind rankle war purposes, and care has lessened his domestic sorrow! Therefore I deem not the loyalty of the Heathobeards nor the alliance with the Danes secure, or the friendship firm! (2033-2069, slightly abridged.)

What a consistent light this passage throws incidentally on the quarrels which, in spite of the Geats and Swedes being bound together in friendship by the marriage of Beowulf's mother, broke out again and again, according to the poem, between the two kindreds—quarrels in which Beowulf himself is represented as taking no part, presumably because, according to tribal custom, his blood relationship to both kindreds was a bar to his taking up the feud or assuming the part of the avenger! And how the whole story of Beowulf's paternal kindred reveals the melancholy fact that, however great the force of tribal custom in controlling feuds, the wild human nature of hot-blooded tribesmen was wont to break through restraints and often ended in the outlawry of tribesmen and the breaking up of kindreds!

Summary of the evidence of Beowulf.

To sum up the results obtained from the study of tribal custom as incidentally revealed in Beowulf:—

(1) There is no feud within the kindred when one kinsman slays another. However strong the natural instinct for avengement, it must be left to fate and natural causes. Accidental homicide does not seem to be followed even by exile. But murder within the kindred breaks the tribal tie and is followed by outlawry.

(2) Marriage between two kindreds is a common

though precarious means of closing feuds between them. The son of such a marriage takes no part in a quarrel between his paternal and maternal relations.

(3) When a marriage takes place, the wife does not pass entirely out of her own kindred into her husband's. Her own kindred, her father and brothers, maintain a sort of guardianship over her, and the son in some sense belongs to both kindreds. He may have to join in his maternal kindred's feuds, and he may become the chieftain of his maternal kindred on failure of direct male succession, even though by so doing he may have to relinquish the right of chieftainship in his paternal kindred to another kinsman.

Finally, in passing from the blood feuds to the composition substituted for them, after what we have learned from Beowulf of tribal custom, there need be no surprise that maternal as well as paternal relations are found to be interested in them. We may fairly judge that tribal custom, in the stage in which we find it in Beowulf and later in the laws of various tribes, would not have been true to itself, had this been otherwise.

CHAPTER IV.

TRIBAL CUSTOM OF THE IRISH TRIBES.

I. THE ERIC FINE OF THE BREHON LAWS.

RETURNING now once more to the examination of tribal custom and the structure of tribal society in the case of tribes belonging to the Celtic group, it might be expected that Cymric customs would be likely most closely to accord with those of the Celtic tribes of Ireland, Brittany, and Gaul. But it must be remembered that the Cymry whose customs are contained in the Codes, whatever their original Continental position may have been, are supposed to have come into Wales from the North, with Cunedda and his sons. The Codes therefore probably represent the customs of the Cymry of ancient Cumbria north of the Solway Frith, rather than those of the Britons, whether Goidels or Cymry, dwelling in South Wales and more or less subject for generations to Roman rule.

Goidelic tribal custom differed from Cymric.

If the theory of the emigration from Wales and Cornwall into Brittany, as the consequence of the Saxon invasion, be correct, the Britons who emigrated into Brittany may never have shared the peculiar customs of the immigrants into Wales following upon the conquests of Cunedda and his sons. They may have had more in common with the Goidelic tribes of South Wales than with the Cymric newcomers into Wales.

These considerations may well prepare the way for the recognition of differences as well as resemblances between Cymric and Irish tribal custom.

The system of payments for homicide amongst the ancient tribes of Ireland as described in the Brehon Laws differed widely from that of the Cymric Codes.[1]

In the first place, the Brehon laws describe no scale of galanas or wergeld, directly varying with the social rank of the person killed. Gradations of rank there were indeed, and numerous enough. But there appears to have been only one *coirp-dire*, or body-fine, the same for all ranks, namely seven cumhals or female slaves—the equivalent of twenty-one cows.

The Brehon *coirp-dire* of all tribesmen the same: six cumhals and one added.

And when this *coirp-dire*, or price of the body or life of a man, is further examined, it is found to consist of two parts: (1) one cumhal of compensation (aithgin); (2) the six cumhals of the *coirp-dire* proper.

In the tract 'Of every Crime'[2] it is stated:—

> If the man who is dead has a son, he takes the cumhal of compensation alone. If not alive, his father is to take it. If not

---

[1] The references in this chapter are to the four volumes of *The Ancient Laws of Ireland*. I regret very much not to have had the advantage of vol. v. edited by Dr. Atkinson and not yet published, but I am greatly indebted to him for his kind help and advice on many difficult points.

[2] iv. p. 259. This passage is abridged.

alive, his brother; if he be not alive, the nearest person to him is to take it. And then the coirp-dire is divided:

3 cumhals to the son and the father;
1 cumhal to the brother;
1 cumhal to the son and father (*sic*);
1 to the geilfine from the lowest to the uppermost man;

—so making up the 6 cumhals of the coirp-dire.

And in the 'Book of Aicill' (p. 537) are these lines:

Three eric fines are counselled:
(1) There is paid full compensation;
(2) And fair honest coirp-dire;
(3) And honour-price is paid.

Besides this coirp-dire, therefore, was the *eneclann*, honour-price or price of the face, *i.e.* payment for insult. And this was the payment, by no means confined to homicide, which varied according to rank.

The *eneclann* or honour-price varied with rank.

These two things then—the coirp-dire of seven cumhals and the honour-price—made up together (with, in some cases, exceptional additions) the eric fine.

The 'eric' fine included both.

Next as to the persons liable for its payment.

In the Corus Bescna[1] the following statement is made relating to homicide in cases where the homicide was one of *necessity*:—

The eric fine is to be paid by the slayer's kindred (fine), as they divide his property (cro). He (the slayer) shall pay a cumhal of restitution (aithgin) and as much as a son or a father of the six cumhals of the dire-fine.

As to crimes of *non-necessity*:—[2]

he himself is to be given up for it, with his cattle and his land.

If he has not enough to pay the eric or is not to be caught, then

The kindred of 'near hearths' were liable for the whole eric.

it is to be paid by his son until his cattle and his land be spent on it (or failing him) by his father in the same manner.

[1] iii. p. 69.

[2] *Ibid.* and iv. 245–248.

Lastly, failing both the son and the father,

it is to be paid by each nearest hearth (teallach) to him until all they have is spent, or full payment of the crime is made up among them.

So that, in the absence or in default of the murderer, at the date of this Brehon tract, his family and kindred were answerable for the whole of the eric in the case of wilful murder.

The 'hearths' liable apparently to third cousins.

The nearest hearths or 'fine who bear the crimes of each kinsman of their stock' were, according to the Senchus Mor (i. p. 261):—

1. *Geil* fine;
2. *Derb* fine;
3. *Iar* fine;
4. *Ind* fine.

I think M. D'Arbois de Jubainville[1] is probably right in explaining these four hearths or fines to be groups or grades of kindred. He divides them thus:—

The *geil* fine	father; son; grandson; brother.
derb fine	grandfather; paternal uncle; nephew; first cousin.
iar fine	great-grandfather; great-uncle; great-nephew; second cousin.
ind fine	great-great-grandfather; great-great-uncle; great-great-nephew; third cousin.

Whether this interpretation of the Brehon scheme

[1] *Cours de Littérature Celtique*, tome vii. *Etude sur le Droit Celtique*, tome i. p. 186.

of the divisions of the Irish fine or kindred be correct in every detail I shall not venture to give an opinion, further than to say that, viewed in the light of other tribal systems, it seems to me to be nearer the mark than the various other attempts to make intelligible what after all are very obscure passages in the Brehon Laws. The seventeen persons making up the four divisions of the fine or kindred must be taken, I think, as representing *classes* of relations and not individuals; *e.g.* under the head 'first cousin' must be included all 'first cousins,' and so on throughout.

So understood, the four hearths or groups of kindred liable for the eric would include the sixteen grades nearest of kin to the criminal. He himself, or the chieftain, would form the seventeenth person on the list.

The tract 'Of every Crime' seems to confirm the view above taken. It states (iv. 241) that 'for the crimes of every criminal' he himself was first liable.

> If he has absconded it goes upon his chattels; living chattels or dead chattels.

The four 'fines' or 'hearths' were groups of kinsmen in grades of relationship.

The liability falls next upon his father and his brother, but, according to the commentary, upon his son first, if he have one. These seem to be the *geilfine* relations or nearest hearth. And after them it falls, according to the text, upon his 'deirbhfine relations.' And 'if they have absconded so that they cannot be caught, his crime goes upon his chief.' But before it goes upon the chief the iarfine and other fines come in, according to the commentary, and the *chief* is said to be that of the *four fines.*

> The reason why the crime goes upon the deirbhfine division and the iarfine division here before it goes upon the chief is

because it is one chief over them. . . . *His chief—i.e.* the chief of the four families (p. 243).

On the whole, therefore, according to whatever rules of kinship a fine may have been divided into the 'four nearest fines or hearths,' we can hardly be wrong in considering them not as four artificial groups including in all seventeen individuals, but as four *family groups* arranged in the order in which liability for a kinsman's crime was to be shared.

The same groups both received and paid eric.

The full liability for the eric would then, as in the Cymric case, fall upon the four groups or hearths as a whole. But, again as in the Cymric case, the amount falling upon each of them was defined and divided among the individuals composing it. The same family division held good both as regards payment and receipt of eric.[1]

The general correspondence between the obligation to pay and the right to receive a share in fines is shown by another passage from the Senchus Mor:

> The feini charge the liability of each kinsman [comfogius] upon the other in the same way as he obtained his eric fine and his inheritance.[2]

[1] The view here taken, that the four fines in the geilfine division are classes or grades of relationship, makes more intelligible the rules laid down in the Book of Aicill (iii. 331–335), especially the one which determines that 'if one person comes up into the "geilfine" so as to make it excessive, a man must go out of it into the "deirbhfine," and a man is to pass from one division into the other up as far as the indfine, and a man is to pass from that into the community.' Obviously, as a fresh *generation* comes into the nearest hearth, a generation at the top naturally moves out of the group. The great-grandfather becomes a great-great-grandfather, and so on.

[2] i. p. 263, and iv. p. 245.

The penalties for any other crime than homicide fell in the first instance upon the criminal alone, and the person injured took the whole of the compensation for his injury.

But it was not so in the case of homicide. It was not a matter for the individual alone. Both in payment and receipt it was, as with the Cymry, a joint interest of the kindred

The following passage makes this clear :—

> What is the reason that it is upon himself alone every crime that a person commits goes, *except killing*, provided he has the means of paying it?
>
> *Answer*. Because, though it be against him alone evil is done, *except killing*, it is to himself alone it shall be paid. Every *killing*, however, which he commits, it is not he alone that shall pay for, though he has the means of paying for it, but it goes upon the family (fine), and this is now the reason: because though it were himself or his son that had been killed, it is the whole family (fine) that would take the body fine (coirp-dire) of either of them, and not his son or father.[1]

The solidarity of the kindred.

A still clearer indication of this solidarity of the family or kindred occurs in the Book of Aicill (p. 541) in regard to the right of the several members, according to relationship, to share in composition for a kinswoman abducted without their consent. If taken without her own consent, honour-price was to be paid to herself, and also honour-price was to be paid to her chiefs, and her relations, according to the nature of their relationship to her. This presumably was for the breach of their protection. Should death overtake her before she was restored, coirp-dire and honour-price were to be paid to her family. In case

[1] iv. p. 245.

of her consent it was the same except that she could claim no honour-price for herself.

So far, then, we have felt our way to the following conclusions:—

Summary of the rules as to eric.

(1) That the eric for homicide in Ireland was shared by the family in grades of relationship elaborately fixed, but which it is not necessary to discuss further.

(2) In cases of innocent homicide the family, *i.e.* four nearest hearths or grades of kindred, shared the eric with the slayer, *i.e.* the slayer was only liable to pay a share of the eric.

(3) In cases of intentional homicide the goods of the murderer all had to go first, and only the remainder was thrown upon his kindred. But (except *inter se*) they were liable to the kindred of the slain for the whole of what the slayer could not pay.

(4) The eric consisted of two parts—the coirp-dire and the honour-price. The coirp-dire was seven cumhals, one of which was for restitution (*aithgin*), the other six cumhals being the *coirp-dire* proper.

(5) As in other laws, there were sometimes additional payments for breach of protection or privilege &c.

II. THE HONOUR-PRICE (ENECLANN).

It is necessary next to direct special attention to the honour-price (eneclann).

The question at once arises, *whose* honour-price had to be paid?

In the first place, according to a passage in the Book of Aicill, it is the honour-price of the *slayer* that had to be paid, *i.e.* the higher the rank of the slayer the greater the payment to the kindred of the person slain.

The honour-price of the slayer.

The passage alluded to occurs almost at the beginning of the Book of Aicill (p. 99). The heading, literally translated, is: 'Fines are doubled by anger (ferg).' Then follows a long commentary, in which the point seems to be limited to *secret* murder, and the doubling seems to be the result of the *concealment*. This is quite consistent with tribal feeling as shown in other laws, concealment of the slain person on the part of the murderer being considered a grave aggravation. The passage is as follows:—

> *Fines are doubled by anger (ferg).*
>
> The double of *his own honour-price* is due of each and every person, whether native freeman, stranger, foreigner, daerman, or looker-on, for the crime of *secret* murder.[1]

And then the commentary goes on to say that if it was the same person who killed and concealed

> a fine of 7 cumhals and full honour-price for the concealing, and 7 cumhals and full honour-price for the killing, which is twice 7 cumhals and double honour-price upon a native freeman for secret murder.

Obviously the *honour-price* in both cases is that of the murderer, for a little further on is a statement that

> the same fine is upon a native freeman for looking on at the killing of a native freeman, or a stranger, or a foreigner, or a daerman.[2]

The honour-price of the slain or of his kinsmen.

But besides this honour-price of the criminal, as we have seen, other payments had apparently to be made to the relatives of the slain, for breach of their protection or for injury sustained, and these were

[1] iii. p. 99.

[2] p. 101.

measured by the honour-price of the recipients and not by that of the criminal.

It is not quite clearly stated that these payments were a part of the eric, but we may suppose that they were in a sense a buying off of the right of feud, and accepted in lieu of the right of joining in the avengement of the crime and in the feud, for which the eric was the composition.

The honour-price of the protector of the slain.

A passage in the Book of Aicill (p. 107) incidentally seems to show that the son of a person slain could choose whether to claim honour-price on the scale of his own social rank, according to right of property, or of the status of his father or grandfather, or that of the chieftain under whose protection he lived.

> If, having been given his choice of taking honour-price in right of property, or honour-price in right of his father and his grandfather, he made choice of honour-price in right of his property, and decay came upon his property so that he has [left] but the kingship of the three handles—the handle of his flail, the handle of his hatchet, and the handle of his wood axe; he is (then) entitled to but one screpall for his worthiness if he be worthy; and if he be not worthy he is entitled to nothing, unless children have been born to him afterwards which he had not before on the day of making his choice, and if they have been born he has honour-price in right of them.

The passage goes on to mention the case of his having made choice 'to have honour-price in right of his relations or in right of his chief.'

In the Senchus Mor (i. p. 275), without direct mention of the case of homicide, is the following statement:—

> The honour-price is fourfold. Full honour-price is due to one for his father, half honour-price for his father's brother, one third honour-price for his son or his daughter, one fourth honour-price for his grandson.

On the whole it may be gathered from the Brehon

tracts that, whilst the coirp-dire or body fine was a fixed amount, the eric or full payment was complex, involving, besides the coirp-dire, the honour-price of the slayer according to his rank, and also payments to the relations of the slain, regulated by their honour-price and rank, and nearness of relationship to the slain person, by way of reparation for the insult or injury involved, or for breach of their protection, &c.

In order to judge how much these payments of honour-price added to the eric, we must seek to learn something of the character of the various grades and ranks, and the amount of the honour-price of each.

III. THE GRADATIONS IN RANK UNDER THE BREHON LAWS.

The gradations in the honour-price, as stated in the 'Crith Gabhlach,' become very important from the light thrown by them upon the structure of tribal society in Ireland.

The 'midboth' or ordinary freeman and his food allowance.

At the bottom of the list of these grades is mentioned the *midboth* man or ordinary freeman without land or cows (?). He is said to be entitled, as food allowance, to the humblest fare of 'milk and stirabout' and for himself alone (iv. 301).

His honour-price is only a dairt heifer or colpach heifer, and his honour-price (as that of other grades) is also the limit of the value of his oath or pledge. He is a man who has not yet attained to a household of his own. When he has done that he seems to rise to the next rank of an *og-aire*, *i.e.* a young *aire*.

Suddenly, we are told of the og-aire that he has seven cows and a bull, seven pigs, seven sheep, and a horse. He also has a cow land, *i.e.* land to graze seven cows, for which a cow is paid every year by him to his chief. He has an ox, and a fourth part of the needful for ploughing: *i.e.* presumably he joins with others in making up a plough team of four oxen. Surely these have been supplied to him by his chief, as in the case of the Cymric 'da.' His proportionate stock (turcreicc) is eight cows, which with his land he gets from a bo-aire, possessed of surplus cattle, and he pays to him a food-rent 'bes tigi' (like the Welsh gwestva) of a cow and a pig, &c. Should his stock increase he does not always become at once a *bo-aire*, 'because four or five such may occupy the land of a bo-aire, and it would not be easy for each of them to be a bo-aire' (iv. pp. 305–309).

The 'bo-aire.'

So in the same way a *bo-aire* has land of twice seven cumhals, and he has half of a full ploughing apparatus, and his proportionate stock (from his chief) is twelve cows; and a colpach heifer is his food-rent; and his honour-price is five seds.

A bo-aire may have a full and complete plough team and twenty cows and other things, and he may even rise to the giving of proportionate stock to tenants of his own if his stock should have grown too much for his land. But he still may remain a bo-aire. He may, however, rise from a bo-aire into a *flaith* (or chief), when he has double as much as an 'aire desa' and has established himself with a *green* round his homestead, and so surrounded his house with a *precinct* in which he can give protection to cattle taken in distress, this being one of the important duties and functions of a chief (flaith) (iv. pp. 309–317).

It would seem that even when a man had risen to be the chief of his kindred (fine) he might still be simply a bo-aire, and not necessarily yet a *flaith chief*.

In another tract, among other disconnected items are the following :—

> Whatever number of the divisions of the bo-aires happen to be contending, though one of them be older than the others, the grade which is most wealthy, *i.e.* in point of wealth, it is it that takes precedence.
>
> He is a hill of chieftainship in the third person.
>
> Unless his father and grandfather were flaith, though he may be of the same race as to his origin, his chieftainship is lost to him.
>
> A plebeian chief is one whose father or grandfather was not a chief (flaith). (iv. pp. 379–381.)

It would seem from these statements that to become a flaith from the rank of bo-aires something like an election was needful, and that wealth weighed most in the election. It shows, however, that it was election out of a class or family in which the flaithship descended from father to son, and that one of the qualifications was that a man's father and grandfather before him must have been flaiths.

So too in the 'Crith Gabhlach' (iv. p. 321) the *aire desa* must be the son of an aire and the grandson of an aire. He has (probably a minimum of) ten tenants, five *giallna* and five *saer*, and gets a food-rent from each. But he himself takes proportionate stock from his chief, for which he pays food-rent in the same way. The 'aire desa.'

The *aire ard* has twenty tenants, ten *giallna* and ten *saer*, and in his turn he takes proportionate stock from his chief (iv. p. 325). The 'aire ard.'

The *aire tuisi* has twenty-seven tenants, fifteen giallna and twelve saer, and he takes himself propor- The 'aire tuisi.'

tionate stock from a king, 'and he makes corus-arrangements *in the raith right of his father and grandfather,*' whatever this may be (iv. 325).

The 'aire forgaill.'

Above him is the *aire forgaill*, with forty tenants; and at the head of the flaith or chieftain grade comes the *Ri-tuaithe*, who is the chief or King of a Tuath.

The 'Ri-tuaithe.'

The lower grades take stock from the higher and pay food-rents to them.

We need not attempt to discuss the details of this hierarchy of chieftains. It is enough that, throughout, the lower chieftain takes stock from and pays food-rents to the higher chieftain, or the Ri-tuaithe, as the case may be. So that the grades of tribal rank were connected by the link formed by the receipt of an allotment of stock from, and the payment of food-rent to, the next superior grade.

Concentrating attention now on the 'fine' or group dependent upon a single flaith or chief, we have seen that it consisted not only of his kindred, but also of other dependents.

The other tenants of a chieftain.

We have seen that the chief had both *giallna* and *saer* tenants, and that he supplied these tenants with stock, and received food-rent and services in return.

In the second volume of the Senchus Mor[1] are two chapters on *Saer-raith* and *Daer-raith*. And the two kinds of tenancy are explained somewhat as follows.

In the *saer*-raith the stock is given without any pledge, and the return for it is one-third in value as food-rent every year, and the tenant has to perform what is translated as homage, and to do service on the dun-fort, at harvest time, and on military expeditions, but he does no manual labour. The

[1] ii. p. 195.

saer tenant cannot separate from his own hereditary tribal chieftain, or refuse to take stock from him, and to that extent he seems to be *adscriptus glebæ*. But if he chooses to receive stock from another chief he can give it up when he likes, unless not having returned it *for three lifetimes*, he has let the chief get a permanent hold on him, but this must not be so as to rob his own tribe of their innate rights (p. 219). This freedom to take stock from other chieftains does not, therefore, seem to alter his posi tion or that of his successor as permanent tenants of their own hereditary chieftain. And this applies both to his higher chieftain of *kingly* rank, and his own lesser chieftain of *flaith* rank.

Effect of continuance of tenancy for three lives.

He cannot separate from his own king (ri) at any time, either in *saer*-rath or *daer*-rath, unless the chief be indigent. . . . His own *aire* of the *flaith* grade is in the same position as his own *king* (p. 211).

On the other hand, whilst in the case of stock taken from another chieftain the contract can be ended on either side (except after three lives), the hereditary king or chieftain cannot, without good reason, withdraw the stock from the tenants.

If he be his own king he can never take away either his *saer* stock or *daer* stock unless the tenant be indigent, and there are no life separations between the tenant and his own hereditary king unless either of them act illegally, &c. . . .

The tightness of the tribal bond is shown still more clearly by the statement that the chieftain himself is not competent to forgive, so as to bind his successors, the food-rent due from the tenant.

The food-rent is free to the successors of the chief; for the chief is not competent to forgive the payment of what supplies his house (p. 213).

So much we gather from the chapter on *saer*-rath. Now as to *daer*-rath (p. 223). No one was bound to take *daer* stock from any one, not even from his own chieftain or king. Taking daer stock was therefore a matter of contract, and a contract by a tribesman affected his *fine* or kindred.

> The stock is received by the tenant either with or without the knowledge of the *fine*, for if it was unknown to them they could impugn his contract, but if it was within their knowledge, though the stock be ever so great, it is fastened upon them.

The fine had a voice, presumably lest it should be found that cattle in their family herd, unknown to them, might belong to some outside chieftain. And further, if continued for three lives, the obligation might become permanent, as in the case of saer stock.

'Fuidhir' tenants become *adscripti glebæ* after three generations.

Besides these *daer* and *saer* tenants who had taken stock from their chieftain or king, and who seem to have been to a great extent *adscripti glebæ*, there is mention of *fuidhir* tenants. They seem to be strangers, admitted, like the Cymric alltuds, upon a chieftain's land, and, like the Cymric alltuds, free to move away, until by residence for three generations they also have become recognised as freemen, and at the same time *adscripti glebæ*.

In the tract, 'Divisions of the Tribe of a Territory,'[1] is the following mention of the fuidhir tenants, confirming what has been said above.

It occurs in the commentary :—

> His fuidhir tenants, *i.e.* they become free during the time of three persons ; the fourth man is called a daer-bothach person ; the *fifth is a sencleithe* person.

---

[1] iv. p. 283.

The fifth person would be the great-great-grandson of the original fuidhir. Further on (p. 287) is the following :—

> The families of the fuidhir tenants are subject to manifold divisions. The son is enriched in the same ratio as his father, and the father does not sell anything to the prejudice of his sons, grandsons, great-grandsons, or great-great-grandsons.

The fifth generation become 'sencleithe.'

The chief point of interest is that the men of the fourth generation of fuidhirs, according to the above-quoted passages, became *daer-bothach* persons—half free men—and the fifth generation *sencleithe*, so that the family, like the Cymric stranger, grew into freedom in four or five generations.

This gradual growth of fuidhirs into sencleithe tenants in five generations of occupation is illustrated by the retention of rights for a corresponding period. In the Book of Aicill (p. 157) is a statement that the land of an imbecile person (a fool's land) is not lost to his descendants, though they be also imbeciles, 'till five persons :' that is, till the fifth generation.

The number of generations required does not, however, seem to have been absolutely uniform.

The following is from the 'Crith Gabhlach' (p. 321):—

> If there be service from them (cottier and fuidhir tenants which he, the chief, brings upon the land) to 'flaith' chiefs to nine times nine (years ?), they are cottiers and fuidhir tenants; they are *sencleithe* tenants from that out.

In the Editor's note (p. 350) to the sequel to the 'Crith Gabhlach,' there is a statement that the sencleithe tenant was a man who came from his natural chief to settle under another chief; and if he or his successors continued away during the time of three successive chiefs, with the knowledge of the former chief, and unclaimed by him or his successors, he or they then became 'sencleithe,' and could not go away of themselves nor be claimed by the other.[1]

Comparison with Cymric custom as to strangers.

These passages, taken together, seem to imply that after five, or sometimes three, generations of tenancy under the same chieftain or his successors, the fuidhir tenants became in some sense *adscripti glebæ*, like the Cymric alltuds, and at the same time formed a group of kindred very much like a Cymric gwely.

Beyond this it is not easy to realise the position of the *sencleithe* person. The text of the Brehon law tracts is often very obscure, and the commentary so imperfect that the suggestion again and again occurs to the student that the commentator may sometimes himself be groping in the dark. Moreover, all the Brehon tracts have not yet been published, so that we have as yet only part of the evidence before us. Still it seems to be safe to say that there are indications that, as in Wales, there were rungs in the social ladder by which the stranger or unfree tenant might, after a certain number of generations, climb into something like freedom and tribal rights at the cost of becoming at the same time attached to the land of the chieftain; and that to the freeman also the grades of social rank were in some measure dependent upon the social position of fathers and grandfathers and great-grandfathers as well as upon the acceptance of stock and the payment of food-rent and the performance of services to chieftains of higher rank.

[1] Dr. Atkinson has kindly given me a reference to MS. H. 3–18, 237 and 485, the former of which ends its paragraph on 'sencleithe' thus:—'If he serve from that onward, till the fifth man come and during the time (*his* time ?), then he is a sencleithe and he cannot go from the heirs [comarba] for ever after.'

Further, without pressing too far resemblances which are not complete between Irish and Cymric custom, it may at least be suggested that the Irish example of the acceptance of stock by the young og-aire from the chief of his family, or some higher chieftain whose man he was or became, may throw some light upon the Cymric provision of *da* or cattle to the young tribesman who became 'man and kin' to the chieftain who gave it for his maintenance. In the Irish instance, this bestowal and acceptance of stock was part of a system which ran through all ranks and grades. And it seems to have formed the natural link connecting one social rank with another, and securing some kind of solidarity in the whole kindred or tribe, in addition to the tie of blood relationship and sometimes as a substitute for it.

and as to the link between chief and tribesmen made by bestowal and acceptance of cattle.

We are now in a position to consider the amount of the honour-price of the various grades in tribal society as exhibited in the Brehon tracts, and to judge how far it was an important addition to the coirp-dire, and whether it raised the Irish *eric* to an amount at all near to that of the *galanas* of the Cymric Codes.

In the 'Crith Gabhlach' the honour-price of each grade is given as below:—

The amount of the honour-price of each grade.

Midboth men . .	a dairt heifer	or colpach heifer
Og-aire . . .	3 seds of cow kind	
Bo-aire . . .	5 seds	or = 1 cumhal
Aire desa . .	10 seds	or = 2 cumhals
Aire ard . . .	15 seds	or = 3 cumhals
Aire tuisi . .	20 seds	or = 4 cumhals
Aire forgaill . .	15 seds (*sic* ; ? 30 seds)	or = 6 cumhals.[1]
Ri-tuaith		7 cumhals

[1] See *Senchus Mor*, i. p. 76 and iii. p. 43.

The honour-price is given in the 'Crith Gabhlach' in seds. The number of cumhals or female slaves is taken from a list in the Book of Aicill (p. 475) and from a statement in the Senchus Mor (i. p. 76) in which the honour-price of the aire forgaill is stated to be 6 cumhals.

It seems, then, that the honour-price of the Ri-tuaith, the highest chieftain, was seven cumhals, whilst the honour-price of the bo-aire only amounted to one cumhal, that of the og-aire to only three two-year-old heifers, whilst that of the simple freeman without land or cattle was only one single heifer.

Difference between the Irish 'eric' and the Cymric 'galanas.'

The whole eric fine for homicide, including the coirp-dire and additional payments of honour price, evidently fell very far short of that of the Cymric galanas. Even in the case of the Ri-tuaith or highest chieftain slain by one of his own rank, the eric can hardly have exceeded the galanas of the young unmarried Cymric tribesman—viz. of sixty cows.

The importance under Irish tribal custom of the honour-price of a tribesman, and its graduation in proportion to rank, position, and wealth in the tribe, is apparent quite apart from the question of homicide.

The honour-price the limit of the power of protection.

It ruled the value of 'his oath, of his guarantee, of his pledge, and of his evidence.' These according to the 'Crith Gabhlach' (p. 307) were the four things in which he acted to the extent of his honour-price, and he was not competent to undertake liabilities beyond this limit. This becomes very important when we realise how large a place the system of compurgation, or the support of a kinsman by the oaths of his fellow-kinsmen, filled in tribal usage.

On the other hand, whilst the honour-price of a

tribesman or chieftain was the limit up to which his power of giving protection to his fellow-tribesmen by oath or pledge or otherwise extended, it also was the measure of his own protection. He was entitled to his honour-price not only in case of homicide. If he was satirised or insulted, or if the protection he afforded to others was violated, or his house was burned, or any one stole from him, out of his house or in it, or forced his wife or his daughter, his honour-price was the measure of the amount of redress he could claim for the wrong. The analogy of this to the Cymric *saraad* is obvious, and something like it is found in most tribal systems.

A typical case of eric from the Senchus Mor.

Finally, imperfect and vague in some points as may be the result of the foregoing examination of the Irish evidence, we are now perhaps in a position to appreciate, for what it is worth, the curious case described in the Senchus Mor.[1] It may be taken so far as it goes as a precedent or indication of the way in which the intricate matters connected with the eric fine and honour-price were worked out in practice, though it is difficult to explain all the rulings of the Brehon experts.

The matter in dispute was between two of the three principal races of Erin—the Feini or 'men of the North' and the Ulaidh or 'men of the South.' Fergus was the son of the King of the Ulaidh. Owing to a quarrel amongst the Feini, Eochaidh Belbhuidhe, being expelled by Conn of the Hundred Battles, had fled from his own tribe and put himself under the protection of Fergus.

[1] i. pp. 65–77.

Whilst under the protection of Fergus, Eochaidh was killed by Asal the son of Conn, and by four sons of Buidhe, and a grandson of Buidhe. The latter, being the son of Buidhe's daughter *Dorn* by a stranger, was not acknowledged by her kindred (fine).

The eric fine for this outrage upon the protection of Fergus was thus arranged:—He was to have three times seven cumhals, *i.e.* seven cumhals in gold, seven in silver, and land of seven cumhals called *Inbher-Ailbhine.*

This was in satisfaction for the crime of the six murderers, viz. the son of Conn, and the four sons and the grandson of Buidhe. Five out of the six slayers apparently were able to pay their share. But not so the sixth, viz. the grandson of Buidhe, the illegitimate son of his daughter Dorn, who, being unrecognised by the kindred, apparently had no claim for help from them. Consequently Dorn, the mother of the illegitimate grandson, was handed over to Fergus as a bondwoman in pledge for her son's share of the eric.

So matters stood for a time. But a new trouble arose, which seems to have upset the whole settlement and made it necessary to consider it over again, from the beginning.

It would seem that after all there was a question whether the land *Inbher-Ailbhine* was permanently handed over, or only for a time, and redeemable within the period of the lives of three chieftains, because there was a question whether such a period had expired or not. And again it was claimed that Dorn was only given in *temporary* bondage as a pledge for her illegitimate son's share of the eric.

Besides these doubts, new circumstances had created a new position. Fergus was unfortunate enough to have suffered a blemish on his face. This, being a serious matter in a chieftain, was studiously kept from his knowledge. Dorn, acting as bondwoman, was one day, according to the story, preparing a bath for Fergus. Fergus complained that she was too slow about it and struck her with his horsewhip. She, being vexed, reproached him with his blemish, and for this insult Fergus slew her on the spot. Very shortly afterwards Fergus himself died.

This then was the new position, causing a new quarrel between the two tribes and involving the reopening of the old one. The interest lies in the way in which it was settled.

A balance was now struck between the crimes on each side, beginning with the slaying of Eochaidh while under the protection of Fergus, as follows :— Final balance of payments agreed to.

Fergus, being king of a province, was entitled to 18 cumhals both as airer-fine and honour-price for the violation of his protection. There were also due to him 9 cumhals for his half airer-fine and half honour-price for Dorn's insult in reproaching him with the blemish ; so that this was altogether 27 cumhals to Fergus.

On the other side the Feini claimed as follows :—

Honour-price was demanded by the Feini for the killing of (Dorn) the pledge, for the pledge they had given was without limitation of time, and for it 23 cumhals were payable by Fergus for airer-fine and honour-price, for the authority of Fergus was opposed at the time.

This seems to have settled the matter between the two tribes ; *i.e.*, so to speak, the public matter between the Feini and Fergus's people. But there were individual rights to be considered also. Besides these 23 cumhals due to his tribe,

> Buidhe was entitled to honour-price for the killing of his daughter, *i.e.* he was an *aire-forgaill* of the middle rank and was entitled to 6 cumhals as honour-price. Her brother was also entitled to honour-price for her death; he was an *aire-ard* and was entitled to 4 cumhals as his honour-price.

Why the other brother had no claim for honour-price does not appear—perhaps the one brother was the representative of the brothers as a class. The total sum demanded on Dorn's side was therefore 23 + 6 + 4 cumhals = 33 cumhals.

> So that this which the men of the South demanded amounted to 33 cumhals, and the men of the North demanded 27; and a balance was struck between them, and it was found that an excess of 6 cumhals was due by the men of the North, for which the land *Inbher-Debhline* was again restored by the men of the North.

The commentary goes on to say:—

> And it is evident from this, that when a man has paid eric fine, should the person to whom it has been paid commit a crime against him, the law orders that his own eric fine should be restored to the former should it be better than the other eric fine.

In this case the land which had been taken by Fergus as 'seven cumhals of land' was returned to pay for the balance due of six cumhals only.

It will be observed that whilst the father and brother of Dorn had their own honour-price allowed for her slaying, no *coirp-dire* was claimed for the life of Dorn herself. The reason is given as follows:—

> What is the reason that the land was restored by the people of the North and that the eric-fine for the woman was not restored, whereas both had been given (to Fergus) as eric-fine for trespass? The reason is the woman committed an offence in the North for which she was forfeited, and the land did not commit any offence for which it could be forfeited, but it was returned in part payment for that trespass (*i.e.* the killing of Dorn).

IV. THE CURRENCY IN WHICH THE BREHON FINES WERE PAID.

Before leaving the Irish coirp-dire and honour-price, allusion must be made to the currency in which they were paid.

The most significant point was the payment in *cumhals* or female slaves. The cumhal was equated with three cows, but the payment was reckoned and stated in cumhals. The female slave was the prominent customary unit of payment, and doubtless a common object of commerce and trade.

Payment in cumhals or female slaves.

The equation of the cumhal and the cow with silver was also remarkable. The cow was equated with the Roman ounce, and the cumhal with three ounces.

Cumhal = three cows or ounces of silver.

From a passage in the Senchus Mor (i. p. 247) and the Book of Aicill (pp. 371–377), the following table of values is evolved :—

8 wheat-grains		=	pinginn of silver
24 „	(3 pinginns)	=	screpall
72 „	(3 screpalls)	=	sheep (B. of A. p. 377)
96 „	(4 screpalls)	=	dairt heifer
576 „	(6 dairts)	=	bo, or cow, or unga
1728 „	(3 bo)	=	cumhal or female slave

These silver values as compared with those of the Cymric Codes seem at first sight to be singularly low. The Welsh cow, as we have seen, was valued in silver at three Saxon ounces, and the male and female slave each at a pound of twelve ounces. The Welsh value of the cow was roughly three times, and that of the slave three and one third times, the Irish silver value.

This Irish equation between cattle and silver must surely have been made at a time when silver was of quite exceptional value in Ireland. But there is some reason to believe that an earlier equation had been made with gold of a very different character.

An older equation with gold.

Professor Ridgeway has called attention to an interesting story from the life of St. Finian in the Book of Lismore (fol. 24, b.c.), in which an ounce of gold was required for the liberation of a captive, and a ring of gold weighing an ounce was accordingly given.

Now, if the ounce of gold is put in the place of the cumhal or female slave, the gold values of the Brehon monetary reckonings would be :—

Cumhal	=	576 wheat-grains	=	ounce
Bo or cow	=	192 ,,	=	stater or ox unit
Dairt heifer	=	32 ,,	=	tremissis

These gold values, if established, would take their place at once as following the gold system of Constantine, and probably might belong therefore to a period in which the Continental ratio of gold to silver would be 1 : 12, and the silver values fairly consistent with those of the Welsh and other tribes. The cumhal or female slave would then equal twelve ounces or one pound of silver as in Wales. This, however, must not be taken as proved. It is with the silver values of the Brehon Laws that we are here concerned. And we should be tempted to refer this silver value to the period of Charlemagne's attempted introduction of the ratio of 1 : 4 were it not that, as we shall see, it seems to date back to a period some centuries earlier.

There is another point of interest in connection with the early Irish monetary reckoning.

We have seen that in the Brehon Laws the

smallest silver unit was the *screapall* or scripulum. And it has already been mentioned that the scripulum was also known as the *denarius Gallicus*, of which 24 went to the Roman ounce of 576 wheat-grains, as in the Brehon Laws, and that a score of ounces made the mina Italica of twice 5760 wheat-grains. It is curious to find in a passage quoted by Petrie[1] from the *Fodla Feibe* in the Book of Ballymote,[2] a full and exact appreciation of the number of wheat-grains in the scripulum and the Roman ounce. The wheat-grains, according to this passage, are to be taken from wheat grown on typically rich soil which produces 'the three roots,' and 24 wheat-grains are the weight of the 'screapall' of silver, and 576 the weight of the 'uinge' or ounce. Further it is stated that the full weight which the *Tinde* or weighing bar is to weigh is—not a pound: there is no mention of the pound—but *seven score ounces*.[3] Now this reckoning, not in pounds, but in *scores of ounces*, has already been alluded to as, consciously or unconsciously, a reckoning in so many of the *mina Italica*. Petrie quotes a passage from the 'Annals of the Four Masters' in which this payment in scores is illustrated.[4]

The reckoning in scores of Roman ounces, *i.e.* the 'Mina Italica.'

A.D. 1029. Amlaff, son of Sitric, lord of the Danes, was captured by Mahon O'Riagain, lord of Bregia, who exacted 1,200 cows as his ransom, together with seven score British horses and three score ounces of gold and the sword of Carlus . . . and three score ounces of white silver as his fetter ounces, and four score cows for word and supplication, and four hostages to O'Riagain himself as a security for peace and the full value of the life of the third hostage.

[1] *Round Towers of Ireland*, p. 219.

[2] Fol. 181, b.b. This will be inserted in Dr. Atkinson's vol. v. of the Brehon Laws.

[3] In one MS. 'six score ounces.'

[4] Petrie, *Round Towers of Ireland*, p. 214.

Apart, however, from the monetary system of the Brehon Laws, the fact remains that the real currency of early Irish custom seems to have been in *cumhals* or *female slaves*. The coirp-dire and the honour-price of the Brehon tracts were reckoned in cumhals, and we shall find that there appears to be good evidence that both payment in female slaves and the equation of the female slave with three Roman ounces of silver go back to a very early period.

V. THE IRISH COIRP-DIRE AND HONOUR-PRICE TRACED FURTHER BACK THAN THE BREHON LAWS.

The evidence regarding the coirp-dire of the Brehon Laws and its payment in female slaves does not rest on those laws alone.

St. Patrick's 'pretium hominis' of 'seven ancillæ.'

St. Patrick, in his 'Confessions,'[1] treats the *pretium hominis* as a well-known unit of value. These are the words of St. Patrick:—

Vos autem experti estis quantum erogavi illis qui judicabant per omnes regiones quas ego frequentius visitabam; censeo enim non minimum quam pretium quindecim hominum distribui illis.	You know by experience how much I have paid out to those who were judges in all the regions which I have often visited; for I think that I have given away to them not less than the *pretium quindecim hominum*.

Further, in the 'Tripartite Life' St. Patrick is represented as putting the alternative between the death of a transgressor and the payment of seven cumhals ('*Aut reum morti aut* VII. *ancillas reddere debet*').[2] The evidence for this coirp-dire and its payment in ancillæ seems to be thrown back by these passages to the fifth century.

[1] *Tripartite Life of St. Patrick*, ii. p. 372. [2] *Ibid.* i. p. 212.

Further, when we turn to the series of 'Canones Hibernenses' published in Wasserschleben's work, *Die Bussordnungen der abendländischen Kirche* (p. 136), we find repeated evidence that the 'pretium hominis,' or 'pretium sanguinis,' of seven ancillæ, was a well-recognised unit of payment in ecclesiastical quarters more or less connected with the Irish and Breton Churches.

Evidence of the 'Canones Hybernenses.'

The first group of these Canons is headed '*De disputatione Hybernensis Sinodi et Gregori Nasaseni sermo de innumerabilibus peccatis incipit.*'

The first clause of this group imposes a penance for parricide of fourteen years in bread and water and satisfaction; or half this only if there was no intention.

The next clause imposes for ordinary homicide seven years' penance in bread and water.

Clauses 8 and 10 fix the 'prætium animæ' of a pregnant woman (including woman and child) at twelve ancillæ.

Clause 9 fixes for us the silver value of the *ancilla* and seems to show that it was the same as the silver value of the cumhal in the Brehon Laws.

Ancilla of same value in silver as the Brehon *cumhal.*

The clause is as follows:—

> XII. Altilia[1] vel XIII. sicli (? XII.) prætium uniuscujusque ancillæ.

Ecclesiastical usage retained to some extent the use of Roman phraseology. The siclus or sicilicus, as we have already seen, was the didrachma of two Roman *argentei* or silver drachmæ And as the drachma after Nero was one eighth of the Roman

[1] Altilia, *i.e.* fattened heifers, Skeat, *sub voce* 'heifer.'

ounce, so the *siclus* was one quarter. The Altilia was the 'fattened heifer' possibly of Irish custom.[1] Twelve fattened heifers or sicli equalled therefore three Roman ounces—*i.e.* the exact silver value of the cumhal of the Brehon Laws. Here, therefore, in these so-called Irish Canons the ancilla seems to be reckoned at the Brehon silver value of the cumhal.

Having gained this point we proceed to examine the other clauses.

In title III., headed '*Synodus Hibernensis decrevit*,' are the following:[2]—

Seven ancillæ the price of a man's life.

Sanguis episcopi vel excelsi principis vel scribæ qui ad terram effunditur, si colirio indiguerit, eum, qui effuderit, sapientes crucifigi judicant, vel VII. ancillas reddat.	The blood of a bishop or high prince or a scribe poured on the ground, *si colirio indiguerit*,[3] the 'sapientes' judge that he who sheds it shall be crucified or pay seven ancillæ.

Here, obviously, the VII. ancillæ are the price of the life of the criminal—the seven cumhals of the coirp-dire. The canon adds the following:—

Si in specie, tertiam partem de argento et comparem verticis de auro latitudinem nec non et similem oculi de gemma pretiosa magnitudine reddat.	If paid in specie, one third must be paid in silver, and of gold of the size of the crown of the head, and also the like in precious stone of the size of an eye.

These passages seem to have a curious corre-

---

[1] The samaisc heifer of the Brehon Laws being $\frac{1}{2}$ oz., and the dairt heifer $\frac{1}{6}$ oz., the fattened heifer would naturally take the middle place between them as $\frac{1}{4}$ oz.

[2] Wasserschleben refers these canons to the fifth century Synod under St. Patrick.

[3] '*Si colirio indiguerit*' seems to be equivalent to the Irish 'that requires a tent.' But Dr. Atkinson informs me that the Irish word literally means 'a plug of lint.'

spondence with the following passage in the Brehon Laws (sequel to the 'Crith Gabhlach,' iv. p. 363):—

> As to the shedding of a bishop's blood, if it reaches to the ground as blood that requires a tent the guilty person is to be hanged for it, or it is seven cumhals that are to be paid for his sick maintenance and his eric.
>
> If the wound be in his face, the breadth of his face of silver is paid, and of the crown of his head of gold.

The canons go on to state that if the blood does not reach the ground *nec colirio indigeat* the hand of the striker is to be cut off, or the half of VII. ancillæ paid, if the act is done with intention; if not, the price of one ancilla is to be paid.

Another clause states that if a bishop be struck or violently handled, without effusion of blood, half the price of VII. ancillæ is to be paid.

In all these cases the fines are reckoned in a unit of VII. ancillæ or the half of it. The cutting off of the hand of the criminal is reckoned as equal to half of VII. ancillæ. The VII. ancillæ is the recognised unit.

When, in other clauses, dealing with the case of the same things done to a *priest*, a lesser punishment is decreed, still *the price of VII. ancillæ* is the price of the life of the criminal. If the blood of a priest is shed and reaches the ground, *donec colorium subfert*, the hand of the criminal is to be cut off, or half of VII. ancillæ to be paid, if the act be intentional. If not intentional, the price of one ancilla is enough.

In title IV., *De jectione*, after a clause stating that he who ejects a poor man kills him, and he who meets a person ready to perish and does not succour him kills him, there follows this clause :—

Si quis jecerit episcopum et si mortuus fuerit, accipiatur ab eo pretium sanguinis ejus L. ancillas reddit, id est VII. ancillas uniuscujusque gradus vel l. annis peniteat et ex his accipiuntur VII. ancille de jectione ejus.	If any one ejects a bishop and if he should be dead, let there be received for him the price of his blood, let him render fifty ancillæ, *i.e.* seven ancillæ for each grade of rank, or do penance fifty years, and from these shall be received seven ancillæ *de jectione ejus.*[1]

'Pretium sanguinis' seven ancillæ.

Here the ordinary '*pretium sanguinis*' or *coirp-dire* is again clearly reckoned at VII. ancillæ, and the bishop, being of the seventh grade of rank in the ecclesiastical hierarchy, is to be paid for sevenfold.

It is also worth notice that in these clauses the cutting off of a hand is reckoned as *half* of the '*pretium sanguinis*.' This is in full accordance with the Brehon rule laid down in the 'Book of Aicill' (iii. p. 349).

Half the eric-fine of every person is to be paid for a foot, a hand, an eye, a tongue.

But inasmuch as the 'eric-fine' in this case might be taken by mistake to include the honour-price as well as the coirp-dire, the commentary adds :—

He is entitled to half 'coirp-dire' and half compensation (aithgin) and full honour-price.

The loss of the hand was reckoned at half the coirp-dire. The full honour-price was due for the insult or assault.

Yet another clause in these canons seems to show that not only the coirp-dire of seven cumhals was

[1] Compare this clause with the 'Book of the Angel,' *Tripartite Life*, ii. p. 355. 'Item si non receperit prædictum præsulem in hospitium eundem et reclusserit suam habitationem contra illum, septem ancillas (cumala) sive septem annos pœnitentiæ similiter reddere cogatur.'

familiar to the makers of the canons, but also the honour-price.

In the Brehon Laws the honour-price was payable for breach of a chieftain's protection, and in the case of the Ri-tuaith or kingly chieftain of a Tuath the honour-price was, as we have seen, seven cumhals. And so also was that of the bishop of the church in his territory.[1]

'Honour-price' of a bishop or king seven ancillæ.'

Accordingly, in the following clause in the canons the bishop is put in the same position as a king, with what was practically an honour-price of seven ancillæ:—

Patricius dicit: Omnis qui ausus fuerit ea quæ sunt regis vel episcopi aut scribæ furari aut rapere aut aliquod in eos committere, parvipendens dispicere, VII. ancillarum pretium reddat aut VII. annis peniteat cum episcopo vel scriba.

Patricius dicit: Every one who shall dare to steal anything belonging to a king or bishop or scribe, or to take away from or commit anything against them heedlessly, shall pay the price of seven ancillæ or do penance for seven years with a bishop or scribe.[2]

So that, though it is not very easy to put an exact date upon these canons, they seem clearly to adopt and confirm for ecclesiastical persons the Irish coirp-dire of seven ancillæ, and the highest honour-price also of seven ancillæ. And further the *ancilla* of these canons was, it appears, of the same silver value as the *cumhal* of the Brehon Laws.

VI. THE BRETON OR GALLIC WERGELD OF THE SO-CALLED 'CANONES WALLICI.'

It is perhaps possible with help from another set of canons to obtain further evidence of Celtic usage

[1] See *Senchus Mor*, i. p. 43: 'Equal dire-fine for a king and a bishop, *i.e.* equal honour-price to the "rig tuath" and the bishop, *i.e.* of the church of a "rig tuath."'

[2] P. 141.

as to the fine for homicide, and what is still more to the point, to trace it back to the Continental side of the Channel.

The so-called 'Canones Wallici' of perhaps the Breton Church.

At the end of the Latin version of the Dimetian Code of South Wales are appended as part of chapter XLIX. several clauses which do not belong to the Code and are quite inconsistent with its provisions. These clauses are carelessly extracted, with variations, from a set of canons which, from their thus partly appearing at the end of the Latin version of the Dimetian Code, have come to be known as the 'Canones Wallici.'

The oldest MS. of this document is referred to the 8th century, and the canons themselves are referred by Haddan and Stubbs to the 7th century.[1]

It is not at all clear that, notwithstanding the name they have acquired, they are of Welsh origin.

The intercourse between the missionary monks and churches of Brittany, Cornwall, Wales, and Ireland was so intimate that there is no difficulty in understanding how a Welsh scribe or copyist falling upon these canons should add extracts from them to a Latin copy he was making of the Dimetian Code. Whether of Welsh origin or not, some of them may have been used, amongst others, by the Church in South Wales.

It may seem presumptuous to doubt their Welsh origin after the opinion expressed both by Wasserschleben and such competent authorities as Haddan and Stubbs, to whose labours the student is so greatly indebted. But that opinion is doubtfully expressed,

[1] i. p. 127.

and reference is made by them to the fact that two of the three MSS. describe the collection of canons not as 'Canones Wallici' but as '*excerpta de libris Romanorum et Francorum,*' and '*excerpta de libris Romanis et Francorum*' while the third, of the 8th century, does not seem to have any heading but '*Incipit justicium culparum.*' Haddan and Stubbs assign the origin of these canons to that period (c. A.D. 550–650) during which both the Welsh Church and the Welsh Principalities appear to have become organised, *i.e.* to the period following St. Patrick and St. Finian, during which the monastic churches of South Wales were the channel of intercourse between the Breton and Irish Churches. This *collection*, according to the same authority, may date from the 7th century.

The Canons may have been meant for use on both sides of the Channel. And as they are '*excerpta*' from books of the Romans and Franks, they seem to originate from the Continental side, however much they may have been used in Wales.

When we come to examine them, they bear every evidence of being '*excerpta,*' and we know from the *excerpta* of Isidor what different materials may be brought together in such a collection. There is no continuous plan or order apparently running through the whole. And certain of the canons, chiefly those relating to *homicide*, seem to be marked off from the remainder by the payments being made throughout in '*ancillæ*' and '*servi*'; whilst in most others the payments are made in *libræ argenti* or in *libræ stagni*, or occasionally in *solidi*, *unciæ*, and *scripula*.

The safer course may be, therefore, to treat them,

not as a consistent and single set of canons, but as *excerpta* from various sources.

The clauses as to homicide.

Following the eighth-century MS. as most likely to be correct in its text, the *excerpta* relating to homicide are these:—

C. 1. Si quis homicidium ex intentione commiserit, ancillas III. et servos III. reddat et securitatem accipiat.

Canon 1. If any one by intention shall have committed homicide, let him pay three ancillæ and three servi and acquire safety.

C. 2. Si quis judicio fuerit competitus et præstando verum durus esse voluerit et ipsam intentionem fuerit interfectus, ancillas II. et servos II. reddi debere præcipimus. Quodsi manum aut pedem vel quemlibet membrum perdiderit similiter duas partes prætii se noverit accepturum.

Canon 2. If any one, being brought to justice, tries to resist the arrest and is slain in the attempt, we declare that two ancillæ and two servi shall be given for him, but if he loses a hand or a foot or any limb let him likewise know that he shall accept two thirds of the price.

C. 3. Si quis homicidii causa fuerit suspicatus et non ei titulus comprobandi, XL. et VIII. viris nominatis, ex quibus XXIV. in ecclesia jurent eum esse veracem, sic sine causa discedat. Quodsi non juraverit, ancillas III. et servos III. reddat et securitatem accipiat.

Canon 3. If any one shall be suspected of homicide, but there are not means of proof ('titulus comprobandi'), 48 men having been named, of whom 24 shall swear in a church that he is right ('verax'), so he shall depart innocent ('sine causa'); but if he [they ?] shall not have sworn he shall pay *three ancillæ and three servi* and be free.

C. 4. Si servus ingenuum occiderit et culpa ingenui fuerit hoc, de fuste aut dextrali aut dubio aut de cultello fuerit interemptus, ipse homicida parentibus tradatur, et quidquid faciendi voluerint habeant potestatem.

Canon 4. If a slave shall kill a freeman and it shall be the fault of the freeman, and he shall have been slain by a cudgel, or a hatchet, or a . . . or a knife, the homicide himself shall be handed over to the parentes and they shall have power to do what they like with him.

C. 5. Si quis dominus servum arma portare permiserit et ingenuum hominem occiderit, ipsum et alium juxta se noverit rediturum.

Canon 5. If any master permits his slave to carry arms and he kills a freeman, let him know that he must hand over the slave himself and another likewise.

C. 6. Si quis ingenuus servum alterius sine culpa occiderit, servos duos domino. Quod si culpa fuerit servi alius, alius servus domino reformetur.

Canon 6. If a freeman shall kill the slave of another without fault (of the slave), he shall pay two slaves to the master. But if it were the fault of the slave, another slave shall be restored in his place.

. . . .

C. 12. Si quis homicidium fecerit et fugam petierit, parentes ipsius habeant spacium intra dies XV., ut aut partem restituant et securi insedeant, aut ipsi de patria vadant; post hoc si ipse interemptor venire voluerit, reddat medium quod restat et vivat securus. Quodsi interim occisus fuerit, mancipium et quæ acceperint faciant restaurari.

Canon 12. If any one shall have done homicide and shall have sought flight, his parentes shall have the space of fifteen days, in order either to make their share of restitution and remain safe, or themselves quit the country. After this, if the slayer himself wants to return, he shall pay the remaining half and be safe. But if in the meanwhile he shall be slain they shall cause the slave [? slaves] and whatever they had received to be restored.

Payments of six *ancillæ* or *servi* for homicide. The slayer to pay half and the parentes half

Here, apparently, is a fairly complete and consistent set of canons relating to homicide. All the payments are to be made in *ancillæ* and *servi*. And the payment for intentional homicide is apparently a fixed payment of three ancillæ and three servi, *i.e.* six slaves in all. Canons 1 and 2 are consistent and conclusive on this point.

Now, looking at these canons alone, two facts point very strongly to an Irish rather than a Welsh connection, or perhaps we ought to say, to a Goidelic rather than Cymric connection. In the Brehon Laws, as we have seen, the payments are made in *cumhals* or ancillæ, and the fixed wergeld or *coirp-dire* is strictly speaking *six* ancillæ, and one added for a special object, making seven cumhals in all. In the Cymric Codes, on the other hand, the galanas is paid in cows and never in ancillæ, and the amount of the galanas is graduated according to rank, that of the lowest and youngest tribesman being 60 cows, nearly three times as great as the six ancillæ and servi of these canons.

The Irish coirp-dire apparently common to South Wales and the Breton churches from fifth to seventh century.

The force of these suggestions of Irish connection is greatly increased by the fact that nowhere else in the collections of Canons and Penitentials except in these so-called 'Canones Wallici' and the 'Canones Hibernenses,' and closely allied sources, do we find the payments expressed in ancillæ. And it must be remembered that the intimacy between Breton and Cornish saints was mainly with South Wales, and through South Wales with Ireland, and further that South Wales, until conquered by Maelguin, was Goidelic rather than Cymric.

But whether the payment for homicide in the 'Canones Wallici' be the coirp-dire of the Brehon Laws or not, if we may recognise in these rules as to homicide the customs current in some degree on both sides of the Channel, let us say from the fifth to the seventh century, we cannot also fail to recognise in them evidence of influences at work which have broken away partly from tribal usage, and which hail, not from the primitive tribal instincts of Irish or Gallic tribes, but from the side of Roman and ecclesiastical law, to which the districts alluded to had long been subject.

We shall see more and more how foreign the tribal instinct of the solidarity of the kindred, and the consequent obligation on the whole kindred for the whole composition for homicide, were to Roman law and Christian feeling, and how soon under these influences the disintegrating process began in Gallo-

Roman districts, causing the solidarity of the kindred to give way.

The solidarity of the kindred is partly recognised in these canons, but it is also partly ignored.

The extent of the liability of the parentes of the slayer.

The 12th canon states, as we have seen, that if the murderer had taken flight his parentes had fifteen days allowed either to pay part and be secure, or themselves leave the country. What part? The clause states that if the murderer wished to return from his exile he might pay the *half* that remained, and thereafter live secure. So that it would seem that the kindred were only liable to pay half, instead of the whole coirp-dire of six ancillæ and servi. If, in the meantime, the murderer was killed, presumably by the parentes of the slain, the slaves, or whatever else had been received by the parentes of the slain from the parentes of the slayer, had to be restored to the latter, the feud having been satisfied by his death at their hands.

In the Brehon Laws as in the Cymric Codes, the solidarity of the kindred was complete. As we have seen, under Irish custom the whole kindred of the four nearest hearths were liable for the payment of the *coirp-dire* for unnecessary homicide. But the fact that the payment of wergelds was foreign to Roman law, combined with the claim of the Church to protect from death criminals taking refuge at the altar, had no doubt in Northern Gaul, as we shall find was the case in Southern Gaul also, already begun to break up to some extent the tribal solidarity on which joint liability for the payment of wergelds was based.

Those criminals who claimed protection at the altar were, under Gallic ecclesiastical usage, as we shall see, saved from death, but at the same time handed over as slaves to the parentes of the slain. And it is not difficult to detect the lines of thought leading to this result. In the 'Penitentials' attributed to St. Finian,[1] the spirit in which the missionary churches of Brittany, Wales, and Ireland, from their clerical point of view, dealt with crime very clearly appears. A layman, in addition to making composition to the injured person, should also do penance; but a cleric who possessed no property of his own could not pay the composition (s. 9, p. 110). What, then, was he to do in a case of homicide? The penitential (s. 23) lays down the rule:—

The cleric who slays is to give himself up to the slain person's parentes.

> If any cleric kills his neighbour he must undergo ten years' banishment with seven years' penance. If after ten years he has acted rightly and is approved by the testimony of the abbot or priest, let him be received back into his country and let him satisfy the friends of him whom he has killed. Let him return to the father or mother (of the slain), if alive, saying 'Behold I, as for your son, will do whatsoever you tell me.' If he does not rightly do this he is not to be received—'in eternum.'

Then in s. 53 is added, 'If any one will propose better rules we will accept and follow them.'

To sum up the evidence of the canons, we can hardly claim to have done more than to have connected the coirp-dire of the Brehon Laws with the *pretium hominis* of St. Patrick, and with the *pretium sanguinis* of the 'Canones Hibernenses,' and with the clauses relating to homicide excerpted by the compiler of the so-called 'Canones Wallici' from the books of the Romans and Franks.

The connection, though traceable only through

[1] *Pœnitentiale Vinnicii*, s. 23; Wasserschleben, p. 113.

ecclesiastical channels, seems to establish a continuity as regards the fixed payment for homicide between the Breton and Irish churches, and possibly the churches of the Goidelic portion of South Wales, of the fifth and sixth centuries.

Continuity of Irish and Breton custom as regards the 'pretium hominis' and payment in ancillæ.

If it were suggested that the *pretium hominis* of seven ancillæ might be an ecclesiastical invention originating with the missionary churches of the Armorican districts of Gaul, we should still have to inquire why these churches differed so much from other Gallic churches. Everywhere else the Church, finding it impossible to get rid of a deep-rooted custom, seems to have made compacts with the secular power, adopting the customary system of wergelds prevalent in each of the conquered and converted tribes, and giving to the several grades in the ecclesiastical hierarchy graduated wergelds placing them on a level with corresponding classes of tribesmen or laymen. Even in these Celtic Canons the clerical instinct, whilst apparently adopting the fixed wergeld or coirp-dire for laymen, claimed for the clergy a graduated wergeld.

The bishop, as we have seen according to the canons, claimed a sevenfold *pretium hominis*—seven times the price of seven ancillæ—because of his rank in the clerical hierarchy. He claimed too the *honour-price* of seven ancillæ—the same as that of the Irish chieftain of a district for breach of his protection or precinct. The bishop seems to place himself here as elsewhere in these matters, on a level with the secular prince or even with the king.

And again, if St. Patrick in his 'Confessions' (a work the authenticity of which is generally accepted) could use, as he did, the *pretium hominis* as a well-known unit of payment, it would seem that at least as early as the end of the fifth century the value of the *pretium hominis* as a unit of payment was perfectly well understood. And this in itself is a proof of further antiquity.

The redeeming of baptized captives from slavery was moreover a recognised method of increasing the number of converts to the Christian Faith. In his equally authentic Epistle to the subjects of Coroticus St. Patrick speaks of the Roman and Gallic custom of Christians to send holy and fit men to the Franks and other nations with so many thousands of solidi for redeeming baptized captives, while Coroticus was killing and selling captives to a foreign people ignorant of God. Mr. Whitley Stokes, in editing this letter, suggests that this passage points to a date before the conversion of the Franks (A.D. 496).[1] The traffic in captives and slaves, and their sale perhaps into a still pagan corner of France, accords with the strangely local use of the *ancilla* as the unit of payment as well in the Canons as in the Brehon Laws.

What, then, are we to make of this fixed wergeld of seven ancillæ? So far, we find it prevalent only in Ireland and in the Goidelic or non-Cymric districts of South Wales and Brittany. And the evidence seems to carry it back to the fifth century.

---

[1] *Tripartite Life*, p. 378 *n.*

VII. THE WERGELD OF ANCIENT GALLIC CUSTOM. THE EVIDENCE OF CÆSAR.

Cæsar does not state the amount of the Gallic wergeld, but the Druids had jurisdiction in cases of homicide.

There seems to be left but one possible further source of evidence as regards the wergelds of the Gallic tribes before the Roman conquest, viz. that of Cæsar. Speaking of the Druids, his words are these :—

> Illi rebus divinis intersunt, sacrificia publica ac privata procurant, religiones interpretantur. Ad eos magnus adulescentium numerus disciplinæ causa concurrit, magnoque hi sunt apud eos honore. Nam fere de omnibus controversiis publicis privatisque constituunt, et, si quod est admissum facinus, *si cædes facta*, si de hereditate, si de finibus controversia est, iidem decernunt, præmia pœnasque constituunt (vi. 13).

There is certainly nothing in these words, when carefully considered, which indicates in the slightest degree whether the Gallic wergeld was fixed, or graduated according to rank. They amount to this :—

> The Druids have cognisance of nearly all public and private controversies, and if any crime has been committed, if a murder has been done, if concerning inheritance, if concerning boundaries there is controversy, it is they who decide, and they fix the compensation and penalties.

On the occasion of any murder committed, there would be plenty of room for controversy whether the wergeld were fixed or graduated according to rank, or even, as is quite possible, left open to the judgment of the Druids. So that we gain nothing from Cæsar's evidence on this particular point, further than that the penalties for slaying were within the jurisdiction of the Druids.

It may, however, be well to notice that this passage has been the subject of controversy upon another point of interest to this inquiry: viz. on the question whether the evidence of Cæsar should be taken as in favour of the theory of the communistic ownership of land in Gaul or that of individual ownership.

M. Fustel de Coulanges[1] has argued with great force that the statement of Cæsar that the Druids were accustomed to settle controversies whether *de hereditate* or *de finibus* implies that in his view there must have been something like private property whether of individuals or of families.

The evidence of Cæsar on tribal land-holding.

Now if a connection may be traced between the liability of the whole kindred for wergeld and the occupation of land by kindreds, with lesser divisions into something like *gwelys*, then, without pressing the point too far, without suggesting that the Welsh or the Irish form of tribal occupation of land may have been exactly that which in Cæsar's time prevailed in Gaul, we may at least say that the analogy of the Welsh and Irish examples would lead us, from a tribal point of view, to judge that the form of land occupation in Gaul was not likely to be either absolute individual or absolute communal ownership. And as under Welsh and Irish tribal custom and forms of land occupation there was plenty of room for public and private controversies both *de hereditate* and *de finibus*, it may fairly

[1] *Questions Historiques*, pp. 105 117.

be suggested that some form of tribal land occupation would at least be more consistent with what Cæsar recorded in the few sentences under review than either complete individual or complete communal ownership would be.

But, passing from the passages already quoted to Cæsar's further statements relating to the Druids, light seems to pour from them into another matter otherwise very difficult to realise.

It is at first sight with something like amazement that we view the arrogance of the pretension of the missionary priests of the Christian Church to impose what must have been galling penances upon chieftains and tribesmen who had committed crimes of murder or incest. Still more surprised might we well be that they had any chance of securing obedience.

The evidence of Gildas and of the Cadoc records quoted in a former volume is sufficient to show that to a most astonishing extent even chieftains submitted to the penalties and penances imposed by priests and monks who were claiming for themselves immunity from secular services and payments. The very fact that the Ecclesiastical Canons contain the rules we have examined as to the payments for homicide by the kindred of the murderer seems to involve the bold claim of the Church to bring the punishment of crime within its jurisdiction. We have seen also how in these Canons the right of the bishop to be placed in social rank on a level with the highest chieftains and princes and kings was already taken for granted in the corner of Gaul so closely connected with South Wales and Ireland.

The position of the Druids paved the way for clerical pretensions.

The statement of Cæsar opens our eyes to the extent to which under the earliest prevalent system of religious belief the way was paved both for these clerical pretensions and also for the submission of chieftains and people to the penances imposed.

After describing, as above, the prerogatives of the Druids, Cæsar adds a few words to describe the nature of the *sanctions* by which obedience to their awards was secured :—

vi. xiii. 5. Si qui aut privatus aut populus eorum decreto non stetit, sacrificiis interdicunt. Hæc pœna apud eos est gravissima. Quibus ita est interdictum, hi numero impiorum ac sceleratorum habentur, his omnes decedunt, aditum sermonemque defugiunt, ne quid ex contagione incommodi accipiant, neque his petentibus jus redditur, neque honos ullus communicatur.

Whoever of them, whether a private person or a people, does not stand to the award, they interdict from the sacrifices. This penalty is with them a most heavy one. Those who come under this interdict are looked upon as in the number of the impious and criminal. These all shun, avoiding touch or speech, lest they should be hurt by the contagion. Nor to these is justice given if they seek it, nor is any honour shared with them.

Then in the passage following Cæsar describes how strongly organised was the power which the Druids represented and which they had at their back :—

His autem omnibus Druidibus præest unus, qui summam inter eos habet auctoritatem. Hoc mortuo aut, si qui ex reliquis excellit dignitate, succedit, aut, si sunt plures pares, suffragio Druidum, nonnumquam etiam armis, de principatu contendunt. Hi certo anni tempore in finibus Carnutum, quæ regio totius Galliæ media habetur, considunt in loco consecrato. Huc omnes

Above all these Druids, there is one who holds the chief authority among them. To him, if dead, if there be one of the others excelling in dignity, he succeeds, or if there be many equal, by the suffrage of the Druids, sometimes even by arms, they contend for the chieftainship.

At a fixed time of year they hold session in a consecrated place in the district of the Carundique, qui controversias habent, conveniunt, eorumque decretis judiciisque parent. . . .

nutes, which region is held to be the centre of all Gaul. Here all, from everywhere, who have controversies, assemble and submit to their decrees and judgments. . . .

Druides a bello abesse consuerunt neque tributa una cum reliquis pendunt: militiæ vacationem omniumque rerum habent immunitatem. Tantis excitati præmiis et sua sponte multi in disciplinam conveniunt et a parentibus propinquisque mittuntur.

The Druids are accustomed to keep away from war, nor do they pay tribute with other people; they have exemption from military service and a general immunity. Induced by so great advantages, many join their order both of their own accord and sent by parents and relations.

It is not necessary here to follow further these familiar passages in the 'De Bello Gallico' or to inquire more deeply into the religion of the Gauls. It is enough that the religion or superstition of the Gauls was sufficient in itself, and sufficiently deeply believed in, to fortify the influence and power of the Druids with the necessary sanction, and to outlive the disintegration which Roman conquest, in spite of its tolerance to tribal religions, must have in degree produced. The testimony of Renan to the deep-rooted superstition of the Breton population, and the lingering presence even to this day of instincts and customs reaching back to a stratum of indigenous ideas underlying Roman and Christian civilisation, shows, as Irish and Welsh legends do also, that feelings of this kind are not subject to sudden change

And when we try to realise the position and work of the early Gallic or Breton or Cornish or Welsh or Irish churches from the fifth century onwards, we seem to see how their position and work were made possible only by the fact that what was technically called the conversion of a people to Christianity was not after all so great a revolution as one might at first sight have thought.

The missionary monks or priests, it might almost be said, *naturally* took the place of the Druids in the minds of the people. They had power to shut out the criminal from the sacrifices of the Christian altar, just as the Druids could from theirs. The conversion, such as it was, meant at least that in the belief of the people the spiritual powers were transferred to the priest, and that the old sanctions of superstition naturally followed the transfer. Thereby was secured to the Church something of the same prestige and power which had once belonged to the priests of the old religion.

The tribes were used to the central power of the Druids and of Imperial Rome and the Church took their place.

When it is considered how the organised and world-wide system of the Church, with its centre in Rome, continuing to some extent the prestige and the civilisation of Imperial Rome, must have appeared to the chieftains and petty kings of uncivilised tribes, it may be recognised that in this respect also it resembled to their eyes the power of the priesthood of the old religion with its centre at Chartres and reaching in its authority from Britain to Southern Gaul. So that in this respect also the way was paved for the Church in the minds of the people. The tribes were used to the idea of a great central spiritual power, and in the Church, by transfer from the old to the new religion, they found it again.

CHAPTER V.

THE WERGELDS OF THE BURGUNDIAN AND WISIGOTHIC LAWS.

I. THE BURGUNDIAN WERGELDS.

The result of contact with Roman and Christian civilisation.

It is not proposed to do more in this chapter than very briefly to examine the laws of the Burgundians and Wisigoths with reference to the evidence they contain with regard to the results of contact with Roman and Christian civilisation upon the solidarity of the kindred as shown in the payment of wergelds.

The remoteness of these tribes from any connection with the Anglo-Saxon invasion of Britain makes it unnecessary to do more than this. Indeed, this chapter might have been omitted but for the useful light it may throw upon the process of disintegration in tribal custom in the case of tribes settling in countries with a long-established civilisation superior to their own. In such cases tribal custom, however hardly it might resist, had eventually to succumb, thus affording a strong contrast with the Cymric and Irish examples, in which tribal custom was so much better able to hold its own, and even succeeded to some extent in forcing tribal rules upon the new Christian institutions.

The Burgundian laws, so far as they belong to those first issued by Gundebald himself, fall between

A.D. 501 and 516, and his reference to his ancestors in his preface shows that, while he may have remodelled the laws to meet altered circumstances, they were in part based upon traditional customs of his people.[1]

But his people were in a new position. Geographically they were sharing with a population still under Roman law the south-western part of the Helvetian Valley—*i.e.* between Neuchâtel and Geneva, and a good part of the old country of the Sequani on the Gallic side of the Jura.

The method of settlement.

They seem to have come into this district not altogether as conquerors, but in some sense as invited guests. According to Tit. 54 of the laws the newcomers, by the munificence of the Burgundian king and his ancestors, had had delegated to them individually, in a particular place, *hospitalitas*, which consisted of two thirds of the land and one third of the slaves of the *hospes* upon whom they were quartered, and by this clause in the laws they were forbidden to take more.[2] It is generally understood that this method more or less closely resembled the Roman method of quartering soldiers upon a district.

The Burgundians therefore came into a district with a mixed population of Romanised Gauls and Germans, already, after long residence and many vicissitudes, living and settled under Roman law, and regarded by the newcomers as Romans.

Thus two sets of laws became necessary, one for the Burgundian immigrants, the other for the old

[1] Pertz, Bluhme's preface, p. 498.

[2] Bindung's *Das Burgundisch-Romanische Königreich von 443 bis 532 n. Chr.* chap. i.

inhabitants who were to continue under Roman law.

Homicide under the 'Lex Romana.'

Now under the Roman law there was no wergeld. And so in the Tit. II. of the Burgundian *Lex Romana* the slayer, whether a freeman or slave, if captured outside a church was condemned to death. If the homicide was in defence of life it was to be referred to judicial decision according to the Novellæ of Theodosius and Valentinian.

If the slayer had taken refuge in a church, *quia de preciis occisionum nihil evidenter lex Romana constituit*, the Burgundian lawgiver decreed that if a freeman by a freeman should be killed, and the slayer should flee to a church, he who confessed the homicide should be adjudged to be the slave of the heirs of the person killed, with half of his property, the other half to be left to the heirs of the slayer.

After this follows a clause, also of Burgundian origin, fixing the payment by a freeman who has killed a 'servus' and fled to a church. The price is to be paid to the lord of the servus on the following scale :

For an 'Actor'	100	solidi
For a 'Ministerialis'	60	,,
ploughman, or swineherd, or shepherd, and other 'servi'	30	,,
goldsmith	100	,,
smith (iron)	50	,,
carpenter	40	,,

'This by order of the King.'

Under the Burgundian Law.

Now if from these clauses of the Lex Romana which relate to the Roman population, we turn to the Tit. II. of the Burgundian law proper of Gundebald 'De homicidiis,' we may gather what the old customary wergelds may have been, but at the same time recognise how strongly Roman law and ecclesiastical influence had led Gundebald to break through what to the Romanised conscience seemed to be the worst features of the system of tribal wergelds.

Original wergelds no longer adhered to.

Homicide punished by death.

From Tit. II., 'De homicidiis,' it appears that the original wergelds were these:

Optimatus nobilis	300 solidi
Aliquis in populo medioeris . .	200 „
Minor persona	150 „
Pretium servi	30 „

These wergelds closely correspond with those of the Alamannic and Bavarian laws; but the first clause enacts that the homicide of a freeman by another, of whatsoever nation, shall only be compounded for by the slayer's blood: thus overriding tribal usage and introducing the Roman law.

The second clause enacts that if the homicide be in self-defence against violence, half the abovementioned wergelds should be payable to the parentes of the slain.

Homicide by a slave.

Clause 3 enacts that if a slave, unknown to his master, shall slay a freeman, the slave shall be delivered up to death and the master free from liability. Clause 4 adds that if the master was privy to the crime of his slave both should be delivered to death. Clause 5 enacts that if the slave after the deed shall have disappeared, his master shall pay 30 solidi—the price of the slave—to the parentes of the slain. And lastly, in clause 6, the parentes of the slain are in all these cases warned that no one is to be answerable for the crime but the homicide himself, 'because as we enact that the guilty shall be extirpated, so we cannot allow the innocent to suffer wrong.'

The new law breaks away altogether from old tribal traditions, and an attempt is made to treat homicide from the new point of view of reason and justice as between one individual and another, with but little, if any, regard to kindred.

The traditional value of animals.

From the law against theft we get a scale for the equation of cattle &c. with gold. If a Burgundian or Roman 'ingenuus' steals away a slave, horse, mare, ox, or cow, he is to lose his life, unless he takes refuge in a church, and from the property of the criminal the price of the stolen animal is, 'in simplum,' to be paid to the person robbed, unless the thing stolen can be found and restored—*i.e.*:

For the slave	25 solidi
For 'best horse'	10 ,,
For moderate horse	5 ,,
For mare	3 ,,
For ox	2 ,,
For cow	1 solidus.

Thus from these traditional values, retained even under new circumstances by the Burgundian law, we learn that the wergeld of the middle class of freemen, 'mediocres in populo,' of 200 solidi, was still regarded as the equivalent of 100 oxen or 200 cows.

There is no doubt in this case that the solidi were those of the Imperial standard. The Burgundian Kingdom was destroyed by the Franks in A.D. 534—*i.e.* before the issue by Merovingian princes of solidi and trientes of the Merovingian standard.

II. THE WERGELDS OF THE LEX WISIGOTHORUM.

The laws of the Wisigoths are too Roman to be taken as evidence of what may have been the ancient tribal wergelds of the Goths.

The tribal polity of the Goths broken up by Roman influences.

Their rule extended to the Loire till they were driven back to the Garonne by the Franks in the sixth century, and lasted in Spain and Aquitaine to 711 when it succumbed to Arab conquest. The Wisigoths conquered a country already under Roman law, with a mixed population of German as well as Celtic and Iberian tribes. They were not the first German intruders. They were invaders, but not altogether at enmity with the Romans. Their princes, after the break-up of the Roman power, issued gold coins—solidi and tremisses—in close imitation of those of the Eastern Empire. Goth and Roman were encouraged to marry on equal terms. And though there are traces of a scale of payments in composition for homicide, it bears little trace of the tribal principle of the solidarity of the kindred.

There is no scale of payments directly under the head of homicide, and we are left to gather incidentally what the wergeld (if it can be so called) may have been.

In a clause[1] added between 653 and 672 it was enacted that upon the kidnapping of the child—son or daughter—of a free man or woman, the criminal was to be delivered over into the power of the child's father, or mother, brother or nearest parentes, so that they may have power to kill him or sell him.

[1] Lib. vii. Tit. iii. s. 3.

And if they desired it, they might demand the composition for homicide from the criminal, *i.e.* 500 solidi (some MSS. 300 solidi), the crime being to the parents no less grave than homicide. If the child could be recovered, half the composition for homicide was to be paid, and if the criminal could not pay he was to become their slave.

This doubtful mention of 500 solidi or 300 solidi finds some explanation in a later clause.

The wergeld graduated according to the age of the individual.

Indirectly, again, we get the scale in force for homicides in L. VIII. Tit. IV. s. 161, of about the same date. It enacted that injuries done by vicious animals, known to be such, were to be paid for *sicut est de homicidiis* by the 'constituted composition'—*compositio constituta*—and then the following scale is given:

Aliquis honestus	500 solidi
Ingenuus persona, 20 years old and up to 50	300 ,,
Ingenuus persona from 50 to 60 .	200 ,,
Older than this	100 ,,
Youths of 15 years	150 ,,
,, 14 ,, ...	140 ,,
,, 13 ,, ...	130 ,,
,, 12 ,, ...	120 ,,
,, 11 ,, ...	110 ,,
,, 10 ,, ...	100 ,,
,, 7 to 9	90 ,,
,, 4 to 6	80 ,,
,, 2 to 3	70 ,,
,, 1 year	60 ,,
Daughter or wife from 15 to 40 .	250 ,,
,, ,, 40 to 60 .	200 ,,
,, ,, older . .	100 ,,

Under 15, half the payment for a male; liberti, half-payments.

It is impossible to look upon this scale as fully representing ancient Gothic tribal tradition. And when we turn to the title '*De cœde et morte hominum*, which seems to belong to the same date, it becomes obvious how far the spirit of these laws had wandered away from any tribal standpoint and from all recognition of the solidarity of the kindred. A homicide committed unknowingly ('nesciens') is declared to be in the sight of God no cause of death. 'Let the man who has committed it depart secure.'[1]

Innocent homicide no longer to be paid for.

Every man who killed another intentionally, and not by accident, was to be punished for homicide. The punishment had, in fact, already become a matter of criminal law. The prosecution for homicide was no longer to be left only to the parentes of the slain, 'for they might be lukewarm' (s. 15). The judex ought to take the matter up, and on neglect of his duty was to be liable for half the payment for homicide, viz. 250 solidi. Strangers in blood as well as relations had already been enabled to bring the accusation.

Homicides fleeing to a church to be handed over as slaves to the family of the slain.

Chindasvinthe, who reigned from 642 to 653, had legislated in the same direction. The question had arisen, what was to be done with homicides who took refuge in a church and committed themselves to the protection of God? Seeing that every one ought to be punished for his crime, he issued an edict to settle this question once for all. He enacted that whatever slayer or evil-doer the law required to be punished, no power whatever should be able to shield from punishment. And although the criminal might flee to the sacred altar, and in that case no prosecutor could drag him away without the concurrence of the priest, yet the priest, having

[1] Lib. vi. Tit. v.

been consulted, the sacrament having been given, was to repel the criminal from the altar, and expel him from the choir, so that his prosecutor might apprehend him. The criminal thus expelled was to be freed from any further death penalty, but short of this was to be in the power of the parentes of the slain, who might do what they liked with him, *i.e.* he became their slave unless presumably the composition required was paid.

Murder of a kinsman to be punished with death.

The successor of this king (653–672) dealt with another point in which tribal instinct was at variance with Roman law. With the dissolution of the kindred disappeared the reason and traditional justification for the rule that there was no feud and no wergeld within the kindred. Tribal custom everywhere left the worst crime of all—murder of a parent or a kinsman—without redress, at the same time unpardonable and unavenged. It became, therefore, needful to promulgate an edict that the judex should punish the murder of a kinsman by death. And in this case, if there were no children, all the murderer's property was to go to the heirs and near relations of the murdered person. But if there were children of another marriage, innocent of their parent's crime, half only of the property was to go to the children of the murdered kinsman, and half to the innocent children of the parricide.

If the murderer had fled to the altar of a church he was to be delivered up to the parentes or propinqui of the slain kinsman, to be dealt with as they chose, short of death, and if there were no such parentes his property was to go to the fisc. The murderer whose life was thus spared was not to have the use of the property.

Lastly there is found in some of the MSS., as an addition to Lib. XII. Tit. II., an edict of King Wamba, who reigned 672–680, which seems to mark the last stage in the process of confining the punishment of the crime to the criminal alone.

The punishment had become a matter of criminal law and was confined to the criminal alone.

Up to this time, as we have seen, the murderer *with all his possessions* was by law to remain the slave of the parentes, or the next heirs of the murdered person, except in the one case of the murderer having children by another wife. Thenceforth, if the murderer, according to the edict, had children or wife free from participation in the crime, he alone was to be delivered up to the parentes or next heirs of the dead. His possessions were not to go to them, but to the children or heirs of the *criminal*, on the ground that the punishment should in justice fall alone upon the sinner, and not upon his innocent family. Clearly the last tie of tribal instinct securing the solidarity of kindreds was now broken. It had lost its ancient significance. Murder had become the crime of an individual against the State, and a matter of criminal law. The only survival of tribal feeling seems to have been that, as some compensation to the family of the murdered man, the murderer whose life the Church had saved was to become their slave.

CHAPTER VI.

TRIBAL CUSTOMS OF THE FRANKS AND OF THE TRIBES CONQUERED BY THE MEROVINGIAN KINGS.

I. THE WERGELDS OF THE LEX SALICA.

IN turning now to the Lex Salica the inquiry will again at first more or less be a study of wergelds.

There are many difficult points in the construction of the Lex Salica, and the capitularies connected with it, which, after all the learned labour expended upon them, still remain unsettled. To attempt to discuss them fully would involve an amount of research and erudition to which this essay can lay no claim. All that can be attempted in this survey of the traces of tribal custom in the laws of the Continental tribes is to approach their text afresh in the light of the Cymric evidence, as a tentative first step towards, at last, approaching the Anglo-Saxon laws from the same tribal point of view and from the vantage-ground of a previous study of the survivals of tribal custom elsewhere.

The district within which the Lex Salica had force.

The Lex Salica had force apparently at first over the Franks of the district extending from the *Carbonaria Silva* on the left bank of the Meuse to the River Loire.

The first sixty-five chapters about A.D. 500, but with later alterations.

The earliest manuscripts of the Lex Salica are considered to belong to the late eighth or early ninth century. And the general opinion seems to be that the first sixty-five chapters may be ascribed to the time of Clovis, or at least to a period before Christianity had become general among the Franks.

The reign of Clovis extended from A.D. 481 to 511, and may perhaps be taken as covering the date when the sixty-five chapters were first framed. There is, however, no proof that they were not modified afterwards. For at the end of the celebrated chapter *De chrenecruda* there is a clause in a later manuscript which implies that it was no longer in force.[1]

If these sixty-five titles, in their original form, really go back to the time of Clovis, the fact that they were allowed to continue in late issues of the Lex Salica along with the additions made to it, is probably enough in itself to excite suspicion that even these may not have been allowed to remain as they originally stood without modification.

Edict of Childebert II. A.D. 599 on homicide discourages receipt and payment of wergelds.

Particularly on the question of homicide and the liability of the kindred of the slayer in the payment of the wergeld, it is difficult to understand how the clauses relating to its payment and receipt, if representing fully more ancient custom, could have been left altogether unaltered after the decree of Childebert II. (A.D. 599), which may be translated as follows:—

> Concerning homicides we order the following to be observed: That whoever by rash impulse shall have killed another without cause shall be in peril of his life. For not by any price of redemption shall he redeem or compound for himself. Should it by chance happen that any one shall stoop to (make or receive ?)

[1] Hessels and Kern, Codex x. Tit. lxi.

payment, no one of his parentes or friends shall aid him at all, unless he who shall presume to aid him at all shall pay the whole of the wergeld, because it is just that he who knows how to kill should learn to die. (Pertz, *Leges*, i. p. 10.)

The logic of this decree is curious. The slayer's kindred were absolved by it from liability if they chose to stand aloof. But, if they stooped to help their kinsman at all, they must see to it that the whole wergeld was paid, no doubt to avoid breaches of the peace from attempts at private revenge if any part were left unpaid. But if the slayer's relations did not pay the wergeld—what then? The slayer was to be left 'in peril of his life.' From whom? It must have been from the vengeance of the slain man's kindred.

One would have thought that this decree would have defeated itself, for apparently, whilst it absolved the murderer's kindred from obligation to assist the murderer to pay the wergeld, it left untouched the right of vengeance on the part of the slain man's relations, thereby, one would have thought, multiplying cases of breach of the peace.

That clauses relative to receipt and payment of wergeld were left in the Lex after this decree shows probably that the system of wergelds remained practically still in force. People went on 'living under the Lex Salica,' after the date of the edict, and in spite of the latter no doubt wergelds were paid and received. But whilst this may have been a reason why the clauses regulating the payment and receipt of wergelds could not be altogether omitted, it may also have made necessary the modification of some of their provisions.

One may even venture to trace motives in the making of modifications in favour of the fisc, which can hardly have had their root in ancient tribal custom.

The system of wergelds was extended to the advantage of ultimately both official and clerical hierarchies, and even from the Franks themselves to strangers and to the Gallo-Roman population amongst whom they dwelt. And the whole character and system of the 'Lex Salica' was so much like a statement of crimes and the composition to be paid for them that it lent itself very easily to the interest of the fisc.

The Lex allowed a tribesman to break himself away from his kindred. And the fisc gained by it.

In the sixty-five titles themselves there is direct evidence that tribal tradition and the solidarity of the kindred had once existed, and that in spite of the edict the fisc was interested in their maintenance. Thus by Tit. LX., *De eum qui se de parentilla tollere vult*, a door was thrown wide open for the Salic tribesman to escape from the obligations of kindred. To secure this object he is to go to the mallus with three branches of alder, and break them over his head, and throw them on four sides in the mallus, and declare that he withdraws from the oath, and the inheritance, and everything belonging to the parentilla, so that thereafter, if any of his parentes either is killed or shall die, no part either of the inheritance or of the composition shall pertain to him, but all go to the fisc. If we take this clause strictly it implies and sanctions the general right of a kinsman of a slain person to share in his wergeld. The share of the kinsman, who under this clause frees himself from the liability to pay, and gives up his right to receive any portion of the wergeld of a relative, does not lapse altogether, but is apparently kept alive for the fisc.

This clause is not perhaps inconsistent with the edict which left the receipt of wergeld still possible, though payment by the slayer's kindred was optional. And so long as the occasional receipt of wergeld was still possible, rules for its division might reasonably remain in the Lex.

The same may perhaps be said of other clauses included in the original sixty-five. Tit. LXII., *De compositione homicidii*, is the one which deals with the division of the wergeld by its recipients, *i.e.* the kindred of the person slain. According to the text of Hessels, Cod. I., it is as follows:— Tit. LXII., 'De compositione homicidii.'

Si cujuscumque pater occisus fuerit medietatem compositionis filii collegant, et aliam medietatem parentes quae proximiores sunt tam de patre quam de matre inter se dividant.	If any one's father be killed, the sons are to take collectively one half of the composition, and the other half is to be divided between the parentes who are proximiores, both of the paternal and maternal kindreds.
Quod si de nulla paterna seu materna nullus parens non fuerit, illa portio in fisco collegatur.	But if there be parentes on neither side,[1] paternal or maternal, then that portion (*i.e.* the second half) is to go to the fisc.

According to this clause, in the absence of the parentes, their half share still has to be paid by the kindred of the slayer, but again the fisc gets control of the lapsed portion which the parentes would have taken had they been forthcoming.

Amongst some clauses said to be added to the Lex Salica by Childebert I. (A.D. 515 to 551) is a very

---

[1] Brunner (*Sippe und Wergeld*, p. 31) prefers the reading of the other codices, 'on either side,' but the principle is the same; the fisc gets whatever share lapses, whether it be $\frac{1}{4}$ or $\frac{1}{2}$.

Addition to the Lex by Childebert I. A.D. 515–551 in the interest of the widow (?) of the person slain.

important one, Tit. CI., *De hominem ingenuo occiso*, which seems to show that, at that date, composition was still encouraged by the law, but that some alteration was necessary in the division of the wergeld amongst the kindred of the slain.[1]

Si quis hominem ingenuum occiderit et ille qui occiderit probatum fuerit, ad parentibus debeat secundum legem componere; media compositione filius habere debet. Alia medietate exinde ei debet ut ad quarta de leude illa adveniat. Alia quarta pars parentibus propinquis debent. Id est, tres de generatione patris et tres de generatione matris. Si mater viva non fuerit, media parte de leudae illi parentes inter se dividant. Hoc est, tres de patre proximiores et tres de matre. Ita tamen qui proximiores fuerint parentes de prædictis conditionibus prendant.

Et tres partes illis duabus dividendam dimittat. Et nam et illis duabus ille qui proximior fuerit, illa tertia parte duas partes prendant, et tertia parte patre suo demittat.

If any one shall have killed a freeman and he who slew shall have been ascertained, he ought to make composition according to the law to the parentes.

The son (Cod. 2 'sons') ought to have half the composition. After that, of the other half it ought to be for her (? the mother), so that she (?) comes in for a quarter of that leuda (or wergeld). The other quarter ought to go to the near parentes, *i.e.* three [parentillæ] of the kindred of the father and three of the kindred of the mother.

If the mother shall not be alive, the half leuda (wergeld) those parentes divide amongst themselves, *i.e.* the three proximiores [*i.e.* nearest parentes] of the father and three of the mother, but so that the nearest parentes under the aforesaid conditions shall take [two thirds].

Three parts again it leaves to be divided between the other two [parentillæ]. For also of those two the nearest [parentilla] takes two thirds and leaves one third for [the parentilla of] the previous ancestor.[2]

There must have been some special object in this addition to the Lex. Brunner, following the

[1] Hessels and Kern, Tit. ci., p. 412. Pertz, *Legg.* 11, 5.

[2] This translation of the final clause does not materially vary in meaning from that of Brunner, *Sippe und Wergeld*, p. 34.

very plausible suggestion of Wilda and Boretius, points out that the 'mother,' who, if alive, is to share in the second half of the wergeld, may be the mother of the son who takes the first half, *i.e.* the *widow of the person slain*, otherwise why should the mother alone be mentioned, and not the father of the slain?[1] If this view may be accepted the object of the clause becomes at once apparent.

Under Tit. LXII. no share is given to the widow. And we have learned from the Cymric example the reason why tribal custom gave no part of the wergeld of the husband to the widow. It was simply because there was no blood relationship between them. The widow and her kindred would have taken no part in the feud, and so took no part of the galanas in composition for the feud.

The silence of Tit. LXII. and the force of the Cymric precedent warrant the inference that it may have been so also under ancient Salic custom. However this may be, the fact that an addition to the Lex was made, whether in favour of the widow or of the mother, seems to show that Roman and Christian influences had introduced other considerations than those of blood relationship, so breaking in upon tribal custom and necessitating special legislation.

The three 'parentillæ' sharing in the wergeld.

If this view may be accepted, and if (as we had to do in interpreting the Brehon rules regarding divisions of the kindred) we may take the word 'son' as meaning all the sons, and insert the word *parentillæ* in explanation of the three *proximiores*, so as to under-

[1] Brunner, *Sippe und Wergeld*, p. 34.

stand them (as in the Brehon *Geilfine* division) to be not three persons but three groups of kindred, then these clauses become fairly intelligible and consistent with Tit. LXII.[1]

The wergeld is divided into two halves and the second half (subject to the newly inserted right of the widow or mother of the slain) goes to the three groups of proximiores. What these three groups or parentillæ may be is not very clear.

The father has been killed and his sons take the first half of the wergeld. The other half is taken by the three nearer parentillæ. The nearest group at first sight would be the descendants of the two parents of the slain. The second group would be the descendants of the four grandparents of the slain. The third group should include the descendants of the eight great-grandparents of the person slain.

The three 'parentillæ' include descendants of great-great-grandparents.

But Brunner has pointed out that the division into paternal and maternal lines of relationship begins with the slain person's grandparents; so that the three proximiores on both sides should go back to the descendants of great-great-grandparents. He also points out that, as at each step the nearer group are to take two thirds and those behind it one third, the division between the three groups would be in the proportions of 6 : 2 : 1. And he quotes a statement regarding the division of wergelds in Flanders in the year 1300, in which the proportions of the payments of the three groups of relatives were still as 6 : 2 : 1. The half falling to the three

[1] *Sippe und Wergeld*, p. 34.

groups being reckoned as $\frac{18}{36}$, the division was as under :—

Rechtzweers (Geschwister Kinder), *i.e.* first cousins.	paternal	$\frac{6}{36}$	
	maternal	$\frac{6}{36}$	
Anderzweers (Ander-geschwister Kinder), *i.e.* second cousins.	paternal	$\frac{2}{36}$	$=\frac{18}{36}$
	maternal	$\frac{2}{36}$	
Derdelinghe (Dritt-geschwister Kinder), *i.e.* third cousins.	paternal	$\frac{1}{36}$	
	maternal	$\frac{1}{36}$	

We may then safely, I think, follow Brunner's cautiously expressed conclusion that it is very probable that also in the Lex Salica under the words 'tres proximiores' are intended relations belonging to three separate parentillæ.[1]

The wergeld from the payer's point of view.

So far we have dealt only with the *receivers* of the wergeld. We have now to consider the wergeld from the *payers'* point of view. When at last we turn to the title '*De chrenecruda*,' which deals with the *payment* of the wergeld by the slayer and his kindred, we seem all at once to breathe in the atmosphere of ancient tribal custom before it had been materially tainted by the new influences, which the conquest of a Romanised country and migration into the midst of a mixed population necessarily brought with them. The force of tribal instinct survives in this clause even though since the edict of Childebert II. it may have been allowed to remain in the Lex partly on sufferance, and even though some of its details

[1] *Sippe und Wergeld*, p. 36. 'Es dünkt mir sehr wahrscheinlich, dass auch in der Lex Salica unter den 'tres proximiores' Verwandte von drei verschiedenen Parentelen gemeint sind.'

Later examples of division of wergelds in other districts quoted by Brunner show that the division of the kindred into three similar grades or groups was prevalent also in Frisian and Saxon districts.

have been made incoherent by the mutilation it may have undergone. It was probably left in its place in the Lex, together with the clauses regarding the receipt of wergeld, because, even though the assistance of the kindred in the payment of wergeld had been made optional and discouraged, the instincts of kindred were not to be extinguished all at once. To save the life of a kinsman, kinsmen will sometimes exercise the option. And the slayer, before he flees for his life, will make his appeal to his kinsmen. The old traditional rules for payment will have force in the feelings of those who, under all the discouragements of the law, still choose to assist the slayer. Moreover, the Mallus, it appears, still exercised jurisdiction over the option.

This celebrated clause may perhaps therefore be quoted as evidence for so much of ancient tribal custom as to wergelds as the royal edict was unable to extinguish all at once.

The title 'De chrenecruda.'

Difficulty arises chiefly from the imperfect condition of the text of one of the clauses. But, keeping close to Codex I. of Hessels and Kern's edition, the following translation may pass for our purpose (Tit. LVIII.):

(1) Si quis hominem occiderit et, totam facultatem data, non habuerit unde tota lege conpleat, xii juratores donare debet [quod] nec super terram nec subtus terram plus facultatem non habeat quam jam donavit.	If any one shall kill a man and, having given up all he possesses, he yet shall not have enough to satisfy the whole legal requirement, he ought to give the oaths of twelve co-swearers that neither above the earth nor under the earth he has any more property than he has already given up.
(2) Et postea debet in casa sua introire et de quattuor angulos terræ in pugno collegere et sic	And afterwards he ought to enter into his house and to gather earth in his hand from its four

postea in duropullo, hoc est in limitare, stare debet intus in casa respiciens, et sic de sinistra manum de illa terra trans scapulas suas jactare super illum quem proximiorem parentem habet.

(3) Quod si jam pater et fratres solserunt, tunc super suos debet illa terra jactare, id est super tres de generatione matris et super tres de generatione patris qui proximiores sunt.

(4) Et sic postea in camisia, discinctus, discalcius, palo in manu, sepe sallire debet, ut pro medietate quantum de compositione diger est, aut quantum lex addicat, illi tres solvant, hoc est illi alii qui de paterno generatione veniunt facere debent.

(5) Si vero de illis quicumque proximior fuerit ut non habeat unde integrum debitum salvat; quicumque de illis plus habet iterum super illum chrenecruda ille qui pauperior est jactet ut ille tota lege solvat.

(6) Quam si vero nec ipse habuerit unde tota persolvat, tunc illum qui homicidium fecit qui eum sub fidem habuit in mallo præsentare debent, et sic postea eum per quattuor mallos ad suam fidem tollant. Et si eum in compositione nullus ad fidem tullerunt, hoc est ut redimant de quo domino[1] persolvit, tunc de sua vita conponat.

corners, and after this he ought to stand on the threshold, looking back into the house, and so from his left hand throw across his shoulders some of that earth over *him* [? those] whom he has nearest of kin.

But if father and brothers have already paid, then over his (relations) he ought to throw that earth, to wit over three [parentillæ] of the kindred of the mother and over three [parentillæ] of the kindred of the father who are nearest of kin.

And likewise after that, in his shirt, ungirded, unshod, stake in hand, he ought to leap the fence, so that for that half those three shall pay whatever is wanting of the composition or what the law adjudges: that is, those others who come of the paternal kindred ought to do so.

But if any very near kinsman shall be unable to pay the whole amount due, then whoever of them has more, on him again let the one who is poorer throw the chrenecruda, so that he may pay the whole amount due.

But if not even he shall have the wherewith to complete the required amount, then those who held him under oath ought to produce him who committed the homicide in the Mallus, and in the same way again afterwards four times in the Mallus hold him to his faith. And if no one take up his faith concerning the composition, *i.e.* to redeem him by payment, then let him make composition with his life.

[1] Codices 3, 7, 8, 9 have 'de quod non.'

Now, if we are here dealing with actual tribal custom, it is natural to place some weight upon the picturesque incidents which testify to its traditional origin. These picturesque incidents can hardly be other than proofs of antiquity.

The slayer and his co-swearers declare that he has given up everything.

Let us try, then, in spite of some confusion in the text, to make out the probable meaning of the action described. Clause 1 makes it clear that the first public step taken on the part of the slayer was to go to the Mallus with twelve co-swearers, who with him pledge their faith that he has given up everything, above ground or below it, towards the wergeld. There must have been previous negotiations with the kinsmen of the slain, and a stay of vengeance must have been conceded on the understanding that if possible the wergeld will be paid. Having thus obtained legal security for a time, the next stage in the proceeding is one between the slayer and his kinsmen, without whose help he cannot pay the wergeld.

The family gathering to arrange for payment of the rest of the wergeld.

The graphic details of the second clause seem to involve the presence of a family gathering met within the enclosure containing the house of the slayer, and, for anything we know, other houses of near relations. In this enclosure the kindred have met to deal with a family catastrophe in which they themselves are involved as well as the slayer. Even if they have to find only their half of the wergeld, fifty head of cattle from the family herd or their separate herds, as the case may be, must be to them a matter of importance. Standing on the threshold of the house from the four corners of which the slayer has gathered a handful of earth, he throws it over the representatives of his paternal and maternal kindred. He has done his part, and now the responsibility rests on them.

The vagueness and difficulty of the next clause result from a text which has probably been tampered with. But with the help of Tit. LXII. and the addition of Tit. CI., giving further details, it becomes at least partly intelligible. The rule that the payment of wergeld was made by the relatives in the same proportions as they would receive it, if one of their kinsmen had been slain, is so general that we may fairly assume that it was followed also by the Salic Franks. We have seen that according to these clauses, if a father was killed, the sons took the first half of the wergeld, and that the other half was divided between three sets of *proximiores*—the three parentillæ or sets of relatives of both paternal and maternal kindreds—in certain proportions. The slayer and his sons should pay the first half, and his father and brothers apparently help them to pay it. The other part ought to fall upon the three parentillæ nearest of kin on both the paternal and maternal side.

So that Clause 3 becomes partly intelligible. 'If the father and brothers have already paid' what the slayer could not pay of the first half, the earth has to be thrown upon the three parentillæ nearest of kin of the mother's kindred and the three parentillæ nearest of kin of the father's kindred. These seem to be the 'proximiores' who should pay the other half.

The phraseology of the titles LXII. and CI. and the analogy of other tribal custom seem to warrant the conclusion that here also the *three proximiores* on the paternal and the maternal side were originally not three persons next of kin, but the three *parentillæ*, *i.e.*, according to Brunner, the descendants of the grandparents, the great-grandparents, and the great-great-grandparents of the slayer on both the paternal and maternal sides.

The next clause is the one which bears clearest marks of having been tampered with. It makes no sense when strictly construed, but it seems to contain two ideas: first that there may be a deficiency as regards the second half of the payment, and secondly that the persons who ought to make it up are '*those others who come of the paternal kindred*.'

The question who are intended by these words is one not easily answered decisively. Nor is it one upon which we need to dwell. It is to be regretted, however, that at this critical point the text is so sadly confused. For it must be borne in mind that if no relative was liable beyond those included in the phrase 'the three proximiores' then the liability to pay and receive wergeld under Salic custom was restricted to the descendants of the paternal and maternal great-great-grandparents. And whether it was so in ancient custom is just what we should like to know.

Having cast the responsibility upon his kindred, the slayer leaps over the fence.

Be this as it may, the slayer has done what he could in throwing the responsibility upon his kindred. He knows not, perhaps, whether they will fulfil the obligation thus cast upon them. He has given up everything he himself possessed, and now, in his shirt, ungirded, and unshod, he leaps over the fence of the enclosure with a stake ('palus') in hand, to wander about in suspense until it transpires whether the rest of the wergeld will be found or not: whether those who ought to assist him, whoever they may be, will help him in his need.

Clause 5 seems to state merely that the liability of the 'proximiores' is collective and not individual, so that the poorer in each group of relatives are to be assisted by the richer, and we need not dwell upon it.

If his kindred do not pay, the slayer pays with his life.

Lastly, Clause 6 brings the slayer, after all his efforts and appeals to his kindred, face to face with the final result. Four successive times his co-swearers have brought him up to the mallus to hold him to his faith, and now at last, if no one steps in to complete payment of the wergeld, he must pay with his life.

This is the best we can make of the famous title in the Lex Salica regarding the payment of wergeld. But perhaps it is enough when taken together with the clauses relating to its receipt to reveal the main points of early Salic tribal custom. We may state them thus:—(1) That the wergeld was divided into two halves, for one of which the slayer, helped by his father and brothers, was responsible, and for the other of which the three grades of kindred, extending apparently to the descendants of great-great-grand-parents, were responsible. (2) That if the addition of Tit. CI. in this respect represented ancient tribal custom, the payments, like the receipts, of the second half, were so distributed that the nearer parentilla or group of relatives paid and received, in relation to those behind them in kinship, in the proportion of two thirds and one third. (3) That, if we may take the addition of Tit. CI. as giving a share to the *widow*, and as an innovation, then it may fairly be concluded that, under ancient Salic custom as under Cymric custom, the widow originally took no share in the wergeld of her husband, not being a blood relation to him.

Position of the wife and her kindred.

Further, as in the title *De chrenecruda* there is no mention of any share in the *payment* of wergeld falling upon the wife of the murderer or her family, we may conclude that however closely two families might be united by a marriage, the wife, for the purpose of wergeld, still belonged to her own kindred, and that marriage did not involve the two families in mutual obligations for each other's crimes of homicide, until both paternal and maternal kindreds became sharers in payment and receipt of wergelds in the case of the children of the marriage.

What became of the slayer's rights in the land.

It is not needful to follow the speculations of various authorities as to what became of the homestead and landed rights abandoned by the slayer when he threw the chrenecruda upon his kindred and leaped, ungirt and unshod, over the fence of the inclosure. It is begging the question to call it his *Grundstück* in the sense of a plot of land individually owned. Whether it was so, or whether under Salic custom land was held by family groups, as in the case of the Cymric gwely, is what the clause *De chrenecruda* does not tell us. The question may perhaps have easily solved itself. The homestead and grazing rights, under tribal custom, might probably simply merge and sink into the common rights of the kindred, *i.e.* the neighbouring kinsmen would get the benefit of them. Even if the slayer, now himself slain or an exile, had held a privileged or official position as chief of his family, it would not follow that his successor (having doubtless already a homestead of his own) would care to succeed to the one left vacant. It is much more likely that tribal superstition would leave the murderer's homestead to decay. Even the sons of a person, whose kindred had left him to perish by refusing the necessary help in the payment of the wergeld of his victim, might well refuse to 'uncover' the haunted hearth of their father, whilst if the wergeld were paid the slayer would return to his old homestead. Finally it must be remembered that in the tribal stage of land occupation the value of land itself bore a very small proportion to the value of the cattle upon it. And so the 'Grundstück' of the slayer would be as nothing compared with the value of the hundred cows of a normal wergeld.

II. THE DIVISION OF CLASSES AS SHOWN BY THE AMOUNT OF THE WERGELD.

Turning now to the amount of the wergeld, something may be learned of the division of classes under the Lex Salica.

Tit. XLI. fixes the amount of the wergeld of the typical freeman who is described as 'the Frank or the barbarian man who lives under the Lex Salica.'

The wergeld of the freeman living under Salic law 200 solidi.

The amount, as throughout the Lex are all the payments, is stated in so many denarii and so many solidi—8,000 denarii, *i.e.* 200 solidi. And that the Frank or barbarian living under the Lex Salica was the typical freeman is shown by the title *De debilitatibus*,[1] which fixes the payment for the destruction of an eye, hand, or foot at 100 solidi. Half the wergeld is the highest payment for eye, hand, and foot ever exacted by the Continental laws, and 100 solidi

[1] Tit. xxix.

certainly cannot apply to any grade of persons with a lower wergeld than 200 solidi.

Tit. XLI. is as follows :—

Si quis ingenuo franco aut barbarum, qui legem Salega vivit, occiderit, cui fuerit adprobatum viii. *M.* den. qui fac. sol. cc. culp. jud.	If any one shall kill a freeman —a Frank or barbarian man who lives under the Lex Salica—let him whose guilt is proved be judged to be liable for viii. M. denarii, which make cc. solidi.

As this clause probably dates before the issue of Merovingian solidi of diminished weight, the 200 solidi of the wergeld may be taken to have been at the date of the law 200 gold solidi of Imperial standard.

So that the wergeld of the Frank or the free 'barbarus living under the Lex Salica' originally, when paid in gold solidi, was neither more nor less than the normal wergeld of a heavy gold mina.

Officials had a triple wergeld.

We learn from clause 2 of the same title that if the homicide was aggravated by concealment of the corpse the composition was increased to 24,000 denarii or 600 solidi, and that the wergeld of a person 'in truste dominica' was again 600 solidi. The Royal Official thus, as in several other laws, had a triple wergeld.

Then lastly under the same title are three clauses describing the wergelds of the 'Romanus homo conviva Regis,' as 300 solidi, of the 'Romanus homo possessor' as 100 solidi, and of the 'Romanus tributarius' in some texts 45, and in others 63, 70, and 120 solidi. In Codex 10 the 'Romanus possessor' is described as the man who in the pagus in which he lives *res proprias possidet.*

The natural inference from these lesser wergelds

is that the Gallo-Romans were not 'living under the Lex Salica,' but under their own Gallo-Roman law, with wergelds one half the amount of those of the Frankish freemen.

Another of the 65 titles, viz. LIV., gives a further set of wergelds. The wergeld of a *grafio* is to be 600 solidi, that of a *sacebaro* or *ob-grafio* who is a *puer regis* 300 solidi, and that of a *sacebaro* who is an *ingenuus* 600 solidi. The *sacebaro* was apparently the lowest in rank of judicial officials except the *rachinburgus*, and the clause adds that there ought not to be more than three sacebarones in each malberg.

We may conclude from these statements that, the wergeld of the freeman living under the Lex Salica being 200 gold solidi, the higher wergelds up to 600 solidi were the threefold wergelds of public officials, *i.e.* threefold of the wergeld of the class to which they belonged. The wergeld of the sacebaro who was a *puer regis* was three times that of the Romanus possessor. The sacebaro who was an *ingenuus* had a wergeld three times that of the ingenuus living under Salic law.

Strangers in blood had only half wergelds *Romanus possessor* 100 solidi.

We are thus brought into contact with an interesting question. These laws, made after conquest and settlement on once Roman ground, ought to be good evidence upon the tribal method of dealing with strangers in blood: *i.e.*, in this case, the Gallo-Roman conquered population. And these clauses seem to show that half wergelds only were awarded to them under Salic law.

M. Fustel de Coulanges held indeed the opinion that the term 'Romanus' of the laws was confined to the *freedman* who had been emancipated by process of Roman law.[1] But here the contrast seems to me to be between Franks and barbarians 'who live under Salic law' on the one hand, and the Gallo-Romans, whether freedmen or Roman possessores, living under Roman law on the other hand. We shall come upon this question again when the Ripuarian laws are examined, and need not dwell upon it here.

It is interesting, however, to notice that in Codex 2, Tit. XLI. the Malberg gloss on the clause regarding the wergeld of the '*Romanus tributarius*' is '*uuala leodi*,' which Kern (208) explains to mean the wergeld of a *Wala*—the well-known name given by Teutonic people to their Gallo-Roman and Romanised neighbours.

III. TRIBAL RULES OF SUCCESSION IN 'TERRA SALICA.'

The question of the payment of wergeld is now generally admitted to be distinct from that of inheritance in land.

The persons who receive and pay their share of the wergeld are those who would have taken part directly or indirectly in the feud. They are not confined to the expectant heirs of the slayer or the slain.[2]

If we are to learn anything directly upon the question of the method of landholding under Salic custom it must be, not from the clauses relating to the wergelds, but mainly from the Title LIX. *De Alodis.* It is the next title to the *De*

[1] See his essay on this subject in his *Problèmes d'Histoire*, pp. 361 &c.

[2] Brunner, in his *Sippe und Wergeld*, shows this clearly, pp. 1–3.

chrenecruda and can hardly be passed by without some attempt to recognise the bearing of its clauses upon the present inquiry.

Its text is very variously rendered in the several manuscripts, and it has been the subject of many interpretations. But if it may be legitimate to approach it from a strictly tribal point of view, it will not be difficult, I think, to suggest an interpretation consistent with what we have learned of tribal custom from the Cymric example, and therefore worthy at least of careful consideration.

The title 'De Alodis.'

According to Codex 1 of Hessels and Kern the clauses are as follows:—

(1) Si quis mortuus fuerit et filios non demiserit, si mater sua superfuerit ipsa in hereditatem succedat.	If any one shall have died and not have left sons, if his mother shall have survived let her succeed to the inheritance.
(2) Si mater non fuerit et fratrem aut sororem dimiserit, ipsi in hereditatem succedant.	If the mother shall not be [surviving] and he shall have left brother or sister, let them succeed to the inheritance.
(3) Tunc si ipsi non fuerint, soror matris in hereditatem succedat.	Then, if they shall not be [surviving], let the sister of the mother succeed to the inheritance.
(4) Et inde de illis generationibus quicunque proximior fuerit. ille in hereditatem succedat.	And further concerning these generations, whichever shall be the nearer, let it succeed to the inheritance.
(5) De terra vero nulla in muliere hereditas non pertinebit, sed ad virilem secum (leg. *sexum*) qui fratres fuerint tota terra perteneunt.	But concerning *land* no inheritance shall pertain to a woman, but to the male sex who shall be brothers let the whole land pertain.

The last clause in Codex 10 (Herold's) is amplified as follows:

(5) De terra vero Salica in mulierem nulla portio hæreditatis	Concerning, however, *terra Salica*, let no portion of the in-

transit, sed hoc virilis sexus acqviret: hoc est, filii in ipsa hæreditate succedunt. Sed ubi inter *nepotes aut pronepotes* post longum tempus de alode terræ contentio suscitatur, non per stirpes sed per capita dividantur.

heritance pass to a woman, but let the male sex acquire it: *i.e.* sons succeed to that inheritance. But where after a long time dispute may arise between *grandsons* or *great-grandsons* concerning the alod of land, let the division be not *per stirpes*, but *per capita.*

The 'alod' embraced the whole inheritance—land and cattle, &c.

Now, in the first place, what is meant by the term *alod?* In the Lex Salica it occurs again in Tit. XCIX. *De rebus in alode patris*, which relates to a dispute about the right to a certain thing, as to which the decision turns upon the proof that can be given by the defendant that he acquired the thing *in alode patris.* He has to bring three witnesses to prove '*quod in alode patris hoc invenisset*,' and three more witnesses to prove '*qualiter pater suus res ipsas invenisset*,' and if after failure of proof and the interdiction of the law the thing be found in his possession he is to be fined xxxv. solidi.

From this clause the inference must apparently be that the '*alod* of the father' was the whole bundle of rights and possessions, personal as well as real, which passed to descendants by inheritance. Indeed, it seems to be generally admitted that in the title 'de alodis' all the clauses except the last apply to personal property, and only the last to realty.[1]

There are titles 'de alodibus' both in the Ripuarian Law [2] and in that of the 'Anglii and Werini.'[3] In both laws the 'alod' includes personalty, and the latter defines the personalty as '*pecunia* et *mancipia*,' thus reminding us that the personalty of the

[1] Blumenstock, i. 266. [2] Tit. lvi. [3] Tit. vi.

alod mainly consisted of cattle and slaves. In the title 'de alodibus' of the Ripuarian Law, the hereditary or ancestral character of the alod is emphasised by the application to it of the words 'hereditas *aviatica*.' There may, however, be some doubt whether the term *hereditas aviatica* included the whole alod or only the land of the alod.

It was an ancestral family inheritance.

Regarding, therefore, the 'alod' as in some sense a bundle of rights and property, let us try to consider these clauses with a fresh mind in the light of what we have learned of Cymric tribal custom.

The position of females and modifications made in their favour.

Under this custom, speaking broadly, as we have seen, daughters did not share in the landed rights of the gwely. They received instead of landed rights in the gwely their *gwaddol* or portion, mostly, no doubt, in cattle, and they were supposed with it to marry into another gwely, in whose landed rights their sons were expected to share by paternity. If women inherited landed rights at all, it was exceptionally in the case of failure of male heirs, and then only so that their *sons* might inherit. The heiress in such a case, under Cymric as well as Greek tribal law, was in quite an exceptional position, and, as we have seen in Beowulf, the sister's son might be called back into the mother's family to prevent its failure for want of heirs.[1] The exclusion of female successors from terra Salica is therefore quite in accordance with tribal custom.

That the clauses as to personalty in the 'de alodis' were modifications of ancient Salic custom, made

[1] The clause *De reipus* is very important in regard to some of these points. But the subject is too difficult a one to be discussed here.

in favour of females, is rendered almost certain by the position of the last clause as a saving clause, apparently inserted with the object of protecting the rights of the sons in the land of the alod, by preventing the application to it of the previous clauses.

The land of the alod was *terra*

Codex 1 does not describe the land as *terra Salica*. It is content to protect *land* without qualification from the application of the previous clauses, which, if applied to land, would transgress against tribal custom. And the same may be said of Codices 3 and 4. But in the Codices 5 to 10 and in the 'Lex emendata' the words 'terra Salica' are used.

This is a point of importance, because it goes far to show that the whole of the land of the alod was terra Salica, and protected by the saving clause from participation by females. The use of the word *land* alone in Codex 1 forbids our thinking that part of the land of the alod was terra Salica and the rest not terra Salica.[1] And this consideration seems to show that to import into the clause any explanation of the term derived from the word *Sala*, so as to confine its meaning to the '*Haus und Hofland*' or the '*Väterliches Wohnhaus*,' as Amira[2] and Lamprecht[3] would do, would be misleading. The homestead of the chief of a tribal family holding, on terra Salica, may, like the Roman villa, have passed by

[1] Guérard, on the other hand, says: 'C'est l'alleu d'un Salien défunt que la loi divise en deux parts: dans l'une est la terre salique, et dans l'autre la terre non salique; mais ces deux terres sont également partie de la succession du défunt.' *Polyptique d'Irminon*, i. p. 487. But he does not seem to have noted the use of 'land' unqualified in the saving clause of the first 4 codices.

[2] *Erbenfolge*, &c., pp. 12–14.

[3] *Deutsches Wirtschaftsleben*, i. p. 39.

various and even natural stages into the '*Herrengut*,' or '*terra indominicata*' of later manorial phraseology, and the term *terra Salica* may have clung, as it were, to it. But to reason backwards to the Lex Salica from the instances of its later use, given by Guérard in his sections on the subject, seems in this case, if I may venture to say so, to be a reversal of the right order of inference. Lamprecht carefully guards himself against the view that the *terra Salica* of the Lex was as yet a 'Herrengut,' and Guérard, in his careful sections on the subject, admits three stages in the evolution of the *terra Salica*: (1) 'l'enceinte dépendant de la maison du Germain;' (2) 'la terre du manse seigneurial;' (3) 'simplement la terre possédée en propre, quelquefois donnée en tenure.'[1]

This may in some sense fairly represent the line of evolution subsequently followed, and I have long ago recognised the embryo manor in the 'Germania' of Tacitus; but, for our present purpose, this does not seem to help to an understanding of the term as used in the Lex Salica.

When all the Codices are taken together into account, *terra Salica* seems to include the whole of the land, or landed rights, of the alod. From the whole, and not only the chief homestead, the succession of females is excluded, and it is the whole, and not the chief homestead only, which is to be divided between the nepotes and pronepotes of the deceased tribesman.

Approaching the Lex Salica, as we are doing, from a tribal point of view, we seem to get upon quite other and simpler ground.

[1] *Polypt. d'Irminon*, i. p. 495.

Terra Salica was land held under the rules of the Lex Salica and subject ultimately to division *per capita* between great-grand-children.

The emphasis laid in the Lex Salica upon the distinction in social status between persons 'living under the Lex Salica' and those living under Roman law suggests that *land* held under the Lex Salica was not held under the same rules as those under which the 'Romanus possessor' held his 'res propria.' It would seem natural, then, that *terra Salica* should be land held under Salic custom as opposed to land held under Roman law. And if this be the simple rendering of the term *terra Salica* in the Lex, then returning to the likeness of the Salic 'alod' to the Cymric family holding some likeness might be expected in the rules of succession to the land of the alod when compared with the Cymric rules of succession to the 'tir gweliauc' or family land of the gwely.

We have seen that in the gwely the descendants of a common great-grandfather were kept together as a family group till, after internal divisions between brothers and then between cousins, there was at last equal division of landed rights between second cousins, *i.e.* great-grandsons of the original head of the gwely. The fact of this right of redivision at last between great-grandchildren was apparently what held the family group together till the third generation.

The last clause of the 'de alodis,' even as it stands in Codex 1, coincides with Cymric custom in so far as it excludes females from landed rights and confines inheritance in the land of the alod in the first instance to *sons* '. . . *qui fratres fuerint.*'

And when at last later Codices call the land of the alod *terra Salica*, and the addition in Codex 10 is taken into account, the evidence becomes very strong indeed that under Salic custom the land of the alod or terra Salica was held as a family holding, and, like the land of the gwely, divisible, first between sons, then between grandsons, and at last between great-grandsons.

> But when among grandsons or great-grandsons contention arises, after long time, concerning the alod of land, they [the lands of the alod] should be divided, not *per stirpes*, but *per capita*.

The later the date at which this sentence was added to the final clause of the 'de alodis,' the stronger becomes the evidence of what ancient Salic custom on this matter was.

The final clause protects the family holding.

Assuredly the object of these words is not to introduce a new principle. They obviously describe ancient Salic custom in order to protect it. And how could a division *per capita* amongst great-grandsons take place unless, as in the Cymric gwely, the holding of terra Salica had during the whole period of the three generations been kept in some sense together as a family holding?

It would be unwise to press analogies between Cymric and Salic tribal custom too far, but I have before pointed out that a system of wergelds, to which paternal and maternal relatives each individually contributed their share, seems to imply an original solidarity of kindred, which must, wherever it was fully in force, have been connected with a corresponding solidarity in the occupation of land, together with its complement, an individual ownership of cattle. And in the light of the 'de alodis' it does not seem unlikely that it may have been so under ancient Salic custom.

Distinction between land under Salic and land under Roman law.

If the foregoing considerations be accepted, may we not recognise in the term *terra Salica*, as at first used, a meaning analogous to that which Professor Vinogradoff has recently so brilliantly given to the Anglo-Saxon term 'folc-land'?[1] In both cases surely it was natural that there should be a term distinguishing land still held under the rules of ancient tribal custom from land held under the Romanised rules of individual landownership.

It is not necessary to do more than allude here to the various clauses of the Lex Salica from which the existence of individual holdings is clearly to be inferred. If, from this single mention of *terra Salica* and its ultimate division among great-grandsons *per capita*, the continued existence of tribal or family holdings held still under Salic law may be legitimately inferred, it is at least equally clear that the *Romanus possessor* who lived and held his possession as *res propria* under Roman law also existed. And if so the two classes of holders of land must often have been neighbours. The vicini, 'qui in villa consistunt,' of the title 'de migrantibus' (XLV.) may some of them have been of the one class and some of them of the other. The objection of a single person living under Salic law to the interloper would have a new meaning and become very natural if the conflict between the two systems were involved. And when we have reminded ourselves of these facts the title *De eum qui se de parentilla tollere vult*, to which allusion has already been made, which enabled the tribesman, by the somewhat theatrical action of

[1] *English Historical Review*, January 1893.

breaking the four sticks of alder over his head, to cut himself loose from his parentilla, takes its proper place as evidence of the temptation which must have beset the young tribesman in close contact with Gallo-Roman neighbours to free himself from what had come to be regarded as a bondage, and to take an independent position as an individual under the new order of things which was fast undermining the old.

Besides the title 'de alodis' there is another source of information which must not be overlooked —viz. the Edict of Chilperic (A.D. 561–584).[1] Edict of Chilperic A.D. 561–584.

This edict appears to have been issued soon after the extension of the Frankish boundary from the Loire to the Garonne, and specially to apply to the newly conquered district.

This conquest would necessarily extend the area within which Salic settlements would be made among non-Salic neighbours, and multiply the cases in which even a Salic Frank might find himself less securely surrounded by kinsmen than of old. Under these altered circumstances instances would become more and more frequent of the close neighbourhood of tribesmen still holding under Salic custom and strangers living under Roman laws of succession. The clauses of the edict seem accordingly to be directly intended to prevent lapsed interests of Salic tribesmen in land from falling to the vicini when there were brothers or female relations surviving. In old times in purely Salic settlements lapsed

[1] Hessels and Kern, Tit. 78; Pertz, *Leg.* ii. p. 10.

interests must usually have become merged in the general rights of the kindred, the vicini being kinsmen. And no harm might come of it. Landed rights would seldom have passed away from the kindred. But as the stranger element increased in prominence the kindreds would more and more suffer loss. Hence probably the extended rights given by the edict to female relatives. It allows them to succeed in certain cases so as to prevent the land, or, as we should rather say, the landed rights, from lapsing to the vicini.

Admission of female succession to prevent Salic land from passing from the family group to strangers.

Clause 3 is as follows :—

Simili modo placuit atque convenit, ut si quicumque vicinos habens aut filios aut filias post obitum suum superstitutus fuerit, quamdiu filii advixerint terra habeant, sicut et Lex Salica habet.

Likewise we will and declare that if any one having *vicini*, or sons or daughters, shall be succeeded to after his death, so long as the sons live let them have the land as the Lex Salica provides.

So far evidently no change is made; old custom still holds good. But in the rest of the clauses a modification is made evidently to meet altered circumstances, and specially to shut out the *vicini.*

Et si subito filii defuncti fuerint, filia simili modo accipiat terras ipsas, sicut et filii si vivi fuissent aut habuissent. Et si moritur, frater alter superstitutus fuerit, frater terras accipiat, *non vicini.* Et subito frater moriens frater non derelinquerit superstitem, tunc soror ad terra ipsa accedat possidenda. . . .

And if suddenly the sons shall have died let the daughter receive those lands as the sons would have done had they been alive.

And if he [a brother] should die and another brother should survive, let the brother receive those lands, *not the vicini.* And if suddenly the brother shall die not leaving a brother surviving, then let a sister succeed to the possession of that land. . . .

The remainder of the clause is very difficult to construe in the imperfect state of the text, and it is not necessary to dwell upon it. It seems to apply to newcomers ('qui adveniunt') and their rights *inter se*.[1]

We have then in these clauses an allusion to ancient tribal custom as well as to the change made necessary by the new circumstances.

Analogy of Cymric custom.

The implication is that under the rule of ancient custom, on a brother's death without children, *his brothers did not succeed to his land, but the vicini.* Now the brother is to succeed, *not the vicini.*

At first sight this seems unnatural and unlikely. But it ceases to be so if we may regard the alod of terra Salica as a family holding under conditions somewhat like those of the gwely. For under Cymric custom the brother did not succeed to the childless brother as his heir. The co-inheritors, as far as second cousins, were his heirs. In other words the lapsed share went to his *vicini*, but they were the kinsmen of his own gwely.[2]

Nor did a brother succeed to his brother's *da*, and the grazing rights and homestead connected with it. He had received this *da*, as we have seen, from his chief of kindred by 'kin and descent,' *i.e.* by tribal right in his kindred, and therefore if he should die without children his *da* and everything he had by kin and descent went, not to his brothers, but back to the kindred or the chief of kindred from whom he received it.

---

[1] See note in Hessels and Kern, and Amira in his *Erbenfolge*, p. 16 (München, 1874).

[2] See *supra*, pp. 26, 27.

> If the son die after 14 years of age and leave no heir, his 'argluyd' is to possess all his *da* and to be in place of a son to him and his house becomes a dead-house. (*Ven. Code*, i. p. 203.)[1]

The lapse of landed rights in family holdings to the kindred was one thing. Their passing out of the kindred to vicini who were strangers would be quite another thing.

When after a time, let us say under cover of the title 'de migrantibus' or upon extended conquests, others, perhaps 'Romani possessores,' had taken places in the villa side by side with the tribesmen living under the customary rules of *terra Salica*, or when Salic Franks had settled among strangers, the new element would have to be reckoned with.

In the clause 'de migrantibus' the protection of ancient Salic custom was sought by the exclusion of strangers at the instance of a single objector from terra Salica. In the Edict of Chilperic, on the other hand, the presence of stranger vicini was taken for granted, and the protection of terra Salica sought by extending the right of succession to brothers and females, so that at least fewer cases might arise of lapsed inheritances falling away from the kindred into the hands of the *vicini* who might be strangers.

The breaking up of tribal custom thus was not all at once, but by steps. At first *terra Salica* was limited to men, then female succession was allowed,

[1] This is repeated, ii. p. 391. 'The argluyd takes him as a son, and if he die receives his *da* unless he leaves a son.' Up to 14 his father was his 'argluyd.'

and lastly, in default of kindred, stranger vicini under certain conditions were admitted to the lapsed inheritance.

IV. THE WERGELDS AND DIVISION OF CLASSES IN THE 'LEX RIPUARIORUM.'

The customs of the Ripuarian Franks as to wergelds, as might be expected, do not seem to have varied much from those of the Salic Franks. They were probably neighbours in close contact with each other, and, judging from the laws, the population of the district was a mixed one.

Wergeld of freeman as under the Lex Salica, 200 gold solidi. That of the official threefold.

The wergeld of the Ripuarian ingenuus, like that of the Salic Frank or barbarian living under the Lex Salica, was 200 gold solidi, and 12 co-swearers were required to deny the homicide (Tit. VII.).

Here again official position seems, as under the Salic law, to be protected by a triple wergeld. The *grafio* or *comes*, who was a fiscal judge, had a wergeld of 600 solidi (Tit. LIII.). The payment for one *in truste regis* was also 600 solidi (Tit. XI.).

On the other hand, the wergeld of a '*homo regis*' (Tit. IX.), like that of the '*puer regis*' of the Salic law, was only 100 solidi, and that of the 'man' of the Church the same (Tit. X.), *i.e.* half that of the Ripuarian ingenuus.

Consistently with this, the triple payment for killing a woman between childbearing and 40, as also in the Salic Law, was 600 solidi, whilst the wergeld of the 'femina regia' or 'ecclesiastica' was only 300 solidi.

There are apparently hardly any indications as to

how or to whom the wergelds were to be paid. There is only one reference to the *parentes*, and that is not connected with the wergelds. In Tit. LXXXV. it is stated that he who shall disinter a corpse and rob it shall pay 200 solidi and be 'expelled till he shall satisfy the *parentes*.'

The murderer alone seems to be responsible, unless indeed the few words added to the clauses imposing the triple wergeld of 600 solidi upon the murderer of a woman may be taken to be of general application. The words are these:—

> 'If the murderer shall be poor, so that he cannot pay at once, then let him pay *per tres decessiones filiorum*.'

Has it really come to this, that since the Edict of Childeric II. came into force the parentes are released, and the descendants of the murderer, for three generations, are to be in slavery till the wergeld is paid? It may be so, for the penalty in default of payment of the wergeld probably included his own slavery, which involved with it that of his descendants.

The fisc gradually takes the place of the kindred.

The ancient tribal tradition that within the family there could be no feud or wergeld, but exile only, was still apparently in force. In Title LXIX. there is a clause which enacts that if any one shall slay one next in kin ('proximus sanguinis') he shall suffer exile and all his goods shall go to the fisc. This exile of the slayer of a near kinsman and forfeiture of his goods to the fisc seems to be almost the only distinct important survival of tribal feeling, apparently neither wergeld nor the death of the slayer being admitted. But in this case the fisc was, as usual, the gainer. Parricide under any system of criminal law would be a capital crime. The pertinacity with which the custom that, being a crime *within* the kindred, there could be no feud and therefore no wergeld, was adhered to in the midst of manifold changes in circumstances, feeling, and law, is very remarkable.

There is not much else in the Ripuarian laws throwing light upon tribal customs as regards the solidarity of the kindred. But there is a good deal of interesting information upon the important subject of the treatment of strangers in blood.

Distinction between persons living under Salic law and those living under Roman law who were treated as strangers in blood.

We have seen that in the Lex Salica the definition of the *ingenuus* with a wergeld of 200 solidi was the *Francus* or *barbarus* living under Salic law. The 'barbarus' who lived under Salic law was no longer a stranger; he had in fact become a Frank. As we should say, he had been *naturalised.* Hence there was no inconsistency in the apparent occasional indiscriminate use of the words 'Francus' and 'ingenuus.' They meant the same thing. But there is nothing to show that the ordinary Gallo-Roman was included under the term '*barbarus* who lived under Salic law.' On the other hand, we find him living under the Roman law.

In considering the method of dealing with people of so mixed a population as that of the Ripuarian district it is very important to recognise how, under tribal custom, every man continued to live under the law under which he was born, until by some legal process his nationality, so to speak, was admitted to be changed. The Cymric example has shown us how strictly the tribal blood and admission from outside into the tribe were guarded. In such a mixed population as that of the Ripuarian district, the strictness may have been somewhat relaxed, and the formalities of admission less difficult. But there is evidence enough, I think (with great deference to M. Fustel de Coulanges' doubts on the subject), to show that to some extent at any rate social distinctions were still founded upon 'difference of blood.' At all events it is worth while to examine the additional evidence afforded by some clauses in the Ripuarian laws.

Strangers of allied tribes have wergelds according to the law of their birth, but if they cannot find compurgators must go to the ordeal.

In Tit. XXXI. it is stated that Franks, Burgundians, Alamanni, and others, of whatever nation, living in the Ripuarian country, are to be judged and dealt with, if guilty, according to the law of the place of their birth, and not by the Ripuarian law, and it is significantly added that (living away from their kinsmen as they often must be) if they cannot find compurgators they must clear themselves by the ordeal of 'fire or lot.'[1]

Here we come upon one of the strongest tests of tribal custom in its insistence upon the necessity of a man being surrounded by a kindred before he can be a fully recognised tribesman. Unless he be surrounded by kinsmen who can swear for him, under tribal custom, he must have recourse to the ordeal in case of any criminal charge.

There is a clause, not inconsistent, I think, with Tit. XXXI., which seems to draw a clear distinction in

[1] Sohm, in his preface to the *Lex* in Pertz (dated 1882), p. 188, concludes that this clause and clause 36 must be referred to the sixth century. There is a Formula in Marculf's collection in which instructions are given to a newly appointed official, *inter alia*, to judge Franks, Romans, Burgundians, and those of other nations 'secundum lege et consuetudine eorum' (Marc. *Form.*, Lib. i. 8.

favour of tribes more or less nearly allied in blood with Franks, viz. the Burgundians, Alamanni, Bavarians, Saxons, and Frisians, resident in the Ripuarian district, as contrasted with the *Romanus*, who surely must be the Gallo-Roman.

In Title XXXVI. the following wergelds are stated, the slayer being a Ripuarian in all cases :—

A stranger	Frank	200 solidi
" "	Burgundian	160 "
" "	Romanus	100 "
" "	Alamann	160 "
" "	Frisian	
" "	Bavarian	
" "	Saxon	

Thus the Roman stranger is placed in the lowest grade. His wergeld is only 100 solidi—half that of the Ripuarian or Salic Frank—whilst those tribes nearer in blood to the Frank are classed together with a wergeld of 160 solidi, not much less than that of the Frank. Indeed, there is reason to believe that these were the wergelds of the several tribes in force in their own country according to their own laws.[1]

Wergeld of the *Romanus* 100 solidi instead of 200 or 160 solidi.

In this connection the view of M. Fustel de Coulanges, that the term 'Romanus' is confined to the libertus freed under Roman law, hardly seems natural. The evidence seems to show that the man freed under the formalities of Frankish law thenceforth lived under Salic law and became a Frankish freeman with a freeman's wergeld of 200 solidi, whilst the man who

[1] In the Burgundian Law the wergeld is 150 solidi; in the Alamannic Law, 160 solidi; in the Bavarian law, 160 solidi. That this was also the wergeld of the Frisian and Saxon see *infra*.

became a freedman under process of Roman law thenceforth lived under Roman law, and became a Roman freeman—a Romanus—with a wergeld of only 100 solidi. The inference that the difference in status was the result of difference in blood is not altered by the fact that the social status awarded to the Gallo-Roman was the same as that of the libertus in some other laws.

The fact relied upon by M. Fustel de Coulanges, that under the laws of the Burgundians and the Wisigoths the Gallo-Roman was placed in a position of equality with the Teutonic conquerors, need not, I think, affect the view to be taken of his position under the Salic and Ripuarian laws. Tribal custom had to meet in Burgundy and the Wisigothic district with Roman law and Roman institutions still comparatively in their full strength. Marriages with the Gallo-Roman population were encouraged, and the system of wergelds almost entirely superseded. The Frankish conquest was of another kind, and the Frank was hardly likely to care to meet the Gallo-Roman on equal terms.

Position of the freedman or *denarialis* under Frankish law. His wergeld 200 solidi.

Passing now from the position of the stranger who was recognised as a freeman, let us try to get a clear idea of the position of the *freedman* under the Ripuarian law, taking the cases of the Frankish freedman and the Roman libertus separately.

In Tit. VIII. the payment for slaying a *servus* is 36 solidi. In Tit. LXII., if any one makes his servus into a *tributarius* or a *litus* and he is killed, the penalty is the same—36 solidi, but if he chooses to make him into a *denarialis* (*i.e.* a freedman under Frankish law) then his value shall be 200 solidi.

The tributarius or litus has gained but one step up the ladder of Frankish freedom. But the denarialis, with nearly six times his wergeld, has as regards his wergeld reached the highest rung at a single leap.

But till he has a free kindred, if he has no children the fisc is his heir.

Though, however, as regards wergeld he has done so, in another sense he has by no means done so. Under tribal custom he would not attain to full tribal rights till a kindred had grown up around him. So under Tit. LVII. the 'homo denarialis,' notwithstanding his wergeld of 200 solidi, is recognised as having no kindred.

> (s. 4) If a 'homo denariatus' shall die without children he leaves no other heir than our fisc.

And in full accord with this statement is the following clause in the 'Capitulare legi Ripuariæ additum' of A.D. 803.

> Homo denarialis non ante hæreditare in suam agnationem poterit quam usque ad terciam generationem perveniat.

So that more of tribal custom still prevails in his case than at first appears. Only in the third generation are full rights of inheritance secured to his successors.

Wergeld of the *libertus* under Roman law 100 solidi.

If now we turn to the *libertus* under Roman law, Tit. LXI. states that if any one shall make his servus into a libertus and Roman citizen, if he shall commit a crime he shall be judged by Roman law, and if he be killed the payment shall be 100 solidi: but 'if he shall die without children he shall have no heir but our fisc.'

Thus, as regards inheritance, the Frankish

denarialis and the Roman libertus seem to be treated alike, notwithstanding the difference of wergeld.

Turning to another matter, the Ripuarian laws, being of later date than the Lex Salica, made provision for the wergelds of the clergy.

Wergelds of the clergy, and of their 'men.'

Tit. XXXVI. provided that the clergy should be compounded for according to their birth, whether of the class of servi, or men of the king or of the Church, or liti, or ingenui. If *ingenui*, they were to be compounded for with 200 solidi. Then the wergelds of the higher clergy are stated as follows:—

Subdeacon	400 solidi
Deacon	500 ,,
Priest	600 ,,
Bishop	900 ,,

And there is a long clause *De Tabulariis* (Tit. LVIII.) providing that servi may be made under process of Roman law *tabularii* of the Church, so that they and their descendants shall be and remain servants of the Church, and render the proper services of tabularii to the Church, without any one having power further to enfranchise them. In case of their death without children the Church is to be their heir. These appear to be the 'men of the Church' whose wergeld was 100 solidi.

The Tit. LVI. *De alodibus* is as follows:—

The clause 'De alodibus.'

Si quis absque liberis defunctus fuerit, si pater materque superstites fuerint in hereditatem succedant.	If any one shall have died without children, if father and mother survive they shall succeed to the *hereditas*.
Si pater materque non fuerint, frater et soror succedant.	If there are not father and mother, brother and sister shall succeed.

Si autem nec eos habuerit, tunc soror matris patrisque succedant. Et deinceps usque ad quintam genuculum, qui proximus fuerit, hereditatem succedat.	But if he has not these either, then the sister of the mother and the sister of the father shall succeed. And further, up to the fifth knee, whoever is nearest shall succeed to the inheritance.
Sed cum virilis sexus extiterit, femina in hereditatem aviaticam non succedat.	But as long as the male sex survive, a woman shall not succeed to the *hereditas aviatica*.

All that need be remarked regarding this title is, first its close resemblance to the clause 'de alodis' in the Lex Salica and the confirmation given by the phrase 'hereditas aviatica' to the family character of the 'alod,' and secondly that it seems to belong to the time when female succession was favoured.

Whether the 'hereditas aviatica' included the whole alod or only the land of the alod, on failure of male heirs, females were now to succeed.

There remains only to be noticed the interesting addition to Tit. XXXVI. which enacts that if any one ought to pay wergeld he should reckon, *inter alia*:—

The traditional value of animals in payment of wergelds.

The ox, horned, seeing, and sound, for . .	2 solidi
The cow, horned, seeing, and sound, for [3 or]	1 solidus
The horse, seeing and sound, for . . .	6 solidi
The mare, seeing and sound, for . . .	3 „

The wergeld of 200 solidi = 100 oxen.

And this is followed by a final clause which is found only in some of the manuscripts and which is probably an addition made under Charlemagne:—

> If payment shall be made in silver, let 12 denarii be paid for the solidus, *sicut antiquitus est constitutum.*

Thus our consideration of these laws ends with the fact that, before the disturbance in the currency made by Charlemagne, the wergeld of the Frankish freeman of 200 gold solidi or heavy gold mina was still, in the Ripuarian district at all events, a normal wergeld of 100 oxen.

V. THE ALAMANNIC AND BAVARIAN LAWS.

These laws have an interest of their own, but only those points come directly within the range of this inquiry which are likely to throw light upon the interpretation of the Anglo-Saxon laws.

Beginning at once with the wergelds, there are two distinct statements.

The wergelds of the early Alamannic 'Pactus,'

According to the 'Pactus,' which is assigned to the sixth or seventh century, and which is considered to represent customs of the Alamanni before they were conquered by the Franks,[1] the wergelds were as follows:—

Baro de mino flidis . .	170 solidi (? 160)
Medianus Alamannus . .	200 „
Primus Alamannus . .	240 „

And for women:—

Femina mino flidis . .	320 „
Mediana	400 „
Prima Alamanna . . .	480 „

These wergelds correspond very closely in some points with those of the Burgundian laws and should be compared with them.[2]

The wergeld of women was double that of men of the same class. In the Lex Salica and Lex Ripuariorum, women were paid for threefold.

and of the later 'Lex Hlotharii.'

In the Lex Hlotharii, s. LXIX., the wergelds are stated as follows:—

> If any freeman ('liber') kills a freeman, let him compound for him twice 80 solidi to his sons. If he does not leave sons nor has heirs let him pay 200 solidi.

[1] See Merkel's preface to the laws in Pertz, p. 14.

[2] In the Burgundian laws the division is into 'optimatus' with a wergeld of 300 sol., 'mediocris' with 200 sol., and 'minores' with 150 sol.

Women of theirs, moreover, always in double.

The medius Alamannus, if he shall be killed, let 200 solidi be paid to the parentes.

It is not clear that there has been any change in the wergelds since the date of the 'Pactus.'

The wergeld of 160 solidi accords with the statement in the Ripuarian law.

The wergeld of the medius Alamannus, 200 solidi, is the same as before. That of the liber, 160 solidi, seems to be the same as that of the baro de mino flidis in the 'Pactus.' It is also the wergeld of the Alamannus according to the clause mentioning strangers in the Ripuarian law. The use of the term 'medius Alamannus' seems to imply that there should be a primus Alamannus as in the 'Pactus.' But what these two classes of Alamanni with higher wergelds than that of the liber were does not appear.

This later statement of the wergelds seems also to contain a provision which can, I think, only be explained by tribal custom. It occurs again in clause XLVI., which enacts that the same payment has to be paid to the parentes of a person sold out of the country beyond recall as if he had been killed. This rule is the same in the Salic and Ripuarian codes. But in this law a distinction is made between the case of a slain man leaving an heir, and the case of his leaving no heir.

Wergeld of 200 solidi if no heir of the person slain.

If he cannot recall him let him pay for him with a wergeld to the parentes. That is twice 80 solidi if he leave an heir. But if he does not leave an heir let him compound with 200 solidi.

The explanation must be that if the lost kinsman leaves no heir, the loss is all the greater to the kindred. This looks like a survival of tribal custom. The dread of a family dying out lay, as we have seen, at the root of the widespread custom which brought in the sister's son to fill the vacant place when there was no one else to keep up the family. This addition in the later statement, though omitted in the 'Pactus,' pointing back as it appears to earlier custom, seems to show that the Lex as well as the 'Pactus' may in the matter of wergeld be traced to Alamannic rather than Frankish sources.

Wergeld of women.

In both the 'Pactus' and the Lex, as we have seen, the wergelds of women were double those of men. The Bavarian law gives the reason of the rule (IV. 29) and also the reason why sometimes an exception was made to the rule.

> Whilst a woman is unable to defend herself by arms, let her receive a double composition; if, however, in the boldness of her heart, like a man, she chooses to fight, her composition shall not be double.

In titles XXIX. and XXX. of the Alamannic law it is enacted that if a man be slain in the *curtis* of the Dux a threefold wergeld must be paid, and that if the messenger of the Dux be killed within the province his triple wergeld must be paid.

The freeman's wergeld of 160 solidi under Bavarian law.

In the Bavarian law the wergeld of the freeman is stated to be 160 solidi, thus:—

> If any one kill a free man ('liberum hominem') let there be paid to his parentes, if he have any, or if he have no parentes to the Dux or to him to whom he was commended whilst he lived, twice 80 solidi: that is, 160 solidi. (Tit. IV. c. 28.)

There are no wergelds mentioned in the Bavarian law corresponding to those of the *medius Alamannus* and the *primus Alamannus* of the Alamannic laws.

Higher wergelds of certain families.

According to Tit. III. 1, there were certain families who were held in double honour, and had double wergelds. The Agilolvinga had fourfold wergelds, being the family from whom the Dux was chosen. The Dux himself had a fourfold wergeld with one third added. If the life of any of his parentes were taken the wergeld was, according to one manuscript, 640, and according to another 600 solidi.

These wergelds of the Alamannic and Bavarian laws are not on all fours with those of the Salic and Ripuarian Laws. But in both cases the ordinary freeman's wergeld is 160 solidi (unless there be no heir to inherit), so that in both cases the wergelds correspond sufficiently with the clause in the Ripuarian Laws which accords to them a wergeld of 160 solidi, after having before stated that strangers are to be judged according to the laws under which they were born.

Wergelds of the freedman and the servus.

In the Bavarian law there is special mention of the freedman and the servus, and it is worth while to dwell a moment on the position assigned to them as compared with the ordinary freeman.

There are three titles headed as under:—

Title IV. De *liberis*, quo modo componuntur.
„ V. De liberis qui per manum dimissi sunt liberi, quod *frilaz* vocant.
„ VI. De *servis*, quo modo componuntur.

These clauses relate to injuries as well as to homicide. As regards all minor injuries, the freedman is paid for at one half, and the servus at one third, of the payment to the liber for the same injury.

Payments for eye, hand, or foot one fourth the wergeld.

But when the payment comes to be for the eye, hand, or foot, the difference is, roughly speaking, doubled. The payment for the liber is 40 solidi, for the freedman 10 solidi, and for the servus 6 solidi (? 5 sol.). And these payments are seemingly intended to be one quarter of the respective wergelds for homicide. We have seen that the wergeld of the freeman was 160 solidi. These clauses state that the freedman's wergeld was 40 solidi, and that of the servus 20 solidi, and that in both these cases the lord took the payment.

In Tit. IV. 30, *De peregrinis transeuntibus viam*, the passing stranger's death was to be paid for with 100 solidi to his parentes, or in their absence to the fisc.

Bavarian wergelds.

The wergelds of the Bavarian laws may therefore be thus stated:—

Ducal family (4 fold) . .	640 solidi
Families next in honour . .	320 ,,
Liber	160 ,,
Stranger	100 ,,
Freedman	40 ,,
Servus	20 ,,

And all these solidi were gold solidi of Imperial or Merovingian standard, it does not matter much which.

No wergeld within the family.

The crime of homicide within the near family was dealt with in the Alamannic law in conformity with ancient tribal custom. There was no wergeld in such a case.

> If any man wilfully kills his father, uncle, brother, or maternal uncle (avunculus), or his brother's son, or the son of his uncle or maternal uncle, or his mother, or his sister, let him know that he has acted against God, and not fulfilled brotherhood according to the command of God, and heavily sinned against God. And before all his parentes, let his goods be confiscated, and let nothing of his pertain any more to his heirs. Moreover, let him do penance according to the Canons. (Tit. XL.)

Once more in these laws the parricide (the fisc having taken his property) goes free, but for the penance required by the Canons of the Church.

As regards the wergelds of the clergy in the

Alamannic law the Church seems to claim triple penalties. The wergelds of the clergy are as follows, according to the Lex Hlotharii (XI. to XVII.):— Wergelds of the clergy.

Bishop as that of the Dux or Rex.	
Priest, parochial	600 solidi
Deacon and monk	300 „
Other clerics like the rest of their parentes.	
Liber per cartam (the Ripuarian tabularius) .	80 „

The free colonus of the Church as other Alamanni.

According to the Bavarian law (Tit. I. c. x.) a bishop's death was to be paid for by the weight in gold of a leaden tunic as long as himself, or its value in cattle, slaves, land, or villas, if the slayer should have them; and he and his wife and children are to be *in servitio* to the Church till the debt is paid.

The lower clergy and monks were to be paid for according to their birth *double*; parochial priests threefold. (I. c. viii. and ix.)

In the *Liber secundus* of the Alamannic law is an interesting clause which throws some light upon the position of married women.

The wife's inheritance goes back to her kindred if no children born alive.

(XCV.) If any woman who has a paternal inheritance of her own, after marriage and pregnancy, is delivered of a boy, and she herself dies in childbirth, and the child remains alive long enough, *i.e.* for an hour, or so that it can open its eyes and see the roof and four walls of the house, and afterwards dies, its maternal inheritance then belongs to its father.

This is natural, but it seems to show that if the child had been born dead and the wife had died without children her paternal inheritance would have gone back to her kindred and not to her husband.

In the absence of other evidence this is perhaps enough to show that in accordance with tribal custom the kindred of the wife had not lost all hold upon their kinswoman, and therefore that she by her marriage had not passed altogether out of her own kindred.

Traditional value of cattle stated in gold tremisses.

Lastly, there are clauses in the same *Liber secundus* which declare the value of the solidus in equation with cattle.

LXXX. Summus bovus 5 tremisses valet. Medianus 4 tremisses valet. Minor quod appreciatus fuerit.

LXXVII. Illa mellissima vacca 4 tremisses liceat adpreciare. Illa alia sequenteriana solidum 1.

These clauses show that the solidi in which the wergelds were paid were gold solidi of three tremisses.

In the Ripuarian laws the ox was equated with 2 gold solidi, *i.e.* 6 tremisses, so that we learned from the equation that the wergeld of the Ripuarian liber, 200 solidi, was really a wergeld of 100 oxen. But the above equations show that under Alamannic law the wergeld of the liber was not so.

In the Alamannic laws the best ox was valued only at five tremisses instead of six, so that the wergeld of 200 solidi of the medius Alamannus was really a wergeld of 120 oxen; and the 160 solidi of the wergeld of the *baro de mino flidis* of the 'Pactus,' or simple 'liber' of the Lex Hlotharii, was a wergeld of 96 oxen or 120 Alamannic '*sweetest cows.*'

Any one who has seen the magnificent fawn-coloured oxen by which waggons are still drawn in the streets of St. Gall will appreciate what the 'summus bovus' of the Alamannic region may have been. Why it should have been worth in gold less than the oxen of other lands does not appear.

CHAPTER VII.

TRIBAL CUSTOMS OF THE TRIBES CONQUERED BY CHARLEMAGNE.

1. THE EFFECT UPON WERGELDS OF THE NOVA MONETA.

The *nova moneta* of Charlemagne.

WE have reached a point in our inquiry at which it becomes necessary to trouble the reader with further details concerning the changes in the Frankish currency, made by Charlemagne.

We are about to examine the customs as regards wergelds of those tribes which owed their laws, in the shape in which we have them, to the conquests of Charlemagne. The alterations in the currency, made literally whilst the laws were in course of construction, naturally left marks of confusion in the texts relating to wergelds, and we have to thread our way through them as best we can.

A change from gold to silver.

The change which we have to try to understand was in the first place a change from a gold to a silver currency—*i.e.* from the gold currency of Merovingian solidi and tremisses to the silver currency of Charlemagne's *nova moneta*.

There had been a certain amount of silver coinage in circulation before, but the mass of the coinage had been hitherto gold, mostly in gold tremisses.

In all the Frankish laws hitherto examined the monetary unit was the gold solidus with its third—

the tremissis. And the only question was whether the solidi and tremisses were of Imperial or of Merovingian standard—whether the solidus was the Merovingian solidus of 86·4 wheat-grains and the tremissis 28·8, or the Imperial solidus of 96 wheat-grains and the tremissis 32.

Merovingian kings first used and then imitated Imperial coin.

As regards the Lex Salica, originally the solidus was probably of the Imperial standard, because the Merovingian kings at first in their coinage copied the Imperial coins both in type and weight. And before they issued a coinage of their own they made use of Imperial coins, both gold and silver. Numismatists point in illustration of this to the fact that in the tomb of Childeric at Tournay were found no Frankish coins, but a large number of Roman coins, gold and silver, of dates from A.D. 408 to those of the contemporary Emperor Leo I. (457–474). And for proof that these Roman coins were afterwards imitated by Merovingian princes M. Maurice Prou had only to refer the student 'to every page' of his catalogue of 'Les Monnaies Mérovingiennes.'[1]

The denarius of the Salic law first the scripulum and then the Merovingian silver tremissis of 28·8 w.g.

Now, if the gold solidus was at first of 96 wheat-grains, then the denarius (one fortieth) would be 2·4 wheat-grains of gold, and at a ratio of 1 : 10 the denarius would be the scripulum of 24 wheat-grains of silver, which was called by early metrologists the 'denarius Gallicus.' Further, at 1 : 12 the denarius would become the Merovingian silver tremissis of 28·8. So that probably the denarius of the Lex Salica may originally have been the scripulum, and under later Merovingian kings their own silver tremissis. Thus

[1] Introduction, p. iv.

these silver tremisses had probably been regarded as the denarius of the Lex Salica for a century or two at least before Charlemagne's changes.

Up to this time, therefore, there was apparently a distinct connection between the reckoning and figures of the Lex Salica and the actual Frankish coinage. The Merovingian coinage of gold and silver tremisses of 28·8 wheat-grains was therefore, from this point of view, so to speak, a tribal coinage for the Franks themselves, but not one adapted for currency, over a world-wide Empire such as Charlemagne had in view, and with which at last, when adopting the title of Emperor, he had practically to deal.

The changes he made in the currency were intimately connected, not only in time but in policy, with the extension of his kingdom and his ultimate assumption of the Imperial title.

Charlemagne, on conquest of Italy, raised the gold and silver tremissis to the Imperial standard of 32 w.g.

His raising of the weight of the Frankish gold tremissis and silver denarius from the Merovingian standard of 28·8 to the Imperial standard of 32 wheat-grains was probably the result of his conquest of Italy. He seems to have arranged it with the Pope, for they issued silver denarii of the higher standard with the impress of both their names upon them.[1]

It was natural that he should wish his coinage to obtain currency throughout his dominions, and this could not be expected if it was continued at a lower standard than that of the Byzantine Emperor.

Not only in the currency, but also in other matters, extended empire involved the breaking down

[1] Martini, *Metrologia*, *sub* 'Roma.' See also *Traité de Numismatique du Moyen Age*, par A. Engel, vol. i. p. 222.

of tribal peculiarities and greater uniformity in legal provisions and practice.

The Lex Salica still in force for Franks. And its family holdings not yet extinct.

To mention one instance suggested by our previous inquiry, we have noticed how the extension of Frankish rule in Gaul from the Loire to the Garonne increased the difficulties of maintaining two laws as to land. Strangers under Roman law, as in the 'de migrantibus,' one by one were settling among Franks holding alods or family holdings of terra Salica. Extended conquests reversed the process, and in conquered provinces immigrants living under Salic law became strangers amongst vicini living under Roman, Burgundian, or Wisigothic law.

The family holdings of terra Salica must have now become the exception and not the rule. This becomes evident in the provisions made for the army.

In the Capitulare of A.D. 803,[1] *de exercitu promovendo*, it was ordered that every free man ('liber homo') who, *de proprio suo* or as a benefice, had four *mansi vestiti*, that is mansi occupied by tenants, should equip himself and attend 'in hostem.' And those not having so many mansi were to club together so that for every four mansi a soldier should be found. The possession of mansi had apparently become sufficiently general to be taken as the typical form of landholding.

In A.D. 807[2] special arrangements were made for the case of the recently conquered Frisians and Saxons.

If help should be needed in Spain, every five of the Saxons were to equip a sixth. If the need arose

---

[1] Pertz, p. 119.

[2] Pertz, p. 149.

nearer home, every two were to prepare a third. Or if the need arose still closer at hand, all were to come. Of the Frisians, counts and vassals and those who held benefices, all were to come, and of those who were poorer every six were to equip a seventh. There is no mention of mansi in the case of the Saxons and Frisians.

The Capitulare of A.D. 803 seems to show that in the longer settled districts of the Empire the possession of so many mansi, *de proprio suo*, was the prevalent form of landownership. So that, although the lex Salica remained still in force, the number of Franks living under it seems by this time to have borne a very small proportion to those living under Roman and other laws.

Family holdings under the Lex Salica were, however, probably not quite extinct. In the 'Capitula generalia' of A.D. 825[1] was inserted the following clause providing specially for family holdings, which may possibly have been holdings of *terra Salica*, though it is not so directly stated.

De fratribus namque qui simul in paterna seu materna hereditate communiter vivunt, nolentes substantiam illorum dividere, hac occasione, ut unus tantum eorum in hostem vadat, volumus ut si solus est vadat: si autem duo sunt similiter: si tres fuerint unus remaneat: et si ultra tres numerus fratrum creverit, unus semper propter domesticam curam adque rerum communium excolentiam remaneat. Si vero inter eos aliqua orta fuerit con-	Concerning brothers who together live in common in the paternal or maternal inheritance, unwilling to divide their substance, when occasion comes that one of them only should go *in hostem*, we will that if there be one only he should go, and if there be two the same: if there be three let one remain; and if the number of brothers grows to more than three, let one always remain on account of domestic care and to attend to their common concerns

[1] *Hludowici et Hlotharii Capitularia*, Pertz, p. 251

tentio, quis eorum expeditionum facere debeat, prohibemus ut nemo illorum remaneat. In ætate quoque illorum lex propria servetur. Similiter et in nepotibus eorum hæc conditio teneatur.

But if among them any contention shall have arisen which of them ought to go on the expedition we prohibit that any one of them shall remain. During their lives also let the *lex propria* be preserved. In the same way let this condition be kept to even among their grandsons.

When we reflect that the Franks living under the Lex Salica must have thus sunk into a small minority, it becomes obvious that wider views must of necessity have entered into the minds of Charlemagne and his advisers, not only as regards land, but also as regards the currency.

The currency of the Lex Salica only a local one.

The currency of the Lex Salica, with its solidi of 40 denarii, was, as has been said, after all a local one. And outside the old Frankish boundary, in the Wisigothic region, as well as probably in Italy, the Roman currency or local modifications of it apparently more or less prevailed. Ecclesiastics, as we have seen, even Alcuin himself, still used the terms of Roman currency in writing on monetary matters to their friends outside the Empire.

The Roman drachma or *argenteus* of 72 w.g. the silver denarius of the Empire.

To them the denarius was still the Roman drachma of 72 wheat-grains of silver, commonly called the *argenteus*, in contrast to the gold solidus or *aureus*.

Gregory of Tours, when he has occasion to mention monetary payments, speaks of *aurei*, *trientes*, and *argentei*. In one story he speaks of *solidi*, *trientes*, and *argentei*.[1]

[1] *De Mirac. S. Martini*, l. i. c. 31. Mention of the *aureus* occurs twenty-four times in the index to his works. Mention of *trientes* occurs twelve times, and of *argentei* five times.

Further, in a supplement to the laws of the Wisigoths[1] is a statement under the name of *Wamba Rex* (A.D. 672–680), which apparently represents the monetary system in vogue south of the Frankish boundary. It states that the pound of gold equalled 72 gold solidi, so that the gold solidus was not the Merovingian solidus but that of Constantine. It then states that the 'dragma' of gold = 'XII argentei.' The argenteus being the silver drachma, the ratio of gold to silver was 1 : 12.

To Isidore of Seville, from his Spanish standpoint, the silver drachma was still the denarius.[2]

Dragma octava pars unciæ est et *denarii* pondus argenti, tribus constans scripulis.

Solidus apud Latinos alio nomine 'sextula' dicitur, quod his sex uncia compleatur; hunc, ut diximus, vulgus *aureum* solidum vocat, cujus tertium partem idco dixerunt tremissem.[2]

The drachma is the eighth part of an ounce, and the weight of the silver denarius containing three scripula.

The *solidus* with the Romans is otherwise called the *sextula* because it is one sixth of the ounce; hence, as we have said, the vulgar call the *solidus* the *aureus*, the third part of which is called the tremissis.

Thus the solidus was the typical gold unit or aureus, and the drachma was the silver denarius or argenteus.

It is remarkable that at a ratio of 1 : 10 twelve Wisigothic or Roman argentei or drachmas of silver equalled exactly in wheat-grains the Merovingian gold solidus current on the Frankish side of the Garonne or the Loire.[3]

Twelve drachmas of silver = at 1 : 10 the Merovingian gold solidus.

[1] In some codices placed at the end of Lib. xii., Tit. ii. See edition of Walter (1824), p. 669.

[2] 'Ex Isidori Etymologiarum Libris, c. De ponderibus.' Hultsch, ii. 113.

[3] Twelve argentei (12 × 72 w.g.) = 864 w.g., or at 1:10 the Merovingian solidus of 86·4 w.g.

It would seem, then, probable that traditionally and 'according to ancient custom' outside the Frankish kingdom the Merovingian gold solidus had been equated with twelve silver argentei or denarii of this reckoning, whilst within Frankish limits 40 of the silver tremisses and now of the pence of the nova moneta were reckoned as equal to the gold solidus of the Lex Salica.

But even to the Frank the 40 denarii of the Lex Salica may have become antiquated except for wergelds and other payments under its provisions.

The silver solidus of 12 silver tremisses already in use in accounts, as $\frac{1}{20}$ of the pound of silver of 240 pence.

The practice apparently had already grown up of reckoning 12 of the silver tremisses as a solidus of silver, twenty of which went to the pound of 240 pence, without, however, any pretence being made that this solidus of twelve silver pence was to be reckoned as equal to the gold solidus in making payments.

In the 'Capitulare Liftinense' of A.D. 743[1] a payment is enacted *de unaquaque cassata solidus, id est* 12 *denarii.* It was necessary to make this explanation.

It is not known how much earlier the practice of reckoning in pounds of silver of 20 solidi of 12 denarii came into vogue, but it was long before the issue of the nova moneta.

It might at first sight be thought that these twelve denarii may have been twelve *argentei* or drachmæ, but 240 drachmæ would make far more than a pound. And by an edict of A.D. 765[2] Pippin had enacted that out of a pound of silver not more than 22 solidi were to be made, one of which was

[1] Pertz, p. 18. [2] Pertz, p. 31.

to go to the monetarius, and this clearly forbids the supposition that the solidus could be of twelve drachmæ. The pound would contain only eight such solidi.

Another Capitulare of A.D. 779 [1] proves that the twelve denarii were Merovingian denarii of 28·8 wheat-grains.[2]

The issue of the new denarii of 32 wheat-grains was apparently made before A.D. 781, for in that year an edict was passed forbidding the currency of the old denarii.[3]

There was nothing very remarkable in this raising of the silver denarius from 28·8 to 32 wheat-grains. It was merely adopting the Imperial standard. But the extraordinary thing was that Charlemagne seems to have thought that he could, by law, substitute the solidus of 12 of his silver denarii for the *gold solidus* hitherto in use. The gold currency was going out and the silver currency was taking its place; but it was quite another thing to make the solidus of 12 silver denarii of 32 wheat-grains legal tender in the place of the gold solidus of the Lex Salica of 40 silver denarii of 28·8 wheat-grains. Yet this was what Charlemagne did, though perhaps only by degrees.

The pound of the *nova moneta* was 240 pence of 32 w.g. = 7680 w.g.

The change was made under the pretence of the

---

[1] Pertz, p. 39.

[2] In this Capitulare three grades of payments are stated, a pound, a half-pound, and five solidi. Five solidi in this scale should be ¼ lb., and in wheat-grains the scale would be 6912, 3456, and 1728. 1728 wheat-grains is 5 solidi of 12 denarii of 28·8.

[3] Capitulare Mantuanum, s. 9, 'De moneta: ut nullus post Kalendas Augustas istos dinarios quos modo habere visi sumus dare audeat aut recipere: si quis hoc fecerit, vannum nostrum conponat.'

Charlemagne enacted that the silver solidus should be legal tender to the gold solidus.

sanction of ancient custom. In the addition made to Tit. XXXVI. of the Ripuarian law the wording of the clause as to the payment of wergelds was 'Quod si cum argento solvere contigerit, pro solido duodecim denarios, *sicut antiquitus est constitutum.*' And this allusion to antiquity was repeated.

What was meant by this appeal to ancient custom it is not easy to see, unless it might be the probably long-established equation already mentioned between 12 Roman drachmæ or argentei and the Merovingian gold solidus. Very possibly this equation was older than that of the 40 denarii to the solidus of the Lex Salica.

In a series of remarkable articles contributed to the *Forschungen zur Deutschen Geschichte* of 1862,[1] Dr. Ad. Soetbeer endeavoured to show, and with considerable force, that the introduction into the Lex Salica of the round numbers of denarii—forty to the solidus—was of comparatively late date ; and if this hypothesis be correct, then it may be that Charlemagne was appealing to an earlier Frankish custom of reckoning 12 silver denarii or drachmæ to the gold solidus. But even if it could be so, obviously the denarii of 12 to the solidus of ancient custom cannot have been the same denarii as those which afterwards were reckoned at 40 to the solidus.[2]

Economically speaking, the substitution of the solidus of 12 denarii for the gold solidus, if they had been Roman drachmæ, would have been reasonable and might have made no change in prices ; but the

[1] *Beiträge zur Geschichte des Geld- und Münzwesens in Deutschland.*

[2] Forty argentei or drachmæ to the solidus would have meant a ratio of about 1:30.

substitution of 12 of the new denarii of 32 wheat-grains for the forty denarii of 28·8 wheat-grains, involving a ratio between gold and silver of 1 : 4, could only be justified by such a scarcity of silver as would prevent a rise in prices. That it was not so justified became very soon apparent.

This involved a ratio of 1 : 4.

Following the order of date, the Capitulare of A.D. 785, 'de partibus Saxoniæ,' shows that prices when quoted in the solidus of 12 pence immediately rose. The ox, the traditional value of which was two gold solidi, is reckoned as worth ten silver solidi. And M. Guérard has shown from the various instances given in the 'Polyptique d'Irminon' that on the estates of the Abbey of St. Germain-des-Prés the price of oxen remained at an average of eight silver solidi long after the death of Charlemagne.[1]

The Lex Salica continued in force with all its fines and wergelds stated in gold solidi of 40 denarii. And a Capitulare of A.D. 801[2] contains the following section which reveals the beginning of confusion :—

Exception made as to Saxons and Frisians.

Ut omnis solutio atque compositio, que in lege Saliga continetur, inter Francos per duodecim denariorum solidos componatur, excepto hubi contentio contra Saxones et Frisones exorta fuit, ibi volumus ut 40 dinariorum quantitatem solidus habeat quem vel Saxo vel Frisio ad partem Salici Franci cum eo litigantis solvere debet.	That every payment and composition which is contained in the lex Salica between Franks shall be paid by solidi of twelve pence, except that where a dispute has risen up against Saxons and Frisians we will that the solidus shall be of the amount of 40 pence which either a Saxon or a Frisian ought to pay to a Salic Frank at law with him.

[1] *Polyptique d'Irminon*, Introduction, i. 151. See also No. 82 of St. Gall Charters (Wastmann, i. p. 78), in which is an annual payment of 'i bovem v solidos valentem' sub anno A.D. 778.

[2] Pertz, p. 85.

In A.D. 803 a clause was inserted in a Capitulare to the effect that all debts to the King should be paid in solidi of 12 denarii 'excepta freda quæ in lege Saliga scripta sunt.'[1] This looks like a general reservation of the fines and wergelds of the Lex Salica. But it does not seem to have been so intended, or perhaps there was vacillation in the Councils of the Emperor.

A Capitulare of A.D. 816[2] contained the following:—

De omnibus debitis solvendis *sicut antiquitus fuit constitutum* per duodecim denarios solidus solvatur per totam Salicam legem, excepto leudis, si Saxo aut Friso Salicum occiderit, per 40 dinarios solvant solidum. Infra Salicos vero ex utraque parte de omnibus debitis sicut diximus 12 denarii per solidum solvantur, sive de homicidiis sive de omnibus rebus.	In the payment of all debts *according to ancient custom* the solidi shall be paid by 12 denarii throughout Salic Law, except in the case of wergelds, if a Saxon or Frisian shall kill a Salic Frank let the solidus be paid by 40 denarii. Among Salic Franks, however, on both sides as to all debts, as we have said, 12 denarii shall be paid for the solidus, whether in the case of homicides or anything else.

As between Salic Franks, therefore, the solidus of 12 denarii was to be legal tender in payment of wergelds and everything else.

The *nova moneta* enforced by penalties.

This was all very well for debtors, but it was not so satisfactory to creditors. The exception that, when a Frank was killed by a Saxon or a Frisian, the wergeld was still to be paid in the solidus of 40 denarii, was an admission that to receive it in solidi of 12 denarii would have been a hardship. And as to the general public, the acceptance of payment

[1] Pertz, p. 114.

[2] Pertz, p. 116.

of debts in the denarii of the nova moneta had to be secured by penalties. A clause was introduced into the Capitulare of A.D. 794 [1] according to which freemen refusing the new denarii were to be fined 15 solidi; whilst servi refusing them were to be publicly beaten naked at a post.

And it became permanent and was adopted by Offa and Alfred.

The permanent result was very remarkable. The new currency was maintained as legal tender in France, and the gold currency practically disappeared. Charlemagne and his successors coined very few more gold solidi and tremisses. King Offa and after him Alfred raised the English sceat to the penny of 32 wheat-grains, probably in imitation of the nova moneta, and Charlemagne's pound of 240 of these pence—*i.e.* of 7680 wheat-grains of silver—became generally recognised as the pound of monetary reckoning in Western Europe.

But the ratio between gold and silver went back to 1 : 12.

So far Charlemagne triumphed. But in the meantime the artificial ratio of 1 : 4, sought to be established between gold and silver, could not be maintained. The pound of silver remained the standard in accounts, but one of Charlemagne's successors restored the Imperial ratio of 1 : 12 and enacted that the pound of pure gold should no longer be sold at any other price than 12 pounds of silver. The date of the edict by which this restoration of the old ratio was secured was A.D. 864.[2]

These were the changes in the currency which

[1] Pertz, p. 72. Refusing to receive the new denarii must have meant as 12 to the solidus, for the new denarii themselves were heavier than the old ones, 32 wheat-grains instead of 28·8.

[2] Pertz, p. 494. *Karoli II. Edictum Pistense*, A.D. 864: Ut in omni regno nostro non amplius vendatur libra auri purissime cocti,

took place during the period of the formation of the Lex Frisionum and Lex Saxonum which we have next to examine.

No wonder that they should have introduced confusion and alterations in the text of the various clauses. And in order that we may be able to feel our way through them it now only remains that we should realise the actual difference between the amount of silver in the 40 denarii of the solidus of the Lex Salica and the amount of silver in the 12 denarii of the new solidus of the *nova moneta* which had thenceforth to take its place as legal tender in the payment of debts and wergelds.

In the first place, we know that the denarius of the nova moneta was a silver penny of 32 wheat-grains, so that Charlemagne's solidus of 12 silver pence contained 384 wheat-grains of silver.

All debts could be paid in one third of the weight of silver required before.

In the next place, whatever the denarii of the Lex Salica may originally have been, we know that the Merovingian silver denarii which had long been current in France and in England were of the same weight as the Merovingian gold tremisses, viz. 28·8 wheat-grains. Forty of these would contain 1152 wheat-grains of silver—*i.e.* exactly three times as much silver as the twelve denarii of the nova moneta.

So that if a wergeld were paid in silver it could now be paid in exactly one third of the weight of silver hitherto required under the Salic law, and so of every other debt.

---

nisi duodecim libris argenti de novis et meris denariis.

Illud vero aurum quod coctum quidem fuerit, sed non tantum ut ex deauratura fieri possit eo libra una de auro vendatur *decem* libris argenti de novis et meris denariis.

Finally, not only was the ratio between gold and silver disturbed, but also the ratio between money and cattle. And this was an important matter in the payment of wergelds, for, as we have seen, the normal wergeld was 100 head of cattle. Obviously, wergelds would no longer be paid, as of old, either in gold or in cattle, when they could be paid at a third of the value in silver.

In which currency are the wergelds of the Frisians and Saxons recorded in the laws?

In framing new laws representing the old customs of the newly conquered Frisians and Saxons, the question would certainly arise whether the wergelds were to be stated in the equivalent of their old customary value in cattle, or reduced to one third of their old value by retaining the traditional number of solidi as if they were still of the gold value.

We have seen that Frisians and Saxons were exceptionally dealt with; but they had now become a part of the Empire, and, with the best intentions, how was the framer of their laws to describe their ancient wergelds which had hitherto been paid in gold solidi or in cattle? No one of the courses open to him would be without its difficulties.

He might record the customary wergeld as still to be paid in gold solidi; in which case the wergeld would be three times that of neighbouring tribes who could now pay their wergelds in silver.

Or he might divide the amount of the ancient wergeld by three, so as to reduce it to the lower level; in which case the number of animals in which by long custom the wergeld had been paid would be worth three times the wergeld payable in gold.

These would be the alternatives if the payment in gold were continued, and never as yet in any of the laws had the wergelds been stated otherwise than in gold.

There was only one other way open to the legislator, if he wished to keep up the old customary values, viz. to translate the gold values at the old ratio into the new silver solidi: that is, to treble the gold figures of the ancient customary wergelds and make them payable in silver solidi. This would probably be the best course if he wished to continue the old relation of the wergelds to the animals in which they had hitherto been mostly paid. But then it might be difficult to enforce the payment of wergelds in silver in districts where the currency was still gold.

The legislator would, in any case, have to make up his mind whether to lower the ancient wergelds of the newly conquered tribes to a third of what they had been, or to keep up the value of the wergelds and the number of cattle in which they had from time immemorial been paid.

The wergeld in the popular tribal mind was a thing so fixed and so sacred that the makers of the Lex Frisionum and the Lex Saxonum were almost certain to find themselves between the horns of a dilemma.

II. THE LEX FRISIONUM.

The tribes conquered by Charlemagne, whose laws we have now to examine, differed from those whose laws and wergelds have been already considered in one important particular. They were not conquering tribes which had migrated into districts already under Roman law.

The conquests of Charlemagne over the Frisians and Saxons were conquests of German tribes settled as of old in their own countries. They were, moreover, conquests of still pagan tribes by Christian and partly Romanised Franks.

Frankish conquest had extended far into Frisian and Westphalian territory under the Merovingian kings. In Frisia Frankish influence was shown by the existence of Merovingian mints at Duurstede.[1] In Westphalia, at Soest and Paderborn, there were already Christian churches under the jurisdiction of the Archbishop of Cologne. But neither the conquest nor the conversion was completed till the time of Charlemagne.

Was the wergeld 160 solidi?

We have already learned from Titles XXXI. and XXXVI. of the Ripuarian law that there were Frisians as well as Saxons, Burgundians, Alamanni, and Bavarians resident in the Ripuarian district. Moreover, it was directly stated that these immigrants were to be judged, not by Ripuarian law, but by their own law and custom. Further, being often isolated and without kindred near them to swear for them, if charged with crime they were to clear themselves by the ordeal of fire or lot. And finally their wergeld was stated to be 160 solidi, the inference being that this was the wergeld of the Frisian freeman in his own country, by the law and custom of which he was to be judged.

So that we approach the text of the Frisian law with this valuable earlier knowledge in our possession.

[1] *Traité de Numismatique du Moyen Age*, par Arthur Engel (Paris, 1891), vol. i. pp. 329 332.

Two centuries before the date to which the collection of Frisian laws is assigned, the Ripuarian law bears witness that the Frisian wergeld was 160 solidi. Even if these clauses were not a part of the original text and did not date back to the sixth century,[1] the inference would be strong, and perhaps all the stronger, that such must have been the wergeld at the later date of the Frisian law. This earlier evidence is important, as, without the clue it gives us and with nothing but the Frisian law to guide us, we might very easily have been led to a wrong conclusion.

The laws are of different dates.

There seems to be no text of the Frisian laws earlier than that published by Herold at Basle in 1557, and he does not state from whence he obtained the text followed by him.[2]

Moreover, it is clear from internal evidence that the laws as we have them are by no means of one single date. They form, in fact, a collection of the customs of the three districts into which Frisia was divided, with modifications and various additions made to the original collection at different times.

At first sight there are inconsistencies in the statements of the wergelds, and, as in other cases, the key to an understanding of them is to be found, to some extent, in close attention to the currencies in which the amounts of the compositions are stated.

It is not necessary to enter into any discussion of the various theories suggested to meet the diffi-

[1] Sohm, in his preface to the Ripuarian law in Pertz, against his own former opinion, concludes that clause xxxvi. did go back to the sixth century, and was originally a part of the Lex (p. 188).

[2] See Richthofen's preface to the Frisian Laws in Pertz, p. 631.

culties caused by the confusion of the various currencies. The knowledge already obtained in the course of this inquiry will, I think, if adhered to, suffice to clear the way sufficiently for our purpose. Bearing in mind that the 'Lex Frisionum' as we have it is a compilation with various additions, the inconsistencies in the text will be no surprise provided that the reason for their occurrence is apparent.

The three districts of Frisia and their local solidi.

Frisia was divided into three divisions, and in certain glosses which appear late in the laws [1] we are told that each division had a separate solidus of its own.

(1) Between the *Laubach* and *Weser* (the Northern division) the solidus is described as of two denarii, *i.e.* tremisses, of the nova moneta.[2] This solidus, we shall find, was like that of the Saxon tribes on the Eastern side of the Weser. The solidus, being of two tremisses, contained sixty-four wheat-grains of gold.

(2) In the middle division, between the *Laubach* and *Fli*, the solidus is said to have been of three denarii, or tremisses, of the nova moneta,[3] *i.e.* ninety-six wheat-grains of gold. This solidus is the gold solidus of three tremisses after it had been raised by Charlemagne to the standard of the Eastern Empire.

(3) In the Southern or Western divisions, between the *Fli* and the *Sincfal*, the solidus was 2½ denarii

[1] They appear in the *Additio Sapientium,*' Tit. ii., clauses lxiii. and lxxviii.

[2] 'Inter Wisaram et Laubachi, duo denarii novi solidus est.'

[3] 'Inter Laubachi et inter Flehi, tres denarii novæ monetæ solidum faciunt.'

or tremisses *ad novam monetam*, *i.e.* eighty wheat-grains of gold.[1]

But it seems to be clear that the statements of the wergelds and other fines in earlier clauses of the laws are not made in these local solidi.

Thus in Title XVI. we are told that *Inter Laubachi et Sincfalam*, *i.e.* in both Middle and Southern divisions, in cases of homicide the payment to the lord for breach of his peace (*de freda*) was thirty solidi, '*which solidus consists of three denarii*,' although the local solidus of the Southern division was that of $2\frac{1}{2}$ tremisses. Sometimes the fines are stated in solidi of three tremisses and sometimes in solidi of 20 to the pound. There is no difficulty, after what we have seen in other laws, in recognising in the solidus of three tremisses the *gold solidus*, and in the solidus of 20 to the pound the *silver solidus* of the Frankish Empire.

Again, we at once recognise in the term *nova moneta* the new standard of Charlemagne, and in the term *veteres denarii*, which also occurs in the laws, the gold or silver tremisses of the Merovingian currency before the monetary reform of Charlemagne.

All this is exactly what might be expected in laws of somewhat different dates, some of them perhaps going back to the time of the Merovingian conquests, and others following upon the conquests of Charlemagne.

---

[1] 'Inter Flehi et Sincfalam solidus est duo denarii et dimidius ad novam monetam.' That the word *denarius* was applied to gold as well as silver coins, see mention of the 'gold penninck' of Gondebald in *Chronijck van Vrieslandt*, *sub* A.D. 739.

Having thus so far cleared the way, we pass on to the amounts of the wergelds as stated in the Lex. Wergelds in gold solidi under Tit. I.

Title I. is headed *Incipit lex Frisionum, et hæc est simpla compositio de homicidiis.* And the wergelds of the three districts as stated in the text and glosses may be tabulated as follows:—

(1) *Between the Laubach and the Weser.*[1]

Nobilis	106 solidi	and 2 denarii (or tremisses)
Liber	53 „	„ 1 denarius
Litus	26½ „	„ ½ tremissis

(2) *Between the Laubach and the Fli.*[2]

Nobilis	80 solidi	Payable ⅔ to the heir of the slain and ⅓ to his 'propinqui proximi.'
Liber	53 „	and 1 denarius (*i.e.* tremissis).
Litus	27 „	less 1 denarius (payable to his lord).
„	9 „	less ⅓ denarius, payable to the propinqui of the slain.

(3) *Between the Fli and the Sincfal.*[3]

Nobilis	100 solidi	of three denarii [*i.e.* tremisses] *novæ monetæ*
Liber	50 „	
Litus	25 „	

These wergelds, with one exception, are alike throughout, so far as regards the proportions between the three classes. The wergeld of the liber is double that of the litus, and that of the nobilis double that of the liber except in the Middle district, in which the wergeld of the nobilis is only 1½ times

[1] 'Inter Laubachi et Wisaram weregildus nobilis 106 solidi et duo denarii, liberi 53 solidi et denarium, liti 26 solidi et dimidius et dimidius tremissis.'

[2] 'Si nobilis [*or* liber *or* litus] nobilem occiderit, 80 solidos componat; de qua mulcta duæ partes ad hæredem occisi, tertia ad propinquos ejus proximos pertineat . . . liberum solidos 53 et unum denarium solvat . . . litum 27 solidos uno denario minus componat domino suo, et propinquis occisi solidos 9 excepta tertia parte unius denarii.'

[3] 'Inter Fli et Sincfalam weregeldus nobilis 100 solidi, liberi 50, liti 25 (solidi denarii 3 novæ monetæ).'

that of the liber. In the same district there is an additional payment to the *propinqui* of the litus, his proper wergeld, half of that of the liber, going to his lord.

It will be observed that in the last district only are the denarii (*i.e.* tremisses) stated to be *novæ monetæ.* The inference is that in the other two districts the tremisses, and therefore the solidi, were of the lower Merovingian standard.

The district in which the tremisses were *novæ monetæ* was the Southern district, first conquered and most thoroughly brought under Frankish influence. The other two districts had apparently not yet so completely come under it.

Accordingly, if we take the $106\frac{2}{3}$ solidi of the nobilis of the Northern district to be of Merovingian standard, the result is ($106\frac{2}{3} \times 86{\cdot}4$ wheat-grains) 9216 wheat-grains, or exactly 16 Roman ounces, *i.e.* the mina called, as we have seen, the Attic mina, which in Scandinavian usage was divided into two gold marks.

The wergeld of the nobilis in the Middle district between the Laubach and the Fli is stated to be 80 solidi instead of 106 solidi and two denarii. But as the wergeld of the liber and litus are the same as those of the Northern district, and therefore also presumably expressed in Merovingian currency, the wergeld of 80 solidi of the nobilis, to be consistent, should also be of the same Merovingian standard. And so it seems to have been, for 80 Merovingian solidi ($80 \times 86{\cdot}4$ wheat grains) make exactly the Roman pound of 6912 wheat-grains or 12 Roman ounces, *i.e.* $1\frac{1}{2}$ gold marks.

In the wergelds of both Northern districts, therefore, an original reckoning in gold marks of the Scandinavian system seems to have been afterwards translated with exactness into an uneven amount and fractions of solidi of the Merovingian standard.

Wergelds in gold marks of the Baltic tribes.

We may therefore state the wergelds of the two districts north of the Zuider Zee in marks of the Scandinavian system thus:

Nobilis . .	2 or $1\frac{1}{2}$	gold marks.
Liber . .	1	„ mark.
Litus . .	$\frac{1}{2}$	„ mark.

That these wergelds could be stated thus evenly in gold marks of the Scandinavian system, whilst in Frankish solidi they could be stated only in uneven numbers and fractions, is an interesting fact. It seems to show that the original wergelds went back to a time when the trade intercourse of Northern Frisia was connected mainly with Scandinavia, the Baltic, and the Eastern trade route. In 'Beowulf' we found that Frisia was on the horizon of the area included within the vision of the poet, the interest of whose story lay chiefly in the Baltic.

Only one third of 160 solidi.

Now let us compare the wergeld of the liber in these districts, viz. 53 solidi and 1 tremissis of Merovingian currency, with what the statement in the Ripuarian law would lead us to expect it to have been, viz. 160 of the same solidi. It is exactly one third of what it ought to be. And the inference from what we have learned in the last section would be that the maker of the laws had divided the wergeld of ancient custom by three.

But for the moment we pass on to follow further the text of the Frisian laws.

In s. 11 of Tit. I. it is enacted that if any one, whether nobilis, liber or litus, or servus, shall slay the servus of another, he shall compound for the servus according to his value. And in s. 13 of the same title it is stated that if a slave shall kill either a nobilis or liber or litus, unknown to his lord, the lord of the slave shall swear that he did not order it and pay twice the value of the slave. But if the lord cannot deny that he ordered it he must pay for the homicide as if he had done it with his own hand.

Slave to be paid for at his value.

In Title IV. it is again enacted that if any one shall kill the slave of another he shall be compounded for at the value put upon him by his lord. And the same rule is made to apply to the case of a horse, ox, sheep, goat, pig, and all domestic animals, except the dog: they are all to be paid for at the owner's estimate of value, or the alleged slayer must clear himself with as many oaths as the judge may require.

Value of the dog.

The *dog* is the only animal whose value is fixed by the law. And its value at first sight was not the same in the several divisions.

Between Laubach and Sincfal.		*Between Laubach and Weser.*
Dog for hawking . .	4 sol.	8 solidi and 12
Wolfhound accustomed to kill wolves . . .	3 sol.	
Wolfhound which wounds but does not kill . .	2 sol.	8 ,,
Shepherd dog . . .	1 sol.	4 ,,

The difference between the value of the dog in the Northern and the other divisions can hardly be other than one of different currencies. Probably the values for the Northern division may be silver values. It may, however, be remarked in passing that the value of a dog in any case is not lightly to be regarded as excessive. Its high value in the Frisian laws, and also in other laws, shows how dependent the tribes surrounded by forests were upon its help. In the Cymric Codes, as we have seen, the herdsman's dog was worth as much as an ox. In the Alamannic Laws the shepherd dog which could kill a wolf was valued at 3 gold solidi, or half as much again as the 'best ox,'[1] and in the Lex Salica the *canis pastoricalis*[2] was valued at 3 solidi. It is not difficult, therefore, to understand how in Frisia the dog which could kill a wolf should be worth 3 gold solidi, and the ordinary shepherd dog a gold solidus.

We now come to a set of clauses in which the differences between the three districts again appear, and in one of which, viz. again the district between the Laubach and the Weser, we meet with values stated in *silver solidi* of 20 to the pound, *i.e.* of twelve pence.

Methods of compurgation and ordeal.

These clauses are interesting as illustrating Frisian methods of compurgation, the ordeal of the lot and of hot water, and trial by battle, all of which evidently belong to ancient tribal custom.

Title XIV. relates to the slaying of a man in a crowd, and describes the means taken to ascertain whose deed it was. Each division had its own custom. That of the *Middle district* is first described :—

> The relative of the slain may summon seven men and charge each of them with the crime, and each is then put upon his oath with eleven co-swearers. Then they are to go to the church,

---

[1] ii. lxxxiv. [2] Tit. vi.

and lots are to be cast upon the altar, or if the church be too far off the lots are to be cast upon relics.

The lots are to be two pieces (tali) cut from a rod and called *teni*, on one only of which is the sign of the cross, the other being left blank. A clean cloth is to be spread over the altar or the relics, and then the priest (or if none, an innocent boy) ought to take one of the lots from the altar and pray God to show by some evident sign whether those seven who have sworn have sworn truly. If he takes up the lot marked with the cross, then those who have sworn were innocent. But if he takes up the other, then each one of the seven makes his own lot, from a rod, and marks his own sign on it, and so that both he and those standing by can recognise it. And the lots shall be wrapped up in clean cloth and laid upon the altar or relics, and the priest, if he be there, and if not the innocent boy, as above, shall take up each of them one by one from the altar, and shall ask him who knows it to be his own lot. And he whose lot happens to be last shall be compelled to pay the composition for the homicide. The rest, whose lots have already been taken up, are absolved.

But if, in the first trial of the two lots, he takes up the one marked with the cross, the seven shall be innocent, as aforesaid, and he (the accuser), if he wishes, shall summon others for the same homicide, and whoever may be summoned ought to clear himself by complete oath with 11 co-swearers. And this shall be enough for the accuser, nor can he bring any one further to the lot.

This law prevailed between the Laubach and the Fli. But between the Fli and the Sincfal for a case of this kind the following was the custom :—

He who seeks composition for a homicide shall swear on saints' relics that he will not summon in this matter other than those who are suspected by him of the actual homicide: and then he shall summon for the homicide one or two, or even three or four, or however many there be who have wounded him who was slain. But though there were twenty, or even thirty, yet not more than seven are to be summoned, and each of those summoned shall swear with eleven others, and shall, after the oath has been tested by the judgment of God, show himself innocent by the (ordeal of) boiling water. He who swears first shall go to the ordeal first, and the rest in order. He who shall be found guilty in the ordeal shall pay the composition for the homicide, and to the king twice his own wergeld: the rest of his co-swearers shall be treated as above concerning perjurers.

Between the Laubach and the Weser the following was the custom :—

He who seeks composition for homicide shall summon one man, declaring him to be the homicide of his kinsman, and saying that he ought to pay the 'leud' of the slain man. And if he, in reply, says that he is willing to purge himself on oath with his co-swearers, let him who has summoned him as homicide say that he wishes to summon him *in placito publico*, and let him so do. Let him summon him *in placito* before judges, and let him who is summoned, if he cannot deny, show another defendant for the homicide of which he is accused. And this ought to be done thus :

Let him produce the man he wishes, and let him swear "he is guilty of the homicide for which I am summoned," holding him by the hem of his cloak. But if he wishes to deny this oath let him swear and go forth to wager of battle against him. And whichever of them in that battle is conquered (*et sibi concrediderit*) shall pay the 'leud' of the slain. But if he be slain his next heir shall pay the composition of the homicide. But in this battle it is lawful for either to pay a champion for himself if he can find one. If the hired champion is slain, let him who hired him pay sixty *solidi* (*ie. three libræ*) to the king, and over and above pay the 'leud' of the slain man.

The payment of *sixty solidi—i.e. three libræ*—clearly indicates that the solidus of this clause was the Frankish silver solidus of 12*d*., of which 20 made the pound of silver. And this helps us to understand that the compositions described in the immediately succeeding and closely connected clause are also silver values. (Tit. XV.)

Wergelds stated in silver.

This is the custom in the same region observed for the composition of wergeld :—

(1) Composition of a *nobilis homo* 'per denarios veteres'	. 11 lbs.
(2) Composition of the *liber* 'per denarios veteres'	. 5½ lbs.
(3) Composition of a *litus*. of which two thirds pertains to the lord, one third to his kinsman	. 2 lbs. 9 oz.
(4) Composition of a *servus*	. 1 lb. 4½ oz.

There can, I think, be no doubt that the libræ of this clause are silver pounds, and further, that as they are stated to be pounds 'per denarios veteres' they must be pounds of Merovingian and not of Carlovingian weight.

These silver values equal to the gold ones at the Norse ratio 1 : 8.

The pounds of this statement are therefore Roman pounds, of 240 Merovingian pence. Let us compare then the wergeld of the liber of $5\frac{1}{2}$ such pounds of silver with the wergeld of the liber as stated in Tit. I., which we saw was equivalent to one mark of gold. Following the Scandinavian ratio of 1 : 8, the mark of 8 ounces of gold would equal 64 ounces of silver —*i.e.* $5\frac{1}{3}$ pounds instead of $5\frac{1}{2}$. The silver wergeld of the nobilis would equal $10\frac{2}{3}$ pounds instead of 11. The reckoning is rough, but near enough to justify the conclusion that what was aimed at was the nearest even pound of silver, and that therefore the wergeld of the one statement is the equivalent of the wergeld of the other statement.

At the same time the fact of the reckoning being throughout in Roman, *i.e.* Merovingian pounds, and not in those of Charlemagne's *nova moneta*, is instructive. It shows that this clause belongs to the period during which the silver currency was pushing its way into Frisia. A reckoning in silver had become necessary, although, as we happen to know, the Frisians had a special liking for gold. They continued to coin gold much longer than the Franks, and some years later than the date of the laws. The Frisians were in close contact with the mint at Duurstede, which was in fact the commercial metropolis of the North at the date of the laws. The mint at Duurstede continued to coin gold coins till the city was destroyed by the ravages of the Northmen in A.D. 837, and it was from these Duurstede Frisian coins that the types were taken of the first Scandinavian coinage.[1] In the meantime the close connection between Frisia and the Scandinavian district is quite sufficient to account for the Scandinavian ratio of 1 : 8 being the one used in the translation of the gold wergeld of the district next to the Weser into a silver equivalent.

Let us now at last translate the wergelds of the three Frisian districts, as stated in Tit. I. in gold solidi of three tremisses, back again into what they must have been when reckoned in the local solidi. If originally they were reckoned in these local solidi the result should be in even numbers.

The wergelds in the local gold solidi.

Between the Laubach and the Weser.

Nobilis (9216 w.g.)	=	144 solidi of 2 tremisses	or 2 gold marks.
Liber (4608 w.g.)	=	72 ,,	or 1 gold mark.
Litus (2304 w.g.)	=	36 ,,	or ½ a gold mark.

Between the Laubach and the Fli.

Nobilis (6912 w.g)	=	72 solidi of 3 tremisses	or 1½ gold mark.
Liber (4608 w.g.)	=	48 ,,	or 1 gold mark.
Litus (2304 w.g.)	=	24 ,,	or ½ a gold mark.

Between the Fli and the Sincfal.

Nobilis (9600 w.g.)	=	120 solidi of 2½ tremisses.
Liber (4800 w.g.)	=	60 ,, ,,
Litus (2400 w.g.)	=	30 ,, ,,

It is interesting to observe that the wergelds of the two districts north of the Zuider Zee, when translated back again into local solidi, turn out to have been in even numbers of such solidi, as well as in even gold marks of the Scandinavian district,

[1] Engel's *Traité de Numismatique du Moyen Age*, i. 233 and 329.

whilst those of the Southern district, most under Frankish influence, make even numbers of the local solidus but not of the mark.

When these Frisian wergelds in local solidi are regarded in connection with the fact that the wergelds on the east or Saxon side of the Weser were, as we shall find, also paid in a local solidus, and that this Saxon local solidus, like the solidi of the North Frisian district, was of two tremisses, and further that it represented the value of the one-year-old bullock, we are led to conjecture that the Frisian local solidi also may have represented the animal in which the wergelds were originally reckoned and paid. And this may perhaps be confirmed by the fact that, down to comparatively modern times, the East Frisian silver currency consisted chiefly of the *gulden* and its one-tenth the *schaap*. Possibly the *gulden* of this silver currency may point back to a time when the 'gold piece' was reckoned of the value of ten sheep.[1] But this is conjecture only. The dog, as we have seen, was the only animal whose value was fixed in the laws.

Why only one third of 160 solidi?

The fact that the gold and the silver values of the wergelds of titles I. and XV. of the lex seem to correspond leads up once more to the difficult question why the wergeld of the liber should be exactly one third of what the Ripuarian law apparently declared it to have been.

Richthofen, in his preface and notes to the Frisian laws in the edition of Pertz, points out that in later

---

[1] Martini's *Manuale de Metrologia*, *sub* 'Emden.' And compare Ridgeway, p. 371. He shows that in Italy and Sicily 10 sheep = 1 cow.

additions to the laws there is a curious duplication and triplication of figures which has to be accounted for. The facts seem to be these:—

In Tit. XXII. *De Dolg*, relating to the Middle district and forming part of the more ancient law, the fines for wounding are first given for the *liber*, and then an explanation is made in the Epilogue that those for the *nobilis* were one third higher and those for the *litus* one half less. The composition for the eye is stated to be half the wergeld.

Fines and perhaps wergelds trebled afterwards.

Then, under the heading *Additio Sapientium*, Tit. II., the amount for the hand is stated to be '25 solidi et 5 denarii.' And after the mention of the amounts for the several fingers are the words, '*Hoc totum in triplo componantur*.' The payments for hand and eye are generally alike, and three times 25 solidi and 5 denarii = 80 solidi, *i.e.* half a wergeld of 160 solidi.

Immediately following these words Tit. III. begins with the statement that the foot entirely cut off is to be compounded for as the hand, *i.e.* by 53 solidi and 1 tremissis, being double the previous amount. The payment for the eye put out is 'ter quadraginta solidi,' *i.e.* 120 solidi. Then whilst in the title *De Dolg* the ear is valued at 12 solidi, in Tit. III. of the Additio it is valued at '*ter* duodecim solidi.' Again, according to the title *De Dolg*, if both testicles were destroyed, the whole wergeld was to be paid: and in Title III. of the Additio the fine has become *ter* 53 solidi and 1 tremissis, three times the wergeld of the liber in Tit. I.

It is not needful to pursue the comparison further than to point out that Richthofen had some reason at any rate to form the opinion that in the additions to the law made, as he thinks, after A.D. 785 and probably about A.D. 802, the *wergelds* were trebled, as well as some of the payments for wounds; and that the inference from the Ripuarian laws that the Frisian wergeld was 160 solidi was therefore correct.[1]

So far Richthofen's contention is, I think, a correct one.

But what was the reason of this trebling of the wergeld in the additions to the laws?

The wergeld of 'liber' was probably 160 solidi.

Was it that the ancient wergelds were originally one third of those of neighbouring tribes and trebled at some auspicious moment to make them correspond with others; or have we not rather to do with the results of that confusion in the currency which was caused by the endeavour to force into use the silver solidus of 12 pence as the equivalent of the gold solidus?

This conjecture standing by itself on the evidence of these laws alone would be too hazardous to build upon, and it is not necessary to consider it further in this place. The matter of chief importance is that, all things considered, there seems to be fairly sufficient evidence that the wergelds of Tit. I. represent the ancient wergelds divided by three, and that accordingly we may take the wergeld of the liber in the two Northern districts of Frisia to have

[1] It is true that in the clauses trebling the amounts for wounds it is not directly stated that the *wergelds* were also trebled; but the use of the words in Tit. I., '*in simplo*,' suggests that it may have been so; whilst the facts that the triple payment for the loss, *e.g.* of the eye, which in the title *De Dolg* was a half wergeld, would otherwise exceed the full wergeld, and that, in the one case in which in the 'De Dolg' the whole wergeld was payable, the amount in the Additio is the *treble* wergeld, make it almost certain that it was so, otherwise the injury would be paid for at three times the value of a man's life.

been three gold marks or 160 Merovingian gold solidi,[1] as stated in the Ripuarian laws.

Division of wergeld among grades of kindred.

With regard to the distribution or division of the wergeld amongst the relations of the person slain, the laws mention only the custom of the Middle districts, according to which two thirds of the wergeld went to the heir of the slain and one third 'ad propinquos proximos.' They give no information as to how the 'propinqui proximi' divided their third amongst themselves, or to what grade of kinship this class of relations extended.

Happily, however, Dr. Brunner, in his informing essay on 'Sippe und Wergeld' already quoted, has been able to supplement the meagre information given by the laws as to wergelds with further details gained from later local sources.

In his section (p. 25) on 'Die Friesen zwischen Zuidersee und Weser,' he gives an illustration of the way in which under later custom the payment of the wergeld was divided amongst the relations of the slain. He states that the North Frisian *tale*, *i.e.* the third share which the kindred had to pay, was known as the *mentele* or *meitele* (magzahl).

Later example.

In a legal document of 'Westerlauwersches Friesland' the *mentele* of the kindred is described as 4 lbs. 5 oz. $6\frac{2}{3}$*d.*, and the *erbsühne*, or two thirds to be paid by the heirs, as 8 lbs. 10 oz. $13\frac{1}{3}$ pfenning. The pound, we are told, is 12 oz. of 20*d.*, so that here we have clearly Frankish currency and *silver*. The

[1] 4608 × 3 = 13824, *i.e.* 160 solidi of 86·4 wheat-grains. The wergeld of the Island of Gotland was also 3 gold marks or 160 solidi of Merovingian standard. See also on the whole question Dr. Brunner's article 'Nobiles und Gemeinfreie der Karolingischen Volksrechte' in *Zeitschrift der Savigny-Stiftung* &c., vol. xix.

third and the two thirds together make a whole wergeld of 13 lbs. 4 oz. of silver. Now in the first place if, as we probably should do, we were to consider this wergeld to be stated in pounds and ounces of Charlemagne's nova moneta, it would be not very far from treble the amount of the wergeld of the liber in Titles I. and XV. of the laws. And this, so far as it goes, confirms the Ripuarian statement that the ancient Frisian wergeld was one of 160 solidi.[1]

Let us now see how the third falling on the kindred was divided.

The one third of the *mentele* of the kindred (moeg) was divided thus :—

	lbs.	oz.	p.
1) The *brother*, or if none, the *brother's son*, or if none, the sister's son	0	12	0
(2) The *uncle* on the father's side (fedria)	0	9	0
The *uncle* on the mother's side (eem)	0	4	0
Or in default of these the *cousins* of the slain, or in default the cousins of the uncles.			
(3) The *eftersusterbern* or cousins descendants of grandparents:			
(*a*) On the side of the father's grandfather	0	3	8
(*b*) On the side of the father's grandmother	0	3	8
(*c*) On the side of the mother's grandfather	0	2	5
(*d*) On the side of the mother's grandmother	0	2	5
(4) The rest falls on the cousins—the eight stems which descend from the great grandparents			
The four stems from father's side	0	7	12
" " mother's side	0	7	8
	4	3	6

This interesting illustration of the payment of a Frisian wergeld, though of later date than the laws, confirms the statement in the laws that in its division the immediate heirs of the slain took two thirds and the *propinqui proximi* one third. It shows that at

[1] It would exactly equal 200 of the local solidi of two tremisses at a ratio of 1 : 8, or 160 solidi of 80 wheat-grains instead of 86·4.

a later date the immediate 'erbsühne' was two-thirds, and the share of the kindred one third. And it adds the important point that the kindred who paid, and by inference shared in the receipt of the one third, were confined to the descendants of the great-grandparents, both paternal and maternal, of the slayer or of the slain.

III. THE LEX SAXONUM.

In turning from the Frisian to the Saxon district, we have again to notice that, as in the Frisian instance, so in the Saxon, the territory over which the law had force was divided into several districts belonging to allied but separate tribes with their own peculiar customs.

Divisions of the Saxon tribes.

The Westfali and the Ostfali and the Angrarii were the chief tribes with which the Lex Saxonum and the Capitularies had to deal. The 'Saxones Bortrenses' and 'Septentrionales' are also mentioned in one of the Capitularies, but these do not appear to be of much importance to our inquiry.

The stubborn resistance of the Saxon tribes to the Frankish conquest, and the sanguinary character of the Saxon wars of Charlemagne, may well have made a cleaner sweep of local custom from these districts than had taken place in others. And this may explain to some extent the disappointing silence of the Lex Saxonum upon questions of custom which might otherwise have been expected to afford useful and interesting points for comparison with the Kentish and Anglo-Saxon Laws. Moreover, the wergelds as stated in the text are, like those of the Frisian Laws at first sight so misleading that only a very careful regard to the changes in Frankish currency can make their amounts intelligible, and bring them into line with those of neighbouring tribes.

Statement of wergelds of *nobilis* and *litus*.

Happily, in approaching the wergelds of the Lex Saxonum, we can do so, as in the case of the Frisian wergelds, with the statement of the Ripuarian Law in mind, that the Saxon as well as the Frisian wergeld was 160 solidi. And it is well that we can do so, for otherwise we might very easily lose our way.

The Lex Saxonum begins with a title 'de vulneribus' which describes the payments to be made for the different wounds inflicted upon a *nobilis*. Title II., 'de homicidiis,' next follows with a statement of the wergelds.

Qui nobilem occiderit, 1440 solidos conponat; ruoda dicitur apud Saxones 120 solidi et in premium 120 solidi . . .	Let him who shall kill a *nobilis* make composition 1440 solidi; the Saxons call 'ruoda' 120 solidi, and 'in premium' 120 solidi . . .
Litus occisus 120 solidis componatur . . .	The *litus* killed is compounded for with 120 solidi.

Much controversy has arisen upon the two extra payments 'ruoda' and 'in premium;' but whatever they may have been, they need not surprise us. Though we may not be able to identify them with the 'halsfang' or the 'wites' and 'bots' of Anglo-Saxon laws, they were probably payments of something of the same kind, additional to the wergeld.

It is more important to remark the absence altogether of any mention of the ordinary 'liber' or 'ingenuus' between the nobilis and the litus, especially as in the title on theft the three classes are all mentioned.

According to Clause 2 of the Tit. II. of the Lex, married women had the same wergelds as men. Those unmarried were to be paid for with a double wergeld. And by Clause 4 a servus slain by a nobilis was to be paid for with 36 solidi.

By Clause 5:

Litus si per jussum vel consilium domini sui hominem occiderit, ut puta nobilem, dominus compositionem persolvat vel faidam portet. Si autem absque conscientia domini hoc fecerit, dimittatur a domino, et vindicetur in illo et aliis septem consanguineis ejus a propinquis occisi, et dominus liti se in hoc conscium non esse cum undecim juret.

If a litus shall slay a man, *e.g.* a *nobilis*, by the order or counsel of his lord, the lord shall pay the composition or bear the feud. But if the litus shall do this without the knowledge of the lord, he shall be dismissed by the lord and avengement made on himself and seven others of his blood by the near kindred of the slain, and the lord of the litus shall swear with eleven [compurgators] that he had no knowledge of the deed.

Value of the ox 2 solidi.

Title IV. on Theft is interesting as, besides mentioning the *liber*, it fixes the value of the four-year-old ox at the date of the clause at 2 solidi, *i.e.* the old ox-unit.

VI. He who by *night* steals a four-year-old ox, which is worth 2 solidi, shall be punished by his head.

Theft of bees from within another's fence or of things to the value of two solidi by night from a house, or of things of any kind, day or night, of the value of *three* solidi, was to be capitally punished. Theft of things of less value than three solidi was to be compounded for ninefold, and *pro freda* the nobilis was to pay 12, the liber 6, and the litus 4 (? 3) solidi.

In Clause 6 of Title II. is the following:—

Si mordum totum quis fecerit, componatur primo in simplo

If any one commit murder with aggravation of conceal-juxta conditionem suam; cujus multæ pars tertia a proximis ejus qui facinus perpetravit componenda est, duæ vero partes ab illo; et insuper octies ab eo componatur, et ille ac filii ejus soli sint faidosi.

ment he (the murderer) makes composition first *in simplo* according to his condition, of which payment one-third part is to be paid by the next of kin of him who has perpetrated the crime, and two-thirds by himself; and besides eight times (the wergeld) is to be paid by him, and he and his children alone shall be in feud.

Murderer pays two thirds and his kindred one third of wergeld, as in Frisian law.

This clause is valuable as showing that, as in the customs of Frisia and most other Low German tribes, the murderer paid two thirds and his kinsmen one third of the wergeld in ordinary cases.

The murderer and his children alone had to pay the eight parts added for the aggravation of the crime by concealment.

That the Lex Saxonum is in some things at least a record of local custom is shown by the fact that, as in Frisia, varieties were recognised in the several divisions of the country.

The payment for taking a wife, in all the divisions, was 300 solidi (Tit. VI.), to be paid to her parentes if with their consent. If with *her* consent, but not with theirs, the payment was doubled. If she were seized without the consent of either, she must be restored to her 'parentes' with 300 solidi to them and 240 to her. Tit. VIII., however, shows that with regard to dower the customs of the several districts varied. Among the Ostfali and the Angrarii, if a wife bore children, she, the mother, retained the dower received on marriage for her life and left it to her children. Should she survive her children *her* next heirs received it. If there were no children, the

Local customs as to dower of wife.

rule was *dos ad dantem*, *i.e.* it went to the husband, or, if he were not alive, to *his* heirs. Amongst the Westfali, after a woman had borne children she kept the dower till her death. After her death, *dos ad dantem*, it went to the husband or the husband's next heirs. Further, Tit. IX. states that as regards what had been acquired by man and wife together, amongst the Westfali the wife received half, but amongst the Ostfali and Angrarii nothing: she had to be content with her dower.

The final clause of the laws, which describes the currency in which the payments were made, is important. According to the best manuscripts it was as follows: [1]—

Wergelds to be paid in solidi of two tremisses, i.e., value of the bullock.

Tit. XVIII. *De Solidis.*	
(1) Solidus est duplex; unus habet duos tremisses, quod est bos anniculus duodecim mensium: vel ovis cum agno.	(1) The solidus is of two kinds; one has two tremisses, which is the one-year-old bullock, or a sheep with lamb.
(2) Alter solidus tres tremisses id est, bos 16 mensium.	(2) The other solidus, three tremisses: that is, the ox of sixteen months.
(3) Majori solido aliæ compositiones, minori homicidia componuntur.	(3) Other compositions are compounded for with the greater solidus, homicide with the lesser one.

This was originally the final clause. But the following additions were afterwards made. In the Corvey Code:—

Quadrinis bos duo solidi. Duo boves quibus arari potest 5 solidi. Vacca cum vitulo solidi duo et semis. Vitulus anniculus sol. 1. Ovis cum agno et anniculus agnus, si super adjunctus, sol. 1.	The four-year-old ox, two solidi. Two oxen by which one can plough five solidi. Cow, with calf, two-and-a-half solidi. Year-old calf, one solidus. Sheep with lamb, if a year-old lamb be added, one solidus.

[1] Pertz, p 83.

And in the Codex Lindenbrogius :[1]—

Westfalaiorum et Angrariorum et Ostfalaiorum solidus est secales sceffila 30, ordei 40, avenæ 60 ; apud utrosque : duo sicle mellis solidus ; quadrimus bos duo solidi : duo boves quibus arari potest quinque sol., bos bonus tres solidi ; vacca cum vitulo solidi duo et semis.	The solidus of the Westfali and Angrarii and Ostfali is 30 sceffila of rye, 40 of barley, 60 of oats ; with both : two siclæ of honey a solidus ; four-year-old ox two solidi ; two oxen, with which one can plough, five solidi ; good ox, three solidi ; cow with calf, two-and-a-half solidi.

According to the original final clause, if it had been followed in the text of the Lex Saxonum the wergelds ought to have been stated in gold solidi of two tremisses, representing the bullock, or a sheep with her lamb. And the lesser penalties for wounds, &c., should have been stated in solidi of three tremisses, representing the ox of 16 months. These values in gold tremisses would then have been consistent with that of the full-grown four-year-old ox as stated in Tit. VI. at two solidi—*i.e.* the normal value of the ox before the change in the currency.

But, as it is, the text is not consistent throughout. Returning to the statement of the wergelds :

Nobilis	1440 solidi.
Litus	120 ,,

we are struck at once with the excessive amount of that of the nobilis. But if the solidi were of two tremisses, as they should have been, then, translated into solidi of three tremisses, the amounts would stand thus :—

Nobilis . . .	960 solidi,	or 1440 bullocks.
Litus . . .	80 ,,	or 120 ,,

These amounts appear to be still far too large ; whether regarded in cattle or in gold.

[1] Pertz, p. 84.

The statement of wergelds seems to be in silver solidi.

It seems probable that, in spite of the last clause, the wergelds of the Lex Saxonum, in the text as we have it, are described in Charlemagne's *silver solidi of* 12*d.*—the solidi which at the moment he was trying at a ratio of 1 : 4 to substitute for gold.

Very nearly contemporary with the Lex Saxonum is Charlemagne's *Capitulare de partibus Saxonie*, A.D. 785.[1] In this document no wergelds are mentioned, but other fines are described which may be compared with them. And it will be noticed that three classes are mentioned—nobilis, ingenuus, and litus.

In s. 19, for refusal to baptize an infant within a year of birth :—

Nobilis	120 solidi to the fisc.
Ingenuus	60 " "
Litus	30 " "

So again in s. 20 for illicit marriage, and in s. 21 for engaging in pagan rites :—

Nobilis . . .	60 solidi.
Ingenuus	30 "
Litus	15 "

These fines were evidently payable in the silver solidus, for in s. 27 the penalty for a man remaining at home contrary to the bann was to be 10 *solidi* or *one ox*. Obviously this is the value of the ox in silver solidi before they were made legal tender. Its gold value was only 2 solidi, as stated in Tit. VI. of the Lex. And, as we have seen, the value of the ox in the silver solidus of twelve pence was maintained at an average of about 8 solidi.

Twelve years later in date another Capitulare was issued, entitled *Capitulare Saxonicum* and dated

[1] Pertz, p. 34.

Capitulare of A.D. 797.

A.D. 797.[1] It was the result of a conference and contract between Franks and Saxons of the three tribes, Westfali, Angrarii, and Ostfali. According to s. 3 the Saxons agreed that whenever, under the laws, Franks had to pay 15 solidi, the Saxon nobiles should pay 12 solidi, ingenui 5 solidi, and liti 4 solidi.

Then follows a clause which is interesting as showing that the payment of wergelds still was a general practice. It enacted that when a homicide had occurred and a case had been settled in a district by the neighbours, the pacificators should, according to custom, receive 12 solidi for their trouble (*pro districtione*), and in respect of the wergeld (*pro wargida*) they should have sanction to do what according to their custom they had been used to do. But if the cause had been settled in the presence of a *royal Missus*, then it was conceded that on account of that wergeld the neighbours should still have their 12 solidi; and that the Missus of the King, for the trouble taken in the matter, should receive another 12 solidi, *ad partem Regis*. In clause 7, homicide of a *Missus regalis*, or theft from him, was to be paid for threefold.

Further, in Clause 9, the King, with the consent of Franks and Saxons, was to have power at his pleasure, whether *propter pacem*, or *propter faidam*, or for greater causes, to double the amount of the usual *bann* of 60 solidi, making it 120 solidi, and to insure obedience to his commands by any amount up to 100 or even 1000 solidi.

---

[1] Pertz, p. 84.

Lastly, in the final clause is the following :—

Moreover, it is to be noted what the solidi of the Saxons ought to be, *i.e.*:

Wergelds payable in cattle &c. or in the silver solidi of 12 pence.

The one-year-old bullock of either sex in autumn, as it is sent into the stable, for 1 solidus. Likewise in spring, when it leaves the stable, and afterwards as it grows in age, so its price increases. *De annona bortrinis* let them give for a solidus 40 *scapili*, and of rye 20.

Septentrionales for a solidus, of oats 30 scapili, of rye 15.

Bortrensi 1½ sicla of honey for a solidus. *Septentrionales* 2 sicla of honey for a solidus; also of clean barley they give the same as of rye for a solidus.

In silver let them make twelve pence the solidus. (*In argento duodecim denarios solidum faciant.*) In other things at the price of estimation.

So that in this Capitulare of A.D. 797, issued just before Charlemagne became Emperor, there is the clear statement that the one-year-old bullock is still to be reckoned as one solidus, and the further statement that in silver 12 pence make the solidus. And this in a clause headed with the words: 'Moreover it is to be noted what the solidi of the Saxons ought to be.'

The fact therefore seems to be that these Capitularies relating to the Saxons, and the Lex Saxonum, following upon the Conquest of the Saxons, date from the middle of the time when the change in the currency from gold to silver was taking place, and the silver solidus of 12 pence, first of Merovingian standard and ultimately of the *nova moneta*, was by law made equivalent for payments to the gold solidus of the Lex Salica of three gold tremisses or of 40 pence.

Now, having derived this information from the Capitularies, let us turn back to the laws.

Destruction of eye &c. paid for with a half wergeld.

In Tit. I. *De vulneribus*, the penalty for destroying another's eye is 720 solidi, exactly half the number of solidi in the wergeld of the nobilis, and for both eyes 1,440 solidi—*i.e.* exactly the amount of the whole wergeld of the nobilis. These proportions are found in several other laws, and were quite natural if the payments were made in both cases in the *same* solidi. But these wounds ought, according to the final clause in the law, to have been paid for in the solidus of three tremisses, while the wergelds should have been paid in solidi of two tremisses.

Clearly they are *not* stated in different solidi, for if for a moment we take them to be so, then the two eyes of the nobilis would be paid for at a higher value than his life.

The solidi must be silver solioi.

Further, if we look at these payments for wounds carefully, it becomes clear that they cannot be *gold* values. Three hundred and sixty gold solidi for a thumb and 260 for the little finger of a nobilis are quite impossible fines. The little finger of the Saxon nobilis cannot have been valued at more than the ordinary freeman's wergeld under the Salic and Ripuarian Laws.

We conclude then that, in spite of the last clause in the law, these values, both for wounds and homicide, are silver values, and that the figures in the text have at some date or other been substituted for the original ones to meet the change in the currency.

Let us try to realise what the effect upon the wergelds of the Lex Saxonum would be of Charlemagne's substitution of the silver solidus of 12*d*. for the gold solidus.

Up to this time the wergelds had been paid in

bullocks valued in gold at the solidus of two tremisses, and the equation was one no doubt of ancient custom. Now the Capitularies made them payable in silver at 12*d.* to the solidus.

One result became at once apparent. In the Saxon district the value of the ox went up, as we have seen, from two of the gold solidi to ten of the new silver solidi—an excessive rise, no doubt, and one likely to startle everybody. As regards most debts the change did not matter very much. The debtor got the advantage. But as regards wergelds hitherto payable in cattle and in gold it mattered very much indeed. It meant that a wergeld of 100 head of cattle could be paid in silver at one third of their value. And Charlemagne's advisers soon found this out. What if a Frisian or a Saxon killed a Frank? Was he to be allowed to escape with a silver payment of one third the value of the cattle? Certainly not; and so, as we have seen in the Capitularies of 781 and 801 enforcing the receipt of the silver solidus of 12*d.* for all debts, an exception was made of wergelds payable by Saxons and Frisians who killed a Salic Frank. These were still to be paid for, as heretofore, in the solidus of 40*d.* of the Lex Salica—*i.e.* the gold solidus of three tremisses.

Confusion in the currency.

This, so far as the wergelds were concerned, set the matter right when a Saxon killed a Frank; but it did not set it right in the ordinary case of a Saxon slaying a Saxon.

How could this be remedied but by altering the figures of the wergeld and the compositions for wounds, and inserting silver values instead of the gold ones? This seems to have been clumsily done,

The wergelds must be divided by three to obtain value in gold solidi.

the other clauses in the laws being apparently left unaltered or only partially altered. But assuming that the wergelds as they appear in the present text of Tit. II. are stated in silver solidi of twelve denarii, let us divide them by three, so as to restore them to gold values in solidi of three tremisses.

The wergeld of the nobilis of 1440 solidi divided by three becomes 480 solidi of three tremisses. And if, following very common precedents, we take this wergeld of the nobilis, whether from his noble birth or natural official position, to be a triple wergeld, then the missing wergeld of the *liber* or *ingenuus* would be 160 solidi, as the passage in the Ripuarian laws so often quoted declared it to be.

The wergelds would then stand thus :—

Wergeld of 'liber' then 160 solidi.

Nobilis	480 solidi of three tremisses.			
[Liber	160	,,	,,	]
Litus	40	,,	,,	

or in the local solidi of two tremisses :—.

Nobilis	720 solidi or bullocks.			
[Liber	240	,,	,,	]
Litus	60	,,	,,	

These then are the figures which, if we are right, were the original figures of the Title *De homicidiis*.

IV. LEX ANGLIORUM ET WERINORUM, HOC EST THURINGORUM.

We may probably follow Richthofen [1] in his conclusions that the Thuringians of these laws were the tribes settled with the Anglii and Werini in North Thuringia, and that they were promulgated under Charlemagne about A.D. 802.

[1] Pertz, p. 118.

Wergelds of the Anglii and Werini.

In the first title the wergelds for homicide are stated :—

Adaling	600 solidi.
Liber	200 solidi.
Servus	30 solidi.

These are evidently unaltered gold values.

A half wergeld for destruction of an eye, hand, or foot.

The rest of the first five titles relate to wounds, and we need only mention that the destruction of an eye, hand, or foot, or a blow causing loss of hearing, was to be paid for with *half* the wergeld of each class, following in this respect the custom of the Frisian and Saxon tribes.

These five titles in the Corvey Manuscript of the tenth century constitute a whole under the title 'Lex Thuringorum.' The remaining titles are, in this manuscript, added to the Lex Saxonum, to which, however, they do not appear to belong.

Triple wergeld of the Adaling.

The triple wergeld of the Adaling of these laws may have been the result either of noble birth or official position, or both combined. The wergeld of the *liber* of 200 gold solidi, presumably of three tremisses, seems to connect the customs of the Thuringian tribes of these laws with those of the Salic and Ripuarian Franks rather than with those of the Saxons and Frisians. It is worth notice, too, that, while in the Lex Saxonum and the Lex Frisionum the figures seem to follow a duodecimal system, in these laws the more usual decimal reckoning is retained as in the Lex Salica.

The fact that among the additional titles there is one 'De alodibus' connects still further these laws, notwithstanding their later date, with the Salic and Ripuarian laws which contain similar titles. And it is worth while, for purposes of comparison, to give it at length. (Tit. v.)

The title 'De Alodis.'

(I) Hereditatem defuncti filius non filia suscipiat. Si filium non habuit, qui defunctus est, ad filiam pecunia et mancipia, terra vero ad proximum paternæ generationis consanguineum pertineat.

(I) Let the son of the deceased and not the daughter receive the inheritance. If he who has died had no son, to the daughter shall go the cattle and slaves, but the land shall pertain to the next blood relation of the paternal generation.

(II) Si autem nec filiam non habuit, soror ejus pecuniam et mancipia, terram proximus paternæ generationis accipiat.

(II) But if he had no daughter either, his sister shall take the cattle and slaves; the next of the paternal generation shall take the land.

(III) Si autem nec filium nec filiam neque sororem habuit, sed matrem tantum superstitem reliquit, quod filia vel soror debuerunt, mater suscipiat, id est, pecuniam et mancipia.

(III) But if he had neither son nor daughter nor sister, but he left a *mother* only surviving, what daughter or sister should have had, let the mother take, *i.e.* the cattle and slaves.

(IV) Quodsi nec filium nec filiam nec sororem aut matrem dimisit superstites, proximus qui fuerit paternæ generationis, heres ex toto succedat, tam in pecunia atque in mancipiis quam in terra.

(IV) But if he leaves neither son nor daughter nor sister nor mother surviving, he who shall be next of the paternal generation shall succeed as heir of the whole as well in cattle and slaves as in land.

(V) Ad quemcumque hereditas terræ pervenerit, ad illum vestis bellica, id est lorica, et ultio proximi et solutio leudis debet pertinere.

(V) And to whomsoever the inheritance in the land shall come, to him ought to pertain the coat of mail, *i.e.* the birnie, and the avenging of the next of kin and the payment of wergeld.

(VI) Mater moriens filio terram, mancipia, pecuniam dimittat, filiæ vero spolia colli, id est murenulas, nuscas, monilia, inaures, vestes, armillas, vel quicquid ornamenti proprii videbatur habuisse.

(VI) A mother dying shall leave her land, slaves, and goods, to her son, but to her daughter her neck-treasures, *i.e.*, necklaces, buckles, collars, earrings, robes, bracelets, or whatever personal ornaments she appeared to have.

(VII) Si nec filium nec filiam habuerit, sororem vero habuerit, sorori pecuniam et mancipia,

(VII) If she had neither son nor daughter, but had a sister, to the sister shall she leave the proximo vero paterni generis terram relinquat.

(VIII) Usque ad quintam generationem paterna generatio succedat. Post quintam autem filia ex toto, sive de patris sive de matris parte, in hereditatem succedat; et tunc demum hereditas ad fusum a lancea transeat.

cattle and slaves, but the land to the next of the paternal kin.

(VIII) As far as the fifth generation the paternal kin succeed. But after the fifth, a daughter, whether on the father's or on the mother's side, may succeed to the whole inheritance; and then finally let the inheritance pass over from the spear to the spindle.

The alod included both land and cattle.

As in the other laws so under these rules the alod clearly embraced both the land and the 'pecunia' and 'mancipia' upon it. Its object, like that of the similar clauses in the other laws and also like that of the Edict of Chilperic, seems to have been to protect the land in ordinary cases from passing over 'from the spear to the spindle,' while at the same time sanctioning inheritance by females even in the land of the alod when otherwise there would be danger of its passing away from the kindred altogether.

In certain cases the land of the alod was made to go to male heirs while the 'pecunia' and 'mancipia' upon it went to females.

Whether the word 'pecunia' in such cases should be translated by 'cattle'[1] or the wider word 'chattels,' it must have included the cattle, and at first sight it is not easy to see how the rule would work which gave the cattle of the alod to a female and the land to a distant male heir. The cattle must in the nature of things have remained or be put upon land, and the awkward question arises upon whose land

[1] See Du Cange *sub voce* 'Pecunia,' and the cases there mentioned in which the word = *pecudes*, *grex*, &c.

they remained or were put. And so we are brought once more to the practical question of the position of women in relation to the land. That in certain cases in default of male heirs they could inherit land is one thing; but this question of the cattle and slaves involves quite another.

Male next of kin takes the land and chieftainship, but females may have cattle upon the land.

When a sister received her portion or gwaddol under Cymric custom, and when she received so many cows for her maintenance from the chief of kindred, she must have had rights of grazing for her cattle in the family herd of her gwely. Till she married, her cattle would graze with the cattle of her paternal gwely; and when she married, with the cattle of her husband's gwely. And so under the rules of this clause 'De alodibus' it does not follow that the distant male heir succeeding to the land of the alod was to evict her and her cattle from it. With the land he had to take also the responsibilities involved in the family holding. Clause V. states that to whomsoever the inheritance of the land shall come, to him ought to pertain the coat of mail, *i.e.* the birnie, and with it the duty of the chief of the kindred to avenge his kin and to see to the payment of wergeld if any one of the kin should be slain. Read from this point of view this clause 'De alodibus' becomes good evidence that, whatever changes may have been made as to female inheritance, the *land* of the alod had not yet lost all its tribal traits. It had not yet become the 'res propria' of an individual possessor under Roman law.

V. THE SO-CALLED LEX CHAMAVORUM.

This document, according to most recent authorities, relates to a district between the Frisians and Saxons to the North and East, with the river Meuse to the South.[1]

The Chamavi under Frankish law.

Its real title seems to be *Notitia vel commemoratio de illa euva quæ se ad Amorem habet*, and it seems to be not so much a code as a memorandum of the wergelds and fines of a Frankish people settled in the district alluded to. Probably in date it may belong to the time of Charlemagne, but before his changes in the currency.

It is of some interest to this inquiry because of its peculiar position, as relating to a tribe or people under Frankish rule, and yet with customs of its own which have survived Frankish conquest.

The Notitia starts with the declaration that in ecclesiastical matters, as regards the *bannus dominicus*, the same laws prevail 'as other Franks have.'

Wergeld of the Homo Francus three times that of the ingenuus.

And then it at once describes the wergeld, as follows :—

The wergelds of this law are as under. Whoever kills—

Homo Francus . .	600 solidi	et pro fredo	200 sol.
Ingenuus	200 ,,	,,	66⅔ ,,
Lidus	100 ,,	,,	33½ ,,
Servus	50 ,,	,,	16⅔ ,,

Then follows a clause (VII.) which states that if any 'Comes' be slain in his own 'comitatus' the wergeld is to be three times that according to his birth.

[1] See *Études sur la Lex dicta Francorum Chamavorum et sur 'Les Francs du Pays d'Amor,'* par Henri Froidevaux. Paris, 1891, chap. ii.

The *Homo Francus* thus has a triple wergeld, like the Comes. But the *Comes* may possibly be not *ingenuus*. He may be a lidus with official position, and so presumably, according to Clause VII., with a threefold wergeld of only 300 solidi.

In the next clause the Royal 'Missus' is put in the same position while on the King's business. His wergeld is also to be trebled.

What, then, is the *Homo Francus* with a wergeld three times that of the ordinary *ingenuus* of the district of Amor?

The wergeld of the latter is the full normal wergeld of 200 solidi. The Homo Francus in this district was therefore very much above the ordinary freemen of other laws. He was evidently a Frankish landowner on a large scale, towering in social position above the ordinary freemen of the district.

The *casa* and *curtis* of the Homo Francus alone were protected by special clauses (XIX. and XX.), and of him alone are any hints given as to kindred or inheritance. Clause XLII., in the following few words. enlightens us as to his social position:—

> If any Francus homo shall have sons, his inheritance in woods and in land shall pass to them, and what there is in slaves and cattle.
>
> Concerning the maternal inheritance, let it go in like manner to the daughter.

We must probably consider the privileged position of the Homo Francus as presumably the result of Frankish conquest. The great landowner may have been the holder of a benefice, or a tenant *in capite* placed upon the royal domain with ministerial and judicial duties, and the triple wergeld may fairly be assigned to his official position.

But to return to the wergelds.

The payment *pro fredo* seems to have been equal to an additional one third of the wergeld.

From clauses XX. and XXXII. it appears that the value of an eye or hand or foot was one quarter of the wergeld, instead of half as in the Salic and Ripuarian Laws.

Payment for the eye etc. one quarter the wergeld.

Theft was to be paid for ninefold with four solidi *pro fredo*.

The further clauses regarding theft in this border district of forests and cattle and mixed population are not quite easily understood, nor need we dwell upon them.

In c. XXX. the penalty for letting a thief go without bringing him before the Comes or centenarius was 60 solidi, as in the Ripuarian Laws.

VI. CONCLUDING REMARKS.

Before passing from the laws, the compilation of which seems to date from the conquests of Charlemagne, it may be well to note that, regarded from the point of view of the wergelds, the tribes whose customs have been examined in the last two sections seem to have belonged to the Frankish group with wergelds of 200 gold solidi, while on the other hand the Frisians and Saxons seem to have belonged to the other group with wergelds of 160 gold solidi.

This grouping of the tribes may not be exactly what might have been expected.

The two groups of tribes with wergelds of 200 and 160 solidi.

Geographically the Frankish group is sufficiently compact. The other is widely extended and scattered. Frisians and Saxons remain in their ancient homes. The Alamannic, Bavarian, and Burgundian tribes have wandered far away from theirs. But in their northern home they may have been once sufficiently contiguous to have shared many common customs and among them a common wergeld of 160 solidi.[1] Settled in their new quarters, the Rhine and its tributaries seem to have been the great highways of commercial intercourse and the connecting links between them. Immigrants from them all met as strangers (*advenæ*) in the Ripuarian district, and, as we have seen, we owe our knowledge of some of their wergelds very much to the recognition of them in the Ripuarian law.

[1] It has already been stated that the wergeld of the Island of Gotland was three gold marks or 160 Merovingian solidi. But owing to the late date of the Gotland laws it cannot be regarded as certain that the amount was the same at the date of the Ripuarian laws.

CHAPTER VIII.

THE TRIBAL CUSTOMS OF THE OLDEST SCANDINAVIAN LAWS.

I. THE MONETARY SYSTEM OF SCANDINAVIA.

THE facts needful for the understanding of the monetary system of the Scandinavian tribes need not detain the reader very long.

The weight system applied to gold and silver was that evidently derived from the Eastern Empire.

Marks, ores, and ortugs.

It consisted of the mark, the ore, and the ortug. The mark was divided into eight ores or ounces, and the ore or ounce into three ortugs, which were in fact staters or double solidi. The ounce being the Roman ounce of 576 wheat-grains, the ortug contained 192 wheat-grains, and was the exact counterpart in wheat-grains of the Greek stater, *i.e.* Professor Ridgeway's ox-unit. Reckoned in wheat-grains, two Scandinavian marks of 8 ounces were, as we have seen, exactly equal to what the early metrologists called the (light) *Mina Attica*, which consisted of 16 Roman ounces or 9216 Roman wheat-grains. Four gold marks thus made a *heavy* gold mina, traditionally representing a normal wergeld of 100 head of cattle.

The ortug the Greek stater or ox-unit.

But this heavy gold Mina of four marks had been seemingly twisted from its original Greek character to bring it into consistency with Roman methods of reckoning. It was divided no longer into 100 staters, but now into 96 ortugs, so as to make the ortug double of the solidus and one third of the Roman ounce, thus throwing it out of gear, so to speak, with the normal tribal wergelds of 100 head of cattle. It was thus made to contain only 96 ox-units, although in actual weight its 32 Roman ounces really did contain, so long as the standard of the Roman ounce was adhered to, 100 Attic staters or ox-units.

That the light mina of two marks or 9216 wheat-grains had found its way by the Eastern trade routes into Scandinavia appears from its survival in the monetary system of countries on both sides of the Baltic to quite modern times.

The pound of two marks.

In Northern Europe the pound of twelve ounces was not, as elsewhere, the usual larger unit. The pound of two marks or sixteen ounces had taken its place. And except in Norway and Denmark, which sooner or later adopted the monetary and weight system of Charlemagne, the ounce remained the Roman ounce of 576 wheat-grains. At the same time, as in the case of the Merovingian system, in spite of the Imperial influence of the gold solidus, there were evident marks of a tendency towards the ancient Eastern standard of the stater rather than the heavier standard of the double solidus. The ortug of 192 wheat-grains seems to have often sunk in actual weight below even the Attic weight to that of the ancient Eastern stater of 8·18 grammes.

Thus when the Russian weight system was recorded in the time of Peter the Great the unit both for precious metals and goods was found to be the *Zolotnic* or gold piece. Thus—

Dolja	=	·0444 grammes	=	wheat-grain.
Zolotnic	=	4·265 ,,	=	96 w. g.
Funt	=	409·511 ,,	=	96 zolotnic, or 9216 w. g.

Here, then, *in wheat grains* the Funt is the light Mina Attica over again, Romanised in its divisions. The Zolotnic is the solidus or half-stater. But in actual weight the pound is exactly half of the ancient Eastern gold mina of 818 grammes.

The Pfund of Silesia (Breslau), according to Martini, was 405 grammes, and that of Poland (Cracow) the same. Only Sweden and Riga seem to have adopted or preserved higher standards, the double mark of Sweden being 425 and that of Riga 419 grammes; but even these fell far short of the standard weight of 16 Roman ounces, viz. 436 grammes. But throughout, low as the standard of the Baltic *Funts* or double marks may have been, they were divided according to the Roman commercial weight system into *ores* or ounces and *loths* or half-ounces, and *gwentschen* or drachmas of one eighth of an ounce, just as if they were of full Imperial weight. The marks and the ores remained, but the old division of *ores* into ortugs or staters had long ago disappeared.

The division into marks, ores, and ortugs was, however, in full force at the time of the Norse laws, both for gold and silver. And the evidence of actual weights seems to show, not only that for the purposes of the Eastern trade routes, reckoning in marks, ores, and ortugs was in common use, but also that the standard, like that of the Merovingian coinage, was the ancient Eastern standard.

Thus the following weights, believed to belong to

the Viking period, from the island of Gotland, are now in the Royal Museum at Stockholm (Nos. 4752 and 5984).

The ortug in weight = Eastern stater or two Merovingian solidi.

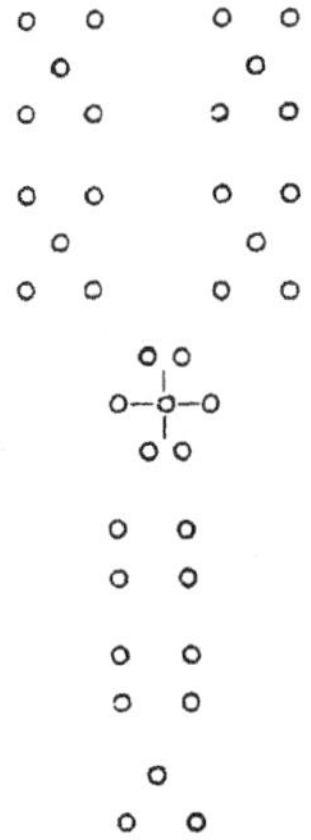

819	grammes	=	100	staters or ortugs	of	8·19
57·25	,,	=	7	,,	,,	8·1
32·65	,,	=	4	,,	,,	8·16
32·4	,,	=	4	,,	,,	8·1
24·35	,,	=	3	,,	,,	8·12

The unit of these weights is exactly the Eastern stater of 8·18 or two Merovingian solidi.[1]

[1] The depreciation in weight cannot have been the result of ignorance of the Roman standard. We learn from the excellent table given by Montelius in his *Remains from the Iron Age of Scandinavia* that the gold solidi of the Eastern Empire found their way into the Islands of Gotland, Oland, and Bornholm in considerable numbers, between A.D. 395 and 518. He shows that, while no silver coins of the Republic or before Nero have been found in Scandinavia, coins belonging to the silver currency of Rome after Nero found their way northwards in considerable numbers. Of Roman coins A.D. 98–192 only four gold coins are known to have been found and 2304 silver coins. Then the gold currency begins, and of dates between A.D. 235–395, sixty-four gold coins have been found and only one solitary silver coin. Lastly came the gold currency of the solidus of Constantine and his successors A.D. 395–518, and of this period 286 gold coins and one silver coin are recorded as having been found in Scandinavia. It is clear, then, that the Roman standard as well as the Roman system of division of the lb. was known in the North. For a long period no doubt the chief trade of the Baltic was with the Byzantine Empire and the East.

Whether this standard had been arrived at independently of the Merovingian standard, or adopted from it, we must not stop to inquire. It is enough that the ortug at the date of the laws through Roman influence had come to be reckoned as one third of the ounce.

Whatever may have been the early Byzantine influences and that of Eastern trade routes, long before the date of the Norse laws, Scandinavia had come under Frankish influences also.

Already during Merovingian times, chiefly through the Frisian mint at Duurstede, Merovingian currency had become well known on the Baltic, and we have seen that the first Scandinavian coins were copies from those of the Duurstede type. Hence it came to pass that in the most ancient of the Norse laws the old Scandinavian reckoning in gold and silver marks, ores, and ortugs had become connected with the Frankish currency. During the period of Merovingian influence the Merovingian ounce and the Norse ore were both, reckoned in wheat-grains, the ounce of the Roman pound, whatever may have been their actual weight. The mark of eight ounces contained 4608 wheat-grains of gold or silver. But at last, as the result of Charlemagne's conquests in the North, his *nova moneta* with its higher standard was brought into contact with Scandinavia. His mark of eight of his ounces or 5120 wheat-grains ultimately superseded in Norway and Denmark the old mark of eight Roman ounces. Hence, as all the Scandinavian laws as we have them, are of later date than Charlemagne's conquests, the question must arise, which of the two marks is the

The mark of 8 Roman ounces and Charlemagne's mark of the *nova moneta.*

one in which the wergelds and other payments are described.

In the oldest Norse laws the wergelds are stated mostly in *silver* marks, ores, and ortugs. The ratio between gold and silver was 1 : 8, so that an ore of gold equalled a mark of silver, and thus the translation of silver values into gold is easy. The laws themselves, as we shall find, make this perfectly clear. A wergeld stated as of so many gold marks is divided in the details of payment into silver marks, ores, and ortugs at the ratio of 1 : 8.

II. THE WERGELDS OF THE GULATHING AND FROSTATHING LAWS.

The Gulathing law.

In approaching the consideration of the Scandinavian custom as to wergelds and the structure of tribal society as disclosed in the ancient laws, I do it with great diffidence, especially as, for the translation of Old Norse, I am dependent on others.

On the whole it seemed best to concentrate attention upon the *Gulathingslög* as the oldest of the Norse laws. The Danish and Swedish laws and the Grágás of Iceland no doubt under competent hands would yield valuable additional evidence, but the oldest of the Norse laws may probably be fairly taken as the most representative of early Northern custom, and at the same time most nearly connected with the object of this inquiry.

Geographically the Gulathing law was in force in the southern portion of Norway. It seems to have embraced, in about the year 930, three, and afterwards six, *fylkis* or districts each with its own *thing* and local customs.[1] In this respect it resembled the Frisian and Saxon laws, both of which recognised, as we have seen, the separate customs of tribal divisions contained in the larger district over which the laws had force.

The Gulathing law must therefore be regarded as in some sense a compilation or collection of customs rather than one uniform law. For instance, there are three or four separate descriptions of the wergeld and the modes of its payment and receipt. One of these is avowedly of later date. The older ones may probably describe local variations of general custom, belonging to one or another of the divisions, and even these bear marks of later modification and additions.

As usual, the introduction of Christianity was the occasion and perhaps the cause of the compilation, and therefore from the time of the formation of Dioceses by King Olaf (A.D. 1066–93) ecclesiastical influence must be expected. But on the whole this Gulathing law presents in some points a far more interesting and instructive picture of social conditions resulting from tribal custom than the laws of other tribes already examined of much earlier date.

The Frostathing law.

The next important of the ancient laws of Norway is the *Frostathingslög* belonging to the more northerly district of Drontheim. Without pretending to have made it the subject of special study, I have here and there found it useful in elucidation of the Gulathing law, and as showing that tribal custom, though with local variations, was in force over a wider district than that under the Gulathing law.

---

[1] *Die Entstehungszeit der älteren Gulathingslög* von Dr. Konrad Maurer, p. 5.

The question of the structure of tribal society and the division of classes in Norway may be most conveniently approached from the point of view of the *rett* or 'personal right,' somewhat analogous to the Irish 'honour-price' and the Welsh 'saraad.'

Grades of personal 'rett.'

Both in the Gulathing law and in the Frostathing law this personal 'rett' lies at the root of the graduated payments for insults, wounding, and homicide. And the statements of it are practically identical in the two laws. They are as follows :—

Gulathing (200)		*Frostathing* (X. 35)	
		Leysing before freedom's ale	4 ores
Leysing	6 ores	Leysing after freedom's ale	6 ores
Leysing's son . .	8 „	Leysing's son	8 ores or 1 mark
Bónde	12 „	Reks-thane[1] . .	12 ores
		A'rborinn man[3]	16 ores or 2 marks
Hauldman[2] . . .	24 „	Hauldman .	24 ores or 3 „
Lendman and Stallare .	48 „		

The chief difference is that the Frostathing law divides the leysings into two classes, a significant point on which important considerations turn.

The things for which full rett was paid may be described as insults. If a man were knocked down, even if he fell on his knees, or if his moustache were seized with hostile hand' (195), or if a man were called 'a mare or bitch,' these were insults for which full rett was to be paid (196).

The payments for inflicting serious wounds (sár) were regulated in the same gradations according to

[1] The Reksthane is an official, and quite a different person from the Bónde.

[2] Elsewhere called the Odal-born-man.

[3] The A'rborinn man seems to be the same as the Aettborinn man, *i.e.* 'a man born in a kindred.'

rank as the rett, but were threefold in amount. These payments were made in 'baugs' or rings, each of twelve ores of silver.

Gulathing Law (185)	
Leysing	1 ring
Leysing's son	2 rings
Bónde	3 "
Odal-born man [1]	6 "
Lend-man and Stallare	12 "
Jarl	24 "
King	48 "

Frostathing Law (IV. 53)	
Leysing	2 rings
Reks-thane	3 "
A'r-borinn man	4 "
Hauld	6 "
Lend-man	12 "
Jarl	24 "
King	48 "

These were the penalties paid by the person inflicting the wound—*i.e. three times his own rett*—and besides this he had to pay *sár-bót* according to the extent and character of the wound, as in other laws. He also had to pay the healing fee (185) of the injured person.

The hauld or odal-man the typical tribesman.

Passing from insults and wounds to homicide, throughout the Gulathing law the hauld, or odal-born man, is taken as the typical tribesman. His wergeld is described, and then the wergelds of other classes are said to vary according to the rett.

But before we consider the wergelds it must be remarked that here, as elsewhere, there is no wergeld for a murder within the family.

In clause 164 under the heading of 'A madman's manslaying' is the following: [2]

Nu hever maðr óðz mannz víg vigit, vigr sunr faður, æða faðer sun, æða bróðer bróðor, æða systkin eitthvert, æða vigr barn móðor sína, æða móðer barn	Now if a man has done the slaying of a madman, if a son slays his father, or a father his son, or a brother his brother or any of his sisters and brothers, or

[1] The hauld seems to have been the same as the odal-born man.

[2] See also the Frostathing Law IV. 31, in which in a similar case the person is outlawed.

sitt, þá firi-vigr hann arve þeim er hann átti at taca. Scal sá þann arf taca er nestr er þá, oc helldr scal konongr hava en hann. En hann være í lande, oc gange til skrifta, oc have sitt allt.	a child slays its mother or a mother her child, then he forfeits the inheritance he ought to take. The one next to him in kin takes that inheritance, and the King shall have it rather than he. But he shall stay in the land and be shriven and keep all that is his.

No wergeld within the family.

In the Gulathing law the kindred within which there is no wergeld is thus the actual family, and it is in full accord with the instance in Beowulf in which the old father is represented as having to put up with the presence of a son by whose arrow another of his sons had been slain, such a crime being one which under tribal custom could not be avenged.

Turning now to the amount of the wergeld of the Gulathing law and the Frostathing law, it must again be remarked that there are in these laws varying accounts of it.

The wergeld of the Frostathing law of later date awarded in marks of gold.

In the first place there are some avowedly of later date than others. Thus, in Frostathing VI. 1 the description of the wergeld is commenced as follows:—

Her hefr upp oc segir í frá því er flestum er myrkt oc þyrftu þó marger at vita, fyrir því at vandræði vaxa manna á millum en þeir þverra er bæði höfðu til vit oc góðan vilja, hvesso scipta scylldi ákveðnum bótum ef þær ero dœmdar, fyrer því at þat er nú meiri siðr at ánemna bœtr, hvesso margar mercr gulls uppi sculu vera epter þann er af var tecinn, oc velldr þat at marger vito eigi hvat laga bót er, er þó at vissi, þá vilia nú fáer því una. En Frostoþings bóc scipter laga-bót hveriom epter sínum burð oc	Here begins and is told that which to most is dark and yet many had need to know, because difficult matters increase among men and those grow fewer who both had the wits and the good-will for it,—how to divide the fixed *bóts* (bœtr) if they are adjudged, *for it is now more the custom to fix the bóts, how many marks of gold* shall be paid on account of him who was slain, and the cause of that is that many know not what the lawful *bót* is, and though they knew it, few will now abide by it. *But the Frosta-*

metorði, en ecki hinum bótum er þeir ofsa eða vansa er í dómum sitia oc sáttmál gera.

thing book divides the lawful bót to every one according to his birth and rank, and not those *bóts* (bœtr) which they that sit in courts and make terms of peace put too high or too low.

Here the writer clearly refers back to the ancient Frostathing book as the authority for the 'lawful bót,' but on examination he seems to add certain additional bóts which the courts now include in the round amount of so many gold marks awarded by them in each case as it comes before them.

The writer takes first the case of an award of six marks of gold and describes how it is to be divided, and then the case of five marks of gold, and so on.

Division of it in silver marks at ratio of 1 : 8.

The division is throughout made in *silver* marks, ores, ortugs, and penningar. But when the items are added up, the total in silver divided at the ratio of 1 : 8 brings back the result as nearly as may be to the number of *gold marks* from which the division started. Thus in the clause describing the division of the wergeld of six marks of gold, the silver items add up to 48 marks exactly, and the division of this by 8 brings back the amount to six marks of gold. And so in the clause dividing five marks of gold, the items seem to add up to one ortug only less than 40 silver marks, and again a division by 8 brings the amount sufficiently near to five marks of gold.

The group of Bauga men.

In each case, however, the writer adheres to the same scheme of division. When he has 6 gold marks to divide he first assigns 18 silver marks to *Bauga* men (*i.e.* the near group of kinsmen of male descent on the paternal side only), and then he adds half as

The other group of Nefgildi-men.

much (*i.e.* 9 marks) to a group of *Nefgildi-men* [1] among whom are included, with others, kinsmen of descent through females on both paternal and maternal sides. So that these two groups of Bauga men and Nefgildi get 27 marks. In all cases he makes the group of Nefgildi receive only half the amount received by the Bauga group, the whole amount being reduced according to the number of gold marks to be divided. After the amount allowed to these two groups, the remainder is made up of additional payments some of which he expressly declares were not included under old law. Thus (in clause 6) he adds an amount which he says was 'not found in the old Frostathing book' and justifies it by saying that there would be danger to the slayer if it was not paid. And so again (in clause 9), there are additions for half-brothers, half-brothers' sons, &c., of the same mother. And these additions are included in the six marks of gold 'according to new law.'

Evidently, therefore, we must not take these wergelds of six and five marks of gold with their divisions as representing the ancient customary wergelds of this class or that in the social scale, but rather as showing the extent to which the system of wergelds had become somewhat arbitrarily expanded and elastic in later times. The total amount with additions was apparently increasing as time went on.

As in the Frostathing law so also in the Gulathing

[1] The Nefgildi-men include the slayer's mother's father, daughter's son, mother's brother, sister's son, father's sister's son, mother's sister's sons, son's daughter's son, daughter's daughter's son, brother's daughter's son, sister's daughter's son.

Later statement in the Gulathing law.

law (clause 316, p. 104) there is a statement of wergeld, avowedly of a late date and added under the name of *Biarne Marðarson*, who lived about A.D. 1223. And this, too, seems to belong to a time when the amount of the wergeld was awarded by some public authority in so many marks of gold. He takes the case of a wergeld of six marks of gold and shows how it ought to be divided; and then the case of a wergeld of five marks of gold and shows how that should be divided—'What each shall take of five marks of gold' and so on—just as was done by the writer in the Frostathing law.

One might have supposed from this that, as the method of awarding fixed amounts and the amounts to be divided in gold marks were the same, so the groups and the persons included in them would have corresponded also. But they differ considerably.

Biarne Marðarson up to a certain point follows the same scheme as the writer in the Frostathing.

In his division of six marks of gold he, too, draws a line at the amount of 27 marks, and he also divides this amount into thirds and gives two thirds to one group and one third to the other. The son of the slain and the brother of the slain form the first group and take 18 marks, and a second group take 9 marks, the two together taking 27 marks.

The group who together take 9 marks, like the Nefgildi-men of the Frostathing, embraces however by no means the same relatives as are included in the latter. The only persons included are the father's brother and his children, *i.e.* first cousins or brœðrungs of the slain, but among them are included the sons of concubines and of female first cousins. And after the mention of these is the statement, '*All that these men take amounts to* 27 *marks and* 2 *aurar*.' Out of the remainder of the 6 gold marks or 48 silver marks other relations take to the 'fifth man' on the male line and the sixth on the female line.

Biarne Marðarson seems, like the writer in the Frostathing law, to have had to some extent a free hand in the division. It is clear that there was much variety in the course adopted. Nor does he seem to have been by any means so systematic and accurate as the other writer. The silver amounts, when added up, do not so accurately correspond with the six gold marks to be divided.

Earlier wergeld of the Gulathing law. In silver marks and cows.

We turn, then, from these later statements to what seems likely to be an older statement of the Norse wergeld, viz. that which commences at clause 218 of the Gulathing law.

It describes the division of the wergeld of a 'hauld' or 'odal-born' man, and it begins with the explanation that the 'mannsgiöld' or wergeld decreases and increases from this as other retts.

It describes the various amounts both in silver marks and in cows, which the other statements do not, and this, so far as it goes, is a sign of antiquity.

In clause 223 is inserted a statement of the various things in which wergelds may be paid. The only item the value of which is given is the cow, which is to be taken at 2½ ores if not older than eight winters and if it be 'whole as to horns and tail, eyes and teats, and in all its legs.' And this silver value of the cow—2½ ores—is the one used in this older description of the wergeld.

The wergeld according to this statement consists

of bauga payments and upnám payments. The first are received in three baugs or rings thus :—

The 64 cows of the Bauga group.

Höfuð (head) *baug*, taken by the son and the father of the slain	10 marks or 32 cows.
Bróður baug, taken by brother, or if none, by the son of the slain .	5 marks or 16 cows.
Brœðrungs baug taken by the father's brother's son, *i.e.* first cousin of the slain. . . .	4 marks or 13 cows – ½ ore.
	19 marks or 60 cows + 2 ores.
To this is added for women's gifts, *i.e.* the mother, daughter, sister, and wife of the slain, or in default to the son of the slain .	1 mark or 3 cows + ½ ore.
Total	20 marks or 64 cows.

After this statement is the declaration, 'Now all the baugs are counted.'

A clause is here interpolated changing the point of view so as to show how, and by whom on the slayer's side the same three baugs were paid.

Nú scal vigande bœta syni hins dauða hafuðbaug.	(222) The slayer shall pay to the son of the dead the *höfuð-baug*.
En bróðer viganda scal bœta brœðr hins dauða bróðor baug, ef hann er til, ellar scal vigande bœta.	The slayer's brother (if he has one) shall pay to the brother of the dead the *bróður baug*; otherwise the slayer shall pay it.
Nú scal brœðrongr viganda bœta brœðrongi hins dauða brœð-rongs baug, ef hann er til, ellar scal vigande bœta.	The brœðrung of the slayer (if he has one) shall pay to the brœðrung of the slain the *brœð-rungs baug*; otherwise the slayer shall pay it.
Sá er sunr hins dauða er við giölldum tecr, hvárt sem hann er faðer æða bróðer, æða hvigi skylldr sem hann er.	He is [reckoned] the son of the dead who takes the giöld, whether he is father or brother or however he is related.

Then follows the declaration, '*Now the baugs are separated*' ('Nú ero baugar skildir').

It seems clear, then, that the slayer was in the last resort responsible for the whole of these baug payments, as it was the son of the slain who would take any part of them lapsing through failure of the designated recipients.

Women's gifts.

The small payments to the mother, daughter, sister, and wife included in the baug payments are evidently additional and exceptional payments in regard to close sympathy. The slayer does not make these payments. It is expressly stated that they are made 'by the kinswomen of the slayer,' but they are included in the even amount of 20 marks or 64 cows.

The recipients of the three baugs, it will be seen, were limited to the nearest relatives on the *paternal* side—fathers, sons, brothers, and first cousins—with no descent through females, while the recipients in the next set of groups or 'upnáms' include also relations through females: but, again, *only males receive.*

There is, however, one exception. In clause 231 is the following:—

Nú ero konor þær allar er sunu eigu til sakar, oc systr barnbærar. þá scal þeim öllum telia söc iamna, til þær ero fertogar.	All those women who have sons are in the *sök* (suit), and sisters capable of bearing sons. They shall all be held to have an equal part in it till they are forty.

Evidently they partake, as under Cymric custom, only in respect of possible sons who if born would partake themselves. Indeed, the sons only appear in the list of receivers and in no case the mother, except among the women's gifts included as above in the baug payments.

Clause 224 describes the upnám set of recipients as under. It will be seen that they include descendants of great-grandparents, but no more distant relations.

The upnám group includes descendants of great-grandparents.

'Sac-tal of upnáms or groups *outside bauga men.*'

1st upnám.

The slain person's —
- Father's brother (*i.e* uncle).
- Brother's son.
- Mother's father.
- Daughter's son.

Each gets a mark from the slayer if a hauld be slain; and this amounts to 4 *marks*.

2nd upnám.

The slain person's —
- Father's brother's son (*brœðrung*).
- Brother's daughter's son.
- Mother's brother.
- Sister's son.
- *Systling* (? Father's sister's son).

Each gets 6 ores from the slayer if a hauld be slain; and this amounts to 3 *marks* 6 *ores*.

3rd upnám.

- Mother's sister's son (*systrung*).
- Brœðrung's child.
- Father's brœðrung.
- Mother's mother's brother.
- Sister's daughter's son.

They get half a mark from the slayer if a hauld be slain (probably ½ mark each): *i.e.* 2 *marks* 4 *ores*, making the total of upnáms 10 *marks* 2 *ores*.

Then follows the declaration, '*Now all the upnám men are counted.*'

Total wergeld 30 marks or 96 cows.

If we add up the amount of the two sets of payments the result will be as follows:—

The three *bauga* payments of near relatives, with addition of women's gifts	20 marks	or 64 cows.
The *upnám* payments within descendants of paternal and maternal great-grandparents	10 marks 2 ores	or $32\frac{4}{5}$ cows.
	30 marks 2 ores	or $96\frac{4}{5}$ cows.

As in the Frostathing law the *nefgildi-men* took as a group an amount equal to one half the amount of the bauga group, so here the *upnám* men do the same. Evidently this is the intention.

Wergeld of the hauld at 1:8 200 gold solidi, or roundly, 100 cows.

Now if we may take the bauga payments and the upnám payments as representing in intention 30 silver marks or 96 cows, then, at a ratio of 1:8, the 30 silver marks equalled, in wheat-grains, exactly 200 Merovingian gold solidi.[1] And this may have been the ancient wergeld of the hauld.

There is, however, in clause 235 a further payment mentioned extending 'to the fifteenth degree of kinship' and amounting to about 1 mark and 3 ores. Possibly (though I hardly think it likely) this formed a part of the original wergeld, and if it be added, it would increase the wergeld to 31 marks, 5 ores, and at $2\frac{1}{2}$ ores to the cow the wergeld would be increased to $101\frac{1}{5}$ cows. If we might take this as roughly aiming at the round number of 32 marks and 100 cows, the wergeld of the hauld would be, at the ratio of 1:8, four gold marks or 100 cows: *i.e.* in actual weight the heavy gold mina of 32 Roman ounces, which under Greek usage was divided into 100 staters or ox-units. The confusion between 96 and 100 cows is so likely a result of the application of Roman methods to the division of the mina that we need not regard it. That the one or the other of these amounts may have been the original wergeld of the hauld representing originally 100 cows is consistent at least with widely spread tribal usage.

This view is confirmed by the fact that the

[1] $4608 \times 30 = 138240$, and this divided by $8 = 17280$ w.g. of gold, *i.e.* 200 gold solidi of 86·4 w.g.

further payments mentioned in the Gulathing are distinctly abnormal ones, and so presumably added at a later date like those mentioned in the Frostathing law.

We are justified in so considering them, because in the laws themselves the persons to whom they were made are expressly called *Sak-aukar*, or 'additional persons in the sak or suit.' And when we examine them further we find that they were hardly likely to have been included among the original recipients of the wergeld.

Among those of clause 236 are the thrallborn brother and thrallborn son of the slain, and the half-brother by the same mother; and clause 239 extends the number to the son-in-law, brother-in-law, step-father, stepson, oath brothers, and foster brothers. Evidently in these exceptional cases the rules of strict blood relationship have been broken away from, and additions have been made to the normal wergeld to stay the vengeance of persons sufficiently nearly connected in other ways to make them dangerous if left unappeased.

It was probably these additional payments, added from time to time in contravention of the strict rules of blood relationship, which caused the uncertainty of the later laws, and led to the new system of awarding a round number of gold marks as the total wergeld, included in which were additions intended to meet the introduction of half-blood and foster relations and others the risk of whose vengeance it seemed needful apparently in later times to buy off.

Returning, then, to the original wergeld of the hauld without these additions, we have seen that it consisted of two sets of payments, bauga payments and upnám payments, and possibly the small addition of those of more distant relations.

Now in the Gulathing law there are two other descriptions of the amount of the bauga payment, and it will be useful to examine them.

Another statement makes the bauga men pay 18 marks.

The first is to be found in clauses 179 and 180.

In clause 179 the payment for cutting off a hand or foot and for striking out an eye is said to be a half 'giöld,' and it is added :—

En ef allt er af einum manni höggvit hönd oc fótr, þá er sá verri livande en dauðr ; scal giallda sem dauðr sé.	But if both hand and foot be cut off the same man, he is worse living than dead, and is to be paid for as if he were dead.

And then in the next clause, under the heading '*About Giöld,*' is the following :—

Nú ero giölld töld í Gula ; giallda haulld xviii mörcom lögeyris. Nú scolo þeðan giölld vaxa oc svá þverra sem rétter aðrer.	Now shall be told payments in Gula. A *hauld* shall be paid for with 18 marks of lawful aurar. Starting from this, the payments shall increase or decrease as other retts.

Now it would seem that this payment for the death of a hauld was not the whole wergeld but only the *bauga* part of it. No details even of the bauga payments of eighteen marks are given in this clause. It seems to be inserted in this place simply with reference to the full limit of payments for injuries. Liability for wounding, under Cymric custom, was confined to the kinsmen of the gwely, and so it may well be that under Norse custom it was confined to the bauga group.

But the amount in this clause is only eighteen marks, while that of the bauga payments of the wergeld we have just been considering, as probably the earlier one, was twenty marks. How is this to be accounted for? The answer surely must be that eighteen marks of Charlemagne, reckoned in wheat-grains, were exactly equal to twenty of the Roman or Merovingian marks of the earlier period.

The other statement alluded to is also a statement avowedly of the bauga payments, and begins with almost the same words, 'Now the giöld for the hauld shall be told.' In this case the details are given and the detailed payments add up between eighteen and nineteen marks, and yet the total is given as a little more than twenty marks.

Another detailed statement makes the bauga payment 18 or 20 marks.

This statement differs from the older one in its divisions, but it has an air of antiquity and reality about it which suggests that it may represent a local custom actually in force. Little touches of picturesque detail seem to bring it into contact with actual life, and to show how local custom might work out a common object by its own peculiar method.

It meets us abruptly in clause 243 under the heading '*On baugar*,' and commences thus:—

> Now the giöld for the hauld shall be told—
> 6 marks (of 12 ells to the ore) in the *head-baug*,
> 4 marks in the *brother's-baug*,
> 2½ marks in the *brœðrung's baug*.

It then introduces quite another element, viz. the *tryggva-kaup* (truce-buying).

Nú scolo fylgia tvau tryggva kaup baugi hverium.	Two tryggva-kaup shall go with every baug.
hvert scal eyrir oc fimtungr eyris tryggva kaup.	Each tryggva-kaup shall be 1⅕ ore.
En tryggva kaup scal fara bauga manna í mellom.	Tryggva-kaup shall go between *bauga-men*.

In the next clause it is explained that this 'peace-price' (*sættar-kaup*) is paid when the kinsmen come together to make peace, and that three marks are also paid as *skógar-kaup*—'forest price,' *i.e.* payment to release the slayer from being a *skógar-maðr*, or outlaw living in the forest.

The slayer pays a *baug* to the son of the dead, and two *truce-prices*, one to the brother and the other to the '*brœðrung* of the dead. And the slayer's brother pays a *baug* to the brother of the slain and again two truce-prices, one to the son of the slain and the other to the *brœðrung* of the slain. And the *brœðrung* of the slayer pays a *baug* to the *brœðrung* of the slain and again two 'truce-prices,' one to the son and the other to the brother of the slain. All this is for peace-buying (*sættar-kaup*) when the kinsmen are met together to make peace.

Then, in clause 245, the women's gifts are described. The slayer, his mother, his daughter, and his wife each give a gift of $1\frac{1}{5}$ ore to the wife, mother, and daughter of the slain—making twelve gifts. The sister of the slayer gives a half gift to the sister, wife, daughter, and mother of the slain (two gifts), and the slayer, his mother, wife, and daughter, each give a half gift to the sister of the slain, making the number of women's gifts sixteen in all.

The amounts thus stated add up as follows:—

Baug payments	12	marks	4	ores
6 truce payments	—		$7\frac{1}{5}$	,,
Forest price	3	,,	—	
16 women's gifts	2	,,	$3\frac{1}{5}$	,,
	18	marks	$6\frac{2}{5}$	ores

The amount aimed at seems to be 18 marks (the upnám payments being 9 marks), and yet the total is stated as follows:—

Now with *baugar* and with *tryggvakaup* and *skógar-kaup* and women's gifts it is 20 marks and 2⅔ ores.

Absolute accuracy need not be expected, but there must be a reason for the difference between eighteen and twenty marks—between the detailed payments and the total—and it is difficult to suggest any other than the one already mentioned.

The total amount of the bauga payments seems to be the same in this as in the other statement, but a new element is introduced with an obvious and interesting object.

The bauga-men, as before, consist of three groups. The slayer pays the *baug* to the son of the slain and appeases the other two groups by payment to each of them of a truce-price, so that to all the three bauga groups of the relations of the slain he has acknowledged his wrong and desire to make composition. And so in each case the representative of the other two groups of slayer's relations pay the *baug* to the corresponding group of the relatives of the slain and a truce-price to the other two, so that no relation of the slain could after this point to any individual as not having joined in the payment to himself or his group.

The women most deeply concerned on both sides are also present at the gathering. And each of those connected with the slayer is prepared with her gift of 1⅓ ore for the corresponding relative of the person slain.

Women's gifts were included in the bauga payments in the other statement also.

The clauses relating to the bauga payments are followed by three others, headed 'On saker,' and the further recipients of wergeld, as before, seem to be divided into *upnáms* and *sakaukar*, but in this case there is a strange mixture of the two. The mother's brother and the sister's son are excluded from the upnáms to make way for the half-brother by the same mother of the thrallborn son.

Clause 246, 'On saker,' gives twelve ores to each of the following, who in clause 250 are called *upnám* men.

Father's brother	12 ores
Brother's son	12 "
Brother by the same mother	12 "
Thrallborn son	12 "
Daughter's son	12 "
Mother's father	12 "
	72 ores = 9 marks.

So that the bauga and upnám payments — two thirds and one third—added together once more make a normal wergeld of twenty-seven marks, that is, thirty of the Merovingian standard.

Then clause 247, 'Further on saker,' gives to—

Mother's brother	9 ores
Sister's son	9 "
Thrallborn brother	9 "
Father's sister's son	6 "

The whole wergeld 2 marks of *nova moneta* or 30 Roman marks.

And in clause 248 'further on saker,' a thrallborn father's brother and a thrallborn daughter's son by a kinborn father, take each a mark.

The traditional wergeld seems, therefore, once more to be 27 marks of Charlemagne or 30 Merovingian marks, and the additional payments appear to be *sakaukar*. But the upnám group in this case includes the brother by the same mother and the thrallborn son, leaving outside as sakaukar the mother's brother and the sister's son and the father's sister's son along with the thrallborn brother.

Payments to outsiders additional to secure safety, and varied locally.

It is not within the scope of this inquiry to attempt either to explain, or to explain away as of no moment, the variations in the persons included under the various schemes in the groups of bauga and nefgildi or upnám men. Even such a question as that of the exclusion from the upnám group of the mother's brother and the sister's son, to make way for the illegitimate half-brother and thrallborn son, is not necessarily to be disposed of as a later alteration in favour of those of illegitimate birth. For the Cymric precedent might well lead us to an opposite conclusion, inasmuch as in the laws of Howell, in spite of strong ecclesiastical opposition, the ancient pagan custom of admitting illegitimate sons to share in the father's inheritance was defended and retained as too fully established to be given up.[1] Looked at from the point of view of the feud, they were naturally more on the spot and therefore of much more moment than the mother's brother or the sister's son.

Professor Vinogradoff[2] has suggested that the evidence of Norse and Icelandic wergelds seems to point to an original organised group of agnates who were bauga men and formed the kernel of the kindred

[1] The following is from the *Venedotian Code*, i. p. 179. 'The ecclesiastical law says that no son is to have the patrimony but the eldest born to the father by the married wife: the law of Howell, however, adjudges it to the youngest son as well as to the oldest (*i.e.* all the sons), and decides that sin of the father or his illegal act is not to be brought against a son as to his patrimony.' Bastards were not excluded till the Statute of Rothllan.

[2] 'Geschlecht und Verwandtschaft im alt-norwegischen Rechte,' in the *Zeitschrift für Social- und Wirthschaftsgeschichte*, vol. vii. (Weimar). To this essay I am much indebted.

liable for wergeld as contrasted with after additions of relations on both paternal and maternal sides and others more or less nearly concerned. The Cymric precedent would lead us to expect to find thrallborn sons as well as legitimate sons among the bauga men without any special mention as such. Under Christian influences they may have been excluded from this group to find a place ultimately, sometimes with special mention, in the upnám group.

It may or may not have been so, according to the stage of moral growth arrived at in the particular case of this tribe or that, at the particular period in question. Hence, although under Norse custom the amount of the normal wergeld of the hauld may have been constant, the way in which it was divided and the group responsible for its payment may well have varied from time to time and in different districts.

It has already been noticed that even under the later methods of awarding as wergeld an even number of gold marks, both the Gulathing and the Frostathing laws, in the case of the award of 6 marks of gold, draw a line, the one at 18 and 27 marks and the other at 20 and 30 marks, as though these amounts had a strong traditional sanction. Even in the case of the lower awards the scheme of division being the same with proportionately lessened figures, this portion of the wergeld was always divided into two thirds of bauga payments and one third of nefgildi or upnám payments. This seems to be strong evidence that, although the persons forming the groups may have differed, the two groups formed originally an inner and an outer kernel of the wergeld proper, the additions to which may fairly be regarded as sakaukar.

The repetition of evidence in both laws that the bauga payment of two thirds was followed by another third of nefgildi or upnám payments, when connected with the further fact that the two together made an amount which was, at the value of the cow stated in the laws, equated with 96 or 100 cows, seems to confirm the hypothesis that in this amount we have the normal wergeld of the hauld. To Professor Vinogradoff's suggestion that the bauga payments may have formed an original inner kernel of the wergeld we may therefore perhaps add that the nefgildi and upnám payments may have formed an outer shell of the kernel, and that both may have been included in the original normal wergeld of 96 or 100 cows.

Wergelds of the several grades of social rank.

Finally, if this may fairly be taken to be the wergeld of the hauld, then, recurring to the repeated statement in the Gulathing law that the wergeld of the hauld being told, the wergelds of others 'varied according to the rett,' the wergelds of the several classes in Norse social rank may, it would seem, with fair probability be stated as follows :—

—	Rett in silver ores	Wergeld in silver ores	Wergeld in cows
Leysing before freedom ale . .	4	40	
„ after „ „ . .	6	60	24 or 25
Leysing's son	8	80	32
Bónde	12	120	48 or 50
A'r-borinn or Ættborinn-man .	16	160	64
Hauld or Odal-born . . .	24	240	96 or 100

The significance of these gradations in the retts and wergelds of Norse tribal society will become apparent in our next section.

III. THE GRADATIONS OF SOCIAL RANK DISCLOSED BY THE WERGELDS ETC.

We are now able to devote attention to the interesting question of the gradations in social rank under Norse tribal custom. And we are fortunate to have the guidance of Dr. Konrad von Maurer's valuable paper written in 1878 and entitled 'Die Freigelassenen nach altnorwegischem Rechte.'

Grades of social rank in the churchyard.

Although tribal custom, viewed as we view it after the acceptance of Christianity, may not be altogether what it was originally in its actual working, yet still it is worth while to seek for the principles underlying the separating lines between social conditions as revealed in the laws. So far as they can be discovered, they are sure to be instructive, for they cannot have been the result of the sudden change in religion. Their roots at any rate go far back into tribal custom, however much, as in other cases, the Church may have adopted and modified what it could not eradicate.

The hard lines of distinction between social classes were kept up even in the churchyard.

Kirkiu garðe er skipt í fiórðonga til griæftar. Skall grafua lænda menn austan at kirkiu oc í landsuðr undir vxa [*v.r.* upsa] dropa, ef þæir æigu lut í kirkiu giærð. En ef þæir æigu æigi lut í kirkiu giærð, þá skullu þæir	The churchyard is divided into four quarters for burial. Lendmen shall be buried to the east and south-east of the church, under the eaves-drop. if they have taken part in the building of the church. But if they have not done that,

liggia í bónda legho, þá skall grafua hauldzmen oc þæira börn.

they shall lie in the burial place of a *bónde*. Next to them shall be buried *haulds* and their children.

En nest kirkiu garðe, þá skall grafua hión manz, oc þá menn er rekner ero at siofuar strandu oc hafua hárskurði norœna. En ef maðr læggær man í frials-giæfua lego, sæckr vj aurum. En ef maðr græfuer frials-giæfua í lœysinga lego, sæckr xij aurum. Græfuer lœysingia í hauldmanz lego, sæckr iij mörkum.

And next to the churchyard wall shall be buried the servants (thralls) of a man, and those who are cast upon the sea shore and whose hair is cut in the Norwegian manner. If a man buries a thrall in the burying-place of a frialsgiaf, he is liable to pay 6 aurar. If a man buries a frialsgiaf in the burial-place of a leysing, he is liable to pay 12 aurar. If he buries a leysing in the burial-place of a hauld, he is liable to pay three marks. (Borgarthing law 13.)

Referring to the gradations of *rett*, it will be seen that there are apparently two classes of leysings, whose social condition was next above the thrall at the bottom of the ladder.

The two classes of leysings or freedmen before and after making 'freedom ale.'

This was first made clear by Konrad von Maurer. The thrall who by purchase or by gift had been made a 'freedman' (frials-giafi) had only taken the first step towards even that limited amount of freedom which belonged to the leysing. Another step had to be made good before he became a full leysing. And the step was accomplished by the ceremony of 'making his freedom ale.'

The leysing before 'making his freedom ale' was still so far the property of his master that his children did not inherit his goods. They belonged to his master.

Nú ero brœðr tveir fœdder upp ánauðgir at eins mannz, oc

If two brothers are brought up as thralls at one man's house, and ero þeir bæðe brœðr oc fostbrœðr, oc leysasc þeir undan drótne sínum, oc firrasc eigi fóstr, eigu saman verc oc orco, þá kemr hvartveggia þeirra til annars arfs. Börn þeirra koma eigi til, nema þeir geri frælsis öl sitt.

are both brothers and foster brothers, and they are freed by their master and continue in fosterage, and have their work and employment together, then either of them inherits from the other. *Their children do not inherit from them unless they make their freedom ale.* (Gulathing, 65.)

This passage shows that the link of blood-relationship between two brothers and foster brothers, by reason of their being fostered together, in the case of thralls was recognised before that between parent and child. It was the fosterage in this case which had forged the link. Blood-relationship in thraldom counted for nothing.

The 'making a freedom ale,' first step to freedom.

The ceremony of 'making a freedom ale' is thus described, in the two laws.

Nú vill leysingi ráða kaupum sínum oc kvánföngum, þá scal hann gera frælsis öl sitt, þriggja sálda öl hit minzta, oc bióða skapdrótne hans til með váttom, oc bióða eigi sökunautum hans til, ok sissa hánom í öndvege, oc leggia .vi. aura í skáler hinn fysta eftan, oc bióða hánom leysings aura. Nu ef hann tecr við, þá er vel. En ef hann gefr upp, þá er sem golldet sé.

(Gulathing law 62.) If a leysing wishes to have control of his bargains and his marriage, he shall make his freedom ale out of at least 3 sievefuls of malt and invite his master to it, in the hearing of witnesses, and not invite his master's foes, and seat him in the high seat, and lay 6 aurar in the scales the first evening [of the banquet], and offer him the 'leysing's fee.' If he takes it, that is well. If he remits the sum, it is as if it had been paid.

Ef þræll kemr á iörð eða býr, þá scal hann gera frelsis öl sitt, hverr maðr níu mæla öl, oc scera á veðr. Ætborinn maðr scal höfuð afscera, en scapdróttinn hans scal taca hálslausn af hálse honum. Nú vill scapdróttinn hans leyfa honum at gera frelsis öl

(Frostathing law IX. 12.) If a thrall takes up land or sets up house, he shall make his freedom ale, every man of 9 mælar [= $1\frac{1}{2}$ sievefuls of malt], and kill a wether. A freeborn man shall cut off its head, and his master shall take the 'neck-release' off sitt, þá scal hann beiða hann með vátta .ii. at hann megi gera frelsis öl sitt, oc bióða honum með .v. (fimta) mann til öldrs þess er hann gerir frelsis öl sitt [. . . .] þá scal hann þó gera, oc láta öndvegi hans oc cono hans kyrt liggia.

his neck. If his master will allow him to make his freedom ale, he shall ask his leave to make it, in the hearing of two witnesses, and invite him and four with him to his freedom ale. [If they do not come] yet he shall make the ale and let the high seat for his master and his master's wife stand empty.

A master might dispense with this formality. He might take his thrall to church, or 'seat him on the kist,' and if then he proceeded formally to 'free him from all debts and dues' the leysing need not 'make his freedom ale.' (G. 61.)

Social status of the leysing.

Now let us see what change in social position and rights the ceremony of 'making freedom ale' or its substitute produced.

The leysing was still unfree in the sense that he could not leave his master. The following is from the Gulathing law (67).

Nú ferr leysingi ór fylki firi útan ráð dróttins síns, oc aflar sér þar fiár æða kaupa. þá scal scapdróttenn fara efter með vátta. Ef hann vill aftr fara, þá er vel. En ef hann vill eigi aptr fara, þá leiði hann vitni á hönd hánom at hann er leysingi hanns, oc fœri hann aptr hvárt sem hann vill lausan æða bundinn, oc setia hann í sess hinn sama, þar sem hann var fyrr.

Now a leysing leaves the district without the advice [or will] of his master, and earns property or concludes bargains; then his master shall go after him with witnesses. If he is willing to come back, that is well. If he is not willing, he [the master] shall call witnesses that he is his leysing, and bring him back, fettered or unfettered, as he likes, and set him in the same seat that he had formerly.

But, on the other side, the master might not sell even a thrall 'out of the land' (F. XI. 20); so that probably he could not turn his leysing adrift at his pleasure.

The leysing remained under *thyrmsl* towards his master, or obligations involving personal loyalty and duty, and upon any breach of these, he could be put back into thraldom.

En ef hann gerer einnhvern lut þeirra, þa scal hann fara aftr í sess hinn sama er hann var fyrr, oc leysasc þeðan verðaurum. Fé sínu hever hann oc firigort.	Should he make himself guilty of any of these things, he shall go back to the seat in which he sat formerly, and buy himself free out of it with money to his value. And his property is forfeited. (G. 66.)

The leysing must now keep his children.

The reason assigned in a clause above quoted for the desire to 'make freedom ale' was that the leysing might 'have control of his bargains and his marriage.' He gained, therefore, both as regards property and also in family rights.

In Gulathing law (63) is described what happened on his marriage. If he marries a kin-born (*ætt-borin*) woman, and they afterwards separate, all the children go with her. He, not being kin-born, has no kindred. She being kin-born, her kindred have rights over her and obligations as to her children.

En ef hon verðr fyrr dauð, þá scolo börn öll hverva til faður síns aftr, oc eta fé hans meðan þat er til; en þá er þat er allt etet, þá scolu börn öll aftr hverva í hit betra kyn, en hann undir scapdrótten sínn.	If she die first, all the children shall go back to their father, and eat his property so long as it lasts, and after it is all eaten up, all the children shall go back to the better kin, *and he back to his master.*

If one leysing marries another, and both father and mother have made their freedom ale, the children of the marriage inherit from both. This is the beginning of the rights to inherit. But it is accompanied by the obligation to keep the children, who are no longer thralls of the master but leysings like their parents.

What happens, then, if the parents fall into poverty and cannot keep their children? Is the master to keep them or are they to starve?

En ef þau verða at þrotom, þá ero þat grafgangsmenn. Scal grava gröf í kirkiugarðe, oc setia þau þar í, oc láta þar deyia. Take skapdróttenn þat ór er lengst livir, oc fœðe þat síðan.

(63) If they come to extreme want, they are *grafgangsmenn*. A grave shall be dug in the churchyard, and they shall be put into it and left to die there. The master shall take out the one who lives the longest, and feed that one thereafter.[1]

But it is not all leysing families which come to this gruesome pass. It may be presumed that the leysing who had 'made his freedom ale' and married and could make his own bargains and keep what property he and his wife could accumulate was mostly prosperous.

Children could inherit from him, but no other kin.

In clause 106 the rules as to 'leysing inheritance' are described. If the leysing who 'made his freedom ale' afterwards had children they could inherit. But he had no other kin who could inherit: so if he died childless the master took the property. As generation after generation passed and a wider kindred was formed, any one of his (the leysing's) kin took in preference to the master and his descendants. But the rights or chances of inheritance on the side of the master's family did not cease for nine generations from the first leysing who had 'made his freedom ale.' So that if a leysing even of the eighth

[1] Some authorities infer from this that the *parents* alone were put in the grave. K. von Maurer thinks *only the children*, and apologises for it as 'nur eine aus grauer Vorzeit überlieferte Antiquität.'

generation died without kin the inheritance in this extreme case went to the descendants of the master of the first leysing 'to the ninth knee' rather than pass by failure of kin to the king.

Leysings erfð . . . scal taca til niunda knés, fyrr en undir konong gange. Þegar leysings sun tecr efter faður sínn, þá take hverr efter annan. Nú verðr þar aldauða arfr í leysings kyni, oc er engi sá maðr er þar er í erfða tale við hann er andaðr er ór leysings kyninu, þá scal hinn er ór skapdróttens kvísl er, taca til níunda knés fyrr en undir konong gange, þó at sá sé hinn átte er andaðr er frá leysingjanom.

(G. c. 106.) A leysing's inheritance shall be taken to the ninth knee before it falls to the king. When a leysing's son takes after his father, then let one take after the other. If in a leysing's kin there comes to be an 'all-dead' inheritance, and no one has inheritance-right after the deceased man of the leysing's kin, then one of his master's kin shall take to the ninth knee before it falls to the king, even though the deceased man be the eighth from the leysing.

Further steps into freedom at stages of three generations.

Thus we seem to see the family of the leysing who had 'made his freedom ale' gradually growing up into a kindred in successive stages until in the ninth generation a kindred of leysings had been fully formed and might be very numerous.

In the corresponding clause in the Frostathing law (IX. 11) further details are mentioned. If not previously purchased by agreement with the master, the '*thyrmsl*' came to an end after four generations: that is, the fifth generation was free from them. They lasted, therefore, over the first four generations from the original leysing to his great-grandchildren. For these four generations the leysing and his descendants were the leysings of the master and his descendants.

Then the clause goes on to show that the first leysing having 'made his freedom ale' shall take inheritance only of his son and daughter, and of his own freedman. The sons of this leysing take inheritance from six persons, viz. father, mother, sons, daughters, brothers, sisters, and, seventhly, from any freedman of their own.

At the ninth generation the lordship over them ceases.

Svá scal sunr leysingia taca oc sunarsunr oc þess sunr . . . oc svá dóttir oc systir sem sunr oc bróðir, ef þeir ero eigi til. Oc svá scal hvárt þeirra hyggia fyrir öðru.	So shall the son of a leysing take, and his son's son [grandson] and *his* son [great-grandson] . . . and daughter and sister like son and brother, if there are none of these. Each *of these shall provide for the other*.

Failing these leysing claimants, the inheritance rights revert to the master to the ninth knee, and, it is added, '*also providing for these if needed*.'

Analogy of the Cymric gwely.

There is here something very much like the Cymric gwely or family of descendants of a great-grandfather with rights of maintenance under the rules of '*tir gwelyauc*' and mutual liability. Until a kindred has been formed the master's obligation to provide for the leysing remains, and it does not cease altogether until the kindred is complete. In the meantime as the kindred is formed its members are mutually liable for each other's maintenance. In this respect within the group of descendants of a great-grandfather there is solidarity for maintenance as well as wergeld.

We are dealing evidently here with a family of leysings growing into a kindred, as under Cymric custom the family of the Aillt and Alltud grew into a kindred. During all these four generations the family were leysings with a *rett* of six ores. But the fifth generation seems to rise into a second grade of social rank and to attain the rank of '*leysings*'

The lordship over them ceases when a full kindred is formed.

sons' with a *rett* of eight ores. And further in another four generations, those of the ninth generation again rise in social rank and seem to become *árborinn* or *ættborinn* men, i.e. *men born in a kindred*, with a *rett* of sixteen ores. They can now boast of a full leysing kindred. Their father, grandfather, and great-grandfather were born in a kindred, and they have now full rights of inheritance. The master and his descendants have no further hold on them or obligation for their maintenance. Any lapsed inheritance now goes direct to the king.

The *árborinn* or *ættborinn* man, therefore, seems at last, at the moment when a full kindred of his own has risen up to swear for him and protect him by feud or wergeld, to have become clear from any claims on the master's side. And accordingly if any claim be set up he has to prove his freedom by witnesses 'that he can count four of his forefathers as *árborinn* men and himself the fifth.' That is, he shows that his great-grandfather was a man with an *ætt* or kindred. If he can prove this he is free from any claim in regard to his leysing descent.

En ef sá callaz árborinn er fyrir söc verðr, þá teli hann fióra langfeðr sína til árborinna manna, en siálfr hann hinn fimta, oc hafi til þess.ii. búanda vitni árborinna. En ef hann er svá liðlauss at hann fær þat eigi, oc hefir þó þessa vörn fyrir sér, þá sanni ætt sína árborna með guðscírslum. En ef hann verðr scírr með iárne eða vitnisburð, þá gialldi hinn honum fulrétti, en biscopi eiða sect. En ef hann fær sic eigi scírt, þá hefir hann fyrirgort fé sínu öllu við scapdróttin, oc liggia

(Frostathing, IX. 10.) But if the accused calls himself *árborinn* *let him reckon up four of his forefathers as árborinn men*, he being the fifth himself, and have for it the evidence of two árborinn householders. But if he is so supportless that he does not get this, and yet sets up this defence [viz. that he is árborinn], then he shall prove his kin to be árborinn by ordeal. And if he is cleared by iron or evidence, the other shall pay him full atonement, and to the bishop an oath á .iii. mercr sylfrmetnar, nema hann launi af sér. Oc svá um vánar mann.

fine. If he cannot clear himself, he has forfeited all his property to his master, and is liable to pay three marks in silver, unless he work it off. The same applies to a *vánar mann* [man of hope, *i.e.* the higher class of leysing].

So far the conclusions drawn from the laws respecting the leysing do not vary much from the views expounded by Dr. Konrad von Maurer in his 'Die Freigelassenen nach altnorwegischem Rechte,' and confirmed by so great an authority they can hardly have wandered very far from the truth.

The theory of this gradual growth of the kindred of the leysing is so nearly analogous to that of the Cymric alltud, and the Irish fuidhir, and at the same time so logical, when the tribal theory of blood-relationship is applied to it, that we cannot be dealing with the fanciful theory of legal enthusiasts which never had an actual place in practical life. Behind all this imperfect description, in the laws, of social conditions and landholding there was, no doubt, a reality, the features of which may be difficult to grasp from our modern point of view, but which become, I think, fairly intelligible when approached from a tribal point of view.

The leysings have become a family group, and the descendants of the master also.

When we consider that in the course of the successive generations, during which some kind of shadowy lordship seems to have prevailed over the family of leysings, they must generally have multiplied into considerable numbers, and that the descendants of the master of the leysing 'who made freedom ale' must during the same period also have multiplied; and further when we consider that the descendants of the leysing were in some sense, it would seem, *adscripti glebæ*, we have to recognise not merely a relation between individuals but something approaching to a relation between two classes, tribesmen and non-tribesmen, the one in some sense in a kind of servitude to the other. In other words, we have to conceive of a kindred of half-free tenants, living under the joint shadowy lordship of a kindred of fully-free men, probably in some tribal sense landowners, with complicated tribal rights among themselves.

It would seem that this semi-subject class of leysings were mostly the descendants of a class of thralls, it may be perhaps in origin some conquered race, members of which had gradually grown into leysings and were now gradually in successive stages growing into freemen.

Before we can fully understand this process we must examine the other side of the question and learn what was the position of the fully-free class by whom this more or less shadowy lordship over the leysing class was exercised. In the meantime it may be remarked that the shadowy lordship of one class or tribe over another finds parallels enough in Indian experience, and that, coming nearer home, we have only to remember the petty exactions of the cadets of French noble families upon a peasantry over whom their family, or the feudal head of it, held a quasi-manorial lordship.

IV. THE CLASSES OF FREE MEN AND THEIR RELATION TO LAND.

Following again the clue of the statements of the 'personal right' of the different classes, and commencing with the *bónde* or ordinary freeman settled upon land and presumably having in some sense, as in Wales, originally tribal rights to share in the land or its use, the next class which claims attention above the bónde is the *odalman* or odalborn man or hauld, whose wergeld of 96 or 100 cows was taken as that of the full and typical freeman.

The odalman or hauld.

Now, in the Frostathing law there is a statement as follows:—

Engum manni verðr iörð at óðali fyrr en .iij. langfeðr hafa átt, oc kemr undir hinn .iiij. samfleytt.	(XII. 4.) No man's land becomes an odal to him until *three forefathers* have owned it and it falls to the fourth in unbroken succession.

And again in the Gulathing law is the following;—

Nu scal þær iarðer telia er óðrlom scolo fylgia. Sú er ein er ave hever ava leift.	(270.) Now shall the lands be told that are odal. The first is the one which *grandfather* has left to *grandfather*.

His grandfather's grandfather had the land.

The odalborn man inherits land from his grandfather's grandfather. The son of an odalman who claims odal as odal by inheritance counts four or five forefathers who had the land before him.

In Gulathing law c. 266 is a description of the mode of settling a claim as to land. It describes the sitting of the open-air court, from which both bauggildsmen and nefgildsmen and relations by marriage of the claimant are excluded as ineligible, the calling of witnesses all to be odalborn men of the same fylki as that in which the land lies, and so on. The validity of the claim is made to rest according to this statement upon the ability to count up *five forefathers who have possessed that land, while the sixth possessed it both by ownership and by odal.*

Þeir scolo telia tıl langfeðra sinna . v . er átt hava. en sá hinn sétti er bæðe átte at eign oc at óðrle.	(266.) They [the men who claim odal] shall count five of their forefathers who have owned [the land] and the sixth having it both in ownership and odal.

The odalmen were of full kindred on the land.

If, then, at the time of the laws we look at the class of landowners who were prominent as odalmen or haulds—typical men with wergelds originally of 100 cows—they were not only men of full *kindred* whose full pedigree of freedom went back the necessary nine generations, but their grandfather's grandfather must have possessed the land. The sixth generation of owners were the first to hold land *both in ownership and odal.*

The steps in the rank of Norse aristocracy were marked, therefore, as in the case of the more dependent class, by the number of the generations of ancestors through whom they could claim their landed rights.

Nor in the case of the odalborn man any more than in the case of the leysing must we look upon the odalman or hauld merely as a detached individual landowner owning his own separate estate like a modern country squire. Such a conception would be far indeed from the truth. It must be remembered that holdings in odal were subject to rules of division. Moreover, indications appear in the laws that the division was not merely one between the heirs of a single holder, but something more like what took place between the group of kinsmen in the case of the Cymric gwely and '*tir gueliauc.*' How otherwise can this clause be read?

The odal land was held by a family and sub ject to family divisions.

Um óðals iarðer. Nú scal þær iarðer telia er óðrlom scolo fylgia. Sú er ein er ave hefir ava leift. Sú er önnur er gollden er í mannsgiölld . . . þær scolo óðrlom fylgia, oc allar þær er í óðals skipti hava komet með bræðrom oc með frændom þeim [*sic*]. Allar aðrar aurum.	(G. 270.) *Of odal lands.* Now the lands shall be told which *are odal.* One is that left by grandfather to grandfather. Another is that paid as wergeld. . . . These shall be odal and all those *which have come under odal division between brothers and their kinsmen.* All other lands shall be counted *aurar* [money].

At the time of the laws owners of odal had, it appears, certain powers of selling their odal, but even then it was not an uncontrolled right of a man to do what he would with his own. His first act must be to 'go to the "thing" in autumn and offer it to his *odal-sharers*' (*odalsnautr*, one who has odal-right to land in common with others). (G. 276.)

The odal-sharers must consent to a sale of odal land.

If a man buys without its having been thus offered, then 'the odal-sharers may break that bargain' (G. 277). Even when the sale and purchase have been made by the public ceremony of *skeyting*, i.e. by taking earth from the four corners of the hearth and from under the 'high seat,' and where field and meadow meet, and with witnesses at the 'thing' (G. 292), the *odal-sharers* of the seller have the right to redeem it within a twelvemonth (G. 278).

Take, again, the case of two brothers dividing odal, and observe how careful law and custom had been to prevent either of the odal-shares going out of the family. The odal rights between them were maintained for as many generations as must pass before the shares could be united again by a lawful marriage between a son of one family and a daughter of the other (G. 282). One is tempted to say that here again there may be something very much like the Cymric gwely and to suppose that marriage was forbidden within the gwely, *e.g.* between second cousins, and that the odal sharing continued so long as the gwely held together.

The odal-sharers have rights to keep it in the family and to prevent its passing to females.

Nú skipta brœðr tveir óðrlom sín á milli, þá scal þingat hverva í þá kvísl óðol, sem loten ero, bæði at boðom oc at ábúð, bióða því at eins í aðra kvísl ef þá sœker þrot æða aldauða arfr verðe. En eigi skiliasc óðol með þeim at helldr fyrr en hvártveggia má eiga dottor annars.	If two brothers divide their óðals between them, the óðals shall pass into the hands of the branch which receives them by lot, in respect both of right of redemption and of occupation; they shall only be offered to the other branch if this one comes to utter poverty, or the inheritance is left without a legal heir. Yet the latter does not lose its right to the óðals until each of the two can marry the other's daughter.

If the family of one of the brothers sinks into utter poverty or is left without a legal heir, the other family have the right of redemption and occupancy; and yet the poverty-stricken or heirless branch does not lose its rights to the odal altogether. There is still the chance that its rights may be restored when a son on each side can marry a daughter of the other side.

There is a further clause in the Gulathing law which provides that when land falls to a woman the men of the kindred, 'if their relationship be so close as to be *nefgildi* or *bauggildi*'—that is, as we have seen, paternal and maternal relations descendants of great-grandparents—have a right to redeem it from their kinswoman at one-fifth less than its value, 'paying one half in gold and silver and the rest in thralls and cattle.' The men then keep the odal and their kinswoman 'keeps the aurar.' Even if odal has passed 'three times under the spindle' it comes back at last to the male kinsmen (275).

Nú verðr kona baugrygr, verðr hon bæðe arva óðals oc aura, oc á engi maðr undan henne at leysa. Nú ero þær konor er óðals konur ero, oc óðrlom scolo fylgia, dótter oc systir oc faður systir oc bróðor dótter oc sunar dótter. Þær ero baugrygiar tvær, dótter oc syster. Þær scolo baugum bœta oc svá taca sem karlmenn, oc svá eigu þær boð á iörðum samt sem karlar. Nú ero þær arvar faður síns. Nú elr önnur dóttor eina, en önnur sun einn, þá scal sunr leysa undan frendkonom sínum sem lög ero til. En ef enn skiptizt um, oc elr hon sun en þeir dœtr, þá scolo þeir leysa undan þeim slícum aurum sem hann leysti undan mœðr þeirra, oc scal þá liggia iörð kyrr þar sem komin er. Þá er iörð komen þrysvar undir snúð oc undir snælldo.

If a woman is a *baugrygr* [an only daughter who in default of heirs male could receive and pay wergeld] she inherits both odal and aurar and no man requires to redeem it from her. The women who are odalwomen and take odal are daughter and sister and father's sister and brother's daughter and son's daughter. Daughter and sister are two *baugrygiar*. They shall pay and take *baugar* as males, and they may redeem land as men. Now if they are their father's heirs, and one of them gives birth to a daughter and the other to a son, the son shall redeem [the odal] from his kinswomen as the law is. But if things turn round again, and she has a son and they [masc.] have daughters, they [masc.] shall redeem it from them [*i.e.* from the daughters] for the same payment by which he redeemed it from their mother, and the land shall then remain where it is. Then the land has passed three times under the spindle.

Now when these remarkable survivals of tribal custom are found still remaining in the laws as to odal and odal-sharers and the right of kinsmen who would have to pay wergeld to redeem odal, so that it may be kept within the ring of odal-sharers, they can-

These are marks of early family ownership.

not be regarded as laws framed to meet the needs of individual landownership. They come down in the laws as survivals of family ownership under tribal custom, the principles of which are by no means wholly obsolete, even though society may have passed onwards some stages towards individual landownership of the more modern type.

The solidarity of the family shown both by odal-sharing and wergelds.

And when we consider the solidarity of kindreds, as regards the payment of wergelds on the one hand, and the corresponding solidarity in the matter of landownership on the other hand, we can hardly fail to recognise that the two are connected—that both spring from a tribal principle which lies at the root of tribal polity. The solidarity of kindreds, taken together with the liability of individuals to take their share in the payments for which their kindred is responsible, corresponds to the solidarity of odal landholding, taken together with the individual rights of the odal-sharers. Unless every one in a kindred had his recognised tribal rights on the land, unless he were possessed of cattle and rights of grazing for their maintenance, how could he pay his quota of cattle to the hauld's wergeld of 100 cows? The two things seem to hang together as in the Cymric instance, and the one makes the other possible.

V. THE LEX SCANIA ANTIQUA.

The 'Lex Scania Antiqua' might perhaps be selected as fairly typical of Danish [1] ancient custom,

[1] Skåne, being only divided from the island of Zealand by the Sound, during the Viking period belonged to Denmark. It afterwards became a Swedish province, being finally ceded by Denmark in 1658.

as the Gulathing has been taken as typical of Norse custom. But apart from this it contains some chapters which seem to throw further light on odal and family holding, and so can hardly be overlooked in this inquiry.

The Latin and old Danish versions of Scanian law.

There are two versions of the Scanian Law, one in Latin and the other in old Danish. They differ considerably and are certainly not translations one of the other, though an older text may have been the foundation of them both.

They both refer to recently made modifications of local custom which fix their date to the early years of the thirteenth century.

The author of the Latin text was the Archbishop of Lund (A.D. 1206–1215), and from the use made by him of legal terms borrowed more or less from Roman law it may be gathered that Scanian custom required for him more explanation than the Danish writer deemed it necessary to give.[1]

The rules with regard to wergelds cannot be quoted as representing unmodified ancient custom. They avowedly are the result of modifications made to remedy evils which had arisen partly, no doubt, from the gradual loosening of the ties of kindred.

In the same way the clauses as to property represent the results of long-continued conflict between ancient rules of family holding and gradual

[1] The various views upon the relation of the two versions to each other are very usefully discussed in the introduction to M. Beauchet's *Loi de Vestrogothie* (Paris, 1894), pp. 67–75. The Latin version was published in 1846 at Copenhagen as Vol. I. of the *Samling af Danske Love* and both Latin and Danish versions in Dr. Schlyter's *Corpus Juris Sue-Gotorum antiqui*, Lund, 1859.

innovations in the direction of individual ownership. In this they resemble the Lex Salica. Still if family holdings more or less on the lines of the Cymric gwely, or the Salic alod, had once been the prevalent form of occupation, even new rules making alterations could hardly fail to reveal traces of older custom. The special value to this inquiry of the 'Lex Scania antiqua' is that it does so.

Disguised as some of these traces may be in the Latin text, under Roman phraseology, with the Danish version at hand it ought not to be difficult to recognise the meaning of the facts disclosed.

When there was arrangement on marriage widow took half of their joint property if no children.

The first chapter relates to the rights of a wife surviving her husband when there are no children of the marriage.

Omnia que in hereditate sunt mobilia, vel se moventia,[1] vel immobilia, precio tempore matrimonii comparata, equis sunt partibus dividenda, medietate heredes defuncti proximos cum prediis que propria ipsius fuerant et uxorem altera cum suis prediis contingente. . . .	All things in the *hereditas* which are moveable or cattle or immoveable, brought in by value fixed at the time of the marriage, are to be divided in equal parts, one part appertaining to the next heirs of the deceased [husband] with the lands which were his own, and the other part to the wife together with her lands.

This clause may very possibly represent an extension of the rights of a childless widow beyond what tribal custom may have originally given her. But certainly the fact that under Scanian law the childless widow was entitled to half of what by compact at the time of the marriage had become the joint property of husband and wife, while the other half went to the husband's next heirs, is good evidence

[1] See Du Cange, *s. v.* 'Moventes' = *pecudes.*

that marriage was by no means a surrender of the wife and her property once for all into the power of the husband and his family. And evidence of the accord of Scandinavian with other tribal custom on this point is not without value.

It may be observed, however, that in the case mentioned there had been something like a compact or valuation of the property brought under the marriage arrangement at the time of the marriage. The result might therefore have been different if no special compact had been made. The inference might well be that the childless widow in that case would not have been allowed to take her half share with her away from her husband's kindred.

Family holding vested in the grand-father as *pater-familias.*

Chapter III. refers again to a wife's property and adds important information. It brings before us a family group with something like a family holding. And it becomes intelligible only, I think, when approached from this point of view.

Into this family group a wife has been brought apparently without the special 'definition' or arrangement. There are also children of the marriage. And the question asked in the heading of the Latin text is, what shares the grandchildren take on their father's death, not in their parent's property, but in the property of the grandfather.

The grandfather is the head of the family group. In the Latin version he is elsewhere styled the *pater-familias* and in this clause his sons are *filiifamilias.*

In the Danish version the family group is simply that of an ordinary *bonde* and the family character of the holding is taken for granted as not needing special mention or explanation.

The chapter is as follows (divided into sections for convenience in comparison of the Latin and Danish texts):—

De bonis avitis que portio contingat nepotes post obitum filiifamilias.

(1) Filiifamilias[1] in sacris paternis cum uxore constituti, si sine diffinicione certe quantitatis bonis patris addiderit bona, que ipse habuit, cum uxore, quotcumque fuerint filii de communi substantia, eciam prediorum post contractas nuptias comparatorum, cum avo et aliis consortibus post obitum patris viriles et equales accipient porciones, (2) per priorem gradum ab aliis prediis excludendi. (3) Si vero, in mansione patris, bona, que habuit cum uxore, fuerunt diffinita, illa sola, si vivente avo pater obierit, filii, quotcumque fuerint, obtinebunt.

Of the grandfather's property what portion goes to the grandchildren on the death of a *filius-familias.*

(1) If a *filiusfamilias* established with his wife in the paternal rites shall, without definition of the exact quantity, have added to property of his father property which he himself had with his wife; then, however many sons there may be, they shall, after the death of their father, receive *equal shares per capita with the grandfather and other co-sharers* in the common substance even of lands acquired after the marriage was contracted, (2) they having to be excluded from other lands by the prior grade. (3) But if in the *mansio* of his father the property which he had with his wife, had been defined, *that alone*, if the grandfather was alive when the father died, shall go to the sons, however many they may be.

The Danish text (I. 5) is as follows:—

Vm bondæ sun föroer kono sina j bo moeth faþoer sinum.

(1) Far bondæ sön konu oc förær hanæ j bo mæth faþur sinum, oc aflær barn wiþær hana oc læghs æy fælegh theræ i mællin, um tha dör bondans sön,

If a bonde's son brings his wife into the house with his father.

(1) If a bonde's son gets a wife and brings her into the house with his father and begets a child with her and no partnership is made between them,[2] if the

[1] 'Filius-familias' in another MS.

[2] As to the *fælagh* or partnership between husband and wife,

tha taki all hans börn fullan lot æftir theræ faþær æm wæl j köpæ iorth sum j bolfæ. (2) Æn af hans fæthrinis iortho fa the æy wattæ mer æn han will giuæ them. (3) læghs fælagh, tha fa the æy mer æn han atte j bo.

bonde's son dies, then let all his children take a full lot after their father as well in land purchased as in moveables. (2) But of his [the bonde's] father's lands they get not a whit more than he will give them. (3) If partnership is made, then take they no more than he [their father] owned in the house.

This clause, in both the Latin and the Danish version, confirms the inference from the previous one, that there was a difference of destination as to the property of husband and wife according to whether it had or had not been 'defined' and so put in partnership as joint property of the husband and wife separately from the property of the family group represented by the grandfather.

If no arrangement on marriage wife's property merged into the family stock.

If not so defined, it became apparently under ancient custom part of the common family property and so divisible after the grandfather's death among all the *consortes* instead of going solely to the children of the marriage.

The clause pictures for us the family group as bound together by paternal rites (*sacris paternis*). The grandfather is alive and is the *paterfamilias*. A son who is a *filiusfamilias* (*i.e.*, as we shall see presently, not an emancipated son) has married and brought into the *mansio*, or family homestead of the grandfather, property which he had with his wife.

see the Gulathing Law, 53. The word *fælagh* seems to be equivalent to the '*definitio*' of the Latin text, the *definitio* of the property being made at the time of the marriage. The word seems to be allied to the English word 'fellowship.' See Skeat, *sub* 'fellow,' who refers it to Icelandic 'felag,' literally 'a laying together of property.'

This, not having been 'defined' on marriage, so as to keep it separate, has become, in the phrase of the Latin text, 'added to the property of the grandfather.' The husband has died leaving several sons, it matters not how many. The question is, what share these grandsons are to take in the property which their father had with their mother, which, for want of 'definition,' has become added to the grandfather's property, or, in other words, become part of the '*substantia communis*.'

There was no succession by representation to a deceased parent during the grandfather's lifetime.

The answer is that the parents' property does not go exclusively to their children as it would have done if it had been defined and separate property. It has become merged in the family property, and there is no sharing of this till the grandfather's death. But apparently by a compromise, due probably to recent legislation, they are allowed on their father's death, according to the Latin text, to take equal shares in his property *per capita* 'with the grandfather and other *consortes*,' or, according to the Danish text, a 'full lot' in it. We are not told who were the '*consortes*' with whom and the grandfather it was to be shared. The *consortes*, whether uncles or cousins or both, were the co-sharers in the '*communis substantia*' of the family holding.

In the final paragraph of the clause both texts give the alternative rule applying to cases, probably the most frequent, in which proper 'definition' of the wife's property had been made on the marriage. And the rule is stated to be that the property so defined and made joint or partnership property on the marriage, and that alone (*illa sola*), would go to the children of the marriage at their father's death during the life of the grandfather. According to the Latin text, they were excluded from the other family property 'by the prior grade.' As the Danish version puts it: 'not a whit of the other property would they get except what the grandfather chose to give them.'

That this is the true meaning of these clauses is confirmed by other chapters.

Permission to the grandfather to give succession to a deceased son's children.

Chapter XVI. is headed: 'How much may be conferred by a father upon the sons of a deceased son during the lives of the other sons, their uncles.' The text is as follows:—

Licet cuique post mortem filii quantum ipsi deberetur si viveret, ejus filio nepoti conferre.	It is lawful to every one after the death of a son to confer upon a grandson, the son of that son, whatever would have been due to the son had he lived.

This seems to be a special permission to the grandfather during his life to mitigate the injustice of the customary rule excluding grandchildren from succession by representation in their deceased parent's property.

If under Scanian custom the children of a dead *filiusfamilias* had succeeded by right to their father's property, this special permission would not have been needed. But it seems to be clear that no such right of succession was recognised by ancient custom.

Chapter XI. opens with the following general statement, there being in this case no question of a marriage or a wife's property.

therwis no succession given by custom.

Patre superstite defunctus filiusfamilias nullum habet, ac si nunquam fuisset genitus, successorem.	The father surviving, the dead *filiusfamilias* has no successor, as if he had never been born.

This seems to make it clear that, the grandfather being alive, the grandchildren took by right under ancient custom no share in their deceased father's property. It was simply merged in the family holding, and they must wait for their shares in it along with the other co-sharers after the grandfather's death.

The growing feeling of the injustice of this from the individual point of view was probably the reason, not only why the permission in Chapter XVI. was given, but also why, following the example of Roman law, the emancipation of sons was admitted.

Chapter XI. proceeds, after the initial sentence above quoted, to tell what happened in the case of the death of an emancipated son dying without children. But this does not concern us.

Both in Norse and Scanian custom originally on a son's death his share in the odal merged in the common stock.

It may be well before passing from the consideration of these clauses of the Scanian law to bring into notice a short isolated clause from the Gulathing law, which seems to accord with them, and so to connect the Scanian rules of family holdings with somewhat similar rules as to the Norse odal-sharing. The denial of the right of representation in both Scanian and Norse ancient custom suggests that a common principle may underlie the custom in both cases.

The clause of the Gulathing law (294) is as follows:—

Nu ero brœðr tveir oc andast annar fyrr en faðer þeirra oc livir sunr efter hinn dauða. Þa scal hann þann lut leysa oðrla at fimtungs falla, undan faður brœðr sinum, sem faður hans stoð til	Now there are two brothers and one of them dies before their father, and a son lives after his death. He shall redeem from his father's brother, at one fifth less, that part of the odal to which his

efter faður sinn. En eigi ma hann fyrr leysa en faður faðer hans er andaðr.

father was expectant heir after his father. But he may not redeem it till his father's father be dead.

In this case, as before, there are living a grandfather and a son and a grandson (son of a deceased son). The share which the deceased son as coheir with his brother might at first sight be expected to take in the grandfather's odal does not go directly to the grandson. By apparently a new law he has permission after the grandfather's death to redeem it from his uncle at one fifth less than its value.

This can only be explained upon the principle that under ancient Norse custom the sons of a deceased son would not succeed by right of representation to their deceased father's share in the division of the grandfather's property. Evidently the right to redeem it from their uncle was an innovation of later law.[1]

The new rules to amend tribal custom show what it once was.

These and other innovations may have been the result of a new sense of justice brought in with Christianity or under the influence of Roman law. The question for us is the meaning of the ancient custom. And we are brought back to the point that in so far as the family group more or less may have resembled the Cymric gwely, and is approached from this point of view, it must be regarded as the group of descendants of a common grandfather or great-grandfather, who is, in the Archbishop's phrase, the *paterfamilias.* While he is alive the landed rights are vested in him. On his death his sons take his place with divided or

---

[1] See *Untersuchungen zur Erbenfolge &c.*, Julius Ficker, ii. p.143: 'Gulathingsbuch und Frostathingsbuch kennen keinen Eintritt der Sohnessöhne in das volle Recht des Parens.'

undivided equal shares, but still as the representative members of the original gwely or family group. One of them dies, and the question is whether the surviving brothers 'of the prior grade' are to promote into this grade at once the sons of their deceased brother. Such a course might naturally be regarded as preferring these nephews to their own sons. The rights of all the members of the 'lower grade' will come in time when all of the 'prior grade' are gone and the grandsons share equally *per capita* in the family property. In the meantime the sons of deceased parents, like those whose fathers are alive, must wait. So it may have been under ancient custom. But in course of time family ties weaken and individual rights grow stronger in national feeling, as we have seen them everywhere doing. And then little by little compromises are made. The joint property of husband and wife, even if not properly 'defined,' is recognised in the Scanian law as belonging to the sons of the marriage to the very limited extent that they may have equal shares with the other *consortes* whether uncles or cousins. The sons of the deceased brother when the grandfather is dead and division among the brothers comes in question are allowed by the clause in the Gulathing law to buy back their father's share in the odal at a fifth less than its value instead of sharing in it as family property.

Thus the Scanian laws throw light on Norse odal holdings. They were family holdings.

So far the clauses in the Scanian and Gulathing laws considered together seem to throw light upon the traditional principle on which the rights of the odal-sharers of the Norse laws may have been founded.

The rules of Cymric custom may not be identical with those of Scandinavian custom, but we seem to recognise very similar tribal principles at the root of them both.

Finally other clauses in the Scanian law may be alluded to as pointing to the common liability of the family group, *i.e.* of the *paterfamilias* and others '*in communione*' with him.

The *paterfamilias* and those in communion with him.

Chapter IX. is as follows:—

Universos contingit de communi consortio quicquid vel culpa amittitur vel industria conquiritur singulorum.	As regards the common consortium whatever is lost by the fault of or acquired by the industry of individuals concerns all.

And in Chapter LXXXVII. it is enacted that if a person denies that he is in possession of a thing stolen and if afterwards upon scrutiny it is found in his house, double the value of the thing stolen is to be taken, 'not only from the portion of the *paterfamilias*, but also from the common property (*de bonis communibus*), however many there may be with the *paterfamilias in communione*.'

And the reason stated confirms the prevalence of family holdings of the kind already mentioned.

The double value is to be taken,

. . . non de sola patrisfamilias porcione sed de bonis communibus quotcunque fuerint cum patrefamilias in communione. Nam cum omnes lucrum respicerent in detentione non est mirum, si dampnum in ejusdem rei contingat omnibus restitutione.	. . . not from the portion of the paterfamilias alone, but from the common property, however many there may be with the *paterfamilias in communione*. For since all expect gain from the detention [of the thing stolen] it is not strange if all sustain loss in its restitution.

The *paterfamilias* in whose house the stolen property is found is evidently himself a member of a wider family group with common interests and liabilities. And the clause goes on to say that the accused must deny the charge with twelve co-swearers if the thing stolen be worth half a mark, or submit to the test of the ordeal of hot iron.

The resort to the ordeal if no co-swearers.

In Chapter XCIX. the ordeal of hot iron is described as having three forms: (1) that of walking on twelve red-hot plough-shares; (2) that called 'trux iarn,' applied to cases of theft: *i.e.* carrying an iron twelve feet and then throwing it into a basin; (3) that of carrying it nine paces and then casting it down: called, from the throwing, *scuzs iarn.* After the ordeal the feet or hands, as the case might be, were to be wrapped in cloth and sealed to prevent fraud, and so to remain till the sabbath, on which day it should be opened and viewed in order to ascertain the innocence or guilt of the accused.

This is one of the clauses which fixes the date of the Latin version, for the ordeal was abolished in A.D. 1215.[1]

On the whole, we may fairly conclude that the Scanian law when regarded from a tribal point of view affords additional evidence of family occupation or ownership and of the solidarity of the family group in Scandinavian society. But at the same time it shows that in Scandinavia, as elsewhere, family ownership was gradually succumbing to the new rules of individual ownership.

The same process of gradual disintegration of tribal usage is visible also in the chapters relating to wergelds.

[1] Beauchet, p. 60.

In Chapter XLIII. it is enacted that the amount to be paid for homicide is not to exceed 15 marks of silver.

The Scanian wergeld.

In Chapter XLIV. it is stated that the wergeld is to be divided into three equal parts, of which each is commonly called a *sal.* And in the next chapter, 'De Compositione,' we are told that before the time of the last constitution it always lay upon the slayer or his heir to provide the first portion only from his own property. He might then exact the second portion from his agnates, and finally the third and last from his cognates. Then it proceeds to say that, as excessive amounts were levied by violence upon the kindred, King Canute had laid down certain rules for the payments. *Inter alia*, it was enacted that of the two thirds falling on the kindred, both agnates and cognates being computed in their grades of kinship, the prior grade should always pay twice as much as the grades behind it.

How it was divided.

Further, in Chapter XLVII. it is stated that according to ancient law the distribution should be so made that each third should be divided again into subthirds, one of which should be paid to the heirs of the slain, the second to the agnates, and the third to the cognates.

It appears also from Chapter XLV. of the Latin version and s. 84 of the Danish version that special care had been taken to prevent fraud on the part of the slayer in claiming the aid of his kinsmen. He was to pay one 'sal' of his own payment before calling upon them for their portion, which was called the *œttæbot.* He then was to collect together his father's friends and compute with them what each

Later modifications.

was to pay. And when the day for payment came, not a penny was to be paid into the slayer's hands till the hour when he paid it over to the slain man's kindred. Then they were safe. The same course was to be afterwards adopted as regards the payments of maternal relations.

The Latin version (Chapter XLV.) proceeds to say that this legislation not having been successful in extirpating fraud and discouraging murder, King Waldemar II. (A.D. 1202–1241) enacted that the murderer should be liable for the whole wergeld (instead of one third). The agnates and cognates were not to be forced by him to contribute against their will. Within three days the murderer was publicly to offer satisfaction or be outlawed, in which case he would be liable to be put to death by any one. In case, however, of his flight, his relatives, agnates and cognates, were individually to offer their proper share of two thirds of the wergeld or be liable to the vengeance of the relatives of the slain, so that the latter should not be deprived of all satisfaction.

These clauses throw some light on ancient custom, but they are evident signs of the gradual loosening of the ties of kindred.

Payment for the servus and libertus.

In Chapter L. of the Latin version the payment for a *servus* is fixed at three marks, and in Chapter LII. the payment for a *libertus* is fixed at half that of the freeborn man.

It is difficult to judge how far these are to be taken as the ancient wergelds of Scanian custom, or whether they had been altered in amount by changes in the currency or recent legislation.

The wergeld of 15 marks of silver is exactly half

of that of the normal wergeld of the Norse hauld. And yet it does not seem likely that it had been reduced in amount by recent legislation when it is considered that under the Norse laws, as we have seen, the tendency seemed to be to add 'sakauka' to the ancient wergelds rather than decrease them.

It may be noted also that in a later addition [1] to the Danish version it is stated that 'a man's bot is 30 good marks and overbot 26 marks and 16 ortugs.' And also in the 'City Law' of A.D. 1300 the wergeld is stated at 30 marks with an additional 'overbot.' [2]

The Scanian wergeld perhaps that of the 'bonde.'

We seem bound to consider the wergeld of the freeborn man under the 'Lex Scania antiqua' of the previous century as 15 marks of silver.

The explanation probably may be that the *bonde* and not the hauld was taken as the typical freeborn man.

When it is further considered that in the Danish version of the Scanian law there is no mention of the hauld, and that, as we have seen, the *bonde* seems to have been regarded as the ordinary householder or *paterfamilias* of the family holding, the inference becomes probably a fair one that the *bonde* was the typical *ingenuus* or freeborn man for the purpose of the wergelds.

If this may be assumed, then the wergelds of the Scanian law accord well with the Norse wergelds. For in that case the wergeld of the bonde is 15 marks of silver in both laws. And further the wergeld of the *libertus* of the Scanian law and that of the Norse

[1] Addition F. 1.

[2] *Skanska Stadsrätten*, s. 43.

leysing after he had made his freedom's ale also correspond, being half that of the bonde.

It may further be noted that as in the Norse law so also in the Scanian law the payment for an eye or hand or foot was half a manbot, while the full manbot was payable if both eyes or hands or feet were destroyed.[1]

VI. SCANIAN AND LOMBARDIC CUSTOM COMPARED.

Lombardic custom.

Before closing this very imperfect chapter on the Scandinavian laws it may be well to compare with them clauses from the Lombardic laws relating to the family holding of land and property 'in communione.'

The laws of the tribes still remaining on the Baltic were five or six centuries later in date than the laws of the Lombardic emigrants who had left their old home and settled in the South upon Roman ground. And yet in this matter we find traces of the same ancient custom of family holdings underlying them both, notwithstanding wide separation, and what is more, of the same process of change going on notwithstanding the difference in date. Roman and Christian influences had not reached the Scanian district on the Baltic till the twelfth century, and were only then effecting changes which in the seventh century had already been accomplished in Transylvania and Italy.

Edict of Rothar. A.D. 643.

The first clause to which reference may be made is s. 153 of the 'Edict of Rothar' (A.D. 643). It is

[1] See I. s. 92 of the Danish version. The word Manbötær = *mulcta homicidii*, Schlyter, Gloss. *sub voce*.

entitled 'De gradibus cugnationum.' It is interesting as showing that seven generations were necessary to the complete kindred.

Kindred of seven generations.

Omnis parentilla usque in septimum geniculum nomeretur, ut parens parenti per gradum et parentillam heres succedat: sic tamen ut ille qui succedere vult, nominatim unicuique nomina parentum antecessorum suorum dicat.

Let every parentilla up to the seventh knee be named, so that parent to parent by grade and *parentilla* the heir may succeed; so moreover that he who wishes to succeed must tell name by name the names of his antecedent *parentes.*

Seven generations would reach back to the great-grandfather's great-grandfather, an important limit of kindred both in the Norse laws and those of the Cymri.

Another clause of the same edict (c. 167), under the heading '*De fratres, qui in casam communem remanserent,*' enacts as follows:—

Family holdings.

Si fratres post mortem patris in casa commune remanserint. et unus ex ipsis in obsequium regis aut judicis aliquas res adquesiverit, habeat sibi in antea absque portionem fratrum; et qui foras in exercitum aliquit adquisiverit, commune sit fratribus quod in casa dimiserit.

If brothers shall have remained in the common home after the father's death and one of them shall have acquired some property in service of the king or judge, let him henceforth have it for himself without the brothers sharing in it. And if one shall have acquired anything abroad in the army let that be in common to the brothers which he left behind in the home.

Et si quis in suprascriptis fratribus gairethinx fecerit, habeat in antea cui factum fuerit.

And if any one of the said brothers makes a donation, let him to whom it was made have it henceforth.

The rest of the clause refers to payments to a wife brought into the family holding by a brother. The 'meta' or portion has, in this case, been given to her on marriage out of the common property, and so the rights of the other brothers have to be considered.

Et qui ex ipsis uxorem duxerit, et de rebus communes meta data fuerit: quando alteri idem uxorem tollere contigerit, aut quando ad divisionem faciendam venerit, simili modo de cumunes rebus ei refundatur aliut tantum quantum frater in meta dedit. De paterna autem vel materna substantia quod relicum fuerit inter se æqualiter dividant.

And he who of them marries a wife and her *meta* was given from the common property, whenever it happens to another likewise to take a wife or whenever it comes to a division being made, in the same way there shall be refunded to him from the common property as much as the brother gave in meta. But whatever is left of the paternal or maternal substance let them divide among them equally.

Rules of family divisions.

Attempts to settle such questions as these, whether and how far property acquired by one brother is to form part of the common family property or be retained by the brother acquiring it, and again how the fact that the payment for a wife's 'meta' had been taken from the common family property was to affect the rights of the brothers when they came to a division, are in themselves good proof, so far as they go, of the continuance of family holdings. But the changes made by these clauses show the same tendency which we have seen in the Scanian laws towards individual ownership and the breaking up of the family holdings.

Finally, the point which in the Scanian laws was most suggestive of the original completeness of the family community of property, viz. that originally there was no succession of sons to their father's share, but division *per capita* between the uncles on the grandfather's death, appears again in the Lombardic laws and is dealt with in the seventh century practically in the same way as in Scania it was dealt with centuries later.

From the tribal point of view the solidarity of the family group was the chief interest regarded. But the point of view was changed. Under the new influences the interests of the individual came more and more into prominence.

No succession of sons by representation at first, but afterwards allowed.

It now seemed unjust to the sons that their father's property should be allowed simply to lapse into the common stock of the family till the grandfather's death and then left to be divided among the uncles. And to mitigate the injustice the right to succeed was given, in the Lombardic as in the Scanian laws, to the limited extent that upon the grandfather's death the sons took the share of their father with the uncles in the division, as if he had been living at the time.

S. 5 of the 'Leges a Grimowaldo additæ' is headed '*De successione nepotum qui post mortem patris in sinu avi remanserint*,' and is as follows :—

Si quis habuerit filios legitimos unum aut plures, et contigerit unum ex filiis vivente patre mori, et reliquerit filios legitimos, unum aut plures, et contigerit avo mori, talem partem percipiat de substantia avi sui, una cum patruis suis, qualem pater eorum inter fratribus suis percepturus erat si vivus fuisset.	If any one shall have legitimate sons, one or more, and it happens that one of the sons dies, the father being living, and he leaves legitimate sons, one or more, and it happens that the grandfather dies, let him [the son] take such part of the substance of his grandfather together with his uncles as their father if he had been alive would have taken among his brothers.
Similiter et si filias legitimas unam aut plures, aut filii naturales unum aut plures fuerint habeant legem suam, sicut in hoc edictum legitur. Quia in-	Likewise also if there were legitimate daughters, one or more, or natural sons, one or more, let them have their rights as is decreed in this edict. Because it

humanum et impium nobis videtur, ut pro tali causa exhereditentur filii ab hereditatem patris sui pro eo, quod pater eorum in sinu avi mortuos est, sed ex omnibus ut supra aequalem cum patruis suis in locum patris post mortem avi percipiant portionem.	seems to us inhuman and impious that for such a cause sons should be disinherited from the inheritance of their father because their father died in the. mund of their grandfather. But let them take an equal portion with their uncles of everything in the place of their father.

The continued existence of community in the family property is shown by the fact that, even after the concession made in this clause, during the grandfather's lifetime everything fell into the common stock and not till a family redivision was made after the grandfather's death was the new rule admitting the sons' succession along with their uncles to take effect.

To trace further the survivals of tribal custom in the Lombardic laws would lead us too far afield. The clauses already quoted are sufficient to show a remarkable similarity of custom in the case of tribes once neighbours on the Baltic notwithstanding that they had been widely separated and that there was an interval of five or six centuries between the dates of their laws.

CHAPTER IX.

TRIBAL CUSTOM IN SCOTLAND.

1. TRACES OF TRIBAL CUSTOM IN THE LAWS OF THE EARLY KINGS.

Tribal custom in the ancient laws of Scotland.

THE population of Scotland was so various in origin and language that it would be unreasonable to expect uniformity of custom. Even where Celtic custom was best able to hold its own there must naturally have been a mixture of Cymric and Gaelic elements. In districts, on the other hand, where Frisian and Northumbrian and Danish and Norse influences may have once predominated, whatever survivals there may have been of tribal custom from any of these origins may well have been afterwards submerged under legal forms and ideas from Anglo-Norman sources.

It is worth while, however, to examine what scattered survivals of tribal custom may be found in the laws of the early kings, and in the various documents collected in the first volume of the 'Ancient Laws of Scotland.'

That tribal custom as to wergeld existed and was recognised is proved by the necessity to abolish what remained of it.

Thus in the 'Leges Quatuor Burgorum' is the following clause:—

Laws of the Four Burgs.

XVII. *Of bludewyt and siklyk thingis.*

And it is to wyt at in burgh sall nocht be herde bludewyt na yit stokisdynt [styngisdynt] na merchet na heregelde na nane suilk maner of thyng.

This wholesale and disdainful disregard of feudal and tribal customs on the part of the townsmen of the four Burgs was followed somewhat later by an Ordinance of Edward I. (A.D. 1305) which again testifies to the wider survival of more directly Celtic tribal usages by forbidding their continuance.[1]

Ordene est que l'usages de Scots et de Brets desorendroit soit defendu si que mes ne soient usez.

Here we have the usages of the Brets and Scots distinctly recognised as still lingering on so late as the beginning of the fourteenth century in some parts of Scotland.

Laws of King David.

In the laws of King David[2] there are distinct traces of ancient custom as regards wergelds and the connection of the kindred with their payment and receipt. In section XIV. it is enacted:[3]—

If in any place within the peace of the King any one shall attempt to strike another, he shall pay to the King 4 cows and to the other 1 cow. If he shall really strike, but without drawing blood, 6 cows to the King and 2 cows to the other. If blood be drawn, 9 cows to the King and 3 to the person struck. If he slay the other, he shall give to the King '*XXIX ky and a colpindach*' (juvenca).[4] And he shall assyth to the kin of him slain after the assyse of the land.

---

[1] See *Ancient Laws of Scotland*, preface, p. 42.

[2] *Ibid.* i. 8.

[3] These extracts are abridged and put into modern English.

[4] Compare the colpindach with the Irish 'colpach heifer.' In the *Crith Gabhlach*, p. 300, the Irish text has the word *colpdaig* translated 'colpach heifer.' Probably the xxix should be ix^{xx}, *i.e.* 180. See *Ancient Laws of Scotland*, p. 270 (red paging), as to the next clause.

Clause XV. deals with violence done in the king's court:—

> If any one draws a knife to another in the King's Court it shall be stricken through the middle of his hand. If he draws blood, the hand shall be cut off. And if he slay any man, he shall give to the King *XX ky and a colpindach* [ix^{xx}, Ayr MS.] and he shall make peace with the kin of him slain and with the King 'after the assyse of the kynrik.'

In both these clauses the wergeld to the kin is additional to the payment to the king (of 180 cows ?) for breach of his peace.

Clause XVI. forbids the letting off of a thief for money or friendship. An earl or any one having the freedom and custom of an earl who does this is to pay to the king 100 cows, and other great men not of earl's rank 34 cows. The thief is to be 'outlawed through all the king's land.'

It is clear, then, that in the time of King David the system of wergelds payable to the kindred of the person slain was generally in force, though no amount is mentioned, and that payments were made at this date mostly in cows.

Assize of King William.

In the 'Assize of King William' under date A.D. 1180 is the following mention of the *wergeld* to be paid evidently for a thief who has been allowed to escape as above.

> XIV. *Of the law which is called weregylt.*
>
> Of every thief through all Scotland whether that he be bondman or freeman the wergeld is **XXXIV** ky and a half.

The following clause is further evidence of the continued right of vengeance on the part of the kin of a person slain.

> XV. *Of a man slain in the King's vengeance.*
>
> If any one for theft or rapin dies by law of iron or water, and of him right be done, or if he were slain with theft found with him and afterwards if his kin in vengeance of him slew him that

brought him to the law, the King shall have as fully right of such men slayers for the death of him, as of his peace fully broken, without concord or relaxation; unless it be through the counsel or the assent of his kin.

And if it happen by chance that the King grant peace to the adverse party unknown to the kin of him that was slain, nevertheless the kin of him shall take vengeance of them that slew their kin.

Laws of Alexander II.

Among the Statutes of Alexander II. under date A.D. 1220 the following fines were imposed upon persons who held land of the king and who absented themselves from the army. (Clause II., p. 68.)

From a thane, 6 cows and a gillot [*juvenca*].
From an *ochtyern*, 15 sheep or 6*s*. (half to King and half to the thane or the knight).
From a carl [*rusticus*], a cow and a sheep to be divided between the King and the thane or knight, but if with the leave of the thane or the knight, then all to the King.

This clause reveals a social division of classes into thanes, *ochtyerns*,[1] and carls or rustics; to which another clause (IV., A.D. 1230) enables us to add the nativus or '*kind-born bondman*.'

It is not needful to pursue the inquiry into the laws of the later kings of Scotland. But among the 'Fragmenta' in App. V. (p. 375) of the collection there is one which must not be overlooked, although it may be difficult to fix its date. It seems to be made up of two fragments united and is interesting as containing two very different statements of the payment 'for the life of a man.'

Put into modern English, the first part is as follows:—

All laws either are man's law or God's law. By the law of God, a head for a head, a hand for a hand, an eye for an eye, a foot for a foot.

[1] Oc-thigernd' = 'Jung herr,' Windisch, p. 757.

By the law of man *for the life of a man ix^{xx} cows*, for a foot a mark, for a hand as much, for an eye half a mark, for an ear as much, for a tooth 12 pence, for each inch of length of the wound 12 pence, for each inch of breadth of the wound 12 pence. For a stroke under the ear 16 pence, for a stroke with a staff 8 pence, and if he fall with the stroke 16 pence. For a wound in the face he shall give an image of gold [? a coin with the King's head upon it].

The other part is as follows:—

And by man's law for breaking of bones 5 ores, for a wound under the clothes 12 pence. For a wound before the sleeve 16 pence, and for each visible wound except the face 15 pence. *For a man's life* 12 *marks*; for a wound above the chest 6 solidi, and under the chest 60 pence; for a foot stroke 60 pence; for blood drawn 25 shillings, and beyond the sea 6 cows.

Amount of the wergeld doubtful.

Now what are we to make of these 'Fragmenta'? Clearly the two fragments must be taken separately, for in the first the payment 'for the life of a man' is 180 cows and in the second the payment 'for a man's life' is twelve marks.

Mr. Robertson seems to have concluded that the payment of 180 cows was the wergeld according to the Assize of Scotland, or, as he puts it, 'the manbote for homicide throughout Scotia.'[1] But he arrived at this conclusion apparently by connecting this fragment with the clause already quoted in the Assize of King David which states that a person killing another in any place within the king's peace 'shall pay to the king 180 cows and a colpindach.' He concluded that the payment was 180 cows from the reading 'ix^{xx} cows,' as it is found in the Ayr manuscript of one of the clauses, as already stated. But the clause itself shows that this payment to the king was

[1] *Scotland under her early Kings*, i. p. 258 *n.*, and ii. p. 307

not the wergeld, because after making this payment the slayer had still to 'assyth to the kin of him slain after the assyse of the land.'

Nor does it seem any more likely that the payment of twelve marks mentioned in the second fragment was the wergeld of Scottish custom. From its amount it seems much more likely to correspond with the payment already alluded to as the 'wergeld' of the thief allowed to escape, which, however, might possibly represent that of persons of lowest rank.

The evidence of these undated fragments leaves us in the dark as to what the wergeld of the ancient Assize of Scotland may have been. Confused and mixed statements as to the wergelds are not surprising when the mixture of races is taken into account, and, after all, the phrase 'after the assize of the land' or 'after the assize of the Kynrik' may refer only to those portions of the kingdom to which the laws of King David specially applied.

II. THE 'REGIAM MAJESTATEM.'

Further traces of tribal custom are mentioned in the treatise entitled 'Regiam majestatem'[1] apart from the remarkable addition to it, which also appears again as a separate document, under the heading 'Leges inter Brettos et Scotos.'

Scotch version of Glanville.

The 'Regiam Majestatem' itself may be regarded as a version of Glanville's well-known treatise on English law, applied with alterations and adaptations to Scotland by a Scotch writer conversant with local

[1] *Ancient Laws of Scotland*, i. p. 233.

custom, and probably dating between A.D. 1200 and 1230.[1]

As in the laws of King David and his successors, so in the body of this treatise, references to ancient usages occur with occasional survivals of untranslated Gaelic words which seem to refer them back to Celtic tribal custom.

Celtic survivals here and there.

Thus, in Lib. II. s. ix, in reference to the modes by which *nativi* might obtain freedom, a specially Scotch addition is made, to the effect that if a lord has carnal intercourse with the betrothed wife of his *servus*, and this is proved by the visinage, the *servus* is thereupon released from the servitude of his lord; and then follows the phrase 'nec aliud *enache* habebit a domino suo nisi recuperationem libertatis.' This untranslated Gaelic word *enache* has already been met with in the *enec-lann* of the Irish 'honour-price,' and we shall find it used again when we come to the customs of the Bretts and Scots.

So, in Lib. IV. c. 7, in cases of rape the woman (according to the text of Glanville) is to make it known to men in good position (*probi homines*) or to the '*prepositus* of the hundred.' In this Scotch treatise the writer inserts instead of the words '*prepositus* of the hundred' '*vicecomitatus vel le toshederach.*' The Gaelic *Toshach* or chieftain of a district is much in evidence in the marginal records of the 'Book of Deer.'[2]

---

[1] *History of English Law*, Pollock and Maitland, i. pp. 145 and 202. There is an elaborate comparison of this Scotch treatise with Glanville's in the *Ancient Laws of Scotland* commencing at p. 136 (red), which is very helpful.

[2] *Book of Deer*, preface, p. lxxxi. Toshach (toisech). The two officers in a townland were the *mormaer* and the *toisech*. *Ced* in Irish = hundred. Tosh-*ced*-erach possibly may have meant 'head of the hundred.'

Again, in IV. 12, in a passage not found in Glanville, the theft of a calf or ram or whatever can be carried off on the back is described in the local words '*berthinsak* seu *yburthananseca.*'

In the same chapter is inserted the already quoted clause from the Assize of King William as to the wergeld of a thief who has been allowed to escape.

> De unoquoque fure per totam Scociam est *wargeld* triginta vacce et una juvenca sive fuerit liber sive servus.

In IV. xxiii. a pledge is mentioned 'quod vocatur *culrach.*'

Cro and galnes of person killed paid to the *parentes.*

In IV. xxx. of the treatise it is stated that if a person on horseback rides over some one going before him so as to kill him, he must render for the dead man so killed '*cro et galnes*' as if he killed him with his own hands; and it goes on to say that if the rider treads a man to death by riding over him when *backing* his horse (as it would not then presumably be his fault) he is to pay nothing but 'the fourth foot of the horse,' which satisfaction the *parentes* of the man killed ought to accept.

The mention in this treatise of *cro and galnes* payable to *parentes* of the slain seems to imply that the customs relating to payments for homicide were generally in force throughout Scotland and not confined to any particular district. The words 'cro and galnes,' apparently meaning the wergeld, meet us again in the document relating to the customs of the Bretts and Scots.

The final clause (IV. liv.) describes the 'merchet' of women 'according to the assize of Scotland.' It begins by stating that the merchet of a woman, *quecunque mulier fuerit, sive nobilis, sive serva, sive mercenaria*, is 'una juvenca vel tres solidi' with 3 *d.* as *rectum servientis.* Surely a female slave is here intended.

Merchet of several grades of women.

This seems to be the minimum 'merchet,' for the clause proceeds :—

> And if she be the daughter of a freeman and not of the lord of the town (*dominus ville*) her merchet shall be one cow or six shillings and 'rectum servientis' 6 *d.* Likewise the merchet [of the daughter] of a thane's son or *ochethiern* two cows or twelve shillings and 'rectum servientis' 12 *d.*
>
> Likewise the merchet of the daughter of an earl (*comes*) ; and that of a queen ; twelve cows and 'rectum servientis' two solidi.

This clause regarding the 'merchet' is useful as giving a scale of values in cows and shillings.

juvenca = 3 shillings. cow = 6 shillings.

And the merchet scale :

Mulier	*nobilis* [?] / *serva* / *mercenaria*	throughout Scotland .	½ cow.
Daughter	of a *liber*		1 „
„	of a thane's son or ochethiern . .		2 cows.
„	of an earl or of a queen . . .		12 „

Value the cow six Norman shillings : at 1 : 12 = stater.

The solidus of this document can hardly be any other than the Anglo-Norman silver shilling of 12 pence of 32 wheat-grains, *i.e.* 384 w.g. The cow equalled six of these shillings or 2304 w.g. At the Anglo-Norman ratio of 1 : 12 the value of the cow would thus be 192 wheat-grains : that is, exactly the normal ox-unit of two gold solidi of Imperial standard.

This curious result is not only interesting as one more instance of the tenacity of custom in retaining the traditional gold value of the animal used as the unit of payments when made in cattle, but also useful for our present purpose as affording a valuable proof that the Scotch compiler of the 'Regiam Majestatem' in appending the important clauses relating to the customs of the Bretts and Scots which follow closely upon this merchet clause was adding to his work a quite independent document, probably of much earlier date.

Value of the cow in the next document three ores, or at 1 : 8 = stater.

In this added document while the payments are again stated in cows, the value of the cow is reckoned, not in shillings, but in *ores*, which the figures, when examined, show to be ores of 16 pence. This reckoning in ores of 16 pence suggests a Norse or Danish influence. For, although the Anglo-Norman reckoning in shillings of 12 pence ultimately conquered and became the prevalent reckoning in the Scotch statutes, there was no doubt a period when the reckoning in ores of 16 pence was in use in Danish England, probably including Northumbria.

This is shown by a law, probably of Cnut's,[1] which enacted as follows:—

Et ipsi qui portus custodiunt efficiant per overhirnessam meam ut omne pondus sit marcatum ad pondus quo pecunia mea recipitur, et eorum singulum signetur ita quod xv ore libram faciant.

Those who have charge of the towns (*portus*) shall secure that under penalties every weight shall be marked at the weight by which my money is received, and let each of them be marked so that fifteen ores shall make a pound.

The ores of this law, as we shall see, were evidently ores of 16 pence, or 512 wheat-grains (16×32), for fifteen of such ores made the Saxon and Anglo-Norman pound of 240 pence, or 7680 wheat-grains.

The fact that the ore of the document describing the customs of the Bretts and Scotts was the same

[1] See *infra*, c. xi.

ore as that in use with both Danes and English in Danish England and probably Northumbria about A.D. 1000 is an important one. For in this document the value of the cow of the Bretts and Scots is stated to be three ores, *i.e.* 1536 wheat-grains of silver, and at the Scandinavian ratio of 1 : 8 the gold value of the cow would therefore be once more 192 wheat-grains or two gold solidi of Imperial standard. That the Danish ratio was 1 : 8 as in the Scandinavian laws we shall find to be involved in the Anglo-Danish compacts making Danes and English 'equally dear,' while as late as A.D. 1192 the Abbey of Kelso compounded for payments to the Pope at the same ratio, two solidi of sterlings (24*d.* of 32 wheat-grains), or 768 wheat-grains of silver being paid for the gold solidus of 96 wheat-grains.[1]

Danish ratio of 1 : 8.

We may therefore consider that the document relating to the Bretts and Scots belongs to the period of Danish influence, and is of much earlier date than the work to which it was appended by the Scotch editor of Glanville.

Laws of the Bretts and Scots belong to time of Danish influence.

III. LEGES INTER BRETTOS ET SCOTOS.

The remarkable document printed separately in Appendix III. of the 'Ancient Laws of Scotland' under the above title is given in three languages—Latin, Norman French, and Scottish English.

Norman French version thirteenth century.

The oldest version of it is that of the 'Berne Manuscript,' now in the 'Register House' at Edinburgh, which is considered to be of the thirteenth century. It appears in this manuscript as a separate

[1] Robertson's *Historical Essays*, p. 47.

document in Norman French, and therefore it would seem that we owe this statement of ancient custom to a Norman scribe. The Latin version added to the 'Regiam Majestatem' is of later date. The earliest manuscript is of the fourteenth century.[1]

As given in the 'Regiam Majestatem' it consists of four clauses, LV to LVIII.

The clauses are headed 'Quid sit le cro quod anglice dicitur "grant before the King,"' 'De occisis in pace Regis,' 'De Kelchyn regis et aliorum dominorum Scocie,' and 'De effusione sanguinis.'

It is printed in Appendix III. of the 'Ancient Laws of Scotland' among the 'capitula vetustiora' under the heading 'Leges inter Brettos et Scotos.' The Norman French of the Berne manuscript is accompanied by the Latin from the 'Regiam Majestatem' and a Scottish-English version of unknown date.

The first clause is as follows :—

The cro and galnes.

De cro quod anglice dicitur grant befor the Kyng.	De cro le Rey descoce & des altres choses.	Her folowis lee Croo'
Statuit dominus rex quod le Cro domini regis scocie est mille vacce vel tria millia orarum aurearum scilicet tres ore pro vacca. Item le Cro filii regis vel vnius comitis scocie est septies viginti [et decem] vacce vel tres ore pro vacca.	Cro le rei descoce est · mile vaches · u · treis mil ores · e fet a sauer treis ores · a la vache. Cro a vn conte descoce · v del fiz le Rei · vii^{xx} · vaches · ⁊ x · ov · iiii^{c} · ⁊ · L · ores. ·	Þe lord þe king has statut þat þe Croo of þe king of scotland i^{m} ky or iii^{m} orarum aurearum bot iii ar for þe kow. Item þe Croo of þe kingis soune or of ane erl of scotland is vii tymes xx^{ti} ky and ten ky.
Item le Cro filii vnius comitis vel vnius thani est centum vacce.	¶ Cro a vn fiz a cunt ou a vn thayn · est · C · vaches · u · treis · C · ores.	Item þe Croo of þe sone of ane erl or of a than is j^{c} ky.

[1] See preface to the *Ancient Laws of Scotland*.

Item le Cro filii thani est sexaginta sex vacce et due partes vnius vacce.	ℂ Cro a fiz dun thayn · est · lxvi · vaches · ⁊ · ii · pars dune vache · ou · CC · ores.	Item þe Croo of þe sone of a thane is iii^{xx} ky and vi ky and twa-pert a kow.
Item le Cro nepotis vnius thani vel vnius ogthiern est quadraginta quatuor vacce et viginti unus denariorum et due partes vnius denarii. Et omnes bassiores in parentela sunt rustici.	ℂ Cro · del neuu · a vn thain · u · de vn ogettheyrn est · xliiij · vac̃c̃ · ⁊ · xxi · đ · ⁊ deu pars dun deñ. E tu li plꝰ [bas] en le parente sūt vilayns · ⁊ vnt dreit^{z} a vilayn.	Item þe Cro of þe newow of a than or of ane ogethearn is xliiii ky and xxi penijs and twapert of a peny. Item al þir þat ar lawer þan þir in kyn ar callit carlis.
Item le Cro vnius rustici est sexdecim vacce.	ℂ Cro a vn vileȳ · xvi · vac̃c̃.	Item þe cro of a carl is xvi ky.
Item le Cro cuiuslibet femine virum habentis est minor per terciam partem quam le Cro viri sui et si non habeat virum tunc le Cro ipsius est adeo magnum sicut le Cro fratris sui si quem habet.	ℂ Cro a checune fēme q̃ barō at · est de la tierz partie mayns de son barō · et si ele nat nēt de barō · dūkes est le cro ausi g^{r}nt cū vne de se freres.	Item þe Croo of euerilk woman hafand husband is less be þe thridpert þan þe cro of hyr husbande. And gif scho has nocht a husband þan þe cro of hir is alsmekil as þe cro of hir broder gif scho ony broder has.
Item le Cro et le galnys et le enach vnius cuiusque hominis sunt pares scilicet in respectu de le enach feminarum suarum.	le cro ⁊ le galnis · ⁊ le enach a checū hōme sūt peirs · ceo est a sauer le enach · pur sa fēme.	Item þe Cro and þe gallnes and þe enauch of euerilkaman ar lik þat is to say in respic of enauch of þar wiffis.

It will be most convenient to put these payments of the cro and galnes into a tabular form.

King of Scotland	1000 cows = 3000 ores
King's son and comes (earl) . .	140 cows = 420 ,,
Comes' son and thane . . .	100 cows = 300 ,,
Thane's son	$66\frac{2}{3}$ cows = 200 ,,
Thane's grandson or ogthiern . .	44 cows & 21*d.* and $\frac{2}{3}$*d.*
All lower in *parentela* or kin and rustics	16 cows

The cro and galnes seem to be substantially the same thing as the wergeld. The word 'cro' is of uncertain meaning. The 'cro' of the Brehon laws is translated 'property.' It seems also to have had the meaning of 'death.' The word 'galnes' can hardly be other than the Welsh *galanas* or wergeld. Whether the phrase 'cro and galnes' means two things or one thing, and if two things, what the distinction between them was, it is not easy to see. But evidently the two together made a single payment for each grade of rank. The payments, moreover, are expressed in cows as well as in ores and pence, and the payment of 100 cows seems to mark the *thane* as the typical and complete tribesman.

Thane's wergeld 100 cows.

The two explanatory clauses introduce a third element, the 'enach.'

> The Cro of a woman having a husband is one third less than the husband's cro, and if no husband she has the same cro as her brother.
>
> The *Cro* and the *galnys* and the *enach* of every man are alike, that is to say in respect of the *enach* of their wives [*i.e.* one third less than the husband's].

The enach, as already said, seems to be the honour-price of the Brehon law. We have seen that, according to the Scotch addition and Glanville's clause, if a slave was injured by his master, he was to be set free and his freedom was to be in the place of any other 'enach.' This accords well with the Irish enec-laun and the Welsh saraad and the Norse rett, all of which referred to insult rather than bodily injury.

The next clause relates to homicide 'in pace regis' or of other lords. We have already seen that in the laws of King David the manbote or payment to the king for breach of his peace, or for crime committed in his *grith* or precinct, was a thing distinct from the satisfaction to be made to the kin of the person slain 'according to the assize of the Kynrik.' In these early laws the payment for slaying a man in the king's peace was, according to the corrected text, 180 cows. In the following clauses 180 cows are again the payment for breach of the king's peace, but there are payments also for breach of the peace of other classes.

Payments for breach of peace of various persons.

De occisis in pace regis.		Of þhaim þat ar slayn in þe peis of þe king and oþer lordis.
Si quis homo sit occisus in pace domini regis sibi pertinent nouies viginti vacce.	ℭ Si hūme est ocys en la pes le rei · il a feit · ix^{xx} vac̃c̃.	Giff ony man be slayn in þe pes of our lord þe king til him pertenis ix tymis xx^{ti} ky.
Item si homo sit occisus in pace filii regis vel vnius comitis sibi pertinent quater viginti et decem vacce.	ℭ Si hūme seit ocis en la pes · le fiz le rei · v en la pees vn cunte · ilur · a feit · iiij^{xx} · vacc · ⁊ · x.	Item gif a man be slayn in þe pes of þe sone of þe king or of ane erl til him pertenis iiij tymis xx^{ti} ky and x ky.
Item si homo sit occisus in pace filii vnius comitis vel in pace vnius thani sibi pertinent sexaginta vacce.	ℭ Si hūme seit ocis · en la pees · al fiz dun cunt · v · de vn thain · ilur a feit · lx · vachis.	Item gif a man be slayn in þe pes of þe son of an erl or of a thayn till him pertinis iij^{xx} ky.
Item si homo sit occisus in pace filii vnius thani sibi pertinent quadraginta vacce. Item si homo sit occisus in pace nepotis vnius thani sibi pertinent viginti vacce et due partes vnius vacce.	ℭ Si vn seit occis en la pees al fiz dun thain · ili a feit · xxvi · [· *xl* ·] vac̃c̃.	Item gif a man be slayn in pes of þe sone of a thayn til him pertenis xl ky. Item gif a man be slayn in þe pece of a nevo of a thayn til him pertinis xx^{ti} ky and twapert a kow.

The payments were as under :—

If a man be killed *in pace regis*	180	cows.	*To the person in whose peace he was killed.*
In that of the King's son or comes	90	"	
" " comes' son or thane	60	"	
" " thane's son	40	"	
" " thane's grandson	$20\frac{2}{3}$	"	

They seem to be very large, but they are not impossible, seeing that in the Norse law, while the wergeld of the hauld was 27 marks of silver or 96 cows, the payment to the king for the breach of his peace (frith-bot) was 40 marks, i.e. 128 cows.[1]

The Kelchin.

The next two clauses, under the heading 'Kelchin' or 'Gelchach,' seem to refer to insult or wounding, (the Welsh *gweli*=wound). And as the word *enach* does not occur again in the laws of Bretts and Scots it seems probable that it may have been included under this heading, and that the Kelchin or Gelchach, like the Irish *enach* and the Welsh *saraad*, referred quite as much to insults to personal honour as to bodily injuries.

De Kelchyn		*Of lee Kelchyn*
Item le kelchyn domini regis est centum vacce. Item le kelchyn filii regis vel vnius comitis est sexaginta sex vacce et due partes vnius vacce.	¶ Gelchach le rei · a · C · vacc · a cont v al fiz le rei · lx[vi] vacc̃c̃ · ⁊ · ii · pars deune vacc̃.	Item þe kelchin of our lord þe king is j^{c} ky. Item þe kelchyn of a sonne of þe kingis or of an erle is iij^{xx} ky [and sex ky and twapert of a kow]
Item le kelchyn filii vnius comitis vel vnius thani est quadraginta quatuor vacce viginti vnus denarii et due partes vnius oboli. Item le kelchyn filii thani est minor per terciam partem quam patris sui et sunt viginti nouem vacce vndecim denarii et tercia pars vnius oboli. Rusticus nichil habet de kelchyn.	¶ Gelchac · de thayn · v · de fiz a cunt · est xliiij · vacc̃c̃ · & · xxi · đ · ⁊ deus pars deune mayl.	Item þe kelchin of a thane or of þe sone of ane erle is xliiij ky and xxi peniis and twapert of a half peny. Item þe kelchin of þe sonne of a thane is les be thrid part þan of his fader þat is to say þar pertenis til him xxix ky and xi peniis and þe thrid part of a half peny. And a carl has na kelchin.
Item si uxor liberi ominis sit occisa vir uus habebit le kelchyn parentes eius habebunt le cro et le galnes.	¶ Si fẽme a vn franc hũme est ocis · son barõ auera le kelchin · ⁊ ses parens auerũt le cro & le galnis.	Item gif þe wif of a fre man be slayn hyr husband sal haf þe kelchyn. And hir kyn sal haf þe cro and þe galnes.

[1] Gulathing law, s. 152.

De Kelchyn		*Of lee Kelchyn*
Item si uxor rustici sit occisa dominus ipsius terre in qua manet habebit le kelchyn et parentes eius le cro et le galnes.	ℭ Et si fēme a vileyn seit ocis · le seygnur del fe v le vilein meint auera le kelchin · ⁊ le vilein auera le turhochret a sa fēme del kelchin · ⁊ le parens [le cro] et le galnis.	Item gif þe woman of a carl be slayn þe lord in quhais lande he duellis sal haf þe kelchin and hyr kyn sal haf þe cro and þe galnes.
De effusione sanguinis		*Of blude drawyn*
Item sanguis de capite vnius comitis aut filii regis sunt nouem vacce. Item sanguis filii comitis aut vnius thani sunt sex vacce. Item de sanguine filii thani tres vacce. Item de sanguine nepotis thani due vacce et due partes vnius vacce. Item de sanguine vnius rustici vna vacca.	ℭ Le saūc de la teste a vn cūte v · del fiz al rei · est · ix · vaches · del thayn · v del fiz al vn cūte · vi · vachis · del fiz al vn thayn · iij · vac̄c̄.	þe blude of þe hede of ane erl or of a kingis son is ix ky. Item þe blud of þe sone of ane erle is vi ky or of a thayn. Item þe blude of þe sone of a thayn is iij ky. Item þe blud of þe nevo of a thayn is twa ky and twa-pert a kow. Item þe blud of a carl a kow.
De sanguine extracto subtus anhelitum est minus per terciam partem in omnibus supradictis.	ℭ Le saunc de suz le alayn · est de la terce parte meyndre.	Item blude drawyn vnder þe aand is thrid pert les of al þir gangand befor.
Et si mulier non habeat virum ius suum erit sicut ius fratris sui si quem habeat.	⁊ ensemēt de lur fēmes est saunc est del t̃ce part mayndre · mes si fēme seit sen baron · · · dūkes ad ele tel dreitur · com sun frere.	And gif a woman haf nocht a husband hyr rycht salbe as of her broder gif scho ony broder has.
Item percussio sine sanguine effuso decem denarii.		Item strikyn without blud drawyn x penijs.

Payments for blood drawn.

· · · · ℭ Et si hūme est ocis en le ost · sun seingnr · auera le kelchin · ⁊ ses parens le cro · e le galnis · ⁊ le rei · viij · vaches · flatha.

Put into a tabular form these payments are as follows:—

Kelchyn or Gelchach

King	100 cows	
Son of King or comes . .	66⅔ "	
Son of comes and thane .	44 "	and 21 *d.* and ⅔ *ob.*
Son of thane . . .	29 "	" 11 *d.* " ⅓ "
Rusticus or carl . . .	*nil*	

De effusione sanguinis or of blude drawyn.

Blood drawn from the head of a

Comes or King's son	9	cows
Comes' son or thane	6	„
Thane's son	3	„ (? 4)
Thane's grandson	$2\frac{2}{3}$	„
Rusticus	1	cow

Blood drawn *subtus anhelitum* one third less than above it.

If a woman have not a husband her right shall be as her brother, if she has one.

Striking without blood drawn 10*d.*

That we are right in supposing the kelchin to be analogous to the Welsh *saraad* seems to be confirmed by the interesting additional information appended to the clauses.

> And if the wife of a freeman is slain her husband has the Kelchyn and her kin the Cro and galnes.
>
> Item if the woman of a carl be slain, the lord of the fee where he dwells shall have the Kelchin and the vilein shall have his wife's *turhochret* of the Kelchin and her kin shall have the cro and the galnes.
>
> If a man be killed in the host, his lord shall have the Kelchin and his *parentes* the cro and the galnes and the King eight cows *flatha.*

These clauses of explanation are very important when we try to understand the laws to which they are appended as a whole.

The thane's wergeld the normal one of 100 cows.

Commencing with what seems to be the wergeld, the 'cro and galnes' of the thane, who may be taken as the typical freeman, was 100 cows. We have seen that the value of the cow was three ores of silver or, at a ratio of one to eight, 192 wheat-grains of gold. The wergeld was therefore, not only the usual round number of 100 cows, but also in gold value, like that of the Cymric codes and so many others, exactly 19,200 wheat grains or 200 gold solidi.

If we try to trace the connection of this wergeld with those of other tribes, the coincidence with the normal wergeld does not help us much.

It is the same as the Welsh galanas of the uchelwr, and the use in the laws of Cymric and Gaelic words might lead us to look upon the wergeld as a Celtic one. But the equality in the payment is in *gold* and not in the number of cows. The cro of the thane was 100 cows. The galanas of the Welsh uchelwr was 120 cows. Moreover, the cows in which the Welsh galanas was paid were equated with three scores of silver, *i.e.* three Saxon ounces of 20*d.*, while the cows in which the cro was paid were equated with three ores of 16*d.* And this seems to point to a Danish connection.

All these things taken together seem to point to a mixture and confusion of influences rather than to a single origin.

The gradations of rank and position disclosed by the amount of the cro or wergeld seem to be based upon family seniority, and to have a character of their own.

The gradations of rank in the family.

The King of course stands at the head of the list with a cro of 1000 cows. His son takes equal rank with the earl with a cro of 140 cows. The earl's son is of equal rank with the thane, and they have a cro of 100 cows. Then comes the thane's son with a cro of one third less, or $66\frac{2}{3}$ cows, and next the thane's grandson with a cro one third less again, of 44 cows and $21\frac{2}{3}$ pence. All below this in *parentela* or kin are classed with rustics or carls, with a cro of 16 cows.

Looking at the position of persons at any given moment, from the point of view of the thane, he has the earl and the king above him and the earl's son as his equal in rank. Their children and grandchildren belong still to the chieftain class, but they are juniors or cadets of the class. Even the grandchildren of the thane are *ogthierns,* or young thanes. In natural course they may presumably take their father's rank on his death, but not until that happens. And possibly only the eldest son of the earl or of the thane succeeded to the official position of chieftain of his house.

Beyond this there is not much more to be gathered concerning the gradations in social rank. Nor are we told anything about the division of the amount among the members of the kindred receiving or paying the cro as the case might be. We are told only that the cro and galnes belonged to the kin of the person slain.

Turning from the cro and galnes to the *kelchin*: what are we to make of it?

The kelchin like the Welsh saraad for insult.

The gradations resemble those of the cro to this extent, that the kelchin of each grade was one third less than that of the one above, but the kelchin was no direct fraction of the cro. The kelchin seems, as we have said, to be something like the Welsh *saraad* for insult or wounding, the Irish *enec-lann* or honour-price, and the Norse *rett* or 'personal right;' but it does not seem to correspond altogether with any one of them.

All we know is that on the homicide of a person, whoever he might be, in addition to the cro and galnes, the kelchin had to be paid. But it was a payment which, like the Cymric saraad, according to the interesting explanation given, did not go with the wergeld proper to the kindred or relations in blood. When a wife was slain, the husband, who was not a blood relation or of the kindred of the wife, took the kelchin, while the wergeld proper—cro and galnes—went to her kindred.

Each grade had a precinct and a fine for breach of it. But not the carl or rustic.

Turning to the payment which had to be made for breach of the peace or protection of the lord, it was a payment due to the king if the homicide were perpetrated 'in pace regis,' and to a person of each grade in succession, even to the thane's grandson, in case the homicide were committed within his precinct. Only the carl or rustic received no payment, as presumably he was living on the land of a lord, who would, therefore, claim it.

The position of the carl or rustic, or in Norman French the *vilein*, is interesting. If his wife was killed the lord took the kelchin. The homicide was reckoned as an insult and loss to him. The wergeld did not go to the husband but to the kindred of the wife, as in the case of those of higher grade. So that, so far as this at least, there was recognition of kindred in the rustic's position. His 'cro and galnes' was just about one sixth of that of the thane and presumably went to his kin—as his wife's cro and galnes went to her kin.

There is one other point as yet unexplained—what was the 'turhochret'?

It occurs in the clause :—

> Item if the woman of a carl be slain, the lord of the fee where he dwells shall have the kelchin *and the vilein shall have his wife's turhochret* of the kelchin and her kyn shall have the cro and the galnes.

There are so many Gaelic words in this document

that there can be little doubt that the *turhochret*[1] is one of them. It seems to have been the part of the kelchin allowed by the lord to go to the husband in respect of the insult to his wife—i.e. *her* share in the kelchin. Whatever it was, when the wife was slain, the husband retained it, while the lord took the rest of the kelchin, and the wife's kin the cro and galnes of their slain kinswoman. The information given is scanty, but it is difficult to make this passage mean anything else.

The wife belonged to her own kindred.

One thing is made remarkably clear in this document: that the wife of the free tribesman did not among the Bretts and Scots pass upon marriage under the full *potestas* of her husband. On her murder, while it was an insult to him and he therefore could claim the kelchin, the cro and the galnes passed to her kin. The wife, therefore, in a very real sense belonged still to her own kindred.

These rules of tribal custom as regards marriage need no longer surprise us after what we have found elsewhere. They closely resemble in principle Cymric usage and are, after all, what the study of Beowulf prepared us to regard as by no means confined to the Celtic tribes.

IV. RECOGNITION OF THE FOURTH AND NINTH DEGREES OF KINDRED IN SCOTLAND.

In the foregoing sections no distinct reference has been made to the recognition of the fourth and ninth

[1] See Windisch, *Wörterbuch*, sub voce '*ter-fochrice*,' also '*fo-chraic*.'

degrees of kindred. It would be misleading to pass from the Scottish evidence without allusion to the subject.

Strongly influenced as custom in Scotland must have been by both Cymric and Gaelic as well as Norse and Danish traditions, it would be strange if no trace were left in Scotland of so marked a feature of tribal policy.

The nine degrees of kindred.

It will be enough, however, to refer the reader to the interesting chapter on 'The Kin' in the second volume of Mr. Robertson's 'Scotland under her early Kings,' in which he alludes to 'the words in which the Northern St. Margaret is supposed to have formally renounced her kindred ("al my Kun I forsake to the nithe Kne"), and to the "nine degrees of kindred" within which all connected with the Earl of Fife might claim the privileges of the Clan Mac Duff.'

And after what we have seen of the way in which the Norse *leysing* rose by steps of four generations into increasing freedom as a kindred grew up around him, it may be worth while to recall attention once more to the reverse process by which the *nativus* or *villanus* under later law became attached to the land.

The fourth generation fixes the status of *nativi*.

Among the fragments of Scotch laws collected under the heading 'Quoniam attachiamenta'[1] is the clause '*De brevi de nativis*' which may be translated as follows:—

> There are different kinds of *nativi* or bondmen. For some are *nativi de avo et proavo* which is vulgarly called *de evo et trevo*, whom he [the lord] will claim to be his *nativi* naturally, by beginning to narrate their ancestors, if their names are known, to

[1] Vol. i. p. 655.

wit, of his *great-grandfather*, *grandfather*, and *father*, who are convicted by his saying that they all are his *nativi* in such and such a villa of his, and in a certain place within the said villa on servile land, and that they rendered and did to him and his ancestors servile service for many days and years, and this "nativitas," or bondage, can be proved through the parents of the convicted one, if they are alive, or *per bonam assisam*.

Likewise, there is another kind of bondage, similar to this, where some stranger shall have taken some servile land from some lord doing servile service for the same land, and if he die on the same land, and his son likewise, and afterwards *his* son shall have lived and died on the same land, then all his posterity [*i.e.* his great-grandsons] shall be at the fourth grade altogether in servile condition to his lord, and his whole posterity can be proved in the same way.

There is a third kind of *nativitas*, or bondage, where some freeman, *pro dominio habendo vel manutenencia* [*i.e.* for protection or maintenance] from some magnate, gives himself up to that lord as his *nativus* or *bondman* in his court by the front hair of his head (*per crines anteriores capitis sui*).

Whatever may have been the date and origin of these remarkable clauses, they are valuable as showing how tribal tradition became hardened in course of time into Feudal law, and how, the transition from tribal to Feudal principles having been accomplished, what is known everywhere by the name of 'serfdom,' became domiciled in Scotland.

CHAPTER X.

ANGLO-SAXON CUSTOM FROM THE NORMAN POINT OF VIEW.

I. ANGLO-SAXON CUSTOM AS APPLIED TO NORMANS.

The Kentish laws to be treated apart.

In approaching the question of Anglo-Saxon tribal custom it is needful to make a clear distinction between the laws of the Kentish kings and the other Anglo-Saxon laws.

The laws of the Kentish kings are known only in the MS.—the Textus Roffensis—compiled or collected by Ernulf, Bishop of Rochester from 1115 to 1125, and are not included in the other collections containing the laws of King Alfred and Ine.

The evidence for Kentish custom seems, therefore, to be independent of that of Wessex or Mercia or Northumbria. Further, in the so-called 'Laws of Henry I.' at the conclusion of the statement of the customs as to homicide in s. LXXVI. it is distinctly stated that the wergelds in Kent differed much from those of Wessex both as regards *villani* and *barones*.

It will therefore be necessary to examine the Kentish laws separately from the others.

On the whole, with regard to the others, it seems best to resort to the method of proceeding from the later to the earlier evidence and to begin with the

Laws of Henry I.

so-called 'Laws of Henry I.,' as a Norman though unofficial view of what Anglo-Saxon custom was or had been before the Conquest.

When a Norman was killed.

It may be well to inquire first, what in the view of the writer took place, after the Conquest, when a Norman or stranger was killed, because this at once raises the question what should happen in the unavoidable absence of kindred.

Si Francigena qui parentes non habeat in murdro perimatur, habeat precium natalis ejus qui murdrum abarnaverit: Rex de hundreto ubi invenietur xl marc̄ argenti; nisi intra vii dies reddatur malefactor justicie regis, et talis de quo possit justicia fieri. . . .	(lxxv. 6) If a Norman (*Francigena*) be murdered who has no *parentes*, let that person have the price of his birth who made known the murder. The King to have 40 marks of silver from the hundred where he was found unless within 7 days the malefactor be delivered up to the justice of the King in such a way that justice can be had of him. . . .
Ad patrem vero, non ad matrem, generacionis consideracio dirigatur: omnibus enim Francigenis et alienigenis debet esse rex pro cognacione et advocato, si penitus alium non habeat.	(7) Consideration as to birth must be directed to the father, not to the mother, for the King ought to be in the place of maternal kindred (*cognatio*) and of advocate for the Norman or stranger if he absolutely have no other.
Si ex parte patris parentes non habeat qui occiditur, et ex parte matris habeat, quantum ad eum attinet, i. tercia pars weregildi sui reddatur.	(8) If he who is killed has no *parentes* on his father's side and he has on his mother's side, let what appertains to her, viz. one-third of his wergeld, be paid.

These clauses show that when a Norman or stranger was slain, in a certain way the king was to stand in the place of the absent kindred to see that justice was done.

The maternal kindred of the slain, if such were at hand, should receive the third of the wergeld which pertained to them, and so presumably the paternal kindred, if they alone were present, should take the two thirds pertaining to them, the king taking the share of the maternal kindred. In any case the right of the *parentes* was recognised when they were present.

When the slayer was a Norman.

Next with regard to the payment of the wergeld in the case of the slayer being a Norman or a stranger:—

Si quis hujusmodi faciat homicidium, parentes ejus tantum were reddant, quantum pro ea reciperent, si occideretur.	(8) If any one commit homicide of this kind let his *parentes* pay so much wergeld as they would have received if he [the slayer] had been killed.
Si ex parte patris parentes habeat, et ex parte matris non habeat, et hominem occideret, reddant pertinentes ei quantum de ejus interfeccione reciperent, i. duas partes weregildi sui.	(9) If he [the slayer] have *parentes* on his father's side and not on his mother's and kills a man, they pay for him as much as they would have received had he been killed, i.e. two thirds of the wergeld.
Si quis autem paterna cognacione carens male pugnet ut hominem occidat, si tunc cognacionem maternam habeat, reddat ipsa terciam partem were, terciam congildones, pro tercia fugiat.	(10) If any one who has no paternal relations shall fight so wrongly as to kill a man and if he has maternal relations they shall pay one-third of the wer, the *congildones* one-third, and for the other third let him flee.
Si nec maternam cognacionem habeat, reddant congildones dimidiam weram, pro dimidia fugiat vel componat.	If he has no maternal relations the *congildones* shall pay half, and for half he shall flee or pay.
Si quis occidatur ejusmodi secundum legem pristinam, si parentela careat, reddatur dimidium regi, dimidium congildonibus.	If any such person is killed, then *according to ancient law*, if he have no kindred half shall be paid to the King and half to the *congildones*.

Recurrence to Anglo-Saxon custom.

These clauses are valuable as showing that to meet the circumstances arising upon the Norman Conquest there was a recurrence as far as possible to ancient law and Anglo-Saxon custom.

This was not the first time that the difficulty of absence of kindred had occurred and been formally

Protection of the kinless stranger.

recognised in England. The early Danish conquests had made special provisions necessary for the protection of the kinless stranger. And it was declared that 'if any one did wrong to an ecclesiastic or a foreigner as to money or as to life, then should the king or the eorl there in the land and the bishop of the people be unto him in the place of a kinsman and of a protector (for *moeg* and for *mund-boran*) unless he had another.'[1]

Again, as regards the position of the maternal relations and the *congildones* of a stranger, it is clear that the writer of these so-called laws is copying and adopting what he finds in the Laws of King Alfred. In ss. 27 and 28 of the latter, in the absence of relatives the *gegildas* of the slayer were to pay half the wergeld; and also, in the absence of relatives of the slain person, his *gegildas* were to receive half the wergeld.

In both cases an artificial group of organised comrades, 'gegildas' or 'congildones,' seems to have been recognised as in part taking the place of kindred. And the importance of the provision of some such substitute for protection by the oaths of kinsmen is evident enough when it is considered that the ordeal of hot iron or water was the recognised alternative.

On the whole the clauses in these so-called laws relating to Normans and strangers adhere to the principle of the liability of kindred both paternal and

---

[1] This passage is from the last clause in the so-called treaty between Edward and Guthrum, 'when the English and Danes fully took to peace and to friendship, and the Witan also who were afterwards, oft and unseldom that same renewed and increased with good.' Thorpe, p. 71; and see Schmid's *Einleitung*, p. xlii.

maternal in cases of homicide, and this is the more remarkable because long before, especially in the Laws of Edmund, as will hereafter appear, a very strong tendency had been shown to restrict the liability in case of homicide to the slayer himself.

In the meantime the attempt to apply the Anglo-Saxon custom as to wergelds to Normans after the Conquest, taken together with the continued recognition of the liability of both paternal and maternal *parentes*, is a very strong proof that the solidarity of the kindred was not altogether a thing of the past. Tribal custom which at the Norman Conquest could be applied to the conquering class cannot be regarded as dead.

II. NORMAN VIEW OF WESSEX CUSTOM.

We pass on now to clause LXX. of the 'Laws of Henry I.' with the heading 'Consuetudo Westsexe.'

The amount of the wergeld according to Wessex law is thus stated :—

Wessex wergeld of twyhynde or villanus and twelvehynde or thane.

In Westsexa, que caput regni est et legum, twihindi, i. villani wera est iiii lib.; twelfhindi, i. thaini xxv lib.	(lxx. i) In Wessex, which is the capital of the kingdom and of laws, the wer of the twyhyndeman, i.e. of the villanus, is four pounds; of the twelvehyndeman, i.e. of the thane, twenty-five pounds.

The Anglo-Saxon and Norman lb. of silver was 240*d.*, and thus the twelve-hyndeman's wergeld of 25 lbs. was the same thing as the ancient Wessex wergeld of 1200 Wessex scillings of 5*d.* Four pounds was a rough equivalent of the twyhyndeman's wergeld of 200 Wessex scillings.

A little further on in the same clause is the following quotation from Ethelred II.'s compact with Olaf.

Si Anglicus homo Dacum occidat, liber liberum, persolvat eum xxv lib. vel ipse malefactor reddatur, et tantundem reddat Dacus de Anglico si eum occidat.	(lxx. s. 6.) If an Englishman kill a Dane—a freeman a freeman—let him pay for him 25 lbs. or the criminal himself shall be delivered up. And let the Dane do the same if he kill an Englishman.

The English and Danish typical freeman of this clause with his 25 lb. wergeld is clearly recognised in these so-called laws as the twelve-hyndeman and not the twyhynde man, who, though free, is identified with the 'villanus.'

Wife still belongs to her own kindred in respect of wergeld.

In further sections of this clause regarding Wessex customs very important statements are made with regard to the position of the wife in case of homicide, showing (1) that if she committed homicide her own kindred were responsible for her crime and not her husband or his kindred; and (2) that in case of the murder of a wife the wergeld went to *her* kindred and not to the husband or his kindred. In s. 12 of this clause is the following statement:—

Similiter, si mulier homicidium faciat, in eam vel in progeniem vel parentes ejus vindicetur, vel inde componat: non in virum suum, seu clientelam innocentem.	Likewise if a woman commits homicide let it be avenged on her or on her children or *parentes* or paid for from that side, not on her husband, or innocent connections.

And in s. 13:—

Si mulier occidatur, sicut weregildum ejus est reddatur, ex parte patris, sicut observamus in	If a woman be killed, whatever be her wergeld, let it be paid *ex parte patris* just as we have

aliis. (14) Si pregnans occidatur et puer in ea vivat, uterque plena wera reddatur. Si nondum vivus sit, dimidia wera solvatur parentibus ex parte patris.

said in other cases. (14) If a pregnant woman be killed and her child be living let the full wergeld of both be paid. If not yet living let half a wergeld be paid [for it] to the *parentes ex parte patris*, [of the child].

The position of the wife under Wessex custom is further shown by the following :—

Si sponsa virum suum supervixerit, dotem et maritacionem suam, cartarum instrumentis vel testium exhibicionibus ei traditam, perpetualiter habeat, et morgangivam suam et terciam partem de omni collaboracione sua, preter vestes et lectum suum ; et si quid ex eis in elemosinis vel communi necessitate consumpserit, nichil inde recipiat.

(ss. 22–23). If the wife survive her husband let her have permanently her dower and her 'maritagium' given to her by written instruments or production of witnesses, and her 'morgengift' and a third part of all joint acquisition, besides clothes and her bed, and let her receive nothing in respect of what has been consumed in charity or common necessity.

Si mulier absque liberis moriatur, parentes ejus cum marito suo partem suam dividant.

If a woman die without children her *parentes* divide her share with the husband.

These statements are valuable evidence that, in regard to the position of a wife, Anglo-Saxon custom was very nearly the same as Cymric custom and that of the Bretts and Scots. And they are the more important as stating in black and white what is only to be inferred from isolated statements in earlier laws.

We now pass to c. LXXVI., *De precio cujuslibet*, containing information as to the mode of procedure in the payment of wergeld.

After stating that if a man be slain he is to be paid for according to his birth, the clause proceeds thus :—

Sureties for wergeld 8 of paternal and 4 of maternal kindred.

Et rectum est ut homicida, postquam weregildum vadiaverit inveniat wereplegios, sicut ad eam pertinebit, i. de thaino debent dari xii wereplegii, viii de parte patris, et iiii de cognacione matris; et cum hoc factum erit, elevetur inter eos pax regis in omni weregildo, et debet halsfang primo reddi, sicut were modus erit.

And it is right that the homicide after having given pledge for the wergeld should find the werpledges pertaining to it.

From the thane: 12 werepledges, 8 *exparte patris* and 4 *de cognatione matris*, and this done shall be raised among them the peace of the king in every wergeld. And first the *halsfang* should be paid according to the nature of the wergeld.

Following the case of the twelve-hyndeman a little further we learn that:—

Twelve-hynde man's halsfang.

Twelf-hindus est homo plene nobilis, i. thainus cujus wera est duodecies c sol. qui faciunt libras xxv, cujus halsfang sunt cxx sol. qui faciunt hodie sol. l. Et non pertinet alii cognacioni pecunia ista, nisi illis qui sunt intra genu.

The twelve-hyndeman is the man *plene nobilis*, i.e. the thane whose wergeld is 1200 scillings which make 25*l.*

His halsfang is 120*s.* which to-day equals 50*s.*[1] [Norman], and it belongs to no other relations than those who are *intra genu.*

This halsfang had to be paid on the 21st day from the giving of the pledge, and it seems to have been a token in recognition of guilt or earnest money to show that the wergeld would be paid.

Manbot and fightwite and then wergeld.

On the next 21st night from the payment of the halsfang the *manbot* had to be paid, and on the 21st night after that the *fightwite*, and on the 21st night again the first payment of the wergeld.

Et sic omnibus parentibus dominisque emendacionibus iniciatis persolvantur reliquum were, intra terminum quem sapientes instituunt.

Thus for all the *parentes* and lords, amends being set agoing, the rest of the wergeld shall be paid during a term to be fixed by the wise men (*sapientes*).

Turning next to the case of persons twyhynde born—*cyrlisci vel villani*—more details are given:—

---

[1] 120*s.* of 5*d.* = 50*s.* of 12*d.*

After stating their wergeld to be four pounds, the clause proceeds :—

Halsfange ejus sunt v marc. que faciunt xii sol. et vi den.: est autem verbum Anglicum quod Latine sonat 'apprehensio colli.'

Their halsfang is v marks which = 12*s*. 6*d*.; and it is an English word which in Latin means *apprehensio colli*.'

Halsfang of the twyhynde class.

There is evidently here an error. 'V marc' ought to be read 5 *mancuses*. The mancus was 30*d*. or 2*s*. 6*d*. Norman money and the halsfang therefore 150*d*. or 12*s*. 6*d*. Norman money, as stated in the following clause.

Si quis ad iv lib. persolvendus occidatur, et ad id res veniat, ut precio natalis ejus componendus sit, primo debent reddi xii sol. et vi den. et in wera numerari: reddantur vero patri, vel filio, vel fratri, vel qui propinquior est de patre, si predictos parentes non habeat: si omnes istos habeat, et ipsi dividant inter se.

A die qua wera vadiata est in xxi diem, sine omni excusacione et dilacione, debet halsfang reddi, sicut premisimus. . .

Inde ad xxi diem reddatur ipsius manbota: tunc ad xxi diem fuytwhita: inde ad xxi diem reddatur ipsius were frumgildum, i. vii sol. et vi den. ad explecionem xx sol.

(6) If any one is killed to be paid for at 4*l*. and it comes to pass that the price of his birth has to be paid, first should be paid [the halsfang of] 12*s*. 6*d*. to be reckoned in the wergeld, and this is paid to the *father or son, or brother*, or, failing these, whoever is the *nearest of kin to the father*. If he has all these, they divide it between them.

On the 21st day from the giving of the pledge, without any excuse or delay the halsfang should be paid, as we have said. .

On the 21st day after that, is to be paid the *manbot*, then on the 21st day the *fightwite*, and then on the 21st day must be paid the *frumgeld* of the wergeld, i.e. 7*s*. 6*d*., to the completion of 20*s*.

Manbot and fightwite and then wergeld.

Thus we learn that in the case of the twy-hyndeman the halsfang of 12*s*. 6*d*. and the frumgeld of 7*s*. 6*d*. make up the first 20*s*. of the wergeld of four pounds. The clause proceeds :—

Inde componat qui weram solvit, terminum de xx sol.: inde ponant terminum suum parentes mortui de xl ovibus, que pro xx sol. computantur: sint autem oves videntes et cornute, nulla parte corporis diminute: ultimo termino reddatur equus, qui pro xx sol. numerandus est. Hoc secundum legem et nostram consuetudinem diximus: differentia tamen weregildi multa est in Cancia villanorum et baronum.

After that he who pays the wergeld pays at another term 20*s.*

Then the *parentes* of the dead fix a term for 40 sheep which are reckoned as 20*s.*, but they must be sheep seeing and horned and deficient in no part of the body. At the last term a horse is given reckoned at 20*s.* This we have said according to law and our custom. There is, however, great difference in the wergeld of both *villani* and *barones* in Kent.

Thus both in the case of the twelve-hynde and the twy-hyndeman the halsfang is the first beginning of the wergeld, and whatever may be the exact meaning of the word, it is pretty evident that it was regarded as an admission of the wrong done and as a kind of earnest money that the rest of the wergeld would be paid.

But between the halsfang or earnest money and the making up of the first full instalment of the wergeld were the two other payments, the *manbot* and the *fightwite.*

They have already been mentioned, but it is important to recognise what these two payments outside the wergeld mean.

We learn from c. LXXX. s. 6 what the fightwite was:—

Fightwite was for breach of precinct.

In cujuscumque terra fiat homicidium, qui socam et sacam suam habeat, si homicida divadietur ibi vel cravetur, fihtwytam recipiat. . . . Si occisus et locus unius domini sint, qui socnam suam habeat manbotam et fihtwytam.

On whosesoever land the homicide may be committed, he who has soc and sac shall if the homicide there be pledged or remanded receive fightwite. . . .

If the person killed and the place are of one lord, let him who has the soc have [both] manbot and fightwite.

It is clear from this that the fightwite was the payment due to the lord who had the 'soc' of the place where the homicide occurred and the wergeld was pledged. The manbot, on the other hand, was the payment to the lord whose man the person slain was. The lord of the soc might also be the lord of the man slain, in which case both fightwite and manbot were payable to him.

Manbot was value to lord of person slain.

In c. LXIX. the manbot of the twy-hyndeman is stated to be 30*s.* (of 5*d.*, *i.e.* 150*d.*), and that of the twelve-hyndeman 120*s.* (600*d.*) as in the Laws of Ine, s. 70.

In the so-called 'Laws of Edward the Confessor' c. XII. is the following:—

Qui scienter fregerit eam [pacem regis] . . . lege Anglorum suum were, i. precium suum, et manbote de occisis erga dominos quorum homines interfecti erant. Manbote in Danelaga, de vilano et de socheman, xii oras; de liberis hominibus iii marcas. Manbote in lege Anglorum, regi et archiepiscopo, iii marc̃ de hominibus suis; episcopo comitatus, comiti comitatus, et dapifero regis, xx soł; baronibus ceteris, x solid̃. Emendacionem faciat parentibus, aut guerram paciatur, unde Angli proverbium habebant: Biege spere of side oðer bere, quod est dicere, lanceam eme de latere aut fer eam.

He who knowingly breaks the king's peace . . . by the law of the English pays his were, i.e. *pretium suum*, and *manbot* of persons killed to the lords whose men have been killed. Manbote in Danelaga of villanus and socheman xii ores, of *liberi homines* iii marks.[1] Manbot in English law to the king and archbishop iii marks for their men; to the bishop and earl of a county and *dapifer* of the king xx*s.*: other barons x*s.* Let him make amends to the *parentes* or suffer feud. Hence the English have a proverb, 'Buy off the spear or bear it.'

This chapter relates chiefly to the breach of the king's peace on the king's highways &c., but it clearly confirms the meaning of the *manbot* as the payment

[1] Three marks are double 12 ores.

to the lord for his man and as quite distinct from the wergeld to the *parentes* of the slain.

Manbot of socheman and villanus alike in the Danelaga.

It may seem strange at first sight that according to this clause the manbot in the Danelaga of the villanus and the socheman should be alike, viz. 12 ores of silver, and further that the villanus and socheman should not be included as *liberi homines*, the manbot of the latter being double their manbot, viz. three marks or 24 ores.

The explanation of the equal manbot of villani and sochemen may partly be found in the tendency after the Conquest to class together all subordinate tenants rendering manual or agricultural services to the landlord as villani, and to ignore the differences in origin between the various classes of tenants of this kind. Still if at this point of our inquiry the relative positions of the sochmanni of the Danish districts and the villani of ordinary English manors were the question under discussion, it would be fair in explanation of the equality in manbot to point out how very nearly the services of the two classes seem to have corresponded so far as their value to the lord was concerned.[1]

The loss to the lord of the twelve-hyndeman was probably reckoned as of greater money value than that of the villanus or socheman, because of the higher grade or character of his military and judicial services

[1] See the instances of services of sochemen given by Mr. Round in his invaluable chapter on the Domesday book in his *Feudal England*, pp. 30–34, from the 'Ely placitum' of 1072–1075: 'Qui *quotiens abbas preceperit* in anno arabunt suam terram' &c. And again *quotienscunque ipse præceperit* in anno arabunt' &c. These are services of the sochemanni of Suffolk and Norfolk 'qui non possunt recedere.'

as compared with the agricultural services of the villanus and socheman.

However this may be, these considerations confirm the importance of the distinction between the *manbot* which varies according to the value or loss to the lord of the person slain, and is therefore payable to him, and the wergeld payable to the *parentes* of the person slain which varied according to the grade in social rank in which he was born or to which he may have sometimes risen.

Further, this distinction between the wergeld and the manbot becomes all the clearer when we turn to the evidence given in the Laws of Henry I. regarding the custom of Wessex in respect of the homicide of slaves.

In c. LXX. the custom of Wessex is stated thus :—

When a slave is killed, or kills an Englishman.

Si servus servum occidat, domino reddantur xx sol. pro manbota, parentibus interfecti servi xl den.

Si dominus occisoris nec pro eo reddit, nec servus habet unde reddat, dimittere potest eum dominus, ut sibi caveat, nisi forte cravetur dum secum est; quod si eveniat, eum repetentibus reddat vel inde componat.

(s 2) If a slave (*servus*) kills a slave xx*s*. [? of 5*d*.] is paid to the lord for *manbot*, to the *parentes* of the dead slave xl*d*.

(s. 3) If the lord of the slayer pays nothing for him and the slave has nothing to pay with, the lord can dismiss him so that he [the lord] may protect himself from having the slave seized while with him. But if this happen he shall hand him over to the prosecutors or pay for him.

Si liber servum occidat, similiter reddat parentibus xl den. et duas mufflas, et unum pullum mutilatum, domini servi xx sol. pro manbota blodwitam vel fihtwitam sicut acciderit.

If a freeman kill a slave let him likewise pay to the *parentes* xl pence and two 'muffles' and a capon. To the lord of the slave xx*s*. [? of 5*d*.] for manbot, [also] bloodwite or fightwite as it happens.

Si servus Waliscus Anglicum hominem occidat, debet ille cujus servus est reddere eum domino et

If a *slave Waliscus* kills an Englishman he whose slave he is ought to give him up to the lord parentibus, vel dare xl sol. pro vita sua. Si hoc capitale nolit dare pro eo, dimittat eum liberum, solvant postea parentes ejus weram illam, si cognacionem habeat liberam. Si non habeat, observent eum inimici. Non cogitur liber cum servo meggildare, nisi velit ei satisfaccionem facere, nec servus cum libero.

and the *parentes* or pay xl*s.* [? of 5*d.*] for his life. If he does not choose to pay this for his head let him set him free; then afterwards let his *parentes* pay his wergeld if he has free relations. If not let them regard him as an enemy. No freeman is to be compelled to join in payment with a slave unless he wishes to make satisfaction for him nor a slave with a freeman.[1]

Manbot of Wessex slave.

Thus while under the Danelaga the equal manbot of the villanus and of the socheman was 12 ores or 240*d.*, we learn from these clauses that the manbot of the ordinary slave under Wessex custom was 20*s. i.e.* (if of 5*d.*) 100 pence, while that of the twy-hyndeman was, as we have seen, only 150 pence.

At first sight it may seem strange that the manbot or value to the lord of his villanus or socheman should be no greater, or even less, than that of his theow or slave. But a moment's consideration will show that the value of the villanus and the socheman to the lord was mainly their week-work and services amounting to perhaps half their whole time, while that of the slave or theow was the value of his whole time and also that of a marketable chattel.

It may be noticed, too, how in the statements of Wessex custom some slight recognition is made of the *kindred* of the slave, but the amount (40 pence) is so very small that it hardly can be reckoned as any real approach to recognition of family rights or rights of kindred belonging to the relatives of the slave.

[1] Cf. Ine, 74. The xl*s.* to be paid for the 'Waliscus' slave who had committed homicide may be double value by way of penalty.

In the 'Laws of William the Conqueror' the manbot of the slave is stated (perhaps in error) to be twice that of the freeman, and in the case of freemen a concession is made of 10*s.* of the wergeld to the *widow* of the slain, who otherwise, not being of the same blood or kindred with her husband, would under tribal custom have received no part of the wergeld.

Si quis convictus vel confessus fuerit in jure, alium occidisse, dat were suum, et insuper domino occisi, manbote, scilicet, pro homine libero x sol. pro servo xx solid.

(s. vii.) If any one shall have been convicted of or have confessed the slaying of another, let him give his wergeld and over and above to the lord of the person slain, *manbote*: that is, for a freeman x*s.* [? of 5*d.* or 12*d.*] for a *servus* xx shillings.

Est autem were theni in Merchenalahe xx libr.; in Westsaxenelahe xxv libr.; rustici autem c solid. in Merchenelahe, et similiter in Westsaxenelahe.

(viii.) The wergeld, however, of the thane under Mercian law is xx lb. [i.e. 1200*s.* of 4*d.*], under West Saxon law xxv lb. [i.e. 1200*s.* of 5*d.*]; of the rustic c*s.* [? of 5*d.* or 12*d.*] in Mercia and the same in Wessex.

De were ergo pro occiso soluto, primo vidue x sol. dentur, et residuum liberi et consanguinei inter se dividant.

(ix) Of the wergeld thus paid for the slain person, first let x shillings be given to the widow, and the rest let the children and relations divide between them.

Finally, it is interesting to observe that according to the so-called 'Laws of Henry I.' tribal custom was still partly recognised in the method of dealing with the homicide of a kinsman.

Homicide of a kinsman.

In clause LXXV. is the following:—

Qui aliquem de parentibus suis occidet, dignis apud Deum penitencie fructibus emendet; et in modo penitencie sit, si sponte vel casu perpetravit; et excidat emendacio patrini sicut manbota

He who shall slay any one of his *parentes*, let him make amends by fruits of penitence worthy before God. And let the measure of the penance be according to whether he did it willingly or by domini: si non pertineat ei utrumque, et aliorum importunitate, quorum consanguineus est, cogatur eum reddere, sapientum hoc judicio, secundum genus, componatur.

accident. And the correction of the sponsor falls just as the manbot of the lord. If there does not pertain to him either the one or the other and by the importunity of others whose kinsman he is he shall be compelled to pay, let it be compounded for by judgment of wise men whatever that may be.

The homicide of a kinsman was apparently still generally free from judicial interference or criminal law. The slayer is handed over to the Church and his punishment is spiritual penance. Even the manbot to the lord who has lost a man through his crime fails to be paid. But should there be a fear of trouble through the importunity of any of the kinsmen of the slain demanding compensation, then a compromise was to be effected by reference to the judgment of wise men. Tribal feeling is evidently not yet dead, although beginning in this matter to yield to the more modern view of individual responsibility for crime without regard to the question of kindred. There is at the same time recognition of the fact that the weakened tribal feeling is no longer always able to restrain the kinsmen from revenge in the case of wrong done within the kindred.

CHAPTER XI.

DANISH VIEW OF ANGLO-SAXON CUSTOM.

I. THE 'DE INSTITUTIS LUNDONIE'—OF CNUT (?).

HAVING thus tried to obtain, from the so-called 'Laws of Henry I.' (whatever they may be), a Norman view of Anglo-Saxon custom, we recognise that on some points we may have learned more from this Norman view than could directly have been learned solely from the earlier Anglo-Saxon laws themselves.

Fresh point of view.

The reason of this is obvious. Special laws issued at various times by Saxon kings do not profess to cover the whole ground of existing and well understood custom. Rather should special laws be regarded as modifications of custom made necessary at different periods by new circumstances. Thus no one of the sets of laws can be expected to give a general view of custom as a whole.

It is not strange, then, that we should owe some knowledge of early Anglo-Saxon custom to the Norman Conquest and the necessity after such an event to collect in a more connected and intelligible form what had formerly to some extent been matters of custom and tradition. And so it may be that our next chance of learning more may be found in the study of the documents and fragments belonging to the period of the Danish invasion of England, and especially the moment of transition from the English rule of Ethelred II. to the Danish rule of Cnut.

Danes and English live under their own

The founding of the Danish kingdom of Cnut was an epoch in English history, and indeed in the history of Europe. It was followed *inter alia* by the legalisation in England of Scandinavian monetary reckoning in marks and ores which had already for some time been in use side by side with the English reckoning in scillings and pounds. And this was typical of the general position of things. In full coincidence with the working of tribal feeling in other countries, into the idea of conquest the amalgamation of the two peoples into one did not enter. Danes continued to live under their laws and the English under theirs, as Franks and Gallo-Romans did under Frankish rule. Certain things were enjoined upon both, but with a difference. It often happens that in documents of this period the 'law of the English' is specially explained while the Danish law is referred to as already known, thus revealing a Danish point of view.

Danish law assumed to be well known.

In the Laws of Ethelred II. (s. 37) it is enacted that if anyone should be charged with plotting against the king, he must 'clear himself with the threefold ordeal by the law of the English, and by the law of the Danes according as their law may be.' And so in the Laws of Cnut penalties are stated as so many scillings by English law and by Danish law 'as it formerly stood.'[1]

So that, from the Danish point of view, it was sometimes a matter of inquiry and record what the

[1] Laws of Cnut, s. 63 and s. 66.

English law had been, while knowledge of Danish law was mostly taken for granted.

With regard to the coinage this was only partly the case. Not that Anglo-Saxon reckoning in pounds and scillings was abolished or that Danish currency was thenceforth the only one allowed. But, Cnut having styled himself 'King of all England and King of the Danes and Norwegians,' London had become in one sense a Scandinavian port.

London under Cnut a port of the 'greater Scandinavia.'

The large sums paid to 'the army' by Ethelred for respite and peace had flooded Scandinavia with English silver money of his coinage.

This was so to such an extent that while the British Museum is rich in the coins of Ethelred, still more of them are to be found in Scandinavian museums.[1] And one marked result of the increased intercourse with England was an increase also in the Scandinavian coinage, the type of which was chiefly taken from the coins of Ethelred II.[2]

London had become to some extent the commercial capital indirectly of what has been happily called the 'Greater Scandinavia.'

In the words of Mr. Keary:[3] 'The Greater Scandinavia, with older countries, included (counting from the East to the West) a large district in the North and West of Russia extending from Kiev to Lake Ladoga. It included Sweden, Norway, Denmark and a strip of land in North Germany (Mecklenburg),

[1] Mr. Keary's Introduction to the Catalogue of the Coins in the British Museum, Anglo-Saxon series, vol. ii. p. lxxxi.

[2] Engel, vol. ii. p. 849 et seq.

[3] Introduction, vol. ii. p. lvii.

Northern England, Man, most of the Western Scottish Islands, the Orkneys and Shetlands . . . settlements in Ireland and colonies in the Faroes and Iceland—a stretch of territories inhabited by peoples closely allied in blood, in speech, and in customs.'

Was it likely, then, that Cnut in making London the commercial capital of his kingdom should adopt the English monetary system unchanged, without regard to that in use in the North?

Happily, in the document known as the 'De Instituis Lundonie' we have an interesting glimpse into the conditions of the port of London, and in its final clause definite reference to the legalisation of the Danish currency.

The commerce of London.

This document has hitherto been placed doubtfully under the reign of Ethelred II. with some others of about the same period, but there is no evidence to show that it should be so placed rather than under the reign of Cnut. It exists only in Latin and it contains no mention of Ethelred, while its final clause becomes intelligible only, I think, if regarded as enacted after the accession of Cnut.

We learn from the document that Aldersgate and Cripplegate were the two gates which had guards.

Billingsgate, being on the river, was treated as a port. Boats on arrival paid toll according to size, smaller ones a halfpenny, boats with sails one penny, '*a ceol vel hulcus*' fourpence if it should lie there. Ships laden with wood paid 'one timber' from their cargo. Those coming with fish to the bridge also paid toll.

Men from Rouen, with wine or whale, paid six

shillings per ship and the twentieth lump of the whale.

Men of Flanders, Normandy, and France declared their cargoes and paid toll. Goods overland through Holland and Belgium were also examined and paid toll. Men of the Emperor who came in their ships were to be held worthy of the same good laws as 'our people (*sicut nos*).'

From this it would appear that a good deal of the trade from the Baltic was an overland trade and in Frankish hands. The 'men of the Emperor' who were treated on equal terms with 'our people' were probably the merchants whose successors ultimately established the Hanseatic towns and two or three centuries later the Hanseatic league.

The final clause is as follows:—

Cnut's ores of 16d. or $\frac{1}{15}$ of the pound.

(9) Et ut monetarii pauciores sint, quam antea fuerint: in omni summo portu iii, et in omni alio portu sit unus monetarius:	And that there be fewer moneyers[1] than there formerly were, in every chief town iii and in every other town let there be one moneyer.
et illi habeant suboperarios suos in suo crimine, quod purum faciant et recti ponderis, per eandem witam, quam prediximus.	And let them have their sub-workers under their responsibility, so that they make pure [money] and of right weight, under the penalties aforesaid.
Et ipsi qui portus custodiant, efficiant per overhirnessam meam, ut omne pondus sit marcatum ad pondus, quo pecunia mea recipitur et eorum singulum signetur ita, quod xv oræ libram faciant. Et custodiant omnes monetam, sicut vos docere praecipio [? praecepto], et omnes elegimus.	And let those who have charge of the towns secure, under penalties, that every weight shall be marked at the weight by which my money is received, and that each of them is so signed that xv ores make a pound. And let all maintain the coinage in accordance with the orders we have chosen to enjoin upon you and all men.

[1] The word is used in the sense of mint-master or money coiner. See Du Cange, *sub voce* 'Monetarius.'

This clause has already been alluded to in connection with the 'Laws of the Bretts and Scots.' The ore of sixteen pence in which the payments of those laws were to be made was the ore described in this clause, for the ore of one fifteenth of the pound was the ore of sixteen pence.

The wording of the clause is very distinct. There were to be *monetarii* (mintmen) at the several mercantile centres, one at each lesser town and at the chief towns three. And every weight used by them was to be marked to the weight at which 'my money' was received and every one of the weights was to be marked '*so that fifteen ores make a pound.*'

The pound was no doubt the Frankish and English pound which since the time of Charlemagne and Offa contained 7680 wheat-grains and was divided according to English reckoning into twelve ounces of 640 wheat-grains or twenty-pence of 32 wheat-grains. The Danish ore of one fifteenth part of the pound was therefore of 512 wheat-grains or sixteen pence.

And there is good reason to believe that this ore was the ore in general use in Scandinavian commerce. We have seen that the Scandinavian ore, like the Merovingian ounce, when reckoned in wheat-grains was the Roman ounce of 576 wheat-grains, but that in actual weight it had sunk below the Roman standard. The 'ortug' or stater had apparently in actual weight fallen back to the weight of the stater of the ancient Eastern or Merovingian standard, viz. 8·18 grammes, so that the ore or ounce of three ortugs of this weight would weigh 24·54 grammes.

And this was almost exactly one fifteenth of the Anglo-Saxon pound.[1]

We may therefore with some confidence regard the ore legalised by Cnut for commercial use as practically identical in weight of silver with the ore of three ortugs in use in the Baltic and generally in Scandinavian trade.

Cnut divides his ore into 20 light pence.

Moreover, when we turn to the actual coinage of Cnut we find that by a sweeping change he reduced the weight of the silver penny from one twentieth of the Anglo-Saxon ounce to apparently one twentieth of this ore, intending, it would seem, to make his ore pass for payments as an ore of 20 pence instead of 16.[2]

When these facts are taken together, we can hardly, I think, be wrong in assigning the 'De Institutis Lundonie' to the time of the foundation of the Danish kingdom by Cnut and in considering its final clause as recording the legalisation of the Danish monetary system with its marks and ores for use in England and for purposes of international trade.

---

[1] The Anglo-Saxon pound of 240 pence or 364 grammes divided by fifteen = 24·2 grammes.

[2] The normal weight of the English penny of 32 wheat-grains was 1·51 grammes. The coins of Cnut's predecessors sometimes fully reached this standard, though oftener somewhat below it. The exact weight of $\frac{1}{20}$ of the Danish ore would be 1·21 grammes, and Cnut's silver pence seem to aim at this weight. Out of 574 silver pence of Cnut described in the Catalogue of the British Museum 400 weigh between ·972 and 1·23 grammes. Only $1\frac{1}{2}$ per cent. are of greater weight. Ethelred's silver pence were not by any means generally of full standard of 32 wheat-grains or 1·51 grammes, but still, out of 339 in the British Museum 25 per cent. are fairly up to this standard and 90 per cent. are above the weight of the new silver pence of Cnut—$\frac{1}{20}$ of his ore. Cnut also reduced the *size* of the pence. See the B. M. Catalogue plates.

The fact that the 'ore of sixteen' was in use not only in the 'Laws of the Bretts and Scots' but also in the Domesday survey, *e.g.* in the district between the Mersey and the Ribble, is a lasting proof of its use wherever Scandinavian conquest and commerce extended, possibly before and certainly long after it was legalised for English use by Cnut.

II. FRAGMENT 'OF "GRITH" AND OF "MUND."'

Having gained from the 'De Institutis Lundonie' some sense of the greatness of the change to England consequent upon the accession of Cnut and also of the importance of England to Cnut's Scandinavian kingdom, we may now turn to the consideration of certain documents which seem to be attempts made during this period of change to realise and record what had been Anglo-Saxon custom.

Mund-bryce of the king and of the Church five pounds.

The first clauses of Cnut's Church laws refer to the maintenance of the rights of the Church as to 'grith and frith.' [1] 'Because God's grith is of all griths the best, and next thereto the king's, it is very right that God's church-grith within walls and a Christian king's hand-grith stand equally inviolate,' so that anyone infringing either 'shall forfeit land and life unless the king be merciful to him.' [2] A homicide within church walls was to be 'botless,' unless the king 'granted life against full bot.' In this case the homicide must pay his full *wer* to Christ or the king,

[1] 'Grith' seems to be a Danish word of nearly the same meaning as 'frith.' See Schmid's Glossary, *sub voce*.

[2] This is in accordance with Ine, 6.

as the case might be, and so 'inlaw himself to bot.' Then the bot was to be the same as the king's 'mund-bryce' of five pounds.

These clauses seem to be taken from another document of this period,[1] headed 'Of Church grith,' which is printed by Thorpe among the Laws of Ethelred.

Again, the laws decreed by Ethelred and his witan at Wantage[2] respecting 'frith-bot' commence with the decree that 'grith should stand henceforth as it originally stood in the days of his [the king's] fore-fathers.' So that again ancient custom is confirmed rather than new law enacted.

The grith of various moots.

This decree of Wantage relates, not, like Cnut's law, to the grith of the Church, but to the grith of various assemblies or courts. Crimes committed within the grith or peace given by the king's own hand (that is, the king's 'hand-grith' of the other documents) is again *botless*. The grith which the ealdorman and the king's reeve give in the assembly of the 'five-burgs' if broken involves a bot of 1200 (scillings?), that given by a burh-assembly 600, that by a wapentake 100, that in an alehouse 'for a dead man vi half-marks and for a living one xii ores.'

In a further clause (s. 12) it is stated that in a king's suit the deposit or 'wed' was to be of vi half-marks, in an eorl's and a bishop's of xii ores, and in a thane's of vi ores. Here both English and Danish currencies are used. The law is common to both peoples.

The principle of the 'grith' or 'frith' is alike for both English and Danes, and it does not seem that

---

[1] Laws of Ethelred, ix. (Thorpe, p. 145). [2] Thorpe, p. 124.

Cnut had any intention of altering what had been law in this respect under his English predecessor.

Grith-bryce and mund-bryce the same thing.

In s. 3 of Cnut's Church laws, dealing with crimes less than homicide, he seems to treat the 'grith' of his new law and the 'mund-bryce' of old law as practically the same thing, and this clause according to the text of MS. G.[1] contains an interesting allusion to Kentish as well as other English law.

Heafod mynstres griðbryce is æt bot wyrþum þingū be cinges munde. ꝥ is mid · v · pundum on Engla lage ⁊ on cent lande æt þā mund bryce · v · pund þā cingce. ⁊ þreo þā arceƀ. ⁊ medemran mynstres mid · cxx · scill. ꝥæ is be cingres wite. ⁊ þonne gyt læssan þær lytel þeowdom sig ⁊ leger-stow þeah sig mid lx scill. and feald cyricean þær leger-scow ne sig mid xxx scyll.

The grith-bryce of the chief minster in cases entitled to bot is according to the King's mund, that is v pounds by English law *and in Kent for the mund-bryce v pounds to the King*, and three to the archbishop, and of a minster of the middle class cxx scillings, that is according to the King's wite, and of one yet less where there is little service, provided there be a burying place, lx scillings and of a field church thirty scillings.

Further, there is a separate document belonging to this period entitled 'Of *Grith* and of *Mund*'[2] which seems to have been a careful statement of what 'formerly' had been law among the English, the Kentish people, the South Angles, and the North Angles respectively.

It is too long to be quoted at length. It states again that 'God's grith is of all griths' of the first importance, and 'next thereto the king's.' 'Formerly among the English,' when a man fled for his life to the king, the archbishop or the ætheling, he had nine days' 'grith.' If he sought a bishop or ealdorman he

[1] MS. G. British Museum, Cott. Nero A. 1. fol. 5.

[2] Thorpe, p. 141, Schmid, *Anhang iv.*

Reference to Kentish law.

had seven days' 'grith.'[1] Then it goes on to state that in the law of the *Kentish* people 'the king and the archbishop had a like and equally dear *mund-bryce*,' while the archbishop's property according to Kentish law was compensated for elevenfold and the king's ninefold, though 'the mund-byrd of Christ's Church was the same as the king's.'[2]

Grith-law of South Angles.

Next the 'grith-law' of the *South Angles* is described. The king's mund-bryce is stated again to be five pounds by the law of the English; an archbishop and an ætheling's mund-bryce three pounds; other bishops' and an ealdorman's two pounds: and if any one fight in the presence of an ætheling or archbishop the bot was cl scillings, if in that of another bishop or ealdorman c scillings.

Law of North Angles.

Lastly, the document records that in the *North Angles'* law 'it stands that he who slays any one within church walls shall be liable in his life, and he who wounds shall be liable in his hand: and let him who slays any one within church doors give to the church cxx scillings, according to the North-Angles' law. And let a freeman who harms a living person in his "mund-byrd" pay xxx scillings.'

Borh-bryce.

In s. 59 of the secular laws of Cnut under the heading 'Of Borh-bryce' is a statement that if any one break the king's 'borh' the bot is five pounds; an archbishop's or ætheling's 'borh' three pounds; a leod-bishop's or ealdorman's 'borh' two pounds. This is a re-enactment of clause 3 of King Alfred's dooms. In the latter the words 'borh-bryce' and 'mund-byrd'

[1] Compare Æthelstan, iv. 4.

[2] This, from the Kentish Laws, was correctly quoted.

appear to be interchangeable. Both mean the breach of protection or *mund.*

Extent of the area of the grith.

There is finally a fragment[1] which fixes the extent of the king's 'grith' to be 'three miles and three furlongs and three acre breadths and nine feet and nine hand breadths and nine barleycorns from the "burhgeat" where the king is.'

Within this area the 'grith' or protection of the king extends, and the use of the word 'grith' seems to place this fragment among those belonging to the Danish group.

In this 'grith' or *area* of protection, taken together with the grith of various persons in regard to the *duration* of the protection, and the grith of the various assemblies or courts, and, finally, in the *mund* of various persons marked by the amount of the *mund-bryce*, there is surely a foundation in ancient custom for the jurisdiction involved in the sac and soc of the later period.

The soc and sac of later laws.

We have seen in the clauses of the so-called Laws of Henry I. allusion to the 'sac and soc' of the lord on whose land a homicide has been perpetrated and under whose jurisdiction the wed or pledge has been given for the payment of wergeld. According to earlier phraseology, the lord's grith or peace has been broken. He has a territorial jurisdiction over the giving of the wed by which it is to be restored, and he is entitled to fightwite accordingly. If his own man has been slain, whether on his own land or not, his *mund* has been broken and the manbot of his man is payable to him. The phrase 'soc and sac' is probably of Scandinavian origin. It does not seem

[1] Schmid, *Anhang xii.*

to go back earlier than the time of Cnut.[1] It is not found in his laws. But the principle at the root of the 'grith' and the 'mund' was not one newly introduced at this period. We shall find it again in the earliest laws, and we have already found it at work under Irish custom. The Irish chieftain's 'precinct' or area of protection extended on his 'green' as far as he could throw his hammer, and the value of his protection varied, as we have seen, with his 'honour price.'

III. THE 'FRITH' BETWEEN ETHELRED II. AND OLAF TRYGGVASON, A.D. 993.

Frith of A.D. 993.

The real Danish invasion of England, which ended in the accession of Cnut to the kingdom of all England, commenced with the arrival of Olaf (Tryggvason), afterwards King of Norway, in A.D. 991. The fatal battle of Malden had been fought and 10,000 pounds of silver paid for a temporary peace. At length the treaty was made between Ethelred and Olaf on the latter embracing Christianity.

The article on homicide in this '*frith-mal*' is the only one which need be quoted here :—

Freeman's wergeld 25 pounds of silver.

Gif Englisc man Denisсne ofslea, frigman frigne, gylde hine mid xxv pundum oþþon mon þone hand-dædan agyfe, ⁊ do se	If an Englishman slay a Dane, a freeman a freeman, let him pay for him with xxv [2] pounds, or let the slayer be delivered up. And

[1] Pollock and Maitland, i. p. 20. But see Laws of King Edmund, s. 4, 'On Blood-shedding.' 'Also I make known that I will not have to "*socn*" in my "hirede" that man who sheds man's blood before he has undertaken ecclesiastical "bot" and made "bot" to the kindred,' &c. See also in s. 6 the use of the words '*mund-brice* and *Ham-socn*.'

[2] Another reading has xxx. See Schmid, p. 206. The Latin version has xxv, and the quotation in the Laws of Henry I also has xxv.

Slave valued at one pound.

Denisca þone Engliscan eal swa gif [he] hine ofslea. Gif Englisc man Deniscne þræl ofslea gylde hine mid punde ⁊ se Denisca Engliscne eal swa gif he hine ofslea.

let the Dane do the same by an Englishman if he slay him.

If an Englishman slay a Danish thrall let him pay for him with a pound; and so a Dane in like manner, by an Englishman if he slay him.

The free-man is the twelve-hynde-man.

The points to be noted here are these. It is for the crime of a freeman slaying a freeman that the wergeld of twenty-five pounds is to be paid. And this wergeld of twenty-five pounds of silver is the wergeld of 1200 Wessex scillings. So that the free-man of this clause is the twelve-hyndeman.[1]

For the purpose of this 'frith' between Ethelred and Olaf the twelve-hyndeman and not the twy-hynde-man is the typical freeman. And the Dane also is to be paid for by a twelve-hyndeman's wergeld.

The twy-hyndeman escapes without notice. No class is mentioned between the twelve-hynde free-man and the thrall; and the thrall whether Danish or English is paid for with a pound of silver.

Finally, the compact is described in Anglo-Saxon pounds, not in Danish marks and ores.

It is an English statement of the 'frith' between the English king and 'the army that Anlaf (Olaf) and Justin and Guthmund, Stegita's son, were with.' And accordingly at the end of clause 7 is recorded the humiliating admission that 'twenty-two thousand pounds of gold and silver were given to "the army in England for the frith."'

---

[1] 25 × 240 = 6000 pence = 1200 Wessex scillings of 5*d.*

CHAPTER XII.

ANGLO-SAXON CUSTOM FROM THE VIKING OR NORTHMEN'S POINT OF VIEW.

I. THE COMPACT BETWEEN KING ALFRED AND GUTHRUM, A.D. 886.

The earlier Danish or Viking invasions.

AT the date of the compact between Ethelred II. and Olaf Tryggvason more than a century had passed since the earlier compact between Alfred and Guthrum. And during that century the successors of Alfred had gradually succeeded in recovering their hold upon the English nation. During the whole of this time, following Continental tribal usage, both English and Danes had presumably lived under their own laws and customs.

But whether it be right to speak of the Northmen of the time of King Alfred as Danes or not, it is necessary to distinguish the difference between the two invasions.

Cnut's invasion was avowedly intended to establish a kingdom, or rather to bring England within the area of his great Danish kingdom. Olaf was on the point of making himself King of Norway; and the founding of kingdoms was, so to speak, in the air. It was an era of conquest and Cnut's invasion of England was in fact the first step towards the Norman Conquest.

The Vikings who invaded England in the days of Alfred, on the other hand, were independent chieftains —the last of the class of the early Frankish and Anglo-Saxon type. Their invasion was not a Danish invasion in the sense that it came from a Danish kingdom. The Vikings of this earlier period were chieftains of moving armies living upon the country they invaded. Their armies were composed of Northmen, and, again to quote the words of Mr. Keary, 'in the history of the Scandinavian nations they were the representatives in the countries of their origin of a bygone or passing order of things '—' the opponents of the extended sort of kingship which was the new order of the day in Denmark, Sweden, and Norway.'[1]

Let us for a moment follow the course of the movements of these Viking armies which preceded the compact between Alfred and Guthrum.

In 867 the 'army' was in the North, took possession of York, and subdued Northumbria. In 868 Mercia was invaded, and till 871 the incursions were practically confined to Northumbria and Mercia, and parts of East Anglia. In 871 the invasion of Wessex commenced, and in the same year Alfred, on the death of his brother Ethelred, became King of Wessex. In 874 the 'army' was again chiefly in Mercia and Northumbria and began definitely to settle in the latter. The southern half of Northumbria became the Kingdom of York under Halfdan, A.D. 876.

The other part of the army under Guthrum proceeded to attack Wessex, and the winter of 877–8 was

---

[1] Catalogue of English Coins, Anglo-Saxon series. Introduction, p. xxxi, to vol. ii.

marked by the retirement of Alfred into the island of Æthelney.

In 878 came the victory of Æthandune, which was followed by the baptism of Guthrum and the partition of England. In 880 Guthrum and his army settled in what became the Danelaga. And in 886 the final compact was entered into between Alfred and Guthrum the text of which has been preserved. Compact between Alfred and Guthrum.

It will be convenient first to consider this compact and then the various fragments of Northumbrian and Mercian law the production or preservation of which may be traced to this period.

The text of the compact is preserved in the tenth-century Manuscript B. Its first clause defines the boundaries between that part of England which was to remain English and the Danelaga. With this matter at the moment we are not specially concerned. Then follows the most material clause (2):—

English and Danes equally dear.

And hi cwædon. gyf mon ofslægen wurðe, eal we letað efen dyrne, Engliscne ⁊ Denisce. ꝥ is to .viii. healf-marcum asodenes goldes. buton þam ceorle þe on gafol-lande sit ⁊ heora lysingon: þa syndon eac efen dyre. ægðer twa hund scyll::	And they ordained, if a man should be slain we estimate all equally dear, English and Danish, i.e. at viii half-marks of pure gold except the ceorl who sits on gafol land and their [the Danish] lysings, they also are equally dear, either at 200 scillings.
And gyf man cynges þegen beteo man-slihtas. ⁊ he hine ladian durre. do he ꝥ mid xii cynges þegnas ⁊ gyf mon þone man betyhð þe bið læssa maga. ladie hine xi his gelicena ⁊ anum cyninges þegene.	And if a man accuse a king's thane of manslaying and he dare to clear himself, let him do that with 12 king's thanes, and if any one accuse that man who is of less degree let him clear himself with 11 of his equals and with one king's thane.

Now, in the first place, it is evident that this text describes the wergeld of two classes or ranks of persons.

Dane and Englishman of the first class are to be held equally dear at eight half-marks of pure gold.

The other class embraces the Saxon 'ceorl who sits on gafol land' and the Danish lysing. These also are equally dear at 200 scillings.

Englishman put on a level with the Norse hauld, at the normal wergeld of 200 gold solidi or 1200 scillings.

Let us look at these two classes separately. The first class of Dane and English *men* without other definition are to be paid for by eight half-marks of gold. The money is Danish. Eight half-marks contained thirty-two ores. And this, as we have seen, at the Norse ratio of 1 : 8 was the same thing as 32 marks of silver. The wergeld of the hauld of the Gulathing law we found to be most probably 30 marks of silver. The Danish *man* of this clause thus seems to be represented in Norse law by the hauld. In other words, Guthrum from his point of view took the hauld as the typical freeman, just as we found him so taken in the Gulathing law.

It will be remembered that this wergeld of the hauld was equated with 96 cows and that in its gold value reckoned in wheat-grains it amounted to 200 Merovingian gold solidi.

From the English point of view it was not far otherwise. The twelve-hyndeman with a wergeld of 1200 scillings was evidently the typical freeman Alfred had in view. 1200 Mercian scillings of four pence, *i.e.* 4800 pence, at the Norse ratio of 1 : 8 equalled 600 gold tremisses or 200 gold solidi. 1200 Wessex scillings of five pence at a ratio of 1 : 10 would also equal 200 gold solidi.

The equation was therefore well within the range of reasonable compromise. And behind both these wergelds—that of the hauld and of the twelve-hyndeman—there seems to be the curious traditional (conscious or unconscious) reference so often repeated to the ancient normal wergeld of 200 gold solidi and the heavy gold mina. At this normal wergeld Dane and Englishman were to be held equally dear.

English ceorl on gafol land put on a level with the Norse leysing.

Turning now to the other class, the wergeld is described in English scillings and the wergeld is that of the twy-hyndeman—two hundred scillings—*i.e.* one sixth of the wergeld of the other class. On the Danish side the equivalent of the twy-hyndeman was the lysing, *i.e.* the 'leysing' or newly made freedman of the Gulathing law, who had not yet made his freedom-ale and whose wergeld was one sixth of that of the hauld 'according to his rett.'

Here again the correspondence is complete. The English twy-hyndeman is put by this compact on the same standing as to wergeld as the Norse leysing or newly made freedman who had not yet made his freedom-ale.

But we gain another point from this remarkable clause. We are warned by it not to be drawn too easily into a rash generalisation from the use of the Saxon word *ceorl.*

It is not the 'ceorl' *as such* who is the twy-hyndeman and put upon the same social level as the Danish lysing. It is clearly only the 'ceorl *who sits on gafol land.*' It is on the last words that the distinctive emphasis must be put. If we had nothing but this clause to guide us we might conclude that all above the 'ceorl who sits on gafol land' were twelve-hynde.

II. THE COURSE OF PROCEDURE IN PAYMENT OF WERGELD.

There are two statements of the course of procedure in the payment of wergelds which may conveniently be mentioned at this point. The first occurs in the 'Laws of King Edmund,' who reigned A.D. 940–946. And the other is contained in a fragment belonging probably to the time following soon after the Compact between Alfred and Guthrum.

King Edmund makes payment of wergeld voluntary.

King Edmund, in order to abate the 'manifold fightings' resulting from the system of feud and wergeld, made stringent regulations under which wergelds were to be claimed, making it voluntary on the part of the kindred to join in payment of the wergeld.

Gif hwa heonan-forð ænigne man ofslea ꝥ he wege sylf þa fæhðe butan he hy mid freonda fylste binnan twelf monðum forgylde be fullan were sy swa boren swa he sy. Gif hine þonne seo mægð forlæte & him foregyldan nellen þonne wille ic ꝥ eall seo mægð sy unfah. butan þam hand-dædan, gif hy him syþþan ne doð mete ne munde. Gif þonne syþþan hwilc his maga hine feormige þonne beo he scyldig ealles þæs þe he age wið þone cyning ⁊ wege þa fæhðe wið þa mægðe forþam hi hine forsocan ær. Gif þonne of þære oðre mægðe hwa wrace do on ænigum oðrum men butan on þam riht hand-dædan sy he gefah wið þone cyning ⁊ wið ealle his frynd & þolige ealles þæs þe he age.

(Edmund Secular Laws, s. 1.)

If any one henceforth slay any man that he himself bear the feud unless with the aid of his friends and within 12 months he compensate it with the full wer; be he born as he may be. But if his mægd forsake him and will not pay for him, then I will that all the kindred be *unfah* [free from the feud] except the perpetrator, if afterwards they do not give him either food or mund [protection]. But if any one of his kindred feed him, then be he liable in all that he possesses to the king and bear the feud with the kindred because they had previously forsaken him. But if anyone of the other kindred take vengeance upon any other man than the real perpetrator, let him be foe to the king and to all his friends and forfeit all that he owns.

Gif hwa cyrican gesece oþþe mine burh ⁊ hine man þær sece oþþe yflige þa þe ꝥ deð syn þær ylcan scyldige þe hit her beforan cwæð.

(2) If any one take refuge in a church or in my burh, and one there seek him or do him evil, be those who do that liable in the same that is heretofore ordained.

And ic nelle ꝥ ænig fyhte-wite oþþe man-bote forgifen sy.

(3) And I will not that any *fightwite* or *manbot* be forgiven.

This relaxation of the rules as to payment of wergeld seems to leave matters very much as they were, with the one exception that for the sake of peace and to lessen the risk of 'manifold fightings,' a year was given to the slayer's kindred to save his life by helping him to pay the wergeld if they chose, while if they chose to forsake him and did not harbour or help him in any way *they* were free. The kindred of the slain in the meantime were left to pursue their feud but only upon the slayer. This of course was another instance of the partial breaking down of the ancient tribal solidarity of the kindred in favour of the principle, long before adopted in some of the Continental codes, limiting the punishment of crime to the criminal himself.

Whether this innovation of King Edmund's was adhered to the evidence of the Laws of Henry I. may lead us to doubt, but for our purpose the law making the innovation is evidence of the ancient solidarity of the kindred, the attempt to loosen which had become necessary in the tenth century.

A clause which follows shows that it was expected that wergelds would still be paid:—

How wergelds were to be paid.

Witan scylon fæhðe settan ærest æfter folc-rihte slaga sceal his for-specan on hand syllan ⁊ se for-speca magum ꝥ se slaga wille betan wið mægðe. þonne

(7) The Witan shall appease feuds. First according to folkright the slayer shall give pledge to his *forespeca* and the forespeca to the kindred that the slayer will

syþþan gebyred ꝥ man sylle þæs slagan for-specan on hand ꝥ se slaga mote mid griðe nyr ⁊ sylf wæres weddian. Ðonne he þæs beweddod hæbbe þonne finde he þærto wær-borh, þonne ꝥ gedon sy þonne rære man cyninges munde of þam dæge on xxi niht gylde man heals-fang. þæs on xxi niht manbote. þæs on xxi niht þæs weres ꝥ frum-gyld.

make bot to the kindred. Then after that it is requisite that security be given to the slayer's forespeca that the slayer may in peace come near and himself give wed for the wer. When he has given wed for this let him find thereto a werborh. When that is done let the King's mund be levied.

Within 21 days from that day let the *halsfang* be paid.

21 days from that the manbot.

21 days from that the frumgeld of the wer.

Earlier statement of how wergelds were to be paid.

The further course of procedure is best given in the earlier fragment alluded to.

The fragment [1] is headed 'How a twelve-hyndeman shall be paid for.' It opens with the statement, 'A twelve-hyndeman's wer is twelve hundred scillings. A twy-hyndeman's wer is two hundred scillings.' And then it proceeds :—

The werborh.

Gif man ofslægen weorðe gylde hine man swa he geboren sy. And riht is ꝥ se slaga siþþan he weres beweddod hæbbe finde þærto wær-borh be þam þe þærto gebyrige ꝥ is æt twelf-hyndum were gebyriað twelf men to werborge, viii fæderen-mægðe ⁊ iiii medren-mægðe.

If any one be slain let him be paid for according to his birth. And it is right that the slayer after he has given wed for the wer find in addition a *werborh* according as shall thereto belong, that is to a twelve-hynde's wer twelve men are necessary as *werborh*, viii of the paternal kin and iv of the maternal kin.

This is in accordance with the clause in Alfred and Guthrum's compact, which, however, makes the additional provision by way of precaution that one

[1] Thorpe (p. 75) appends this clause to the so-called Laws of Edward and Guthrum. But Schmid considers it as a fragment and places it in his *Anhang vii.*

of the twelve co-swearers must be a king's-thane. The clause continues:—

Ðonne ꝥ gedon sy þonne rære man cyninges munde, ꝥ is ꝥ hy ealle gemænum handum of ægðere mægðe on anum wæpne þam semende syllan ꝥ cyninges mund stande.

When this is done, then let the king's mund be established, that is, that they all of either kindred, with their hands in common upon one weapon, engage to the mediator that the king's mund shall stand.

The king's mund.

The king's mund-byrd, as we have seen, was equal to five pounds according to both English and Kentish custom.

Of þam dæge on xxi nihtan gylde man cxx scill. to heals-fange æt twelf-hyndum were. Heals-fang gebyreð bearnum broðrum ⁊ fæderan ne gebyreð nanum mæge ꝥ [feoh] bute þam þe sy binnan cneowe.

Of þam dæge þe ꝥ heals-fang agolden sy on xxi nihtan gylde man þa man-bote þæs on xxi nihtan ꝥ fyht-wite þæs on xxi nihtan þæs weres ꝥ frum-gyld ⁊ swa forð ꝥ fulgolden sy on þam fyrste þe witan geræden. Siþþan man mot mid lufe ofgan gif man [wille] fulle freondrædene habban.

Eal man sceal æt cyrliscum were be þære mæðe don þe him to-gebyreð swa we be twelf-hyndum tealdan.

In xxi days from that day let cxx shillings be paid as heals-fang at a twelve-hynde's wer. Heals-fang belongs to the children, brothers and paternal uncles: that money belongs to no kinsman except to those that be within the knee.

The heals-fang.

In xxi days from the day that the heals-fang is paid let the manbot be paid. In xxi days from this the fightwite. In xxi days from this the 'frumgyld' of the wer; and so forth till it be fully paid within the time that the witan have appointed. After this they may depart with love if they desire to have full friendship.

The man-bot and fightwite and then the wer-geld.

All men shall do with regard to the wer of a ceorl that which belongs to his condition like as we have said about a twelve-hyndeman.

These steps in the procedure are very nearly the same as those quoted in the so-called 'Laws of Henry I.' and these clauses may probably be looked upon as more or less repeating for the benefit of both peoples what Anglo-Saxon custom may have been before the Viking invasions of England. But of this we cannot be certain.

III. FRAGMENTS OF MERCIAN AND THE NORTH PEOPLE'S LAW.

Fragments preserved of ancient custom.

We now have to consider a group of fragments of uncertain date which seem to belong to the period of the Northmen's settlement in Northumbria and invasions in Mercia.

The settlement of the Viking invaders made it necessary to fix the relation of their wergelds to those of the conquered English, and also to gather up fragments of Mercian custom. As the Dooms of Mercian kings have not come down to us, these fragments have a special value.

The importance of Mercia in King Offa's time gives a special interest to any information on Mercian custom. And in other respects, scanty though it be, the retrospect of early Anglo-Saxon custom from the invaders' point of view could ill be spared.

Under Mercian law the oath of twelve-hyndeman = that of six ceorls.

There are two valuable fragments on Mercian law.

The first is as follows:—

Be Merciscan Aðe	*Of the Mercian Oath*
Twelf-hyndes mannes að forstent vi ceorla að forþam gif man þone twelf-hyndan man wrecan sceolde he bið full-wrecan on syx ceorlan ⁊ his wer-gyld bið six ceorla wer-gyld.	A twelve-hyndeman's oath stands for six ceorls' oaths; because if a man should avenge a twelve-hyndeman he will be fully avenged on six ceorls and his wergild will be six ceorls' wergilds.

This fragment of Mercian law is preceded in the group of fragments 'on oaths' in Thorpe's edition of the Laws by the following, which may or may not be of Mercian origin :—

Mæsse-preostes að ⁊ woruld-þegenes is on Engla-laga geteald efen-dyre ⁊ for þam seofon ciric-hadan þe se mæsse-preost þurh Godes gif geþeah ꝥ he hæfde he bið þegen-rihtes wyrðe.

A mass-priest's oath and a secular thane's are in English-law reckoned of equal value; and by reason of the seven church-degrees that the mass-priest through the grace of God has acquired he is worthy of thane-right.

Mass-priest's oath = that of the thane.

The other fragment of Mercian law is as follows :—

Ceorles wer-gild is on Myrcna lage cc scill. Ðegnes wer-gild is syx swa micel ꝥ bið xii hund scill. Ðonne bið cynges anfeald wer-gild vi þegna wer be Myrcna lage ꝥ is xxx þusend sceatta ⁊ ꝥ bið ealles cxx punda. Swa micel is þæs wer-gildes on folces folc-rihtes be Myrcna lage. And for þam cyne-dome geborað oðer swilc to bote on cyne-gilde. Se wer gebirað magum ⁊ seo cyne-bot þam leodum.

A ceorl's wergeld is by Mercian law cc scillings. A thane's wergeld is six times as much, i.e. xii hundred scillings. Then is a king's simple wergeld vi thanes' wer by Mercian law, i.e. xxx thousand sceatts, and that is altogether cxx pounds. So much is the wergeld in the people's folk-right by Mercian law. And for the 'Cynedom' there is due another such sum as *bot* for *cyne-gild.* The wer belongs to the kindred and the cynebot to the people.

Mercian wergelds.

The Mercian wergeld of both twy-hynde and twelve-hynde men is thus stated in scillings, as usual, and the king's wergeld—six times the thane's—would equal 7200 scillings. The Mercian scilling was 4*d.*, and thus, as stated in the text, the king's wergeld would equal exactly 120*l.* or 28,800 pence or sceatts (in round numbers 30,000 sceatts).

This is useful as evidence that the sceatt of this Mercian wergeld was the silver penny of the Anglo-Saxon currency of 28·8 wheat-grains—*i.e.* of the *Sceatt series*—before Offa and Alfred, following the example of Charlemagne, superseded the 'sceatt' by the 'penny' of 32 wheat-grains.

Fragment of North People's Law.

The fragments printed by Thorpe under the heading 'North People's Law' and by Schmid in his 'Anhang VII.' seem to belong to Northumbria or more generally to the Danelaga. Schmid suggests that the 'North people' were the North folk of East Anglia. This, however, is perhaps more than doubtful, especially when it is considered that the Viking 'armies' had established themselves, not only in East Anglia and Mercia, but still more completely in Northumbria, many years before the struggle with Wessex had ended in the compact between Alfred and Guthrum.

The fragment of 'North People's Law'[1] opens with the statement that the king's gild is 30,000 *thrymsas*—15,000 for the wergeld and 15,000 for the people (*leodum*).

In another MS. the wording follows the statement of Mercian law very closely, and agrees with the above in describing the amount in thrymsas.

Wergelds paid in thrymsas of threepence.

Ðæs cyninges wer-gyld sie mid Engla cynne on folc-riht þryttig þusend þrimsa ⁊ þæra xv .M. sien þæs wæres ⁊ oðra xv .M. þæs cynedomes. Se wære belympað to þam mægðe þæs cyne-cynnes ⁊ ꝥ cynebot to þam land-leod.	Let the king's wergeld be with the English race by folkright, 30,000 thrymsas, and of these let 15,000 be for the wer and the other 15,000 for the *cynedom*. The wer belongs to the kindred of the king and the cynebot to the people.

Now, in the first place, what was the *thrymsa*, which occurs in these clauses for the first time?

A statement a little further on in one of the two

[1] Schmid, *Anhang vii.* 2; Thorpe, p. 79.

texts of the same fragment fixes the value of the thrymsa at three pence.[1]

The statement of 'North People's Law' proceeds as follows: [2]—

Arces ⁊ æðelinges wer-gyld is xv þusend þrymsa.	(2) An archbishop's and an ætheling's wergeld is xv thousand thrymsas.
Biscopes ⁊ ealdormannes viii þusend þrymsa.	(3) A bishop's and an ealdorman's viii thousand thrymsas.
Holdes ⁊ cyninges heah-gerefan iiii þusend þrymsa.	(4) A hold's and a king's high-reeve's iv thousand thrymsas.
Mæsse-þegnes ⁊ woruld-þegnes ii þusend þrymsa.	(5) A mass thane's and a secular thane's ii thousand thrymsas.
Ceorles wer-gild is cc. ⁊ lxvi þrim. ꝥ bið ii hund scill be Myrcna lage.	(6) A ceorl's wergeld is cc and lxvi thrymsas, that is cc scillings by Mercian law.

Put into tabular form these wergelds would be as follows in thrymsas and Wessex and Mercian scillings:—

	Thrymsas		Wessex shillings of 5*d*.	Mercian shillings of 4*d*.
King's wergeld 15,000, cynebot 15.000	30000	=	18000	22500
Archbishop's and Ætheling's . . .	15000	=	9000	11250
Bishop's and Ealdorman's	8000	=	4800	6000
Holdr's and King's high-reeve's . .	4000	=	2400	3000
Mass thane's and secular thane's . .	2000	=	1200	1500
Ceorl's	266⅔	=	160	200

The ceorl has a twyhynde wergeld in Mercian shillings and the thane a twelve-hynde wergeld in Wessex shillings. There seems to be so far some confusion. But on the whole this reckoning seems to justify the opinion generally held that the Northmen coming as conquerors into Northumbria or the Danelaga had, at the date of these fragments, doubled the wergeld of the hold or hauld as compared with that of the English thane.

[1] A ceorl's wergeld is cclxvi thrymsas, *i.e.* cc scillings by Mercian law. $266\frac{2}{3} \times 3 = 800$ pence or 200 Mercian scyllings of 4 pence.

[2] From the text of MS. D.

Wergeld of hauld double that of the thane, but after Alfred's victory both equally dear.

If, as seems reasonable, these fragments may be referred to the period following upon the Viking conquest and settlement in Northumbria and the foundation of Halfdan's kingdom of York (A.D. 876), then the doubled wergeld of the hauld may be perhaps the high-water mark as it were of the invasion —the point of vantage at which it was natural for the conquerors to treat the conquered as a tributary race. And if it may rightly be so regarded, then it gives an added interest to the compact between King Alfred and Guthrum in 886. For then, the tide of battle having turned, the two kings at length met on equal terms and, undoing the earlier unequal settlement, now agreed to make Dane and Englishman equally dear.

A still more interesting point than the doubling of the conquering Hold's wergeld as compared with the conquered thane's is found in the subsequent clauses of this fragment, which seem to refer back to ancient tradition as regards the position of the non-Saxon subjects of Anglo-Saxon kings.[1]

Chance given to the Wilisc man to rise as in the laws of Ine.

And gif Wilisc man geþeo ꝥ he hæbbe hiwisc landes ⁊ mæge cyninges gafol forð-bringan, þonne bið his wergild cxx scill. And gif he ne geþeo buton to healfne hide þonne si his wer lxx scill.	(7) And if a Wiliscman thrive so that he have *hiwisc landes* and can bring forth the king's gafol, then his wergeld shall be cxx scillings. And if he only comes up to a half hide then shall his wer be lxxx scillings.
And gif he ænig land næbbe ⁊ þeah freoh sy forgilde hine man mid lxx scill.	(8) And if he have not any land and yet be free, let him be paid for with lxx scillings.

[1] The fragment itself is a combination of two or more. But the statement of wergelds in *thrymsas* seems to unite them. Schmid also points out that the *eorl* had not yet superseded the ealdorman. See *Einleitung*, p. lxv.

The other version is practically the same :—

And Wealisc-monnes weregild gif he beo to tham gewelegod ꝥ he hyred ⁊ eht age ⁊ þam cyng gafol gyldan mæg hit bið þon ccxx scill. Ac he ne bið butan to healf hyda gerysen þonne sie his were lxxx scill.

Gif he land næbbe ac bið freoh gyld mon lxx scill.

(7) And a Wealisc-man's wergeld if he be so enriched that he has family and goods (*hyred and eht*) and can pay the King's gafol shall be ccxx scillings [? cxx].

And if he be risen ut to half a hide, then shall his own wer be lxxx scillings.

(8) If he have no land but is free let him be paid for with lxx scillings.

Now 'hiwisc' and 'hyred' both seem to mean *family*. In a roundabout indirect way 'familia' and *hide* meant apparently very much the same thing, but as the word *hide* is used in the same clause the more direct meaning may surely in this case be the important one.

It is probable that these clauses are variations or fuller expressions of the tradition described in c. 32 of King Ine's Laws, which is as follows :—

Gif Wylisc mon hæbbe hide londes his wer bið c. xx scill., gif he þonne hæbbe healfe lxxx scill., gif he nænig hæbbe lx scillinga.

If a Wylisc man have a hide of land his 'wer' shall be cxx*s.*, but if he have half a hide lxxx*s.*, if he have none lx *s.*

And the additional information amounts practically to this—that the possession of a hide seems to have been held generally equivalent to the possession of a family homestead—family and goods—enabling a man to pay the king's gafol.

It is when we pass on from these clauses to the next that fresh and welcome light seems to be gained upon the connection of the growth of a family and kindred with rise in status and social rank from a ceorlisc or twy-hynde position to that of the Gesithcund or twelve-hynde position. We are now no longer dealing with the Wylisc man but with the ordinary twy-hynde ceorl. And the mention of the payments in thrymsas reminds us that we are still looking at things from the North people's point of view.

The clauses in the two versions are as follows :—

How under early custom a ceorl could rise into the twelve-hynde class.

ix. And gif ceorlisc man geþeo ꝥ he hæbbe v hida landes to cynges ut-ware ⁊ hine man ofslea forgilde man hine mid twam þusend þrimsa.	ix. Gif ceorl sie gewelegod to þam þ [he] age v hyda landes ⁊ mon hine ofslea gyld hine mon mid ii .M. þrimsa.
x. And þeah he geþeo ꝥ he hæbbe helm ⁊ byrnan ⁊ golde fæted sweord, gif he ꝥ land nafað he bið ceorl swa þeah.	x. And gif he begytað ꝥ he hæbbe byrne ⁊ helm ⁊ ofergyldenene sweord, þeah þe he land næbbe he bið siðcund.
xi. And gif his sunu ⁊ his sunu-sunu ꝥ geþeoð ꝥ hi swa micel landes habban siþþan bið se ofsprinc gesiðcundes cynnes be twam þusendum.	xi. And gif his sunu ⁊ þæs sun-sunu ꝥ begyten ꝥ he swa micel landes habbað sien hiora after-gengas þæs siðcunda[n] cynnes ⁊ gyld þam mon mid ii .M. þrimsa.
xii. And gif hi ꝥ nabbað ne to þam geþeon ne magan gilde man cirlisce.	

And they may be translated thus :—

9. And if a ceorlish man thrive so that he have v hides of land to the king's *utware* and any one slay him, let him be paid for with 2000 thrymsas.[1]	9. If a ceorl be enriched to that degree that he have 5 hides of land to the king's utware and any one slay him, let him be paid for with 2000 thrymsas.
10. And though he thrive so that he have a helm and coat of mail, and a sword ornamented with gold, if he have not that land he is nevertheless a ceorl.	10. And if he acquire so that he have a coat of mail and a helmet and an overgilded sword, if he have not that land he is [? not] sithcund.

[1] 2000 thrymsas of 3*d*. equalled 1200 Wessex scillings of 5*d*., so that the ceorl with five hides to the king's utware became a twelve-hynde man. There is no allusion to the six-hynde status as a halfway step towards the gesithcund status. And the use of the word 'gesithcund' seems to throw back the original date of these clauses to that of Ine's law, the word not being used in later laws. See Schmid's *Glossary*, sub voce 'Gesith.'

11. And if his son and his son's son so thrive that they have so much land, afterwards the offspring shall be of gesithcund race at 2000 (thrymsas).

12. And if they have not that nor to that can thrive, let them be paid for as ceorlish.

11. And if his son and the son's son acquire that they have so much land, let their successors be of the sithcund kin and let them be paid for with 2000 thrymsas.

These passages are very important, as the most direct evidence we possess of the way in which under early Anglo-Saxon custom families became *gesithcund* by the gradual growth of a kindred whose kinsmen, like the odal-men of the Norse laws, could reckon four generations in succession of sufficient landholding.

The evidence is all the more interesting because it seems to come from the point of view of the Norse or Danish invaders making inquiry respecting English tradition and recording what had once been the custom of the conquered districts.

Another precious fragment, with further information.

The same remark applies equally to another of these valuable fragments—'Of people's ranks and law.' It, too, seems to look back and to record what once had been the custom of the conquered people.

Hit wæs hwilum on Engla lagum ꝥ leod ⁊ lagu for be geþincðum ⁊ þa wæron [þeod-] witan weorðscipes wyrðe ælc be his mæðe, eorl ⁊ ceorl, þegen ⁊ þeoden.

1. It was whilom, in the laws of the English, that people and law went by ranks, and then were the Witan of worship worthy each according to his condition, eorl and ceorl, thegen and theoden.

These are the phrases of a writer looking back with regret upon ancient custom which to him is past or passing away.

After this follow clauses in one of which the

word *hyrede* and the phrase 'having so many hides to the king's *utware*' again occur, words that seem to suggest that this fragment, while describing ancient English custom, hails from a somewhat similar source as the 'North People's Law.'

And gif ceorl geþeah ꝥ he hæfde fullice fif hida agenes landes, cirican ⁊ kycenan, bell-hus ⁊ burh-geat, setl ⁊ sunder-note, on cynges healle þonne wæs he þonon-forð, þegen-rihtes weorðe.

2. And if a ceorl thrived so that he had fully five hides of his own land, church and kitchen, bell-house and burh-geat, seat and special duty in the King's hall, then was he thenceforth of thane-right worthy.

This seems to be practically identical with clause 9 of the previous fragment. Then follows :—

And gif þegen geþeah ꝥ he þenode cynge ⁊ his rad-stefne rad on his hirede, gif he þonne hæfde þegen þe him filigde þe to cinges ut-ware fif hida hæfde ⁊ on cynges sele his hlaforde þenode & þriwa mid his ærende gefore to cinge se moste syþþan mid his foraðe his hlaford aspelian æt mistlican neodan ⁊ his onspæce geræcan mid rihte swa hwær swa he sceolde.

And if a thane thrived so that he served the King and on his summons (*rád-stefne*) rode with his household (*hirede*), if he then had a thane who him followed, who to the King's *utware* five hides had, and in the King's hall served his lord [the thane] and thrice with his errand went to the King, he might thenceforth with his foreoath his lord represent at various needs and his plaint lawfully conduct wherever he ought.

And seþe swa geþogenne forwyrht an næfde swore for sylfne æfter his rihte oþþe his þolode.

4. And he who so prosperous a vicegerent had not, swore for himself according to his right, or it forfeited.

And gif þegen geþeah ꝥ he wearð to eorle þonne wæs he syþþan eorl-rihtes weorðe.

5. And if a thane thrived, so that he became an eorl, then was he thenceforth of eorl-right worthy.

These passages we shall have to consider further when we sum up the evidence upon the Anglo-Saxon division of classes.

The ceorl must rise into direct service to the king and to having a kindred around him.

But there are two peculiarities which may be marked here as pointing to the archaic character of these precious fragments. First, the alliteration and rhythmical character of some of them, which points to an early and traditional origin, and, secondly, the direct relations of the classes mentioned to the king. The Wilisc man has to bring forth the king's gafol. The ceorl who has five hides has them to the king's utware and he becomes gesithcund and thane-right worthy with special duty in the king's hall, while the thane is all the greater when he has a thane under him who has himself five hides to the king's utware and goes with his errands to the king.

These are marks of direct relationship and service of the gesithcund classes to the king, to which we shall have to recur. They seem to point to the gesithcund class with its completeness of kindred as a privileged class in a semi-official position and from which the king's officials were chosen. It is not until this relationship by service to the king has become established that a ceorl finds an entrance into the gesithcund class, and he does not become eligible for such service till he is surrounded by an adequate kindred.

In the meantime we may be thankful to the exigences of the Viking invasions for the preservation of these valuable fragments of ancient custom which might otherwise have been lost.

CHAPTER XIII.

EARLY ANGLO-SAXON CUSTOM.

I. KING ALFRED'S DOOMS.

Alfred's laws not earlier than the Compact with Guthrum.

In order that the examination of early Anglo-Saxon custom may be free from the intrusion of elements introduced by the Northmen, it is necessary to go back to evidence of earlier date than the laws of King Alfred. Though collected mainly from earlier sources, these laws took their present form probably after the Compact with Guthrum had been made.

They do not profess to be a full statement of early West-Saxon law. King Alfred himself declares that he dared not add much of his own, 'But those things which I met with either of the days of Ine my kinsman, or of Offa, King of the Mercians, or of Ethelbert—those which seemed to me the rightest I have here gathered together and rejected the others.'

Under these circumstances it will be more convenient to refer back to King Alfred's laws when needful in connection with the earlier evidence than to consider them as a separate whole.

There is, however, one subject upon which the evidence of King Alfred's laws may properly be considered before passing on to the earlier laws.

We have seen that in the Compact with Guthrum the Anglo-Saxon 'ceorl who sits on gafol-land' and who was made 'equally dear' at 200 scillings with the Danish lysing was, if the words may be taken strictly, not necessarily a typical or representative member of the ceorlisc class as a whole. Only some of the ceorlisc class may have been gafol-geldas on other people's land. It is important, therefore, to examine whether King Alfred's laws afford contemporary evidence that the ceorlisc and the twy-hynde classes were practically the same, and whether they were, as a rule, gafol-geldas. We have seen, from the precious fragments before quoted, that under ancient 'English' law a ceorl could rise out of the twy-hynde class and become entitled to a twelve-hynde wergeld of 2000 thrymsas.

Were the terms ceorl and gafol-gelda equivalent?

If such a statement had been found in West-Saxon law, the inference might at first sight be that the ceorlisc class could hardly have been mainly a class of gafol-geldas. The laws of Alfred surely ought to throw some light upon this important matter.

In section 39 is the following :—

The ceorl below the six-hynde-man.

Gif hwa on ciorlisces monnes flette gefeohte mid syx scill. gebete þam ceorl. Gif he wæpne gebrede ⁊ no feohte sie bi healfum þam. Gif syx-hyndum þissa hwæðer gelimpe þriefealdlice [arise be þære ciorliscan bote. xii-hyndum men twyfealdlice] be þæs syx-hyndan bote.	If any one fight in a ceorlisc man's flet with six scillings let him make bot to the ceorl. If he draw his weapon and fight not let it be half of that. If, however, either of these happen to a six-hynde man let it increase three-foldly according to the ceorlisc bot; to a twelve-hyndeman two-foldly according to the six-hynde's bot.

The ceorlisc man in this section takes the place

of the twyhynde man in contrast with the six-hynde and twelve-hynde classes. The payments are the bots payable to the owners for fighting within their sacred precinct or inclosure, and the amounts following the proportions of the wergelds of the three classes are :—

Ceorlisc man's	6 scillings
Six-hyndeman	18 „
Twelve-hyndeman	36 „

In this section the ceorlisc class seems clearly to take the place of the twy-hynde class. They seem to be identical.

Section 40 gives similar evidence, in connection with the *burg-* or *burh*-bryce or breach of the fence of the sacred precinct.

Cyninges burg-bryce bið cxx scill. Ærcebiscopes hund nigontig scill. Oðres biscepes & ealdormonnes lx scill. Twelf-hyndes monnes xxx scill. Syx-hyndes monnes xv scill. Ceorles edorbryce v scill. . . .	The King's burh-bryce shall be cxx scillings. An archbishop's ninety scillings. Any other bishop's and an earldorman's lx scillings. A twelve-hyndeman's xxx scillings. A six-hyndeman's xv scillings. A ceorl's edorbreach v scillings. . . .

The ceorl twy-hynde.

Here again the ceorl takes the place of the twy-hyndeman, and the burh-bryce is graduated accordingly, the twelve-hyndeman's being six times the ceorl's.

King's	120 scillings
Archbishop's	90 „
Ealdorman's or bishop's . . .	60 „
Twelve-hynde's	30 „
Six-hynde's	15 „
Ceorl's edorbreach	5 „

There may well be some delicate significance in the word *burh*-bryce being applied only to the twelve-hynde or six-hynde men, and not to the ceorl, as though the word *burh* could not be applied to the ceorl's homestead. His 'flet,' surrounded by its *edor* or hedge, was perhaps too humble to be classed with the moated or walled enclosure of the *burh* of the higher landed classes without a change of epithet. But there is nothing to show that the ceorl of this clause is not identical with the ordinary twy-hyndeman.

Lastly, in sections 10 and 18 the three classes are again described as twelve-hynde, six-hynde, and ceorlisc; while in sections 29, 30, and 31 they are described as twelve-hynde, six-hynde, and twy-hynde.

All this seems to show that for general purposes 'twy-hynde' and 'ceorlisc' were convertible terms.

It can hardly be said that there is anything in King Alfred's laws making a distinction between the twy-hynde class and the ceorlisc class. There seems to be nothing to suggest that the twy-hynde wergeld was confined to any particular section of the ceorlisc class. And therefore, so far as the laws of Alfred are concerned, the description of the twy-hynde class in the Compact with Guthrum as gafol-geldas equally dear with the Danish lysing would seem to apply generally to the ceorlisc class as a whole. And this being so, it would seem probable that, speaking broadly, by King Alfred's time the chief practical division of classes had already resolved itself into that between the landed classes on the one hand and their gafol-paying tenants on the other.

Ceorls must be mostly gafol-geldas.

It is quite true that under King Alfred's laws there is the six-hynde class between the twelve-hynde and the twy-hynde or ceorlisc class; but his laws tell us nothing about this six-hynde class except what may be inferred from the fact that its members certainly were not included in the ceorlisc class. It can hardly be likely that King Alfred could, in his compact with Guthrum, have confined the twy-hynde class to the 'ceorl who sits on gafol-land,' leaving out the six-hynde class altogether, if, in his laws, he meant by the six-hynde class the ceorls who did not sit on gafol-land. It might have been possible to suppose that he used the word 'ceorl' in his laws in a wider sense, as including both twelve-hynde and twy-hynde, had he not introduced the six-hynde class between them and restricted the meaning of the word 'ceorlisc' to the twy-hynde class. He used it apparently to distinguish the twy-hynde from the other classes which by inference were not ceorlisc.

What the six-hynde class was and what the ceorlisc class was under West-Saxon law two centuries earlier than King Alfred's day must be left to be discovered from the evidence of the Dooms of Ine.

The mund-byrd or borh-bryce of various classes.

In the meantime, the consideration of the position of the ceorlisc class having brought before us the penalties for breach of the precinct and for fighting within the precinct of the various classes, it may be well to consider also the evidence of King Alfred's laws upon the mund-byrd or borh-bryce of what we may regard perhaps as the official classes, and in which apparently, at this date, even the twelve-hynde man had no part.

The mund-byrd or borh-bryce seems to be confined to those in official or judicial position.

Already in King Alfred's laws we have lost the

word 'grith' as we had already in Cnut's laws lost the later phrase 'sac and soc,' but the tribal principle underlying the meaning of the words remains the same and becomes all the clearer as we go back in the evidence.

In s. 3, the borh-bryce and mund-byrd of the king are stated to be *five pounds of* 'mærra pæninga,'[1] an archbishop's three pounds, and those of the ealdorman and lesser bishops two pounds, exactly as they were reported to have been in Cnut's time in the 'grith-law' of the South Angles.[2]

Its tribal origin.

The almost indiscriminate use of the two terms in this clause suggests again the very slight distinction between them. The man who by giving his pledge placed himself artificially, so to speak, under the mund or protection of a person in a judicial position or authority and broke his pledge became guilty of borh-bryce or mund-byrd, it hardly mattered which. The penalty apparently included both crimes in one. If we might use the Brehon phrase it was the *eneclann*, or honour price of the person whose dignity was injured, which had to be paid.

But, as we have seen, these penalties were not only personal but also connected with the sanctity of what under Brehon law was called the 'maigin' or precinct. The Brehon tract which declares the extent of the 'inviolable precinct' of the 'boaire-chief' to reach as far as he can throw a spear or hammer from the door of his house, also states that those of higher chieftains extended by multiples of this accord-

---

[1] *I.e.* of pure silver. Compare the same phrase 'de novis et meris denariis' in the *Edictum Pistense*, A.D. 864, quoted *supra*, p. 191, n.

[2] See *supra*, p. 344.

ing to their honour-price, so that the inviolable precinct of the *ri-tuath* extended to sixty-four spear-casts from his door.[1] We have already quoted a fragment fixing the extent of the king's 'grith' at 'three miles and three furlongs and three acre breadths and nine feet and nine hand-breadths and nine barleycorns from the burhgeat where the king is.'[2]

The ceorl or gafolgelda had a flet the peace of which could be broken.

Under King Alfred's laws, as we have seen, the penalties for breaking into this precinct and committing crimes in it were payable to the person whose 'peace' was thus broken, and were not confined to the official classes as the mund-byrd and borh-bryce were. They went back to the tribal root-idea of the sanctity of the hearth and homestead, of every tribesman. They extended from the king to the ceorl through all grades. The penalties for fighting within the precinct were practically the same in amount as those for the breaking into it. The penalty for fighting in the ceorlisc-man's 'flet' was practically the same as that for breaking through his 'edor' into it.

When all these penalties are put side by side in the form of a table two points become evident.

First, how far removed the social position of the twelve-hyndeman was from that of the ealdorman. The penalty for fighting within his precinct is not much more than a third of that of the bishop and ealdorman, the inference being that his official position was much lower than the ealdorman's.

Secondly, when we compare the figures in the three columns, while the burh-bryce and fightwite of

[1] *Ancient Laws of Ireland*, vol. iv. p. 227.

[2] See *supra*, p. 345.

the twelve-hynde, six-hynde, and twy-hynde classes are both graduated in proportion to their wergelds and very closely resemble one another, it is curious to notice that the fightwite is based upon a duo decimal and the burh-bryce on a decimal system of reckoning, as if they had been derived from different original sources. If King Alfred had originated them he would probably have made them alike.

In the following statement, collected from the several sections of King Alfred's Laws for purposes of comparison and future reference, the amounts are stated in Wessex scillings of five pence.

	Borh-bryce and mund-byrd	Burh-bryce	Fightwite
Of the king . .	(s. 3) (5 lbs) 240 *s.*	(s. 40) 120 *s.*	(s. 7) (in the king's doom)
Of the archbishop .	(3 lbs) 144 *s.*	90 *s.*	(s. 15) 150 *s.*
Of other bishops and ealdorman . .	(2 lbs) 96 *s.*	60 *s.*	(s. 15) 100 *s.*
Of do. in his 'gemot' .			(s. 38) 120 *s.*
Of the twelve-hyndeman . . .		30 *s.*	(s. 39) 36 *s.*
Of the six-hyndeman .		15 *s.*	(s. 39) 18 *s.*
Of the ceorlisc man or twy-hynde man .		5 *s.*	(s. 39) 6 *s.*

II. THE DIALOGUE OF EGBERT, ARCHBISHOP OF YORK A.D. 732–766. ECCLESIASTICAL OATHS AND WERGELDS.

There is a gulf of nearly two centuries in the West-Saxon evidence between the laws of Alfred and the 'Dooms' of Ine.[1]

[1] Ine came to the throne in A.D. 688, and Alfred's treaty with Guthrum was in A.D. 880.

We are taken at a leap, not only beyond all thought of the Northmen's invasions, but also half a century behind another great epoch of European importance.

The Empire of Charlemagne formed a kind of watershed in Anglo-Saxon as in European history, and was marked, as we have seen, by a permanent change in the currency of the Western world.

Position of Northumbria before the time of Charlemagne.

The Courts of Offa and Egbert were intimately connected with the Imperial Court of Charlemagne, and the transition from the early Anglo-Saxon currency of sceatts to that of the heavier pence was a typical result of the influence of the Empire. It may be that the supremacy of Wessex under Egbert was indirectly another result of it.

The kingdom of Egbert did not extend over Northumbria, and Northumbria had its own independent connection with the Court of Charlemagne. It had its own mode of monetary reckoning in 'thrymsas,' and from the Northumbrian fragments already examined we have gained some glimpses into its ancient customs.

The document next to be examined refers to Northumbria, and, as it dates from the period immediately preceding the time of Charlemagne, it helps to bridge over the gulf between the Laws of Alfred and Ine.

Egbert, Archbishop of York, A.D. 750.

It is in the form of a Dialogue or set of questions put to Egbert, Archbishop of York, by his priests, with his answers thereto, and its date may be about A.D. 750.

Egbert, Archbishop of York, was an important figure in Anglo-Saxon history. The brother of

Eadbert, the Northumbrian king, the recipient on his accession to his episcopal dignity of the remarkable letter of Bede describing the religious anarchy of his diocese, the founder of the great school at York, in which his pupil Alcuin was educated and from which he migrated to the Court of Charles the Great, Egbert was an important personage, and the centre of beneficent influence in the Northumbrian church and kingdom.

Moreover, this document, so far as it goes and as regards the matters mentioned in it, deals with the questions raised by it avowedly from an ecclesiastical point of view. The great ecclesiastic comes down upon his diocese from a wider world. He had been educated and ordained deacon at Rome. And just as in the monastic rules of St. Benedict Roman weights and measures were adhered to, so when this archbishop has to speak of money matters, ignoring all local currencies, he still thinks and speaks and calculates in the terms of the Roman Imperial currency, and not in Anglo-Saxon sceatts and scillings, or in the thrymsas of Northumbrian usage.

His Roman and clerical point of view.

The Dialogue contains several interesting clauses.

The first to be noticed is in answer to the question as to the value to be attached to the oaths of the bishop, priest, deacon, and monk. The reply is:—

What to be the value of the oaths of clerics.

Ordines supradicti, secundum gradus promotionis, habeant potestatem protestandi: presbiter secundum numerum cxx tributariorum; diaconus vero juxta numerum lx manentium; monachus	The said orders according to their grade of promotion shall have power of protestation. The priest to the number of cxx tributarii; the deacon up to the number of lx '*manentes*;'

vero secundum numerum xxx tributariorum, sed hoc in criminali causa. Cæterum si de terminis agrorum oritur altercatio, presbitero liceat juramenti sui adtestatione terram videlicet unius tributarii in jus transferre æcclesiæ. Duobus quoque diaconis id ipsum conceditur. Testificatio vero trium monachorum in id ipsum sufficiat.	the monk to the number 'xxx tributarii,' i.e. in a criminal cause. But if the dispute has arisen about the boundaries of lands it shall be lawful to the priest on attestation of his oath to transfer, into the right of the church, land, i.e. of one *tributarius*. To two deacons also the same is conceded. Let attestation of three monks suffice for the same.

Now, it seems very unlikely that such a question as this about the value of oaths should be asked of the Archbishop if it had already been settled by law in Northumbria. And so we seem to see him here making a claim and laying down a principle for the first time in Northumbria the following of which resulted in his priests being put upon a par with the secular thane as regards the value of their oaths.

In Mercia priest's oath of same value as that of the thane.

The principle that one man's oath was worth more than another's we have seen already stated in the undated fragment on 'Mercian oaths,' which very possibly represented ancient tradition.

> A twelve-hynde oath stands for six ceorls' oaths, because if a man should avenge a twelve-hyndeman he will be fully avenged on six ceorls and his wergeld will be six ceorls' wergelds (p. 360).

And, further, the right of the priest to be put on equal footing with the thane we have seen recognised in another fragment.

> A mass priest's oath and a secular thane's are in English law reckoned of equal value, and by reason of the seven church degrees that the mass priest through grace of God has acquired, he is worthy of thane-right (p. 361).

The same principle was recognised in the further fragment on the North People's wergelds.

The usual statement in Continental and Anglo-Saxon laws as regards compurgation is that a man must clear himself by his oath and the oaths of so many oath-helpers. But in the Laws of Ine, with which the Archbishop was doubtless conversant, another method was followed in some cases. A man must clear himself, not with the oaths of so many oath-helpers, but with an oath of so many *hides*. The claim of the Archbishop seems to favour the view, suggested but hardly established by various passages in the Laws of Ine, that the twelve-hynde-man's oath was reckoned at 120 hides.[1]

Oaths of so many hides.

All that one can say is that the Archbishop in claiming that the Northumbrian priest's oath should be regarded as one of '120 tributarii' seems to have had in his mind what was afterwards generally conceded, *i.e.* that the priest should be put, in social position, on a par with the thane or twelve-hynde man. Moreover, the Archbishop's use in this connection of the phrase 'so many *tributarii*' or '*manentes*,' instead of so many 'hides,' is interesting. It helps us to understand that the hide as used in the Laws of Ine was probably the same fiscal or gafol paying unit as the *familia* of Bede.

Another clause in this interesting document bears more directly upon the question of homicide, and it is valuable as giving information quite independent of the Laws.

It is the answer of the Archbishop to the question,

---

[1] See Schmid's Glossary *sub voce* Eideshülfe.' There is only one mention of oaths of so many hides in the later Anglo-Saxon laws, viz. in Alfred, s. 11, in which it is stated that a woman must clear herself from a charge of previous unchastity with 60 hides.

'What if a layman shall kill a cleric or a monk, whether the *precium sanguinis* according to the law *natalium parentum* shall be paid to his near relations or whether his *seniores* are to be satisfied by a larger amount—which does your Unanimity sanction?'

The reply is as follows:—

The wergelds of the clergy to be paid to the church.

Quicunque vero ex laicis occiderit episcopum, presbiterum, vel diaconum, aut monachum, agat pœnitentiam secundum gradus pœnitentiæ constitutos, et reddat precium æcclesiæ suæ; pro episcopo secundum [placitum] universalis consilii, pro presbitero octingentos siclos, pro diacono sexingentos, pro monacho vero quadringentos argenteos; nisi aut dignitas natalium vel nobilitas generis majus reposcat precium. Non enim justum est, ut servitium sanctæ professionis in meliori gradu perdat quod exterior vita sub laico habitu habuisse jure parentum dinoscitur.

Whoever indeed of laymen shall have killed a bishop, priest, or deacon or monk shall do penance according to the constituted scale of penitentials, and let him pay the price to his church—for a bishop according to [the decision] of a general Council:

For a priest . 800 sicli
For a deacon . 600 sicli
But for a monk . 400 argentei[1]

unless dignity of birth or nobility of kindred demand a greater *precium.*

For it is not just that service in a holy profession in a higher grade should lose what secular life in lay dress may be recognised to have by right of parentage.

Stated in Roman silver currency.

The wergelds here stated for the clergy are stated in *sicli* and *argentei.* The Roman argenteus, as we have seen (after Nero's time), was the drachma of silver, and the siclus was a didrachma or quarter of an ounce. The Archbishop, therefore, was claiming 200 ounces of silver as the wergeld of his Northumbrian priest.

Whether he knew it or not, this amounted in value to 4000 sceatts (of 20 to the ounce), *i.e.* 800 Wessex and 1000 Mercian scillings. So that in

[1] The monk's oath was one fourth of the priest's in value: so 400 *argentei* = one fourth of 800 *sicli.*

claiming for his priest a wergeld of 200 ounces of silver he does not seem to have had in his mind either the Mercian or the Wessex twelve-hyndeman's wergeld, of 1200 scillings, of 5 or 4 sceatts, but, possibly, as we shall see, a Kentish wergeld of 200 Kentish scillings of 20 sceatts.

Priest's wergeld to be 200 Roman ounces of silver.

The Archbishop's claim falling short of what was ultimately granted in Northumbria is curious as showing that Northumbrian law, at this time, before the inroads of the Norse invaders, was still unsettled, and that the Archbishop may have been influenced by Kentish rather than by West-Saxon or Mercian precedents. It was after another century, and after the Norse invasion and conquest, that the wergelds of the mass-thane and secular-thane in the 'North People's Law' were stated to be alike at 2000 thrymsas, or 1200 Wessex shillings. How much earlier the equation was made in Northumbria we know not.

The next clause to be noticed is that in reply to question viii., viz. 'If any monks shall mix themselves up with sacrilege, should *you* now prosecute, if the avengement of the crime pertains to laymen who are their relations?'

The reply is as follows:—

[Apostolus dicit,] omnes causas æcclesiæ debere apud sacerdotes dijudicari. Si qui vero æcclesiastici crimen aliquod inter laicos perpetraverint, homicidium, vel fornicationem, vel furtum agentes, hos placuit a secularibus in quos peccaverunt omnimodo occupari; nisi animo fuerit æcclesiæ pro talibus satisfacere. Laici vero

The Apostle declares that all ecclesiastical causes should be settled by priests. But if any ecclesiastics have perpetrated any crime among laymen, homicide or fornication or theft, it has been decreed that they be followed up in every case by laymen against whom they have sinned, unless it be the intention qui sacrilega se contagione miscuerint velatis, non eodem modo quo lex publica fornicarios puniri percensuit, set duplicato xxx siclorum pecunia, hoc est lx argenteos volumus dare ecclesiæ adulterantes, quia graves causæ graviores et acriores querunt curas.

of the Church to make satisfaction for them. But laymen who shall have joined in sacrilegious intercourse with nuns [shall be dealt with] not in the same manner as the public law decrees fornicators to be punished, but *double*—by the sum of xxx *sicli*—i.e. we wish adulterers to give to the Church lx *argentei*, because severe cases require severer and sharper cures.

This passage once again makes it clear that in this ecclesiastical document of the Archbishop of York 30 sicli = 60 argentei or Roman drachmæ.

Ecclesiastical causes to be settled by priests.

And, apart from this monetary question, the clause is interesting as marking the claim that all ecclesiastical causes should be settled by the clergy themselves.

In case of crime by an ecclesiastic against a layman the Church reserved the right to stop the layman's prosecution by payment of the wergeld or other satisfaction. At the same time the Church was to claim double compensation from laymen committing crime against nuns. It is impossible to disassociate this document from the letter of Bede describing the religious anarchy of the diocese caused by the abuses of the loose monastic system in vogue, and urging the newly appointed prelate, who was not yet Archbishop, to undertake their energetic reformation.

But for the present purpose the real worth of these statements is the independent evidence they give of the continued strength of the wergeld system and the force of tribal custom in the Northumbrian kingdom before the Norse invasions. The sense of individualism in Christianity was opposed to the solidarity and joint responsibility of the kindred. But instead of fighting against the wergeld system the Church had actually succumbed to it, and adopted it for its own advantage, placing a money price upon the blood of its several ecclesiastical ranks, making the value of the priest four times that of the monk.

The Church succumbed to the wergeld system.

The system of compurgation, again, was a part of tribal usage. The Church adopted it and graduated the worth of the oaths of its various grades according to secular usage, making the oath of the priest in evidence four times the value of that of the monk.

In other words, in England, as on the Continent, the clergy, instead of combating tribal custom in these matters, took their place in the order of secular rank according to their several grades, bishops claiming the wergeld of princes, and priests that of thanes, with, however, the obviously useful reservation that if their secular rank by parentage and birth should be higher than their ecclesiastical grade, the higher wergeld should be theirs.

All this we see in the course of being introduced into Northumbrian usage in answer to local inquiry and local needs, upon the authority of perhaps the very wisest of Saxon prelates.

The wisdom of such accommodation as this on the part of the Church to pagan tribal usage is not the matter in question. The point of the evidence is the proof it gives of the continued strength of tribal usage in England after many generations of occupation and settlement.

III. THE DOOMS OF INE, A.D. 688–725.

The Dooms of King Ine occupy so important a position as the earliest direct information upon Anglo-Saxon custom apart from Kent that they demand careful separate study.

We ought to be able to learn something from them of the aim and spirit of legislation in Wessex two centuries before King Alfred added them to his laws.

Ine's Dooms apart from Alfred's.

There is no reason, I think, to suspect that the text of the Dooms of Ine was altered by Alfred. The words already quoted in which he says that in his Dooms he collected together what he thought 'rightest' of those things which he met with of the days of Ine and Offa and Ethelbert without adding much of his own are quite consistent with his preservation of King Ine's laws as a whole, though in some points differing from his own.[1]

King Ine came to the throne in A.D. 688, and he states in his preamble that he issued his 'Dooms' with the counsel of Cenred his father and of the Bishops of Winchester and London (who had already had twelve or thirteen years' experience in their sees) and also with the counsel of all his *ealdormen* and his Witan :—

ꝥ te ryht æw ⁊ ryhte cyne-domas þurh ure folc gefæstnode ⁊ getrymede wæron, ꝥ te nænig ealdormonna ne us under-geþeodedra æfter þam wære awendende þas ure domas.	So that just law and just kingly dooms might be settled and established throughout our folk; so that none of the *ealdormen* nor of our subjects should hereafter pervert these our dooms.

[1] See Schmid's introduction, where he states his reasons for placing Ine's Dooms before Alfred's in his edition of the Laws

We mark, then, at once that at this period the most prominent public official was the *ealdorman*. From clause 8 and clause 9 we learn that private revenge for a wrong was forbidden before justice had been demanded from a '"scir-man" or other judge.' And that the ealdorman was a shire-man we learn from another clause (clause 36).

The ealdorman a shire-man in judicial position.

Seþe þeof gefehð · oþþe him mon gefongenne agifð ⁊ he hine þonne alæte oþþe þa þiefðe gedierne forgielde þone þeof [be] his were.	(36) Let him who takes a thief or to whom one taken is given, and then lets him go, or conceals the theft, pay for the thief according to his wer.
Gif he ealdormon sie þolie his scire buton him kyning arian wille.	If he be an *ealdorman* let him forfeit his 'shire' unless the King be merciful to him.

Here, as in Alfred's Laws, the ealdorman is an official with judicial jurisdiction. And we learn more about his social status as compared with that of other classes from s. 45.

Burg-bryce of various classes.

Burg-bryce mon sceal betan c. xx scill. kyniges ⁊ biscepes þær his rice bið. Ealdormonnes lxxx scill. Kyniges þegnes lx scill. Gesiðcundes monnes land-hæbbendes xxxv scill. ⁊ be þon ansacan.	(45) Bot shall be made for the *King's* burg-bryce, and a bishop's where his jurisdiction is, with cxx shillings; for an *ealdorman's* with lxxx shillings; for a *King's thane's* with lx shillings; for that of a *gesithcund*-man having land with xxxv shillings: and *according to this let them make legal denial.*

The *burg*-bryce is the same thing as the *burh*-bryce—the breaking into the *burh*. And if we compare the 'bots' of this clause with the burh-bryce of King Alfred's s. 40 (*supra*, p. 372) we see that he was not merely copying King Ine's clause. Nearly as they may resemble one another, there are marked differences between the two clauses.

The king's burh-bryce in King Ine's Laws is the same as King Alfred's. The ealdorman's is eighty scillings instead of sixty. The king's thane takes the ealdorman's place with sixty, and the gesithcund-man's burh-bryce in King Ine's Laws is practically the same as the twelve-hyndeman's in King Alfred's laws.

The gesithcund-man's judicial position.

The gesithcund-man we have met before in one of the fragments of early English law, but so far as relates to Wessex he appears in the Dooms of Ine for the first and last time, and we shall have to consider by-and-by how far he is the same person as the twelve-hyndeman. But for the present it is sufficient to note that he is mentioned along with the king's thane and the ealdorman apparently in order to state the extent to which his oath was to be taken as valid in judicial evidence, or whatever is meant by the words 'and according to this make legal denial.'

Laws as to theft.

The chief obstacle to the maintenance of the peace seems to have been the frequency of thefts and homicide of all kinds. The connection between homicide and theft is the subject of several clauses in the Laws of Ine. And as they bring into notice the liability of the kindred it may be well to consider them in order.

These are some of the clauses in the Laws of King Ine with reference to the slaying of a thief:—

Gif þeof sie gefongen swelte he deaðe oþþe his lif be his were man aliese.	(12) If a thief be seized let him perish by death or let his life be redeemed according to his wer.
Cierlisc mon gif he oft betygen wære gif he æt siþestan sie gefongen slea mon hond [of] oþþe fot.	(18) A ceorlisc man, if he have often been accused, if he at last be seized, let his hand or foot be cut off.
Gif feorcund mon oþþe fremde butan wege geond wudu gonge &	(20) If a far-coming man or a stranger journey through a wood

ne hrieme ne horn blawe, for þeof he bið to profianne oþþe to sleanne oþþe to aliesanne.	out of the highway and neither shout nor blow his horn he is to be held for a thief either to be slain or redeemed.

The ge-geldas and kindred of the thief.

Then comes the question what happens if a man should seize a thief and slay him as a thief. The next clause goes on to state that in the case of the thief slain in the wood the slayer must declare that he slew the man for a thief, and then neither the lord nor the *ge-gildas* of the slain could demand a wergeld. But if he should conceal the slaying and it became known after a time, the way was open for the kindred of the supposed thief to exculpate him by oath and so claim his wergeld, from the slayer.

Where there is no concealment, the kindred of the thief must swear that there shall be no vengeance on him for delivering up the thief.

Se [þe] þeof gefehð [he] ah x. scill. ⁊ se cyning þone þeof ⁊ þa mægas him swerian aðas unfæhða.	(28) He who seizes a thief shall have ten scillings and the king the thief; and let the kindred [of the thief] swear to him oaths of 'unfæhthe.'

If the man who had seized the thief let him go he was liable to pay 'wite'—and if, as we have seen, an 'ealdorman' did so it was at the risk of losing his 'shire.'

Theft seems to have been an increasing crime, for further on in Ine's Laws there are repetitions of some of these clauses, with slight additions, showing that the Dooms of Ine were added to from time to time (s. 35 and s. 27).

We have seen how severe a penalty was attached to the crime against the king's peace of letting a thief

The ceorlisc and the gesithcund classes.

once seized escape. The following clause is still more severe upon any one harbouring a fugitive thief or other outlaw, and it introduces again the division of classes as regards wergelds into gesithcund and ceorlisc, but without mentioning the wergelds of each class.

Gif mon cierliscne monnan flieman-feorme teo be his agnum were geladige he hine. Gif he ne mæge gielde hine [be] his agenum were ⁊ se gesiðmon [eac] swa be his were.	(30) If a man accuse a ceorlisc-man of harbouring a fugitive [thief?] let him clear himself according to his own wer. If he cannot, let him pay for him according to his own wer, and the gesith-man in like manner according to his wer.

This 'clearing himself according to his own wer' alludes evidently to the oath of himself and his oath-helpers and shows that the oath required to clear the gesithcund-man from the charge was a greater one than that required to clear a ceorlisc-man. This was doubtless the case throughout, but apparently it had become needful to strengthen the oath of both classes. The following clause required that in the oath of both the gesithcund and ceorlisc-man in denial of homicide there should be among the oath-helpers 'a King's oath of 30 hides.'

The oaths to be in their hyndens of co-swearers.

Seþe bið wer-fæhðe betogen ⁊ he onsacan wille þæs sleges mid aðe þonne sceal bion on þære hyndenne an kyning [æðe] be xxx hida swa be gesiðcundum men swa be cierliscum swa hwæðer swa hit sie. Gif hine mon gilt þonne mot he gesellan on þara hyndenna gehwelcere monnan [and, *but not in H*] byrnan ⁊ sweord on ꝥ wer-gild gif he þyrfe.	(54) He who is charged with *wer-fæhthe* and he is willing to deny the slaying on oath; then shall there be in the 'hynden' one king's oath of 30 hides as well for a gesithcund-man as for a ceorlisc-man whichever it may be. If he has to pay him, then may he give the man of any one of those 'hyndens' a coat of mail and a sword in the wergeld if he need.

The last part of the clause is ambiguous, but on the whole, taking into account the Latin of the 'Quadripartitus' and Liebermann's suggested translation and the difficulty of the various other suggested readings, I think it is most probable that the meaning may be, that if the man charged cannot get the required 'king's oath' or that of another hynden without paying for it, he may give 'a coat of mail and a sword' to the 'hynden' if it should be needful. We may have to recur to this section, but without attempting to build anything upon this more than doubtful addition to it. Nothing important, I think, turns upon it.

The following is important as showing that both the gesithcund and ceorlisc classes were under the military obligation to follow to the fyrd. Both classes must follow to the fyrd.

Gif gesiðcund mon landagende forsitte fyrde geselle cxx scill. ⁊ þolie his landes, unlandagende lx scill. cierlisc xxx scill. to fierdwite.	(51) If a gesithcund-man owning land neglect the fyrd, let him pay 120*s*. and forfeit his land, one not owning land 60*s*.; a ceorlisc-man 30*s*. as fyrd-wite.

The recurrence in so many clauses of Ine's Laws of the division of classes into gesithcund and ceorlisc leads to the conclusion that it must have been a very prominent one.

It was accepted in the Laws of Ine as a fact existing and of common knowledge, with no mark upon it of novelty or innovation. The distinction was evidently ancient and radical, and yet the word 'gesithcund' is not met with in any later laws.

Throughout the 76 clauses of the Laws of Ine only one makes direct mention of the division of

Mention of twelve-, six-, and twy-hynde classes.

classes into twelve-hynde and twy-hynde, the distinction so generally made in the later laws, and in this clause, as in King Alfred's Laws, the six-hynde class also appears :—

Aet twy-hyndum were mon sceal sellan to mon-bot xxx scill. æt vi-hyndum lxxx scill. æt twelf-hyndum c.xx.	(70) With a twy-hyndeman's wer shall be given as man-bot xxx scillings with a six-hynde's lxxx scillings, [? lx s.], with a twelve-hynde's cxx scillings.[1]

The man-bot was, as we have seen, the payment to a lord for the loss of his man.

There is an indirect mention of wergelds in s. 34, which states that any one who has been in a foray in which a man has been slain must prove himself innocent of the slaying and make bot for the foray according to the wergeld of the slain. If his wergeld be 200*s.* he must make bot with 50*s.*, and the like justice was to be done with respect to the 'dearer born.'

We may assume from this and the later evidence that already the wergeld of the twelve-hyndeman was 1200 scillings, and that of the twy-hyndeman 200 scillings, though in the Dooms of Ine this is not otherwise directly stated. The laws take it for granted that the amount of the wergelds was common knowledge, as in so many other cases.

The six-hynde class.

The mention of the six-hynde class in addition to the twelve-hynde and twy-hynde classes makes it a matter of importance to learn what manner of persons were included in the six-hynde class.

[1] This is repeated in Henry I. lxix.

The Laws of King Alfred, as we have seen, generally mention the six-hyndeman with the other classes, but without giving any clue to an answer to the question to what social rank he belonged. In the Laws of Ine, however, a distinct clue is given, and it is one which accords with Continental usage and suggests a reason for the disappearance of the six-hyndeman from the later laws. He is mentioned again after King Alfred's time only in the so-called Laws of Henry I.

The clauses relating to this subject are important enough to claim consideration in a separate section.

The gafol-gelda and the gebur.

One other important social distinction, or division of classes, appears already in the Laws of Ine, viz. that which existed between possessors of land and *gafol-geldas* and *geburs* who were, as we should say, *tenants* on the land of others. We shall have to return to the consideration of this distinction and to note the fact that it is in these Laws of Ine that the *gebur* appears as almost the equivalent of the *gafol-gelda*, while they afford incidental evidence also that the typical holding of the gafol-gelda (and thus of the gebur) was the 'yardland' or virgate of open-field husbandry.

The mention of the gafol-gelda and the gebur occurs in s. 6.

Gif hwa gefeohte on cyninges huse sie he scyldig ealles his ierfes ⁊ sie on cyninges dome hwæðer he lif age þe nage. Gif hwa on mynstre gefeohte hund twelftig scill. gebete. Gif hwa on	(6) If any one fight in the *king's house*, let him be liable in all his property and be it in the king's dooms whether he shall or shall not have life. If any one fight in a *minster*,

ealdormonnes huse gefeohte oþþe on oðrer geþungenes witan lx scill. gebete he ⁊ oðer lx geselle to wite.

Gif he þonne on gafol-geldan huse oþþe on gebures gefeohte c.xx scill. to wite geselle ⁊ þæm gebure vi scill.

And þeah hit sie on middum felda gefohten hund twelftig scill. to wite sie agifen.

let him make bot with cxx scillings.

If any one fight in an *ealdorman's* house or in any other distinguished wita's, let him make bot with lx scillings and pay a second lx scillings as wite.

But if he fight in a *gafol-gelda's* house or in a *gebur's*, let him pay cxx scillings as wite, and to the gebur vi scillings.

And though it be fought on midfield let cxx scillings be given as wite.

The gafol-gelda and gebur have only a six scilling fightwite.

This clause is intelligible if we follow the principle that fighting anywhere is a breach of the king's peace. The king, therefore, in every case and wherever it happens is entitled to a wite of 120 scillings. But if it happens within the house or precinct of an ealdorman or of any other chief member of the Witan the amount is divided between the king and his official. If the fighting is in the precinct or house of a gafol-gelda or gebur the king still gets his full wite of 120 scillings, and an additional six scillings is to be given to the gebur, just as in King Alfred's Laws the same amount is to be given to the ceorlisc man for fighting in his 'flet.'

This clause forms a valuable groundwork of evidence as to the position of the gafol-gelda under West Saxon law, and we shall have to recur to it when we further consider the position of the ceorlisc class at the date of King Ine's Dooms. The omission of the gesithcund class from this section, unless included as distinguished members of the Witan, can hardly be accidental, but it is not easy at first sight to divine a plausible reason for it.

Let us for a moment try to recognise the position to which so far the Dooms of Ine have brought us.

We seem able in those already quoted to trace a process at work combining distinctions of classes of different origins and based upon different lines of thought.

We find a very marked and prominent division of classes into gesithcund and ceorlisc alongside of hardly more than incidental mention of the division of classes so prominent afterwards into twelve-hynde and twy-hynde. In King Alfred's Laws we could trace no practical distinction between the twy-hynde and ceorlisc classes. We could not distinguish between them. All distinction at any rate evaded our notice. We have now to ask the double question what was the distinction between gesithcund and twelve-hynde, as well as what was the distinction between ceorlisc and twy-hynde.

The chief question raised by King Alfred's Laws was whether any great distinction existed between the 'ceorl who sits on gafol land' and other members of the ceorlisc class. The Laws of King Alfred gave us no clue on this point. It seemed as though, after all, the ceorlisc class must have been so generally gafol-geldas that practically the twy-hynde and ceorlisc class might be spoken of roughly and inclusively as 'ceorls who sit on gafol land,' and that this 'sitting on gafol land' might be, after all, the fairly distinctive mark of the ceorlisc class for whom King Alfred claimed a twy-hynde wergeld as 'equally dear' with the Danish lysing.

The gafol-gelda and gebur of Ine's laws put in the place of the ceorlisc man of King Alfred.

And now in this clause 6 of King Ine's Laws we find the gafol-gelda or gebur put directly into the place of the ceorlisc man of King Alfred's Laws with the same penalty of six scillings payable to him for fighting in his house or his 'flet.'

King Alfred's Laws, s. 39.	*King Ine's Laws*, s. 6.
If any one fight in a ceorlisc man's flet, with six scillings let him make bot to the ceorl.	But if he fight in a gafol-gelda's house or in a gebur's, let him pay . . . . to the gebur six scillings.

It might be said at first sight that here surely is a clear trace of the degradation of the ceorl into a gafol-gelda during the 200 years between the Laws of King Ine and King Alfred. For, it might be said, the ceorl of King Alfred's Laws has the same bot for the fighting in his house as that which the gafol-gelda had under Ine's Laws 200 years earlier. This may be so. But how do we know that the gafol-gelda of King Ine's time was not already the typical ceorl as he seems to have been in King Alfred's time? In that case there would be no sign of degradation of the ceorl into the gafol-gelda. Or at any rate if there had been a degradation from some original higher position and status it had already taken place before the time of King Ine. Our judgment on the position of the ceorlisc class under King Ine's Laws must still be reserved.

IV. THE POSITION OF STRANGERS IN BLOOD UNDER KING INE'S LAWS.—THE SIX-HYNDEMAN.

Strangers in blood.

The question of the position under West Saxon law of strangers in blood is one of much interest, and we have reserved the clauses relating to it for separate consideration.

There may have been several different classes of strangers.

How far there was a considerable substratum of conquered Romano-British inhabitants is a very vexed question. That there were such in the outlying and recently conquered districts is certain. Mr. Coote's view may not be wholly mistaken that a Romano-British population, living, as on the Continent, under their own laws and customs, existed in most districts, especially in the towns.

How were the earlier conquered inhabitants treated?

These strangers may some of them have had land and some of them not. Certainly not all of them were regarded as theows or thralls.

To what class, then, did they belong? And how were they treated? What degree of freedom was granted them, and what was their wergeld, if they had any?

It is to the Laws of Ine that we must go for the answers to these questions. And we start on the inquiry seeking light also upon the position of the as yet unexplained six-hynde class so often mentioned in the Laws of King Alfred but never in the later laws.

The only hint we have had as yet as to the meaning of the six-hynde class is whether gesithcund-men not having land may not have belonged to it.

The wergelds of the ordinary classes of tribesmen were doubtless too well known to require more than incidental mention in King Ine's Dooms, but there are several clauses or fragments of clauses specially mentioning the wergelds of the *wealh* and of the *Wilisc*-man.

The *wealh* or *Wilisc-man* with five hides was six-hynde.

Wealh gif he hafað fif hyda he bið syx hynde.	24) A *wealh* if he have five hides 'he shall be six-hynde.'

Gif Wylisc mon hæbbe hide londes his wer bið c.xx scill. gif he þonne hæbbe healfe lxxx scill. gif he nænig hæbbe lx scillinga.

(32) If a Wylisc-man have a hide of land his wer shall be cxx scillings, but if he have half a hide lxxx scillings, if he have none lx scillings.

Cyninges hors-wealh seþe him mæge geærendian þæs wer-gield bið cc scill.

(33) The king's 'horse-wealh' who can do his errands, his wergeld shall be cc scillings.

It will be noticed that the wergeld of the *Wilisc* man with one hide of land is one fifth of the wergeld of the *wealh* with five hides, so that wealhs and Wilisc men seem to be treated on the same lines—as if the two words meant the same thing.

The Gallo-Roman '*wala*.'

It is not easy to draw a distinction between the 'wealh' and the 'Wilisc' man. 'Wilisc' is certainly used as the adjective corresponding to 'wealh,' though sometimes (as *e.g.* in 'Wilisc ale') for something specially Welsh. In the Lex Salica, as we have seen, the Gallo-Roman living under Roman law, according to the Malberg gloss was a '*Wala*' with a wergeld half that of the 'ingenuus' living under Salic law. And, without pushing this meaning so far as Mr. Coote was inclined to do, we may fairly, I think, look upon the word 'wealh' as generally embracing not only natives of Wales and West Wales, but also the wider class of persons of the conquered populations, whether Welsh or Britons or Romano-Britons, who were not recognised as of Anglo-Saxon blood.

We may call in the later evidence of the Northumbrian Priest-law [1] in illustration. The use of

[1] Schmid, *Anhang ii.*

ores and half-marks in this document and its being, so to speak, domiciled in York, seem to connect it with the period of the Northmen's conquest of Northumbria, when York was its capital and as yet the tide of battle had not been turned—*i.e.* shortly before the date of the Compact between Alfred and Guthrum. In this Priest-law the penalty for the practice of heathen rites on the part of a king's thane was ten half-marks, and if he wished to deny the charge it must be with ten named by himself, ten named by his kindred (*maga*), and ten *Wallerwente*, and if he failed in the denial he had to pay the ten half-marks, half of which went to the church and half to the king.

The *Waller-wente* of Yorkshire.

And so also in the case of the 'landagende man' who had to pay six half-marks: he too must deny with as many of his like (*gelicena*) and as many *wente* as the king's thane. And so also in the case of a 'cyrlisc' man.

It is quite clear that these *Wallerwente* were *free* inhabitants of the district, for their oaths were taken in evidence, which would not have been done had they been theows. The Wallerwente were, on the other hand, not recognised as 'ceorlisc' Saxons. They were obviously the native Celtic inhabitants of the great plain of York[1]—the *gwent* or basin of the Derwent and the Ouse. The locality is fixed by the clause which restricts the Sabbath day's journey on necessity to six miles out of York.

[1] Schmid, Glossary, *sub voc.* 'Die Britischen Einwohner von Cumberland.' But the mention of York is conclusive.

Under Frankish law the Gallo-Romans had half-wergelds.

Now, we have seen that under Frankish laws the Gallo-Roman population living under Roman law had *half*-wergelds. If the freeman living under Salic law had a wergeld of 200 solidi the 'Romanus possessor' had a wergeld of 100 solidi. And so in the same way, returning to the Laws of Ine, while the gesithcund or other landed Wessex freeman was a twelve-hyndeman, the wealh who had five hides was reckoned as six-hynde.

The wealh with five hides had a half-wergeld.

We have seen that the English ceorl who rose to the possession of five hides and paid gafol to the king, and with coat of mail and over-gilded sword followed to the fyrd, became gesithcund with a wergeld of 1200 scillings. It is quite in accordance with tribal feeling as shown in Continental usage that the stranger in blood, whether Welsh or Romano-British, who had risen in the same way to the possession or occupation of five hides should be six-hynde with a half-wergeld of 600 scillings.

We have quoted the Northumbrian Priest-law and noted that its penalties in half-marks and ores suggest that it belongs to the period before King Alfred's Compact with Guthrum, during which York was the capital of the Northmen's kingdom. It is interesting to see that in the fragment of North People's Law quoted in the previous chapter, belonging probably to the same district and to the same period, some of the clauses with reference to the Wilisc man are evidently copied from the Laws of Ine though with some additional matter and perhaps some slight errors in the figures.

> And if a Wilisc-man thrive so that he have a hide of land and can bring forth the King's gafol, then is his wergeld 120 scillings.

And if he thrive not except to half a hide, then let his wer be 80 scillings. And if he have not any land, let him be paid for with 70 scillings [? 60].

And it is worth notice that it was in this very document that the Northmen as conquerors, while leaving the English wergeld of the thane at 2000 thrymsas or 1200 scillings, gave to their own 'hold' a double wergeld of 4000 thrymsas.

The conquering Northmen gave the hauld a wergeld twice that of the thane.

We may therefore regard the six-hyndeman of King Ine and King Alfred's Laws as probably the Wilisc man with five hides or more. There does not appear to be anything in King Alfred's Laws to lead us away from this conclusion. Any other would leave the complete silence of King Alfred's laws with regard to the Wilisc class unexplained, unless it could be considered that in the turmoil of the Northmen's invasions and the stress of war the Wilisc class had already become more or less amalgamated with the Saxon population by the force of their common interests against the invaders.

The six-hynde class died out.

The silence of the later laws as to a six-hynde class may probably be explained by the same considerations.

Passing from the Wilisc man who was six-hynde in consequence of his landed position to the Wilisc man viewed simply as a stranger in blood, there is further evidence that as a stranger he was regarded as only half as 'worthy' as an Englishman. In s. 46 of Ine's Laws it is stated that an oath-worthy person charged with theft is to deny the charge with an oath of 120 hides if the accuser be an Englishman, but with only 60 hides if the accuser be a Wilisc man.

The Wilisc man under Ine's law only half as worthy as the Englishman.

Đonne mon monnan betyhð ꝥ he ceap forstele oþþe forstolenne gefeormie þonne sceal he be lx hyda onsacan þære þiefðe gif he að-wyrðe bið.	(46) When a man charges another that he steals, or harbours stolen cattle, then shall he deny the theft with lx hides if he be oath-worthy.
Gif þonne Englisc onstal ga forð onsace þonne be twy-fealdum.	If, however, an English charge of theft[1] come forward, let him then deny it with twice as many.
Gif hit þonne bið Wilisc onstal ne bið se að na þe mara.	But if it be a Wilisc charge, the oath shall not be the increased oath.

This clause does not tell us whether the Wilisc man was considered to be oath-worthy or not. Probably he would not be as against a Saxon. It only states that when the charge of theft was made by an Englishman the oath was to be one of twice as many hides as would be required to deny the charge of a Wilisc man.

In the 'Ordinance of the Dun-setas' strangers have only half-wergelds and must go to the ordeal as not oath-worthy.

Corroborative evidence as regards the half-wergelds and oath-worthiness of the wealh class may be found in an ordinance of later date, but belonging to Wessex, and it may be quoted as throwing strong light upon the position of the Wilisc or wealh class (*wealþeode*) in apparently a border district, where Saxons and wealhs met together with a boundary of a river between them. It is entitled an 'Ordinance respecting the Dun-setas.'[2]

The leading fact throughout this document is that the two peoples met avowedly as strangers. Its aim was to keep the peace and to protect the owners of cattle on each side of the stream from the raids of their neighbours on the other.

---

[1] See Schmid's note on this passage, and see also Liebermann's translation.

[2] Thorpe, p. 150; Schmid, *Anhang i.*

They are recognised as strangers to each other and on principle treated reciprocally as such. Denial of a charge by oath and oath-helpers, unless by special agreement, is assumed to be of no use and evidently out of place between strangers in blood. Consequently the ordeal was the only answer to a charge of theft.

Ne stent nan oðer lád æt tihtlan bute ordal betweox Wealan & Englan, bute man þafian wille.	There stands no other purgation in an accusation save the ordeal between Wealas and English unless it be allowed.

This was fully in accordance with tribal custom no less than the further fact that their wergelds were, obviously for the same reason, to be half-wergelds.

Gyf Wealh Engliscne man ofsleane þearf he hine hiden-ofer buton be healfan were gyldan ne Ænglisc Wyliscne geon-ofer þe ma sy he þegen-boren sy he ceorl-boren healf wer þær æt-fealð.	If a Wealh slay an Englishman he need not pay for him on this side except with half his wer, no more than the Englishman for a Wylisc on that side, be he thane-born, be he ceorl-born, one half of the wer in that case falls away.

These wylisc men were in Wessex.

In this document the wealh is treated according to tribal principle as a stranger in blood, both as regards recourse to the ordeal, and the half-wergeld. And the word 'wyliscne' is used as the appropriate adjective distinguishing the wealh from the Englishman. So that in this case 'wealh' and 'wylisc' mean the same thing. Further, this evidence, though later in date probably than King Alfred's Laws, is practically Wessex evidence, because, though the geographical position of the Dun-setas is not accurately known, their connection with the West Saxons is the one thing which is clear.[1]

Returning to the Laws of Ine, as the wergeld of the Wilisc man with five hides was a half-wergeld of 600 scillings it might be supposed that the ordinary Wilisc man's would be a half-wergeld of 100 scillings. But it was not exactly so, for, according to s. 32 above quoted, the Wilisc man with one hide had a wergeld of 120 scillings, one with half a hide 80 scillings, one without any land 60 scillings.

In an isolated clause added to s. 23 a somewhat different statement is made. The wealh gafol-gelda has the same wergeld as if he had a hide of land, and the wealh theow the same wergeld as the Wilisc man without land.

Various classes of wealhs and Wilisc men.

Wealh gafol-gelda cxx scill. his sunu c. Ðeowne lx. somhwelcne fiftegum. Weales hyd[2] twelfum.

(23) A wealh gafol-gelda cxx scillings, his son c: a theow lx: some fifty: a wealh's skin twelve.

That the theow of this passage is the '*wealh-theow*' with a wergeld of 60 scillings is clear from sections 54 and 74, the first of which relates to the '*Wilisc wite theow.*'

Wite-þeowne monnan Wyliscne mon sceal bedrifan be twelf hidum swa þeowne to swingum. Engliscne be feower & þrittig hida.

(54) A Wilisc wite-theowman shall be followed up with twelve hides like a theow to the scourging; an English with four and thirty hides.

[1] The only mark of the geographical position of the district is that in the final clause: 'Formerly the Went-sætas belonged to the Dun-sætas, but more properly they belong to the West Saxons; there they shall give tribute and hostages.'

[2] Translated in the Latin version by 'corium,' the meaning probably being that 12 scillings would buy off a scourging.

The wite-theow was a person who had once been free but from debt or calamity had sunk into thraldom.

The English 'wite-theow' is dealt with thus in the Laws of Ine.

Gif wite-þeow Englisc-mon hine forstalie ho hine mon & ne gylde his hlaforde. Gif hine mon ofslea ne gylde hine mon his mægum gif hie hine on twelf-monðum ne aliesden.

(24) If a wite theow, an Englishman, steal himself away. let him be hanged and nothing paid to his lord. If any one slay him let nothing be paid to his kindred if they have not redeemed him within twelve months.

His free kindred might ignore him if they liked: there was no need for them to pay the wergeld of a kinsman who had forfeited his freedom.

Section 74 relates to the *theow-wealh*, but this term would seem to apply to the case of the *wealh-wite-theow*.[1]

Gif þeow-wealh Engliscne monnan ofslihð þonne sceal seþe hine ah weorpan hine to honda hlaforde ⁊ mægum oþþe lx scill. gesellan wið his feore. Gif he þonne þone ceap nelle fore gesellan þonne mot hine se hlaford gefreogan gielden siþþan his mægas þone wer gif he mæg-burg hæbbe freo. Gif he næbbe hedan his þa gefan. Ne þearf se frigea mid þam þeowan mæg-gieldan buton he him wille fæhðe of-aceapian ne se þeowa mid þy frigean.

(74) If a *theow-wealh* slay an Englishman, then he who owns him shall deliver him up to the lord and the kindred or give 60 scillings for his life. The theow-wealh.

But if he will not give that sum for him, then must the lord enfranchise him. Afterwards let his kindred pay the wer if he have a free *mæg-burh*. If he have not let his foes take heed to him.

The free need not pay 'mæg-bot' with the theow unless he be desirous to buy off from himself the feud: nor the 'theow' with the free.

[1] In the Laws of Henry I. (lxx. s. 5) the 'theow-wealh' is translated 'servus Waliscus,' and is worth double the ordinary slave, unless the amount be a double penalty.

This clause is repeated in the so-called Laws of Henry I. c. lxx., but the amount named is 40 scillings instead of 60 scillings. Sixty scillings is double the manbot of the twy-hynde man in s. 70 of Ine's Laws, and it may be the double value of the wealh-theow to his lord.

V. THE TWELVE-HYNDE AND TWY-HYNDE MEN AND THEIR HYNDENS OF OATH-HELPERS.

The silence of the Dooms of Ine upon some of the most important matters relating to ancient custom is no doubt disappointing, but their position as almost our only direct evidence of the customs of Wessex for the first two or three centuries after the conquest of Britain gives to every hint a value. Some of the clauses are so isolated that if we could not approach them with light from other sources we should lose the right clue to their meaning. It is only by following the course we have adopted of working backwards from the known to the unknown that we can rightly interpret some of the clauses by reading into them some things not directly mentioned by them.

The meaning of twelve-hynde and twy-hynde.

And yet if we try to understand such a fundamental matter as the meaning of the division of classes into *twelve-hynde* and *twy-hynde*[1] it is to the Dooms of Ine that we must go.

[1] The usual explanation of these terms is that they are derived from the number of shillings in the wergeld. Mr. Earle in his valuable *Handbook to the Land Charters* &c. (p. 1) considers 'hynde' to be an old form of 'ten' and to refer to the number of soldiers of whom the twelve-hynde and six-hynde men were captains. 'The former was a captain of 120 and the latter of 60.' Neither of these explanations seems to me to be satisfactory.

It is in these Dooms that the meaning of the words twelve-hynde and twy-hynde is most clearly connected with the system of compurgation and the oaths of the oath-helpers. It is moreover in these Dooms that at first sight the mystery is made still more mysterious by the statement of the value of the oaths in so many hides.

Connected with the system of oath-helpers.

The fact of this connection between the value of the oaths and hides was first brought to our notice in the Dialogue of Archbishop Egbert apparently as a matter already well known and established. And it was his claim that the oaths of his priests should be reckoned as oaths of 120 hides which confirmed what, from the Laws of Ine, was hardly more than doubtful inference that this was the value of the oath of the gesithcund or twelve-hynde class.

Value of oaths in hides.

The Archbishop's mention of it confirmed it, but left its meaning and origin as obscure as ever. And yet the whole question of the structure of Saxon society is so mixed up with the right understanding of the twelve-hynde and twy-hynde division of classes that unless further light can be let into it a good deal of what we should like to see clearly must remain unhappily enveloped in fog.

Archbishop Egbert's substitution of the phrase so many *tributarii* or *manentes* for the 'so many hides' of the Laws of Ine obliges us to regard the *hide* of Ine's Dooms in this connection as equivalent to the 'familia' of Bede. The Saxon translator of the Latin text of Bede translated the word *familia* sometimes by 'hide' and sometimes by *hiwisc* or family. In this connection it is also worth noting that, although writing a century later than Egbert and two centuries

Hides were family holdings.

after the date of Ine's Laws, the translator of Bede had not cast off all traces of tribal tradition, for he consistently used the word *mægthe* as the equivalent of Bede's 'provincia.' He still thought of tribes and peoples rather than of districts and provinces. His ideas in these things ran on tribal rather than on territorial lines. So to him the hide was still the *family* unit, and the greater kindred or tribe, as in Beowulf, was the *mægthe*. In Beowulf we saw that some of them conquered others and made them pay tribute. So they did in Bede's time.

The *familia* of Bede.

Manentes and *tributarii* of Egbert.

While, then, we are obliged to connect the value of oaths reckoned as of so many hides with hides which were family holdings, or, as Egbert calls them, *manentes* and *tributarii*, the original meaning of the connection must be sought for in tribal conceptions.

It seems to be quite clear that in saying that the twelve-hyndeman's oath was an oath of 120 hides, and the ceorl's presumably of 20 hides, we have not yet necessarily struck the real train of thought underlying the connection between oaths and hides. For it is absurd to think that the twelve-hyndeman could pretend to the occupation or possession of 120 hides or family holdings, or the ceorl to 20 hides. They could do no such thing. The ceorl, in later times at all events, who had the twy-hynde wergeld was 'the ceorl who sits on gafol land'—a gafol-gelda on some one else's land. And to the great-grandson of the ceorl who had risen to five hides, the continued possession of five hides was sufficient to qualify him for a *sithcund* status worth a wergeld of 1200 shillings or 2000 *thrymsas*.

The question, therefore, needs closer examination if we would rightly understand the meaning underlying the distinction between the twy-hynde and twelve-hynde social status.

Let us then in the first place try to understand the meaning of the word *hynde* which gives to the distinction between twy-hynde and twelve-hynde its important significance.

The meaning of 'hynden.'

The word separated from its prefix apparently occurs in only two places in the Laws. It occurs for the first time in an important clause of the Laws of Ine. And once more it occurs in the Laws of Athelstan, in the 'Judicia Civitatis Londoniæ.' A word which occurs again in Anglo-Saxon laws after an interval of more than two centuries may and perhaps must have had a well-known original significance as a legal term though found nowhere else in Anglo-Saxon literature.

In Ine s. 54 the word is used twice. The first part of the clause, which has already been quoted, is as follows:—

> (54) He who is charged with werfæhthe [man-slaying] and is willing to deny the slaying on oath, then shall there be *in the hynden* one King's oath of xxx hides as well for a gesithcund man as for a ceorlisc man whichsoever it may be.

The set of oath-helpers.

In this first mention of the *hynden* the word must mean the set of oath-helpers supporting their kinsman with their oaths, and the clause lays down the rule that in every such set of oath-helpers in the case of 'slaying' there must be a 'King's oath of thirty hides.' But what is this King's oath of thirty hides which is to be in the *hynden* of oath-helpers of both the twy-hynde and twelve-hynde man in case of man-slaying?

The 30 hides oath of the King's thane.

In the Compact between Alfred and Guthrum is a clause, already quoted, immediately following the statement of the wergelds of Dane and English, and the declaration that they were to be 'equally dear,' which seems to be almost a repetition of the clause in Ine's Laws, but without using the word *hynden.*

(3) If a King's thane be charged with man-slaying, if he means to clear himself by oath, let him do it with twelve King's thanes, and if a lesser man than a King's thane be charged, let him clear himself with eleven of his like and with one *King's thane.*

We have seen that the King's thane is mentioned in the Laws of Ine (s. 45), and that his social position was much higher than that of the ordinary *gesithcund-man.* The bot for his *burg-bryce* was sixty scillings —*i.e.* halfway between that of the ealdorman at eighty scillings and that of the gesithcundman having land at thirty-five scillings.

The King's thane's oath seems, then, to be what is meant by the King's oath of thirty hides in the Laws of Ine. But the King's thane's oath of thirty hides being the oath of a class higher than that of the gesithcundman, how is it that the oath of the latter could be a 120 hide oath?—*i.e.* worth four times as much as that of his superior, the King's thane.

At first the two statements seem to clash, but on reflection a spark of light seems to come from the collision. The King's thane's oath in this case is only *one oath in the hynden of twelve* oath-helpers supporting the twelve-hynde or twy-hynde man. When a King's thane was himself charged with man-slaying the later law declares that he must clear himself with twelve King's thane's oaths. The full oath of the whole hynden, himself and his co-swearers, would therefore be equivalent to an oath of 360 hides —*i.e.* worth three times the 120 hide oath of—may we not now say?—the twelve oath-helpers forming the *hynden* of the gesithcundman.

The single oath of the twelve-hyndeman was of 10 hides.

The King's thane's official position was sufficient to justify the threefold value of his oath and that of the several oaths of his hynden. And if the 120 hide oath of the twelve-hyndeman be the full oath of himself and his hynden of oath-helpers, then his single oath would be a ten hide oath, which is much more within reason. The analogy would be complete were it not for the necessity of including in the hynden of the gesithcundman a King's thane's oath of thirty hides; but this may have been an afterthought. The mention of it in the law of Ine is in itself presumptive evidence that it was a new and an additional requirement beyond what Wessex custom had originally required.[1]

The oath of himself and oath-helpers was of 120 hides.

So far, then, it seems to be pretty clear that the 120 hide oath of the twelve-hyndeman was the twelvefold oath of himself and his hynden of oath-helpers, each of whose single oaths was, like his own, a ten hide oath.

Adhering, then, to the meaning of *hynden* as the set

[1] This view that the single oath of the twelve-hyndeman was reckoned as a 10 hide oath is confirmed by the translation in the Latin of the *Quadripartitus* of Ine's Laws. s. 46. The Anglo-Saxon 'þonne sceal he be lx hyda onsacan,' is translated by 'tunc debet per lx hidas i. e. *per vi homines* abnegare.' And in s. 19 'potest jurare prò lx hidis i. e. *pro hominibus vi.*' Schmid remarks on these passages: 'Hiernach würde also jeder Eideshelfer 10 Hiden vertreten.'

The oath-helpers were kinsmen.

of oath-helpers, we have next to keep in mind that the oath-helpers were naturally kinsmen representing the slayer's kindred and their responsibility for the wergeld of the person slain if their kinsman was the slayer, and by this consideration we are once more thrown back upon tribal custom.

The twy-hyndeman and leysing's want of kindred.

And when in the Compact between Alfred and Guthrum we see the 'ceorl who sits on gafol-land' put in the same position as the Norse 'leysing' or newly made freeman whose kindred was imperfect, howbeit in course of being widened by each generation, we seem again to be put upon the scent that the twy-hynde condition of the Saxon ceorl may also originally have had something to do with his imperfect kindred.

When further, in the remarkable fragment already quoted, we see the Saxon ceorl himself rising in the social scale, getting land 'to the King's utware,' having a 'coat of mail, helmet, and over-gilded sword' and doing direct service to the King, until at last, his son's son having had that land in succession, the great-grandchildren become of *sithcund* kin with twelve-hynde wergelds, the scent seems to lie all the more strongly in the direction of the tribal rules of kindred. For it is as though we had watched the process of the growth of kindred in this case till the *sithcund* condition was reached, and the full hynden had been produced, thus raising the twy-hynde into a twelve-hynde man.

The leysing, we learned from the Norse laws, being a newly made freedman, had at first no freeborn kin from whom he could inherit or who could inherit from him. He had no one of his kin to swear for him or to fight for him till he had sons and grandsons. For three generations the descendants were leysings still. And though during that time kinsmen enough may have grown up around them to swear for them yet still their oaths may well have been reckoned of lower value than those of the hauld, each of whose oath-helpers had a full kindred behind him to support him. It took another three generations to put the leysing in this position.

The full oath of a man with 12 oath-helpers of full kindred twelve-hynde.

There may, then, perhaps be involved in this matter of imperfect and perfect kindred a principle of tribal custom orginally underlying the terms twelve-hynde and twy-hynde. The oath of full value under tribal usage would be the oath of a man with a full kindred, *i.e.* with twelve hyndens, each of full kindred, behind him. Only with a full kindred to support him was his protection complete, because without it he could not secure a full oath of twelve sufficiently influential and powerful oath-helpers. If he could claim from his kindred such an oath, then he may well have been considered properly a twelve-hyndeman, because such an oath meant practically that he had the support and protection of twelve hyndens of kinsmen in case of need.

This might at first sight seem an unnecessarily large requirement if the *oath* were regarded only as clearing a man from the charge of man-slaying. But going back to tribal usage it seems no longer too large when the alternative is considered. The alternative was the ordeal and, on failure of the test of innocence, the feud or the payment of a wergeld of, as we have seen, normally one hundred head of cattle. In either case the slayer was powerless if alone. He was powerful only in having a full kindred behind him bound by ties of kinship and tribal usage first to swear for him instead of his being put to the ordeal, and secondly to fight for him or to assist him in finding the hundred head of cattle required to buy off the feud, according to the proverb 'Buy off the spear or bear it.' In either case the completeness of his kindred was the measure of the power of protection behind him.

The oath of the ceorl worth only one sixth of that of the twelve-hyndeman and thus only twy-hynde.

The twy-hyndeman considered as the leysing or freedman would not be in this strong position. His social status, resulting from his imperfect kindred, must be a low one. If he slew a twelve-hyndeman, from the point of view of the feud he would be helpless. The kindred of the twelve-hyndeman slain by him could not be satisfied merely by the slaughter of an inferior. Tribal custom of the Continental Saxons allowed vengeance for homicide by a thrall to be taken upon seven thralls. Under Mercian usage, as we have seen, it had been settled that the oath of the ceorl was to be taken as worth one sixth of that of the twelve-hyndeman, because the life of six ceorls was held to be equivalent in the matter of vengeance to that of one twelve-hyndeman. And thus it may be that, in the case of man-slaying, his oath and that of his oath-helpers, all of inferior value, came, under Anglo-Saxon custom, to be reckoned in comparison with that of the man of full kindred as worth only 'two hyndens' as against his twelve.

In the other passage in which the word 'hynden' occurs it has not so distinctly the meaning of 'oath-helpers.' It is not used in relation to homicide or wergelds, but still its use and its meaning are instructive.

The use of the word in the 'Judicia Civitatis Lundoniæ'[1] is in connection with the organisation of 'frith-gegildas' for the prevention and punishment of theft. These 'frith-gegildas' were groups or 'hyndens' with a common purse. And contributions were to be made for the common benefit. In the eighth clause it was enacted that the hynden-men should be collected every month, each twelve to a common meal. 'And if it should then happen that any kin be so strong and so great within land or without land whether xii-hynde or twy-hynde that they refuse us our right and stand up in defence of a thief, that we all of us ride thereto with the reeve within whose "manung" it may be.'

The hynden-men of the city frith-gegildas.

These hyndens were not directly groups of kinsmen and oath-helpers, but they were artificial groups formed and bound by a pledge for mutual protection, and the use of the word 'hynden' in this sense is significant. There were hyndens of oath-helpers under tribal custom, and now in the city hyndens of frith-gegildas were formed for mutual defence against powerful kindreds outside their city who were in the habit of protecting thieves from justice.

This was the way apparently that a substitute was found in the towns for the absent kindreds. And as time went on these artificial hyndens of *gegildas* or *congildones* no doubt in some measure took the place of the hyndens of kinsmen in cases of homicide as well as in cases of theft.

[1] Schmid, p. 157; Thorpe, p. 97.

Wealth and fullness of kindred often concurrent.

Naturally in the course of time the possession of property and social status would gradually take the place of the completeness of kindred, and the two elements in status would easily be associated together in common estimation. The value of a man's oath would depend more and more on the number of hides of land he was reckoned to possess, or for which he was responsible to the 'King's utware.'

If we may follow Schmid's translation of 'utware' as 'Heerbann' and picture to ourselves the ceorl who had risen to the social position of a man with a kindred and having five hides to the King's gafol, with his coat of mail and helmet and over-gilded sword coming up at the call of the King to the fyrd with so many followers, whether kinsmen or tenants, from the five hides under his charge and so becoming 'gesithcund' in regard to the King's service, then there would be force in the further clause which declares that, although he had acquired a kindred and a coat of mail and helmet and over-gilded sword, yet *if he have not that land, he is still but a ceorl.*

The power and strength and status of a person would still depend upon the combination of the two elements, and both would have to be reckoned with. A passage has already been quoted in which the possibility is admitted of a kindred becoming so powerful—*magna et fortis*—as to defy the King's law and defend the thief.[1] There is another passage relating to breaches of the peace in Kent in which the two sources of this power of defiance are mentioned together. The dangerous person may either

[1] *Judicia Civitatis Lundoniæ*, c. 8, s. 2; *Ath. L.* vi.

be *so rich* or be of *so great a kindred* that he could not be punished—'adeo dives vel tantæ parentelæ ut castigari non possit.'[1]

VI. THE GESITHCUND AND CEORLISC CLASSES IN THEIR CONNECTION WITH LAND.

Pursuing the question of division of classes mentioned in the Dooms of Ine we turn now to the consideration of the most prominent distinction which runs through the clauses of the Dooms, viz. that of *gesithcund* and *ceorlisc.*

Roughly speaking, the two distinctions may have been gradually coming more and more to mean much the same thing. As a rule no doubt in King Ine's time ceorlisc men were twy-hynde and gesithcund men twelve-hynde.

The unit of 10 hides of land.

The same class which, regarded from the point of view of the wergeld, possessed completeness of kindred and the twelve-hynde oath, when looked at from another point of view was gesithcund, *i.e.* more or less directly in the service of the King and belonging to the official and landed class. So that the value of the oath of both twelve-hynde and gesithcund men may have become easily associated with a territorial unit of ten hides of land.

Now, the fact of the connection of the value of the oath with ten hides of land is pretty good proof that for practical purposes and in common usage the holding of ten hides was looked upon as in some way or other a typical unit of holding of the

[1] *Decretum Episcoporum et aliorum sapientum de Kancia de pace observanda. Ath. L.* iii.

gesithcund or landed class. There is nothing new in this suggestion, but its lack of novelty does not detract from its value. And an examination from a tribal point of view of the isolated passages in the Dooms of Ine relating to this typical holding of ten hides may possibly throw further and useful light upon the position of the gesithcund class.

While we speak of the gesithcund class as almost equivalent to the landed class it is obvious that it would be wrong to consider every gesithcund-man as a landowner. Attention has already been called to the following clause:

> (51) If a gesithcundman owning land neglect the fyrd, let him pay 120s. and forfeit his land. One not owning land 60s., a *ceorlisc* man 30s. as fyrd-wite.

The gesithcundman *not* possessing land may either be one who has forfeited his land or a cadet of the class not having yet attained to the position of landholding and yet being gesithcund by birth.

Nor would it do to let modern notions of land-ownership intrude themselves so far into the question as to make us regard the gesithcund and landed class as a class of land-*owners* in the modern sense. If the typical holding of ten hides be that of the gesithcundman, we may have to regard him rather as a gesith of the King put into possession of the ten hides by way of stewardship than as anything like the absolute owner of them.

Ten hides the unit for food rents to the chieftain or King.

The typical holding of ten hides may perhaps be usefully regarded, from a fiscal point of view, as a unit for purposes of revenue, at a time when that revenue under tribal custom consisted chiefly of food rents paid in kind for the King's or the chieftain's use.

Clause 70 of the Dooms of Ine fixes in detail the food rent of 'ten hides' 'to fostre' or 'on feorm.'

If the unit of ten hides were not the customary unit for these food rents on the Royal domains why should the details of the food rent of ten hides have been made the subject of an isolated clause like this?

Land grants of 10 hides.

Again, if we turn to the grants made by King Ine to the monasteries, they become intelligible if the system of management of the Royal domains in units and multiples of ten hides may be understood to underlie them. When Ine grants to Aldhelm, then Abbot of Malmesbury, '45 cassati' in the county of Wilts, the grant is found to consist of groups of 'manentes' in four different places. And the groups consist of 5, 20, 10, and 10.[1] When Ine makes a grant to Abbot Bernald of land in Somersetshire it consists of three groups of 20, 20, and 20 *cassati* or *manentes* from three different estates.[2] And when he makes a similar grant to Glastonbury it consists of 10, 10, 20, 20 hides and one hide in five different places in Somersetshire.[3]

So also when Bede mentions the donations by King Oswy to the Abbess Hilda of 12 *possessiuncula terrarum* he adds that six were in the province of Deira and six in Bernicia and that each of them consisted of 10 *familiæ*, so that in all there were 120.[4]

Now it would seem that as ealdormen were set over shires so gesithcund men may have been set over smaller units of 10 hides or multiples of 10 hides, holding them as lænland, not only for services

[1] Birch, No. 102, A.D. 701.
[2] *Ib.* 113, A.D. 705.
[3] *Ib.* 142, A.D. 725.
[4] *Hist. Eccl.* lib. iii. c. 24.

rendered, but also with some kind of subordinate official or even judicial functions.

Official position of the gesithcundman.

Schmid long ago pointed out that the translator of Bede in six passages translated the Latin *comes* by 'gesith' or 'gesithcundman.'[1] This seems to imply that his position was in some sense an official one, subordinate indeed to the ealdorman's, as we may also learn from the translator of Bede. For while he translates the '*villa comitis*' of Bede as the '*gesith's hus*' he translates the '*villa regis*' as the residence of the king's ealdor ('botl cyninges ealdor').[2]

We found in s. 45 of King Ine's Laws above quoted that the gesithcundman's burg-bryce was thirty-five scillings while the ealdorman's was eighty scillings. Still, though the lowest official in the scale, it was something that he should be named with the King, the ealdorman, and the King's thane as having a burg-bryce according to which he was to make legal denial (ansacan).

The omission from this clause as to burg-bryce of classes below him seems to mark that while even the ceorlisc man—*i.e.* even the gafol-gelda or gebur—was responsible for the peace within his 'flet' and received a fight-wite when it was broken by fighting in it, the gesithcundman belonged to the class with some sort of extra jurisdiction beyond that which attached to every man whose homestead was by long tribal custom a sacred precinct.

And there is a clause in the Laws of Ine which seems to refer to the something like judicial duties

---

[1] *Glossary*, sub voce 'Gesith,' and see Bede, iii. 14 and 22, iv. 4 and 10, and v. 4 and 5.

[2] Bede, ii. c. ix.

of the gesithcundman, for it shows that neglect of them causing a suit which he ought to have settled to be carried to a higher court—before the ealdorman or the King—deprived him of his right to share in the 'wite-ræden,' whatever they were, appertaining to the suit.

His judicial and magisterial duties.

Gif gesiðcund mon þingað wið cyning oþþe wið kyninges ealdormannan for his inhiwan oþþe wið his hlaford for þeowe oþþe for frige nah he þær nane witerædenne se gesið forþon he him nolde ær yfles gestieran æt ham.	(50) If a gesithcundman has a suit with the King or with the King's ealdorman for his household or with his lord for bond or for free; he (the gesith) shall not there have any 'witeræden' because he would not correct him before of his evil deeds at home.

That he had special duties to discharge in connection with the 'fyrd' was shown not only by one of the qualifications of the gesithcund status being the possession of a coat of mail, helmet, and over-gilded sword, but also by the fyrd-wite of 120 scillings and the loss of his land if he neglected the fyrd.

That he was put into his landed position under conditions to secure the management of the land for the provision of the King's gafol is shown by the following clauses, which in regard to one important particular at least point out what was expected of him and further suggest that there was reason to fear that sometimes he might be inclined to desert his post without having performed the conditions upon which his land was held.

His duty to secure the King's gafol from his land.

Be gesiðcundes monnes fære.	*If a gesithcund leaves [the land].*
Gif gesiðcund man fare þonne mot he habban his gerefan mid him ⁊ his smið ⁊ his cild-festran.	(63) If a gesithcundman leaves, then may he have with him his reeve [?] and smith and his foster-nurse.

He must settle tenants on the land.

Seþe hæfð xx hida se sceal tæcnan xii hida gesettes landes þonne he faran wille.	(64) He who has 20 hides, he shall show 12 hides of *geset land* if he want to leave.
Seþe hæfð x hida se sceal tæcnan vi hida gesettes landes.	(65) He who has 10 hides shall show 6 hides of *geset land.*
Seþe hæbbe þreo hida tæcne oðres healfes.	(66) If he have three hides let him show one and a half.

These clauses suggest very clearly that the gesithcundman had been entrusted with the ten hides or twenty hides, or sometimes a smaller number, under the special obligation to provide the food rent by settling tenants upon the land.

Method of settling gafol-geldas and geburs on yardlands.

Let us pass, then, to what evidence the Dooms of Ine afford as to the customary method of settling tenants on the land.

The very next sections to those just quoted are as follows:—

Be gyrde londes.	*Of a yardland.*
Gif mon geþingað gyrde landes oþþe mære to ræde-gafole ⁊ geereð, gif se hlaford him wile þ land aræran to weorce ⁊ to gafole, ne þearf he him onfon gif he him nan botl ne selð. ⁊ þolie þara æcra.	(67) If a man agrees for a yardland or more to gafol and ploughs it, if the lord wants to raise the land *to work and to gafol,* he need not take it upon him if he [the lord] does not give him a *botl,* and let him give up (?) the acres.
Gif mon gesiðcundne monnan adrife, fordrife þy *botle, næs þære setene.*	(68) If a man drive off a gesithcundman, let him be driven from the *botl,* not the *setene.*

Working from the known to the unknown, in a former volume we found that under the open-field system of husbandry the hide at the time of the Domesday survey and earlier was generally held to contain four virgates or yardlands, and that so far as arable land was concerned each yardland was a bundle, so to speak, of about thirty scattered strips or acres. Tracing the yardland further back, the interesting point was gained from the tenth-century document known as the 'Rectitudines &c.,' that 'in some regions' the custom in allotting a yardland to a tenant called a '*gebur*' was to give him with his yardland to *land-setene* seven acres already sown and a *pair of oxen*, and certain other things theoretically by way of loan, so that on the gebur's death everything returned to the lord, though in practice the holding and land-setene were no doubt continued to his successor on payment of a 'relief.' And this system of settling gafol-geldas and geburs, or whatever such tenants might be locally called, on yardlands seems to be that alluded to in the Dooms of Ine. The clauses incidentally referring to gafol-geldas, geburs, and yardlands thus become intelligible and important in the light of the later evidence. This I endeavoured to show in a former volume.[1]

The yardland was the usual holding of the *gebur*, with a pair of oxen.

Now, this system of settling tenants on yardlands by allotting to each a pair of oxen, so that four of them should be able to combine in forming the common plough-team of the hide, obviously belongs to a time when agriculture had become sufficiently important for the unit of occupation and so of gafol-paying and services to be generally agricultural rather than pastoral. But while the *hide* thus seems to have been connected in the Dooms of Ine mainly with arable farming, it does not follow that it always had been so everywhere. The word 'hide' may have originally been applied to a holding devoted more to the grazing of cattle than the growing of corn.

The hide of four yardlands agricultural.

[1] *English Village Community*, chap. v.

The remarkable document which has been called 'The Tribal Hidage,' to the meaning and date of which Mr. W. J. Corbett[1] has opened our eyes, shows that forty or fifty years before the date of the Dooms of Ine the whole of England then subject to the Anglo-Saxons was, as we should say, rated in hides according to its tribes or mægthes, possibly for the fiscal purposes of the Bretwaldaship. And it would seem likely that under the common designation of hides pastoral as well as agricultural units for food rents must have been included. This seems to be indicated by the fact that the hides and virgates of the pastoral districts of West Wales in the Exon Domesday book are many times greater than those of other parts of England, and vary very much in area.

In pastoral districts co-aration of the waste.

In the pastoral or grazing districts recently conquered from West Wales early tribal usage would be very likely to survive. And there may well have been some continuity in the methods of tribal agriculture. Judging from what we know from the Cymric Codes, there might not yet be permanent division of the fields into strips and virgates but rather co-aration of such portions of the waste each year as suited the requirements of the tribesmen.

The open-field system of agriculture was in its main principles and chief methods common to German and Celtic tribes. But we are told that the Germans knew nothing of co-operative ploughing and the

---

[1] See *Transactions of the Royal Historical Society*. New Series, vol. xiv.

team of eight oxen on which the agricultural hidage of England was so clearly based. For the team of eight oxen we must go to the Cymric Codes and the practice in the Isle of Man and Scotland. It was common to these Celtic regions, even to its details—the yoke of four oxen abreast and the driver walking backwards in front of the team.[1] In such a matter as the method of ploughing there may well have been continuity.

The team of 8 oxen said not to be German.

We seem to see in the Laws of Ine the process going on of transition from the tribal form of the open-field system—the co-aration of the waste—to the more fixed forms of settled and permanent agriculture.

Thus, without pressing analogies too far, there may be a root of tribal custom discernible even in the system of settling geburs on yardlands. Something very much like it was followed on the Continent under Roman usage. But the case of the veteran to whom a pair of oxen with seed of two kinds was given as his outfit only partly resembled the case of the gebur. In the case of the gebur the outfit of oxen remained in theory the property of the lord, and returned to him on the death of the tenant. This was the essential point which created the semi-servile tenancy. With the homestead went the 'setene' or outfit and the corresponding obligation not only of gafol but also of week-work, and out of the peculiar relation so established may have grown up in West Wales, as in Wales itself and Ireland, very easily the doctrine that after its continuance

The allotment of stock and homestead by the lord to the gebur was the basis of the tenancy.

[1] *English Village Community*, p. 117 *et seq.*

for four generations the tenant became *adscriptus glebæ*.

The allotment of stock by the Irish chieftain formed, as we have seen, in a cattle-breeding rather than an agricultural community the traditional tie between himself and his tenants, whether tribesmen or strangers. The Cymric chieftain of a kindred followed very nearly the same traditional practice when he gave to the young tribesman on his attaining the age of fourteen his *da* (or allotment of cattle) for his maintenance, thereby establishing the relation of 'man and kin' between him and the chief.

The same tribal principles were, moreover, applied to strangers both in Ireland and Wales. The Irish 'fuidhir' thus settled on the chieftain's land became, as we have seen, after four generations *adscriptus glebæ*, and so did the *Aillt* or *Alltud* settled on the Cymric chieftain's land. And the same number of generations attached the *nativus* to the land under early Scotch law.

Now, if under tribal usage this was so, it need not be surprising that in the newly conquered districts of West Wales or more generally in Wessex at the time of King Ine, when the extension of agriculture was an immediate necessity, something like the same traditional system should continue or come again naturally into use, producing something like the same kind of dependence of one class upon the other.

This system of settlement very general.

It is necessary to point out that this method of settling tenants on yardlands with an outfit of a pair of oxen &c. was more or less general, because doubts have been recently thrown upon it. Its prevalence as a custom does not rest entirely on the evidence of the 'Rectitudines' but on several incidental mentions of it in various and distant quarters.

For instance, in the will of a reeve named Abba of Kent (about A.D. 833)[1] is the gift of a 'half swulung'—*i.e.* what elsewhere would have been described as a half hide—and with that land were to go four oxen, two cows, and fifty sheep, that is two oxen and one cow and twenty-five sheep to each *gioc* or yardland. Kent.

And again, the Inquisition of Glastonbury (A.D. 1189)[2] describes the holder of a yardland almost in the same terms as those used in the 'Rectitudines' in the description of the *gebur*. He is said to hold a yardland for 32*d.* (probably 1*d.* per acre), and every Monday he must plough a half-acre and harrow it, and he works every day in the week but on Sunday. He has from his lord one heifer (*averum*) and two oxen and one cow and seven acres of corn sown and three acres of oats (to start with)—ten acres in all sown—and six sheep and one ram. King Ine made grants of land, as we have seen, to Glastonbury, and it is interesting to find the custom of allowing two oxen, one cow, and six sheep to the yardland as described in the 'Rectitudines' still going on in West Wales five hundred years after Ine's time on the estates of the Abbey. Glastonbury.

Take again the charter MLXXIX. mentioned by Kemble (i. p. 216). This charter shows that the Bishop of Winchester (A.D. 902) had leased fifteen hides of land to a relative of the Bishop, requiring that he Winchester.

[1] Birch, 412. [2] Roxburgh Club, p. 138.

must settle there (*inberthan*)[1] men who would be fixed (*hamettan*) to the place. He himself had 'hamet' Lufe and her three bairns, and Luhan and his six bairns, and these must remain on the land whoever might hold it. There were also three *witetheows bur*bærde and three more *theow*bærde belonging to the Bishop, with their descendants (*and hire team*). At this date the settling of new tenants (may we not say?) some of them as geburs and some as theows was still going on in Wessex A.D. 902.

It is quite true that the holders of these yardlands are not everywhere always described as *geburs*. But we are dealing with the *thing*, not the name. The word *gebur*, however, was of much wider use than merely in one or two localities.

Tyddenham.

It is not only in the 'Rectitudines' that the gebur and his services are mentioned. On the Tyddenham Manor of King Edwy on the 'gesetland' there were 'geburs' with yardlands (gyrdagafollandes)—as mentioned in the former volume (p. 150). And other examples may be quoted.

Shaftesbury.

In the will of Wynfled[2] there is mention of lands at Shaftesbury and 'the geburs that on those gafollands sit' (*þara gebura di on þam gafollandes sittað*). And as incidental evidence that the geburs became in course of time *adscripti glebæ*, it is worth while to remember that early in the eleventh century the monks of Ely in connection with their Manor of Hatfield kept record of the children of the geburs on

[1] Compare *ærdian*, to inhabit; and so *bur*bærde and *theow*bærde, as below.

[2] About A.D. 995. Cod. Dip. 1290.

their estate who had married with others of neighbouring manors, so that they might not lose sight of them and their rights over them. And the importance with which their rights were regarded is emphasised by the fact that the record was kept upon the back of an ancient copy of the Gospels belonging presumably to the altar of St. Etheldreda.[1] Hatfield.

Now, if such in part was the relation between the gesithcundman and the tenants of the yardlands of his 'geset-land' arising from the allotment or loan of stock, may not something of the same kind lie at the root of the relation between the gesithcundman himself and the King? Lord as he may have been over his ceorlisc gafol-geldas, was not the gesithcundman himself a servant of the King looking after the King's gafol, a kind of middleman, tied to his post with the ealdorman above him in the hierarchy of Royal service, liable to lose his land if he neglected his duty?

How far the gebur was *adscriptus glebæ.*

It is an interesting question how far the ceorlisc class were *adscripti glebæ* under the Laws of Ine, but when we try to find this out we discover that both classes seem to be under some kind of restraint as to 'going away' (*fære*). If a gesithcundman 'fare' we have seen under what restrictions it must be. There is another clause which deals with the case of persons who shall 'fare' without leave from their lords.

Gif hwa fare unaliefed fram his hlaforde oþþe on oðre scire	(s. 39) If any one go from his lord without leave or steal him-

[1] *Cod. Dip.* mcccliv. See also *Liber Eliensis*, p. 120.

hine bestele ⁊ hine mon geahsige fare þær he ær wæs ⁊ geselle his hlaforde lx scill.	self away into another shire and he be discovered, let him go where he was before and pay to his lord 60 scillings.

Judged in the light of later laws to the same or nearly similar effect, this clause must probably be regarded rather as early evidence of the relation between lord and man established generally for the maintenance of the public peace, than as bearing directly upon the question of the attachment of the smaller class of tenants to the soil.[1] And yet if the relation of the ordinary freeman to, let us say, the ealdorman of the shire was such that he might not move into another shire without leave, and until it was ascertained whether his action was *bona fide*, or perhaps with the object to escape from debt or vengeance for a wrong committed, the restriction would be likely to be still stronger when a tenant was under fixed obligations to his lord, or had, by taking a yardland and homestead, settled on his lord's land and accepted stock under conditions of gafol and week-work regulated by general usage.

The idea of freedom as a kind of masterful independence of the individual was not one inherited from tribal modes of thought, nor likely to be fostered by the circumstances of the times which followed upon the Anglo-Saxon conquest of Britain. When this fact is fully recognised, the gulf between the gesithcund and ceorlisc classes does not seem so deep, after all, as it would be if, instead of approaching the question from a tribal point of view, we were looking for allodial landowners on the one hand and expect-

[1] Alfred, s. 37.

ing the ceorl to be a member of a village community of independent peasant proprietors on the other hand.

The king's food rents or gafol how paid.

But we are not doing this, and, returning to the gesithcundman, perhaps we have after all taken for granted quite enough that the general environment in Wessex was agricultural rather than pastoral. Even as regards King Ine himself, there may have been a good deal of the tribal chieftain still left in his relations to his gesithcund followers and officials. We have spoken of his tribal food rents; but how did he gather them?

The *firma unius noctis*.

No doubt the King's gafol may partly have been paid in money. But so far as it was paid in kind it must have been carried by his tenants to his Winchester palace, or one of his other manors, according to the system prevalent at the time, followed for centuries after in West Wales, viz. the system of the 'night's entertainment' (*firma unius noctis*)—a system followed by tribal chieftains and their Royal successors in Scandinavia as well as in Britain.

When the Domesday survey was made of what was once West Wales there was found still existing, especially in Dorsetshire, the survival of a very practical arrangement of Royal food rents which may have been in use in King Ine's time and date back possibly before the West Saxon conquests.

Some portions of the 'terra Regis' scattered about the county of Dorset are grouped in the survey so that each group might supply the *firma unius noctis*, the money equivalent of which is stated to be 104*l.*, *i.e.* 2*l.* per night's entertainment for one night each week in the year. This mode of providing the *firma unius noctis* is illustrated by the legend which represents King Ine himself and his queen as moving from manor to manor for each night's entertainment, their moveable palace of poles and curtains being carried before them from place to place upon sumpter mules.

Now, if we might regard the gesithcundman as one of a class to whom ten hides or twenty hides had been allotted by King Ine on a system providing in this practical way *inter alia* for the night's entertainments, it would be natural that the food rent of the unit of ten hides should be fixed. And further, it would be natural that if the gesithcundman should wish to throw up his post and desert the land entrusted to his management he should be restricted, as we have seen, by conditions intended to secure that the provision for the King's entertainment or gafol in lieu of it should not materially suffer.

We have seen that as the ealdorman was to lose his 'shire' if he let go a thief, so the gesithcundman was to pay a fyrdwite, and to lose his *land* if he neglected the *fyrd*. It was possible, then, that he might have to be evicted. And a clause in the Dooms of Ine has already been quoted which seems to refer to the eviction of a gesithcundman.

The gesithcundman sometimes evicted.

Be gesiðcundes monnes dræfe of londe.	(68) If a gesithcundman be driven off land.
Gif mon gesiðcundne monnan adrife, fordrife þy botle næs þære setene.	If one drive off a gesithcundman, let him be driven forth from the homestead (*botl*), not the *setene*.

If he was evicted he was to be driven from the *botl*

or homestead, not the *setene*. What can the *setene* have been?

The land granted or intrusted to the gesithcundman for the performance of corresponding duties is not likely to have been mere waste. Part of it might surely already be 'geset land,' let to tenants of yardlands. On the rest of it still held in demesne there would probably be some herds of cattle. In these early days the cattle and corn on the land were far more valuable than the mere land itself. If, therefore, a fixed food rent was payable to the King, may it not be inferred that sometimes the typical holding of ten hides included the stock let with it, just as, according to the 'Rectitudines,' the yardland did? Following strictly the analogy, the original stock on the land and in the hands of the tenants would be the 'setene' of the gesithcundman, theoretically, like the land itself, belonging, not to him, but to his lord? It might have been sometimes so. But at the same time there might be other cases in which the possession of cattle may have led to the tenure. The ceorl or the wealh who had risen to having five hides may have brought the cattle or setene with him. And to evict him from his own cattle and crops as well as from the *botl* might be unjust.

Were the stock and crops always his own?

The text as it stands seems to mean that the gesithcundman is not to be evicted *from* the *setene*, and the clause seems to be intended to protect his rights and to prevent his being evicted from his own stock and crops on the land. The clause is not clear, but it adds to the sense that in the case of the gesithcundman we are not dealing with a landowner who can do what he likes with his own, any more than in the case of the ceorlisc gafol-geldas we are dealing with a class of peasant proprietors.

Position of the two classes in Ine's time.

Difficult as it may be to come to a clear understanding of some of these isolated passages in the Dooms of Ine, they may at least have saved us from the pitfall of a fatal anachronism. Their difficulties, forcing us to think, may in some degree have helped us to realise the point of view from which the two classes—gesithcund and ceorlisc—were regarded in early Wessex legislation.

The gesithcund class the landed class.

Throughout Wessex, speaking generally, they seem to have been regarded as the two prominent classes in practical agricultural life. The general facts of everyday observation marked off the gesithcundman as belonging to the ruling class, holding land direct from the King as the King's gesith, while the ceorlisc man, speaking generally, in his relation to land was the gafol-gelda or gebur sometimes probably holding his yardland on the King's demesne, but mostly perhaps and more and more often as the tenant of the gesithcundman. This, it would seem, had become so general that in King Alfred's day and perhaps even in King Ine's, ignoring the exceptional classes between the gesithcund and the other class, there was no absurdity in King Alfred's claiming that equally dear with the Danish lysing the 'ceorl who sits on gafol land' should have a twy-hynde wergeld.

The ceorlisc class the tenant class paying gafol to the landed class.

The division into gesithcund and ceorlisc classes was doubtless a somewhat rough and wide generalisation. There were, we know, men without land who belonged to the gesithcund class, and ceorls who were not tenants of yardlands. And even among the tenants of yardlands some paid gafol only and others both gafol and week-work. But for our purpose the fact to be noted is that the generalisation was sufficiently near the truth for it to be made.

We must not infer that these two classes included strictly the whole population. Judging from Continental evidence, Wessex must have been very exceptional indeed if there were not everywhere numerous *theows* or thralls. From this class Anglo-Saxon wills and other documents show that there was a constant stream of freedmen or theows who by emancipation were allowed to creep up into the ceorlisc class, partly as the result of Christian impulse, and partly probably from the lack of tenants to occupy the yardlands left vacant by the desolation caused by constant wars.

The ceorlisc class would include newly made freedmen.

Thus while, broadly speaking, the gesithcund and the ceorlisc classes may have corresponded to the twelve-hynde and twy-hynde classes, they were not absolutely identical. The two lines of distinction had not the same origin and did not run absolutely parallel. But they may well have worked in the same direction. The original distinction founded upon the possession or absence of the perfect kindred and 'hyndens of oath-helpers' was rooted in tribal instincts and never wholly extinguished throughout Anglo-Saxon history. The gesithcund class, most perfect in their kindred and nearest in their relation to the King, influenced perhaps by traditions of Roman land management, naturally grew up into a twelve-hynde and landed class, while the ceorlisc class, recruited from outside and from below, just as naturally became their tenants.

The gulf between the two classes existed in King Alfred's time.

Thus in England, as elsewhere, we may easily believe that the gulf between classes resulting from tribal instincts and confirmed by difference in wergelds was hardened and widened by the conditions of landholding in the conquered country, which tended to raise the one class more and more into manorial lords and depress the other into more or less servile tenants. The Compact between Alfred and Guthrum affords the strongest evidence that already in King Alfred's time the process was far enough advanced for a pretty hard line to be drawn between them.

VII. COMPARISON OF WESSEX AND MERCIAN WERGELDS WITH THOSE OF CONTINENTAL TRIBES.

Before passing from the Wessex to the Kentish laws it may be well to mark the position to which the evidence hitherto examined has brought us with regard to the amount of the wergelds.

Continental wergelds of 200 and 160 gold solidi for the full freeman.

We have had again and again to come back to the question of the status of the twelve-hynde and twy-hynde classes as shown by their wergelds. By the Compact between King Alfred and Guthrum the English wergelds were brought into line with Norse and other Continental wergelds. The statement of the higher wergeld in gold made possible a comparison of the Anglo-Saxon with Continental wergelds.

The result of. the inquiry into the Continental wergelds of the full freeman was that they seemed to fall very distinctly into two classes—the Frankish and Norse wergeld of 200 gold solidi, on the one hand, and the Frisian, Saxon, Alamannic, Bavarian, and possibly Burgundian wergeld of 160 gold solidi on the other hand.

The ratio between these two wergelds is as 5 : 4.

Now, this is exactly the ratio between the two twelve-hynde wergelds of the Anglo-Saxon laws, *i.e.* of Wessex and of Mercia. Both were of 1200 scillings, but the Wessex scilling was of five pence and the Mercian of four pence.

The Wessex and Mercian wergelds ancient.

Finding twelve-hynde and twy-hynde wergelds in the Laws of Ine, we seem to be bound to regard the distinctions between the two classes as going back to a time two centuries at least before the inroads of the Northmen.

The position of the Dooms of Ine as they have come down to us annexed to the Laws of King Alfred might possibly have raised a doubt as to whether the incidental mention of the wergelds might not have been inserted in the text by the scribes of King Alfred. But if the Mercian wergelds were of ancient tradition, independently of the Wessex evidence, the statement of the Wessex wergelds in the Dooms of Ine need not be doubted. At the same time, the amount of the Wessex wergeld is confirmed by the wergeld of the secular thane in the Northumbrian statement, for 2000 thrymsas are equal to 6000 pence, and thus the wergeld of the thane accords with the Wessex twelve-hyndeman's wergeld. And as this statement seems to have been rescued from times anterior to the Northmen's invasion, it is so far independent evidence. In the same document the ceorl's wergeld of 200 Mercian scillings is also mentioned.

The concurrence of independent traditions thus

seems to trace back the difference between the Wessex and Mercian wergelds as well as the difference between the twelve-hynde and twy-hynde classes in both cases into the early Anglo-Saxon period. And if we may date them back to the time of King Ine—two centuries before the invasion of the Northmen—they may well go back earlier still. For wergelds which have already become traditional in the seventh century may not improbably have been brought by the invading tribes with them into Britain in the fifth and sixth centuries. The fact that the Mercian and Wessex wergelds differed makes it unlikely that the traditional wergelds were first adopted in Britain or acquired from the Romano-British population. That they differed exactly in the same ratio as the two classes of Continental wergelds differed is a fact which points still more strongly to a Continental origin.

At 1 : 10 Wessex wergeld of 6000 pence = 200 gold solidi, and the Mercian of 4800 pence = 160 gold solidi.

Moreover, the Wessex and Northumbrian wergeld of 1200 scillings of five pence—*i.e.* 6000 pence or sceatts at a ratio of 1 : 10—was equal to 600 tremisses or 200 gold solidi.

The Mercian wergeld of 1200 scillings of four pence—*i.e.* 4800 pence or sceatts—at the same ratio was equal to 480 tremisses or 160 gold solidi.

That the ratio of 1 : 10 was not an unlikely one is shown by its being the ratio under the Lex Salica between the forty scripula of silver and the gold solidus before the Merovingian reduction of the standard weight of the latter and the issue of silver tremisses.[1] It was also the ratio at which twelve Roman argentei

---

[1] See *supra*, pp. 180–185.

or drachmæ of silver were apparently reckoned as equal to the Merovingian gold solidus.

The correspondence at this ratio of the Wessex twelve-hynde wergeld with the Frankish wergeld of 200 gold solidi, and of the Mercian twelve-hynde wergeld with the other Continental wergelds of 160 gold solidi, is sufficiently striking to be taken into account in any speculation as to the respective origins of the West Saxon and Mercian invading tribes. But that is not the object of this essay. It is enough to have noted a fact which may or may not turn out to be of some historical significance.

The value of the wergelds to this inquiry consists in the light they throw upon the solidarity of tribal society and the position in social rank of the various classes of Anglo-Saxon society. But we have yet to examine the laws of the Kentish kings, and it will be best to suspend any further judgment on these points until this remaining part of our task has been done.

CHAPTER XIV.

THE LAWS OF THE KENTISH KINGS.

I. DISTINCTION FROM ANGLO-SAXON LAWS, A.D. 596–696.

THE laws of the Kentish kings, if they had been on all fours with the other Anglo-Saxon laws, would have taken back the general evidence for Anglo-Saxon custom another hundred years earlier than the Laws of Ine, and nearer the time of the conquest of Britain. As it is, however, they have to be treated as in part exceptional.

Belgic agriculture.

It is very probable that for a long period the proximity of Kent to the Continent had resulted in the approximation of its social and economic conditions to those of the opposite shore of the Channel. The south-east corner of Britain was described by Cæsar as having been colonised by Belgæ and as having been for some time under Belgic rule. The Belgic tribes were the furthest advanced of Celtic tribes and, according to Cæsar, had fostered agriculture, while his informants spoke of the interior of Britain as pastoral.

Under Roman rule the prominence of agriculture was continued. Ammianus Marcellinus describes large exports of British corn to supply Roman legions on the Rhine. He speaks of the British *tributarii* in a way which suggests that this part of Britain under Roman rule had become subject to economic arrangements similar to those of the Belgic provinces of Gaul.

The sulungs and yokes of Kent.

The introduction, by invitation, of the Jutes into Kent and their settlement, in the first instance at all events, under a friendly agreement of payment of *annonæ*, may have given an exceptional character to the results of ultimate conquest. The permanent prominence of agriculture is perhaps shown by the fiscal assessment in 'sulungs' and 'yokes' instead of hides and virgates.

The exceptional conditions of the Kentish district were continued by its being the earliest to come into close contact with the court of the Merovingian Franks, and with ecclesiastical influences from Rome. The mission of St. Augustine resulted in the codification of Kentish custom into written laws a century earlier than the date of the earliest laws of Wessex.

Early clerical influences.

The peculiar character of Kentish custom may have been further maintained by the partial isolation of Kent. The kingdom of the Kentish kings, though lessened in Ethelbert's time by the encroachment of Wessex, had maintained its independence of both the Northumbrian and Mercian supremacy or Bretwaldorship.

Apart from any original difference in custom between Jutish and other tribes this isolation naturally produced divergence in some respects from the customs of the rest of Anglo-Saxon England and may perhaps partly explain why the Laws of the Kentish Kings came to be included in only one of the early collections of Anglo-Saxon laws.

Further, when we approach the subject of Kentish

wergelds we do so with the direct warning, already alluded to, of the writer of the so-called Laws of Henry I., that we shall find them differing greatly from those of Wessex.

Wergelds said to differ from those of Wessex and Mercia.

> This we have said according to our law and custom, but the difference of wergeld is great in Kent, *villanorum et baronum.*

Moreover, in after times Kentish custom differed from that of other parts of England in the matter of succession. The custom of Gavelkind prevailed in Kent. And among the statutes after the Norman Conquest there is an undated statement setting forth peculiar customs of Kent in matters where they differed from those of the rest of the kingdom.

Some of these differences may have been of later origin, but a comparison of the laws themselves with other Anglo-Saxon laws is conclusive upon the point that important differences always existed and, what is more, were recognised as existing.

Although the Kentish laws are not included with other Anglo-Saxon laws in any manuscript but that of Rochester, yet they were known to King Alfred. He mentioned them in the proem to his laws as well as the Mercian laws as among those which he had before him in framing his own. Moreover, we have seen that at the time of the Danish invasion certain differences between the Kentish and other laws were known and noted correctly in the fragment 'Of Grith and of Mund.'

Finally, in its system of monetary reckoning the Kentish kingdom seems to have been peculiar from the first. And as our knowledge of the Kentish wergelds is essential to an understanding of the division of classes, a good deal must depend upon a previous understanding of the currency in which the amounts of the wergelds are described. Before proceeding further it is necessary, therefore, to devote a section to a careful consideration of the subject. The experience already gained will not be thrown away if it should help us to understand the meaning of the scætts and scillings of the Kentish laws.

II. THE SCÆTTS AND SCILLINGS OF THE KENTISH LAWS.

All the payments mentioned in the Kentish laws are stated in scætts and scillings—naturally, by far the larger number of them in the latter.

What were these scætts and scillings? First, what were the scætts?[1]

The scætts of 28·8 wheat-grains like Merovingian tremissis.

We have already seen that before the time of Offa the silver coinage current in England consisted mainly of the silver tremisses of Merovingian standard, *i.e.* twenty to the Roman ounce, or 28·8 wheat-grains. These are known to numismatists as silver pence of the *Sceatt* series.

That these silver coins were those known by the name of sceatts we seem to have the direct and independent evidence of the following fragment 'On Mercian Law,' already quoted but sufficiently important to be repeated here.[2]

Ceorles wergild is on Myrcna lage cc scill.	The ceorl's wergeld is in the law of the Mercians 200 scillings.
Þegnes wergild is syx swa micel, þæt bið twelf hund scill.	The thane's wergeld is six times as much, *i.e.* 1200 scillings.

[1] The difference in spelling will be noticed. The Kentish spelling is mostly *scætt*. Elsewhere the spelling is *sceatt*.

[2] Schmid, *Anhang vii.* p. 398.

Þonne bið cynges anfeald wergild six þegna wer be Myrcna laga þæt is xxx þusend sceatta, and þæt bið ealles cxx punda.	Then is the King's simple wergeld six thanes' wergeld by Mercian law, *i.e.* 30,000 sceatts, and that is in all 120 pounds.
. . . .	. . . .

Now, as previously observed, the sum of 30,000 sceatts must evidently be taken as a round sum. The statement that the King's simple wergeld was 120 pounds or six times the thane's wergeld of 1,200 Mercian scillings seems to make this clear, for 7200 Mercian scillings of four sceatts (28,800 sceatts) would amount exactly to 120 pounds.[1]

The sceatts minted by Kentish moneyers.

That the sceatts of this fragment of Mercian law were the same silver coins as the scætts of the Kentish laws is further confirmed by numismatic evidence. The evidence of the coins themselves and of the names of the moneyers impressed on them seems to make it probable that to a large extent till the time of Egbert, who was intimate with Charlemagne, and perhaps even till the time of his grandson Ethelbald, in the words of Mr. Keary, 'Kent still provided all the currency of the South.'[2] It would seem, therefore, that practically during the whole period of the issue of the silver pence of the Sceatt series the greater part of them were minted by Kentish moneyers. And thus numismatic evidence applies not only to the coinage of Wessex but also to that of Mercia.[3]

---

[1] It cannot be right, I think, to reason the other way with Schmid, that as there were 30,000 sceatts in the King's wergeld of 120 pounds, there must have been 250 sceatts in the pound and 4·166 sceatts in the Mercian scilling instead of four.

[2] Catalogue &c., Introduction, p. xviii.

[3] 'We must remember further that many of the coins of the Kings of Mercia were probably likewise struck in Kent, and that when we find, as we do, the same moneyers' names occurring on the

We can hardly be wrong, then, in thinking that this valuable fragment of Mercian law in using the word sceatt referred back to ancient custom before the sceatt had been superseded by the penny, and therefore must be good evidence that the silver coins called sceatts in Mercia were similar to those called scætts in Kent. In other words the Kentish *scœtt*, notwithstanding the slight difference in spelling, was almost certainly the silver *sceatt* of 28·8 wheat-grains, *i.e.* twenty to the Roman ounce.

It is quite true that the word *sceatt* was used in the laws in two senses, sometimes for 'money' or 'property,' and sometimes for the coin.[1] But so also was the *scœtt* of the Kentish laws.[2] And it may not always be easy to ascertain with certainty which meaning is the right one.

But the Kentish and Mercian laws were not alone in using the word for the silver coin. The phrase 'sceatts and scillings' was elsewhere used to denote the typical smaller and larger monetary unit, or perhaps we ought to say the silver and the gold unit.

In the tenth-century translation of the New Testament the word *denarius* is translated by 'pæning;' for long before this the penny of 32 wheat-grains had superseded the old coinage of the 'Sceatt series.' But in the translation of Ulphilas the word '*skatt*' is used for the silver *denarius*.[3]

---

coins of a King of Mercia . . . and on the coins of Ecgbeorht, the probability is that these moneyers were Kentishmen who struck first for one master of their country and then for the other' (*Ib.* p. xvii).

[1] See Schmid's *Glossary*, sub voce.

[2] See Laws of Ethelbert, ss. 77, 78 and 79, and 83.

[3] In translating Luke xx. 24 and Mark xii. 15, 'Show me a

At the same time it is important to observe that the word *scilling* was the Gothic word applied to the *gold solidus* in legal documents of the sixth century during Gothic rule in Italy.

According to the bilingual records in the archives of the Gothic church of St. Anastasia at Ravenna payments were made in so many 'skilligans.'[1] So that probably silver skatts and certainly gold scillings were familiar to the Goths of Italy.

Sceatts and scillings.

Again, sceatts and scillings were evidently the two monetary units familiar to the mind of Cædmon or whoever was the author of the metrical translation of Genesis. In c. xiv. 23 Abraham is made to swear that he would take neither 'sceat ne scilling' from the King of Sodom.

Moreover, in the fragment on Oaths [2] in the Anglo-Saxon Laws (Thorpe, p. 76) the same phrase is used:

On lifiendes Godes naman. ne ðearf ic N. sceatt ne scylling. ne pænig ne pæniges weorð.	(s. 11) In the name of the living God I owe not to N. *sceatt nor scilling*, not penny nor penny's worth.

penny,' the word used to translate 'denarius' is *skatt*.

Again, Luke vii. 41, the two debtors, one owing 500 and the other 50 denarii, are translated by Ulphilas as owing 'skatte finfhunda' and 'skatte finftiguns.'

Again in John xii. 5, 'Why was not the ointment sold for 300 denarii?' 'ccc skatti' are the words used, and so also in the parallel passage Mark xi. 5, 'thrijahunda skatti.'

In all these cases it seems to be clear that the *skatt* is the coin. And that it was a silver coin seems to be shown by the use by Ulphilas of the word *skatt* in reference to the 'thirty pieces of silver' in Matt. xxvii. 6-9.

[1] The word occurs seven times in the five Gothic records from Naples and Arezzo generally appended to editions of 'Ulfilas.' In the edition of Massmann (Stuttgart, 1857) see vol. ii. p. 810. In that of Heyne and Wrede (Paderborn, 1896) see p. 227 &c.

[2] Schmid, *Anhang x.* p. 404; Thorpe, p. 76.

Surely in both cases the phrase 'sceatt ne scilling' refers to coins or units of account of two denominations in current use, as in the Kentish laws.

It is even possible perhaps to find an illustration of the reckoning in sceatts and scillings in the well-known passage in the 'Scald's Tale' already quoted.

se me beag forgeaf	He me a bracelet gave
on tham siex hund wæs	on which six hundred was
smætes goldes	of beaten gold
gescyred sceatta	scored of sceatts
scilling-rime.	in scillings reckoned.

If these words may be properly translated literally 'Of sceatts in scillings reckoned'[1] and are taken to mean '600 sceatts in scillings reckoned,' the phrase accords very closely with the method of reckoning in the Salic laws—'so many hundred denarii, *i.e.* so many solidi.'

Returning to the sceatts and scillings of the Laws of Ethelbert, the most obvious suggestion would be that the currency in Kent was similar to that on the other side of the Channel under the Merovingian princes. The two courts were so closely connected by Ethelbert's marriage, and probably by trade intercourse, that the most likely guess, at first sight, would be that the Kentish scætts were silver tremisses and the Kentish scillings gold solidi like those of the Lex Salica.

We have seen that the Merovingian currency was mainly in *gold tremisses*, and as many of the 100 gold

[1] This may be doubtful: *Sceatta scilling-rim*, 'gold to the worth of 600 scillings,' Grein, ii. p. 408; *sceatta*, gen. plural of 'sceatt,' *nummus*, *pecunia*. Grein, ii. p. 405.

tremisses contained in the celebrated 'Crondale find' are believed by numismatists to have been coined in Kent, by English moneyers, the currency of gold tremisses in England is directly confirmed, though the silver currency seems very soon to have superseded it.[1]

At the date of Ethelbert's Laws (A.D. 596) the Merovingian currency was still mainly gold—*i.e.* gold tremisses, three of which went to the gold solidus of the Salic Laws. And if the scilling of Ethelbert, like the solidus of the Franks, had been a solidus of forty denarii we might have concluded at once that Ethelbert's scilling, like the Merovingian solidus, was a solidus of three gold tremisses, or forty silver sceatts.

The scilling of 20 scætts = one ounce of silver.

But the facts apparently will not allow us to come to this conclusion.

Schmid has shown—I think, conclusively—by inference from certain passages in Ethelbert's Laws, that the Kentish scilling was of *twenty* scætts instead of forty.[2] We therefore must deal with the Kentish scilling on its own evidence.

---

[1] British Museum Catalogue, Anglo-Saxon series, vol. i. xiii.

[2] See Schmid's *Glossary*, sub 'Geldrechnung,' p. 594. The inference seems to be too strong to be disregarded. Comparing s. 54 with ss. 70–72, the great toe is valued at 10 scillings, *i.e.* half the value of the thumb in s. 54, viz. 20 scillings. And it is stated in s. 54 that the thumb nail is worth 3 scillings, and in s. 72 that the toe nail is to be paid for at 30 scætts, which would be half 3 scillings of 20 sceatts. The other toes are said in s. 71 to be respectively worth half the fingers. The finger nail in s. 71 at 1 scilling compares with the other toe nails at 10 scætts in s. 72—again one half. Presuming that the scale of one half is maintained throughout, 30 scætts is half 3 scillings and 10 scætts half one scilling. The scilling, therefore, must be 20 scætts.

This conclusion is strengthened by the graduated scale of payments in ss. 33–36, viz. 50 scætts (*i.e.* 1½ scilling) 3, 4, 10,

Now, twenty sceatts of 28·8 wheat-grains, as we have seen, made the Roman ounce of 576 wheat-grains. The Kentish scilling was therefore the equivalent of an ounce of silver. And so in the Kentish laws, so far as reckoning in silver was concerned, the same method was adopted as that of the Welsh, who reckoned in *scores* or *unciæ* of silver, and that which became the common Frankish and Norman reckoning of twenty pence to the ounce and twelve ounces to the pound.

Indeed, when we consider that under common Scandinavian custom gold and silver were weighed and reckoned in marks, *ores*, and ortugs, it would seem natural that the Kentish immigrants from the North should have been already familiar with a reckoning in *ores* or ounces of silver.

But why did they call the ounce of silver a scilling? We might as well perhaps ask why the Wessex scilling was five pence and the Mercian scilling four pence. But the word *scilling* had, as we have seen, been used by the Goths in Italy for the gold solidus. And on the Continent the gold solidus in the sixth and seventh centuries, and indeed till the time of Charlemagne, was so far the recognised symbol of value that the wergelds of the Northern tribes, whether they remained in the north or emigrated southwards, were invariably stated in their laws in gold solidi. The most natural inference would therefore seem to

20 scillings. See also s. 16, where the scale is 30, 50 (? 60) sceatts and 6 scillings (120 scætts). In ss. 58–60 a bruise is 1 scilling, covered 30 scætts, uncovered 20 scætts. It seems to be impossible to make these figures comport with the Mercian scilling of 4 scætts or the Wessex of 5 scætts or the Salic solidus of 40 scætts. The conclusion must be that the Kentish scilling was of 20 scætts.

be that the Kentish scilling, like that of the Salic law, must have been a gold solidus equated, however, in account with twenty silver pence or scætts.

The Kentish scilling probably a solidus of two gold tremisses like the Saxon solidus.

Now, at the ratio of 1 : 10 the ore or ounce of twenty silver scætts would equal a gold solidus of two gold tremisses instead of three.[1] And when it is considered that the main Merovingian currency on the other side of the Channel was of gold tremisses it seems natural that the ounce of silver should be equated with an even number of gold tremisses.

Nor would there be anything unprecedented or unusual in a gold solidus of two tremisses instead of three. For we have seen that when Charlemagne conquered the Frisians and the Saxons, he found that the solidi in which they had traditionally paid their wergelds were not always, like the Imperial and the Salic solidi, of three gold tremisses, but that each district had its own peculiar solidus. The solidus of the southern division of Frisia was of two and a half gold tremisses. The solidus of the middle district was the ordinary gold solidus of three tremisses. The traditional solidus of the district presumably nearest to the Jutes, *i.e.* on both the Frisian and the Saxon side of the Weser, was the solidus of two tremisses. The Saxon solidus of two tremisses, representing the one-year-old bullock, was that in which according to the Lex Saxonum the Saxon wergelds had been traditionally paid.

We have no distinct mention of a Jutish solidus, but as the Jutes probably came from a district not far from that of the North Frisians and Saxons there

---

[1] 576 divided by 10 = 57·6, *i.e.* two tremisses of 28·8 wheat grains.

would be nothing abnormal or surprising in their reckoning in the same solidus as their neighbours, viz. in the gold solidus of two tremisses, and in the Kentish immigrants continuing the same practice. But this as yet is only conjecture.

So far, then, as the facts of the prevalent coinage and currency are concerned, all that can be said is that the hypothesis that the Kentish scilling was that of two gold tremisses has a good deal of probability in its favour. But there is other and more direct evidence of the truth of the hypothesis.

In the first place, as already stated, in the preface to King Alfred's Laws he expressly mentions his knowledge of the laws, not only of Ine and of Offa, but also of Ethelbert, the inference being that in his own laws he retained, *inter alia*, some of the enactments of Ethelbert which were in his own view worth retaining.[1]

Confirmation by other evidence. The King's mund-byrd of five pounds common to Wessex and Kent.

Now, King Alfred *fixed the king's mund-byrd at five pounds* of silver, *i.e.* 240 Wessex scillings, while he must have known that in the Kentish law the king's mund-byrd was fifty Kentish scillings. The difference in scillings must have struck him, but he probably knew perfectly well what the Kentish scillings were. For when we compare these two mund-byrds we find that at a ratio between gold and silver of 1 : 12 (which, as we have seen, was the Frankish ratio of Charlemagne's successors) fifty Kentish scillings of two gold tremisses did equal exactly five pounds. Fifty

[1] Alfred's words were: 'But those things which I met with, either of the days of Ine my kinsman, or of Offa King of the Mercians, or of Æthelbryht, who first among the English race received baptism, those which seemed to me the rightest, those I have here gathered together and omitted the others.'

Kentish scillings or 100 Merovingian gold tremisses, at 1 : 12 were equal to 1200 silver tremisses or sceatts of the same weight, *i.e.* five pounds of 240 sceatts ; or, in other words, 100 gold tremisses (*nova moneta*) were equal at the same ratio to five pounds of 240 of King Alfred's pence of 32 wheat-grains. The equation was exact.

And further, we have seen that in the time of Cnut the Kentish king's mund-byrd was well known and declared to be five pounds according to Kentish law, although in that law it was stated to be 50 scillings.

The passage has already been quoted from the MS. G of Cnut's Church law, s. 3, in which, after stating that 'the grith-bryce of the chief minster in cases entitled to "bot" is according to the king's mund, that is five pounds by English law,' the additional information is inserted,[1]

On cent lande æt þam mund bryce v pund þam cingce.	In Kent land for the mund-bryce v pounds to the King.

Further in the same MS. G of Cnut's secular law, s 63, is the following : [2]—

Gif hwa ham socne ge wyrce ge bete ꝥ mid .v. pundan. þam cingce on engla lage ⁊ on cent æt ham socne v. þam cingce ⁊ þreo þam arce bisceope ⁊ dena lage swa hit ærsteod ⁊ gif hine mon þær afylle licge ægilde.	If anyone commit hamsocn let him make bot for it with v pounds to the King by English law, and in Kent from hamsocn v to the King and three to the arch-bishop and by Danish law as it formerly stood, and if he there be killed let him lie unpaid for.

It is not very clear what the *ham-socn* was. In the Latin versions it is translated by 'invasio domi.' And it seems to be the same thing as the 'heimsókn' of

[1] British Museum Cott. Nero A. 1. fol 5, and *supra*, p. 346.

[2] British Museum, *ibid.* fol. 33 b.

the Norse laws.[1] It seems to be a breach of the peace within the sacred precinct of the 'heim,' and the penalty seems to place it on the same ground as the borh-bryce and mund-byrd of the king so as to have become in Cnut's time one of the crimes which in Kent also involved a penalty of fifty Kentish scillings.[2]

Here, then, the inference again is that fifty Kentish scillings were equal in Cnut's time to five pounds of silver.

It is quite true that these two statements of Kentish law are not found in the other manuscripts of Cnut's laws, so that in one sense they may be regarded as interpolations, but in the MS. G they are not insertions made afterwards. In both passages the words form an integral part of the text, which throughout is written in a clear and excellent hand.

It is difficult to suggest any reason for the insertion of these two statements of Kentish law other than the deliberate intention to point out that the amount of the Kentish king's mund-byrd of fifty Kentish scillings was the same as the Wessex mund-byrd of five pounds of silver.

In addition, therefore, to the fact that at a ratio of 1 : 12 between gold and silver the two amounts were alike, these passages seem to show that the penalty of fifty Kentish scillings had become permanently recognised in Cnut's time as equal to the English penalty of five pounds of silver.[3]

---

[1] See Gulathing, 178.

[2] Compare Cnut's secular laws, s. 59, on *Borh-bryce*. In both passages the additional words 'and three to the archbishop' do not seem to be taken from Kentish law. It is obvious from the fragment 'Of Grith and of Mund' that it was well known that in Kentish law 'the mund-bryce of the King and the archbishop were the same.'

[3] See also *Anhang iv.* Schmid, p. 385.

If the comparison had been made throughout in silver sceatts, the equation would not have held good so exactly, for 1000 sceatts would not have equalled exactly five pounds, *i.e.* 1200 of the same sceatts. The exact equation seems to have been between fifty Kentish gold scillings of two tremisses, and five pounds of silver at the current Frankish ratio of 1 : 12. So that the direct evidence of these passages from Cnut's laws goes very far to verify the hypothesis derived from numismatic considerations that the scilling of the Kentish laws was a gold scilling of two tremisses, like that of the Continental Saxons and North-East Frisians.

Scætts cannot have been farthings.

It is, however, only fair to say that Schmid, while adhering to the view that the Kentish scilling was of twenty sceatts, has suggested that these sceatts may have been, not silver tremisses or pence, but *farthings*, so that the Kentish scilling of twenty farthings might be identical with the Wessex scilling of 5*d.*[1] Konrad von Maurer held the same view.[2] But if this could be supposed for a moment, the Kentish scætt would then be only one quarter of the sceatt of the fragment of Mercian law, and the mund-byrd of King Ethelbert would be only a quarter of that of the Wessex King, notwithstanding the assertion in MS. G of the Laws of Cnut that the Kentish mund-byrd was five pounds of silver, like those of other English laws. With all deference, therefore, to the view of these great authorities, a careful examination of the evidence seems to lead to the conclusion that it cannot be

[1] See Schmid, *Glossary*, sub 'Geldrechnung,' p. 594.

[2] Konrad von Maurer's 'Ueber 'Angelsächsische Rechtsverhältnisse,' in the *Kritische Ueberschau*, vol. iii. p. 48.

maintained. Nor does there appear to be any reason why the Kentish scilling should be expected to be the same as the Wessex scilling, as we know that the Wessex scilling of 5*d*. differed from the Mercian scilling of 4*d*.

Kentish scilling therefore of two gold tremisses or twenty silver sceatts or Roman ounce.

We adhere, then, to the view that the Kentish scilling was a scilling of two gold tremisses like the Saxon solidus, and that it was equated with the ore or Roman ounce of silver, *i.e.* twenty sceatts.

The reader will be able to form his own judgment as to whether examination of the various clauses of the Kentish Laws and the amounts of the wergelds and other payments now to be considered will confirm this conclusion or not. I think it will be found substantially to do so.

III. THE LAWS OF ETHELBERT.

The Laws of Ethelbert begin with the heading: 'These are the dooms which King Ethelbert established in the days of Augustine.'

Evidence of clerical influence.

This heading probably did not form a part of the original laws, but it may serve to remind us that ecclesiastical influence must be reckoned with in their consideration and that some of their clauses may have been modifications of ancient custom rather than statements of what it originally was.

The first clause is as follows:—

Godes feoh ⁊ ciricean . xii . gylde.	The property of God and of the Church.	12 fold
Biscopes feoh . xi . gylde.	A bishop's . . .	11 "
Preostes feoh . ix . gylde.	A priest's . . .	9 "
Diacones feoh . vi . gylde.	A deacon's . . .	6 ,
Cleroces feoh . iii . gylde.	A clerk's . . .	3 "
Cyric-frið . ii . gylde.	Church frith . .	2 "
M[æþel] frið . ii . gylde.	[Moot] frith . .	2 "

This clause is read by Thorpe and Schmid and Liebermann as enacting that thefts were to be paid for on this scale, so many multiples of the value of the goods stolen.[1]

Clause 2 enacts :—

Mund-byrd of the King 50 scil-lings.

Gif cyning his leode to him gehateð. ⁊ heom mon þær yfel gedo . ii . bote. ⁊ cyninge .l. scillinga.	If the King call his *leod* to him and any one there do them evil, the bot is twofold and 50 scillings to the King.

Here are two distinct things. The bot is the payment to the person called to the King. While thus in attendance any injury is to be paid for two-fold. The payment of fifty scillings to the King is the mund-byrd or payment for breach of his protection or peace.

Clause 3 is as follows :—

Gif cyning æt mannes ham drincæð ⁊ þær man lyswæs hwæt gedo twi bote gebete.	If the King drink at any one's 'ham' and any one there does something wrong, then let him pay twofold bot.

That is, the presence of the King at a subject's house is the same thing as the subject being in the King's protection, and the bot for any wrong done to the subject, while the King is there, is doubled.

Clause 4 enacts :—

Gif frigman cyninge stele . ix . gylde forgylde.	If a freeman steal from the King, let him pay ninefold.

It seems at first sight hardly likely that the Archbishop should be compensated elevenfold and the King only ninefold, but as this is repeated in the

[1] Compare the 'octogild' and 'novigild' of the Alamannic and other laws. The literal meaning of 'xii gylde' seems to be payable with 'twelve times the gylde.'

statement of the Kentish law in the fragment 'Of Grith and of Mund' the text may be taken as correct.

Clause 5 enacts:—

Gif in cyninges túne man mannan ofslea . l . scill. gebete.	If a man slay another in the King's tun, let him make bot with 50 scillings.

The bot here again is evidently the mund-byrd payable to the King for breach of his protection, *i.e.* fifty Kentish scillings.

Clause 6 enacts:—

Gif man frigne mannan ofsleahð cyninge . l. scill to drightinbeage.	If any one slay a freeman, 50 scillings to the King as *drihtinbeag*.

Here again the payment is to the King, but in this case, if the word is to be taken literally, it is not perhaps for breach of his peace, but for the *killing of his man.* He claims it as his 'drihtin-beag' or lord's-ring. It is, to use the later Saxon phrase, the King's manbot or value to him of his man killed.

King's smith and outrider pay a *medume* wergeld.

Up to this point the question of wergeld has not been mentioned at all. But in clause 7 is the following: [1]—

Gif cyninges ambiht-smið oþþe laad-rinc mannan ofslehð. meduman leodgelde forgelde.	If the King's *ambiht-smith* [official-smith] or *laad-rinc* [outrider] slay a man, let him pay a *medume leodgeld.*

Liebermann would insert the word 'man' after 'gif' and so read this clause as stating the wergeld of the King's smith and laadrinc-man when *slain* to be a 'medume wergeld' (mittleres wergeld). But the clause is complete as it stands without the

[1] The division of the words in the MS. is as follows: 'Gif cyninges ambiht smið oþþe laadrinc mannan of slehð medumanleod gelde forgelde.'

insertion of 'man,' and, read as it is, means that the smith and the outriders of the King, if they slay a man, are to pay a 'medume leodgeld.' But what does this mean? The word *medume* was translated by Wilkins by 'moderata.' Thorpe read the phrase as meaning 'a *half* wergeld;'[1] Schmid as a 'fit and proper' one; and Liebermann would take it to refer to the wergeld of a person of middle rank or position. We must leave the true meaning for the present in doubt.

Reason why not a full wergeld. Their dangerous work.

Apart from the amount of the wergeld, if we would understand this passage we have surely first to consider for what reason these two royal officials should be singled out from all others and made liable to pay wergelds. The inference must be that in the performance of their duties they were peculiarly liable to injure others. The King's smith in his smithy forging a weapon, and the outrider forcing a way for the King through a crowd, might very easily through carelessness or in the excitement of work cause the death of another. The necessity apparently had arisen to check their action by making them liable to pay a wergeld.[2] But the wergeld was not to be the usual one. It was to be a 'medume leodgelde.'

For the present the exact meaning may be left open, but whether the true reading be a half-wergeld or not, the inference seems to be that a *full* wergeld was not to be paid. Probably it had come to be recognised that a person engaged in a specially

[1] So also Grimm in his *Deutsche Rechts Alterthümer*, p. 653, 'dimidio, nicht moderato, wie Wilk. übersetzt.' Compare 'medeme mynster,' *supra*, p. 346, and 'medeme thegn,' Cnut, ii. 71, s. 2.

[2] Possibly the King's servants were otherwise exempt for injuries done in carrying out their work.

dangerous trade could not be held responsible to the same extent as in the case of an ordinary homicide.[1] These considerations are important, because the 'medume' wergeld will again claim notice and every hint is valuable when, as in the case of these laws, we have only hints to guide us.

In Clause 8, the King's mund-byrd is declared to be fifty scillings; and the next two clauses relate to injuries done to the King's servants.

Gif man wið cyninges mægdenman geligeð . l . scillinga gebete.	10. If any one lie with a King's maiden, let him pay a bot of 50 scillings.	Bots for harm done to King's servants.
Gif hio grindende þeowa sio . xxv . scillinga gebete. Sio þridde . xii . scillingas.	11. If she be a grinding slave, let him pay a bot of xxv scillings. The third [class] xii scillings.	
Cyninges fed-esl . xx . scillinga forgelde.	12. Let the King's *fed-esl* be paid for with xx scillings.	

These bots are evidently payable to the King for injuries done to him by abuse of his servants of different grades. They were not wergelds.

We have now done with these bots to the King, and the laws turn to consider injuries done and bots due to the *eorl*.

Gif on eorles tune man mannan ofslæhð . xii . scill. gebete.	13. If a man slay another in an *eorl's* tun, let him make bot with xii scillings.	Bots due to the eorl.

[1] Cf. *Book of Aicill*, p. 267, where injury inflicted in *quick driving or at work* has only a half fine; 'the excitement of the work or of quick driving takes the other half fine off them.' See also the elaborate rules with regard to accidents of the smith in his smithy, p. 187 &c. The general rule stated is 'that the person who plies the sledge on the anvil is exempt from penalties for injuries arising from the work he is engaged on;' and again 'if either the sledge or anvil break, he is exempt for injuries to idlers, and he pays one third compensation to fellow labourers, &c.' Clerical influence may perhaps be recognised in both the Brehon and Kentish clauses.

Gif wið eorles birele man geligeð . xii . scill. gebete.

14. If a man lie with an *eorl's birele*, let him make bot with xii scillings.

And then from the bots due to the eorl the laws pass to those due to the ceorl. The following clauses show that under the Kentish laws the ceorl also had a mund-byrd.

Bots due to the ceorl.

Ceorles mund-byrd . vi . scillingas.

Gif wið ceorles birelan man geligeð . vi . scillingum gebete. aet þære oðere þeowan . l. scætta. aet þare þriddan . xxx . scætta.

15. A ceorl's mund-byrd vi scillings.

16. If a man lie with a ceorl's birele, let him make bot with vi scillings; if with the slave of the second class l scætts; if with one of the third class xxx scætts.

Thus we get a scale of mund-byrds or penalties due for breach of the peace or protection of the King, the eorl, and the ceorl:—

Mund-byrd of King, eorl, and ceorl.

King's mund-byrd	. .	50 scillings
Eorl's ,,	. .	12 ,,
Ceorl's ,,	. .	6 ,,

but so far we have learned nothing about the amount of their wergelds.

Clause 17 fixes the bot for inroad into a man's 'tun' at six scillings for the first person entering, three for the next, and one for the rest.

Lending a weapon in a brawl.

Then follows an interesting set of clauses, which I think must be read together, as all referring to the case of what might happen in a brawl in which one man lends a weapon to another.

Gif man mannan wæpnum bebyreþ ðær ceas weorð ⁊ man nænig yfel ne gedeþ . vi . scillingum gebete.

Gif weg reaf sy gedon . vi . scillingum gebete.

18. If a man furnishes weapons to another *where there is strife*, and the man does no harm, let him make bot with vi scillings.

19. If *weg-reaf* [street robbery] be done, let him make bot with vi scillings.

Gif man þone man ofsleæhð . xx . scillingum gebete.

20. If any one slay *that* man [*i.e.* to whom he lent the weapons], let him [the lender] make bot with xx scillings.

Gif man mannan ofslæhð medume leod-gild . c . scillinga gebete.

21. If a man slay another, let him [the lender] make bot with a medume leod-geld of c scillings.

Gif man mannan ofsleahð æt openum græfe . xx . scillinga forgelde ⁊ in . xl . nihta ealne leod forgelde.

22. If a man slay another, let him at the open grave [1] pay xx scillings and in 40 nights pay a full [2] leod.

Gif bana of lande gewiteþ þa magas healfne leod forgelden.

23. If the slayer depart from the land, let his kindred pay a half leod.

These clauses taken together and followed carefully, I think, become intelligible.

A man lends weapons to another who is engaged in a brawl, and the question arises how far he is to be responsible for what happens in the brawl. In the case dealt with in these clauses two things are involved—the lending of the weapons and the joining thereby in the fray. In the later laws there are provisions for both points. Under King Alfred's laws (s. 19) the man who lends his weapon to another who kills some one therewith has to pay at least one third of the wergeld unless he can clear himself from evil intention.

How treated in Alfred's and in Ine's laws.

Under Ine's laws (s. 34) a man who joins in a fray in which someone is killed, even if he can clear himself from the slaying, has to pay as bot (*gebete*) one fourth of the wergeld of the slain person whether twy-hynde or 'dearer born.' Under Alfred (29 to

[1] That the soul-scot in later times was paid at the open grave see Ethelred, v. 12, vi. 20, ix. 13; C. E. 13.

[2] Compare s. 86 and 87, where *ealne weorðe* means a 'whole worth' of an esne, and contrast the 'medume leodgild' of 100 scillings payable as bot by the lender with the 'ealne leod' payable by the slayer.

31) the actual slayer has to pay the wergeld, and in addition each of the others in the fray has to pay as 'hloð-bote' 30 scillings for a twy-hynde man, 60 for a six-hynde, and 120 for a twelve-hynde man.

These later precedents may materially help us in the understanding of the Kentish clauses.

Clauses 18 and 19 make the lender of the weapon pay a bot of six scillings though no evil be done or only street robbery occur.

Clause 20 provides for the case in which the man to whom he lent the weapon was slain, and in this case the bot is raised to twenty scillings.

The lender pays a *medume* wergeld for person slain.

Clause 21 seems to deal with the case of some one else being slain, and makes the lender liable to pay a bot of a 'medume leod-gild' of 100 scillings for mixing in the fray. It would be natural that the bot should be greater if another was slain than if the man to whom he lent the weapons had been slain. And if the later precedents are to guide us, the bot of a 'medume wergeld' should not in amount equal the whole wergeld but only a proportion of the wergeld. If the bot of 100 scillings might be considered as equal to a *half*-wergeld we should gain a clue to what the whole wergeld might be. And this would be a tempting inference. But we are not, it seems, as yet warranted in making it. We must therefore at present content ourselves with the conclusion that the 'medume wergeld' cannot mean a whole wergeld, otherwise the lender of the weapon would pay as *bot* as much as the wergeld would be if he had killed the man himself.

Clause 22 makes 20 scillings payable at the open grave and the whole leod in forty nights. It refers apparently to the actual slayer's liability to pay the whole wergeld (*ealne leod*); and finally clause 23 states that if the slayer depart from the land his kindred shall pay *half* the wergeld of the slain person. We are not told to whom the bot of the 'medume wergeld' of 100 scillings was to be paid, nor whether it was to be a part of the wergeld or additional to the 'ealne leod' paid by the actual slayer. The later laws, as we have seen, afford precedents for both alternatives.

Kindred liable for half the wergeld and slayer for the other half.

Another point of interest arises from the last clause. In the absence of the slayer his kindred had to pay only a half wergeld (*healfne leod*). Does this justify the inference that in all cases of wergelds the liability of the kindred was confined to one half? It will be remembered that in the so-called 'Canones Wallici' (*supra*, p. 109), if the slayer had fled, the *parentes* of the slayer had fifteen days allowed for their payment of one half or flight from the country. And only when they had paid their share could the slayer return and make himself safe by paying the other half—the 'medium quod restat.' It seems not unlikely that in the Kentish case also ecclesiastical influence had limited the liability of the kindred to the half-wergeld.

Clauses 25 and 26 are important, and we shall have to recur to them.

Gif man ceorlæs hlaf-ætan ofslæhð . vi . scillingum gebete.	25. If any one slay a ceorl's hlafæta, let him make *bot* with vi scillings.
Gif læt ofslæhð þone selestan lxxx . scill forgelde. Gif þane oðerne ofslæhð . lx . scillingum forgelde. þane þriddan . xl . scillingum forgelden.	26. If [anyone] slay a *læt* of the best class, let him pay lxxx scillings; of one of the second, let him pay lx scillings; of the third, let him pay xl scillings.

The three grades of læts.

To these three grades of læts we shall have to return when we sum up the evidence on the division of classes.

Edor-breach.

Next follow three clauses upon edor-breach. The first relates to the breach by a freeman of the enclosure or precinct presumably of a freeman, the penalty being the same as the ceorl's *mund.* The second imposes a threefold bot upon theft from within the precinct. And the third refers to a freeman's trespass over the edor or fence.

Gif friman edor-brecðe gedeð vi scillingum gebete.	27. If a freeman commit edor-breach, let him make bot with vi scillings.
Gif man inne feoh genimeð se man iii gelde gebete.	28. If any one take property [? cattle] from within, let him pay a threefold bot.
Gif fri-man edor gegangeð iv scillingum gebete.	29. If a freeman trespass over a fence, let him make bot with iv scillings.

After these clauses about *edor-breach* is the following:

Gif man mannan ofslea agene scætte. ⁊ unfacne feo gehwilce gelde.	30. If a man slay another, let him pay with his own money (scætte) and with any sound *feo* [cattle].
Gif friman wið fries mannes wif geligeð his wer-gelde abicge ⁊ oðer wif his agenum scætte begete. ⁊ þæm oðrum æt þam gebrenge.	31. If a freeman lie with a freeman's wife, let him pay his wergeld, and another wife obtain with his own scætte and bring her to the other.

Bots for injuries.

Then follow chapters relating chiefly to injuries done and wounds inflicted, and the bots payable to the person injured for the same. It is not needful to mention more of these than the most important one, viz. that for the destruction of an eye, hand, or foot. The bots for all these in most other laws were alike. In Ethelbert's Laws the bot for each of the three is fifty scillings, which happens to be the same as the mund-byrd of the King. For eye, hand, or foot 50 scillings.

After the clauses for injuries there are several relating to women.

Gif fri wif locbore les wæs hwæt gedeþ xxx scll gebete.	73. If a lock-bearing free wife does wrong, xxx scillings bot.
Mægþbot sy swa friges mannes.	74. The maiden-bot is like a freeman's.
Mund þare betstan widuwan eorlcundre l scillinga gebete. Đare oþre xx scll, ðare þriddan xii scll. þare feorðan vi scll.	75. The mund of the best eorlcund widow is a bot of l scillings. Of the second rank xx scillings, of the third xii scillings, of the fourth vi scillings.
Gif man widuwan unagne genimeþ, ii gelde seo mund sy.	76. If a man carry off a widow not in his mund, her mund shall be twofold.

Injuries to women.

The clause relating to the mund of the four grades of apparently eorlcund (?) widows does not help us much to an understanding of what the grades of Kentish society may have been. But it emphasises a remarkable trait of these laws of Ethelbert. Every class is divided in these laws into grades. The clergy are divided into grades from bishops to clerks. The female servants of the King's household are divided into three classes, and so are the servants of the ceorl's household. The læts are divided into three classes. And now the widows, whether all eorlcund or not, are divided into four classes for the purpose of their mund. The significance of these divisions will be apparent hereafter. In the meantime the mund is probably the amount to be paid by a second husband to the parents or kindred of the widow.

Passing from the mund of the widow, the

following clauses throw some light upon the position of the wife under Kentish custom.

Position of a wife under Kentish custom.

Gif mon mægþ gebigeð, ceapi geceapod sy gif hit unfacne is. Gif it þonne facne is ef þær æt ham gebringe ⁊ him man his scæt agefe.	77. If any one buy a maid, let the purchase stand if without guile. But if there be guile, let him bring her home again and let them give him his money back.
Gif hio cwic bearn gebyreþ, healfne scæt age gif ceorl ær swylteþ.	78. If she bears a living child, let her have half the property if the husband die first.
Gif mid bearnum bugan wille healfne scæt age.	79. If she wills to go away with her children, let her have half the property.
Gif ceorl agan wile swa an bearn.	80. If the husband wills to have [them], [let her have] as one child.
Gif hio bearn ne gebyreþ fæderingmagas fioh agan ⁊ morgengyfe.	81. If she bear no child, let [her] paternal kindred have the property and morgengift.

It is obvious from these clauses that under Kentish custom the position of the wife was very much the same as under Cymric and continental German custom. The marriage was a fair contract between the two kindreds.

The next clause enjoins a payment of fifty shillings to the 'owner' of a maiden if she be carried off by force.

The Kentish esne.

Lastly there are the following clauses relating to the position of the esne under Kentish custom. The esne is considered to be a 'servus' working for hire rather than a theow.

Gif man mid esnes cwynan geligeþ e cwicum ceorle ii gebete.	85. If a man lies with an esne's wife, the husband alive, double bot.
Gif esne oþerne ofslea unsynnigne, ealne weorðe forgelde.	86. If one esne kills another innocently, let the full worth be paid for.

Gif esnes eage ⁊ foot of weorðeþ aslagen ealne weorðe hine forgelde.	87. If an esne's eye and foot are struck out or off, let the full worth be paid for it.
Gif man mannes esne gebindeþ vi scll gebete.	88. If a man bind a man's esne, vi scillings bot.

There is nothing in these clauses, I think, to show that the bot was payable to any one but the owner of the esne.

What the 'full worth' of the esne was we are not told.

IV. THE LAWS OF HLOTHÆRE AND EADRIC, A.D. 685–6.

Between the date of the Laws of Ethelbert and those of other Kentish kings which have been preserved nearly a century had intervened. So that these later laws of Kent are nearly contemporary with King Ine's Dooms of Wessex.

Eorlcund and ceorlisc classes.

As in Ethelbert's laws, the main division of classes of freemen seems still to have been that between eorlcund and ceorlisc. But we get further valuable information.

The Laws of Hlothære and Eadric open with clauses which seem to fix the wergeld of the eorl at three times that of the ordinary freeman.

The owner's liability for an esne's homicides.

They deal with the liability of an owner of an *esne*[1] for his servant's homicides.

Gif mannes esne eorlcundne mannan ofslæhð. þane þe sio þreom hundum scill gylde se agend þone banan agefe ⁊ do þær þrio manwyrð to.	1. If any one's esne slay an *eorlcund* man, one that is paid for with three hundred scillings, let the owner give up the slayer, and add *three manwyrths* thereto.

[1] That the *esne* was very near in position to the 'theow' see Alf. 43, where Church holidays are to be given to 'all freemen but *not to theow-men and esne workmen*'—'butan þeowum mannum & esne-wyrhtum.'

If an esne slay an eorl.

Gif se bana oðbyrste feorðe manwyrð he to-gedo ⁊ hine gecænne mid godum æwdum ꝥ he þane banan begeten ne mihte.

2. If the slayer escape, let him add a fourth *manwyrth* and let him prove with good compurgators that he could not catch the slayer.

The next two clauses are as follows :—

If he slay a freeman.

Gif mannes esne frigne mannan ofslæhð þane þe sie hund scillinga gelde se agend þone banan agefe ⁊ oþer manwyrð þær to.

Gif bana oðbyrste. twam manwyrðum hine man forgelde ⁊ hine gecænne mid godum æwdum ꝥ he þane banan begeten ne mihte.

3. If anyone's esne slay a freeman, one that is paid for with 100 scillings, let the owner give up the slayer and a second manwyrth thereto.

4. If the slayer escape, let [the owner] pay for him with two manwyrths and let him prove with good compurgators that he could not catch the slayer.

This reading of these clauses is not that of Thorpe or of Schmid, but that approved by the best authorities.[1]

Were the wergelds 300 and 100, or are they half-wergelds ?

Following this reading as philologically the most correct one, the inference at first sight might be that under Kentish law the wergeld of the eorlcundman was 300 Kentish scillings and that of the freeman 100 scillings.

But there may be reason to doubt the correctness of such an inference.

For the present we may leave the question of the amount of the wergelds to consider the meaning of the clauses in their main intention. And this seems to be clear. Henceforth the owner of an esne was

[1] Liebermann considers that the 300 and 100 scillings are the wergeld of the eorlcundman and the freeman. His translation reads: 'welcher steht im 300-Scillwergelde' and 'welcher im 100-Scillwergelde steht.' Whether these payments are the wergelds is the point at issue. Schmid, in his note to this passage, favours the view that 300 scillings was the *half*-wergeld of the eorl and 100 scillings the half-wergeld of the freeman.

not to be accountable for the wergeld of the person slain or any part of it further than that if an eorlcundman payable for with 300 scillings be slain he must hand over the esne and *three* times his manworth in addition; and in the case of the freeman payable for with 100 scillings he must hand over the esne and add *one* manworth in addition. That is to say, the esne was in both cases to be handed over and a manworth for each hundred scillings of the amount at which the person slain is paid for.

The clauses limit and lessen the owner's liability.

Now, I think, we must conclude that these clauses were intended to make an innovation upon ancient custom rather than to confirm it. And therefore it may be well to compare with them the parallel evidence of the laws of other tribes, as to the responsibility of an owner for his slave's homicides.

Under the Welsh Laws (ii. p. 105) the liability of the owner of a slave for his homicides was apparently complete

Under tribal custom at first complete.

> If a bondman commit homicide of whatever kind, it is right for the lord of the bondman to pay for the deed of his bondman as for a murderer, for he is a murderer.

And this probably must be taken as the general rule of tribal custom in its early stages.

In the laws of the Saxons and of the Anglii and Werini the ancient German tribal custom was still preserved. The owner of an animal or a slave was liable for any injury done by either, very much as if it had been done by himself ('Lex Sax.' xii. Ang. and Wer. 16 and 52).

But it would seem that Roman and Christian feeling very early suggested that this was hard upon

Then made a half-wergeld only, and the slave to be handed over for the other half.

the innocent owner. Hence in some of the laws the compromise was made that the owner should pay only a *half*-wergeld and hand over the offending animal or slave instead of the other half.

That this innovation was not altogether acceptable to tribal feeling is shown by clauses in the 'Pactus III.' of the Alamannic laws. The whole wergeld was to be paid by the owner if his horse, ox, or pig killed a man (s. 18). But an exception was made in the case of the dog. If a man's dog killed any one, a *half*-wergeld (medium werigeldum) was to be paid, and if the whole wergeld was demanded, all the doors but one of the house of the person making the demand were to be closed and the dog was to be hung up nine feet from the only one left open for ingress or egress, and there it must remain till it fell from putrefaction. If it was removed or any other door was used, the wergeld was to be returned (s. 17).

Grimm ('D. R.' p. 665) has pointed out that in the *Ostgotalaga* (Drap. 13, 2) a similar archaic practice is described when a *slave* had killed a man. The *owner* of the slave under this law ought to pay the whole wergeld, and if he did not do so the *slave* was to be hung up at *his* (the owner's) house door till the body putrefied and fell. Thus the same archaic method of punishing the delinquent was retained in both cases. But the significant point is that so long as the whole wergeld was due from the owner it was at the owner's door that the body of the slayer was to be hung up, while when the *half*-wergeld only was to be paid, the dog was to be hung up at the door of the person who improperly demanded the whole wergeld. Thus, as in so many other cases, the twelfth-century laws of the North preserved the earlier custom of the payment of the whole wergeld, while the Alamanni, after migration into contact with Roman and Christian civilisation, in their laws of the seventh century modified the custom, at the same time retaining the archaic method of forcing compliance with the modification. It must be remembered that every change which relieved the innocent owner from liability, wholly or in part, robbed the kindred of the person slain of the whole or the part of the wergeld.

The compromise of payment of the half-wergeld and the handing over of the offending animal or slave was not confined to the Alamannic laws.

In the Ripuarian Law xlvi. the animal which had killed a man was to be handed over and received 'in medietatem wirigildi' and the owner was to pay the other half.

So in Codex I. of Lex Salica, but afterwards owner released from the half-wergeld.

In the Lex Salica the same rule was at first applied to the case of homicide by a slave or læt. A half-wergeld was to be paid and the slave or læt handed over for the other half.[1] This was the rule according to the Codex I. But in the later Codices, VII. to X., and in the 'Lex Emendata,' the lord, if innocent, was allowed to get off altogether from the half-wergeld and had only to give up the slave or the læt. This further innovation seems to have been connected with the Edict of Chilperic (*circ.* A.D. 574) and thus probably represented the result of

[1] xxxv. 5. 'Si servus alienus aut laetus hominem ingenuum occiderit, ipse homicida pro medietatem compositionis illius hominis occisi parentibus tradatur, et dominus servi aliam medietatem compositionis se noverit soluiturum.'

ecclesiastical influence at very nearly the date of the earliest Kentish laws.

In the Canons of sixth century the slave was to be given up and another besides.

We have only to recur to the Canons of the Celtic Church of Brittany and South Wales of the sixth and seventh centuries, considered in the earlier part of this volume, to recognise the hand of the Church in these innovations upon earlier tribal custom. They extended to Celtic as well as to German districts. In Canon 5 of the so-called 'Canones Wallici' the rule was laid down that 'if any master should permit his slave to carry arms, and the slave killed a freeman, the owner must hand over the slave and another besides' (*supra*, p. 108).

The half-wergeld here is omitted altogether, and, as in the case of the Kentish freeman, two slaves are to be given up instead of one.

In the Burgundian Law slave to be given up and the owner to be free.

These Canons were nearly contemporary with the later Kentish laws, and the same stage of innovation seems to have been reached in both. A still further and final stage had been reached in the Burgundian Law already quoted (*supra*, p. 124) in which in the case of homicide by a slave, unknown to his master, the slave was to be delivered up to death and the master was to be free from liability. The *parentes* of the slain person were to get nothing, not even the slave, 'because, as we enact that the guilty shall be extirpated, so we cannot allow the innocent to suffer wrong.' The whole process of change had taken place in the Burgundian district by the sixth century. But it would seem that in Kent the middle stage only had been reached at the date of the laws of Hlothære and Eadric.

Evidence that the further stage had at last been

reached in Anglo-Saxon law is perhaps to be found in the nearly contemporary law of Ine (s. 74) which enacts that if a *theow-wealh* slay an Englishman, the owner shall deliver him up to the lord and the kindred or give sixty scillings for his life. Here no further manworths are required. But possibly the peculiar position of the *theow-wealh* may have something to do with it, so that we ought not perhaps to assume as certain that the clause represented a still further general innovation upon tribal custom beyond that described in the Kentish clauses.

Kentish clauses meant to modify the previous rule: which may have been the half-wergeld of 300 and 100 scillings.

Returning to the Kentish clauses and assuming that their direct intention was to modify previous custom, we are now in a position fairly to judge what the *previous* rule may have been.

Reasoning from the analogy of other laws, it seems most likely to have been to make the owner pay a half-wergeld of the person slain and hand over the esne for the other half—the stage of custom reached in the Ripuarian Laws and Salic Laws of Codex I.

And if this were in fact the former custom previous to the enactment in these clauses, then without departing from the correct literal reading of the text it may be that the words in the parenthesis in each clause may refer, not to the eorlcundman's or the freeman's wergild—the word '*leod*-geldi' is not used—but to the amount hitherto payable in the particular case of a man slain by an esne. The 300 and 100 scillings may be the *half*-wergeld hitherto payable, instead of which thenceforth the owner of the esne is to pay three manworths or one manworth in addition to handing over the esne.

If previous to the innovation the eorlcundman

had been paid for in such a case with three hundred shillings and the freeman with one hundred, the words in their strictly correct literal meaning might perhaps rightly be read thus :—

> If any one's esne slay an eorlcundman, one who *is* [now] paid for at three hundred scillings, let the owner [in future] give up the slayer and add *three* manworths [of the esne] thereto.
>
> If anyone's esne slay a freeman, one who *is* [now] paid for at *one* hundred scillings, let the owner [in future] give up the slayer and add one manworth [of the esne] thereto.

This reading of the clauses, putting emphasis upon what is *now* the gild (þane ꝥ sie)—the *three* and the *one* hundred scillings—in contrast with what the owner has in future to do, *i.e.* pay *three* manworths and *one* manworth instead of the *three* hundred and *one* hundred scillings in addition to the handing over of the esne—seems to me more than any other rendering to account for the insertion of the parenthesis stating the amounts payable for the eorlcundman and freeman. If the word *leod-gylde* had been used it might have been different. But I am informed on the best authority that the words *gylde* and *gelde* in the two clauses are not substantives but used in an adjectival sense, and in this case they would apply to a half-wergeld payable as correctly as to a whole one.

Was 100 scillings the half-wergeld and so the medume wergeld of King Ethelbert's laws?

At the same time the mention of 100 scillings, if the payment be a *half*-wergeld, may help to an understanding of the *medume* leodgeld of 100 scillings mentioned in Ethelbert's Laws. It suggests that the *medume* wergeld was a modified or middle one which, like the *medium* werigeldum and *medium* precium of the mediæval Latin of the Alamannic and other laws, had come to mean a *half* one. Perhaps, after all, if we recognise clerical influence in the framing and modification of the Kentish laws, the translation of the Latin '*medium werigeldum*' by the Anglo-Saxon '*medume leodgeld*' is not very unnatural.

Before we leave the laws of Hlothære and Eadric there are one or two further clauses worth notice.

Clause 5 reminds us that, though scarcely mentioned in these laws, the system of compurgation was in force. A freeman charged with a crime has to clear himself by the oaths of a number of 'free æwda-men.' System of oath-helpers.

Clause 6 makes mention of the protection of a woman by her kindred:—

Gif ceorl acwyle be libbendum wife ⁊ bearne riht is ꝥ hit ꝥ bearn medder folgige ⁊ him mon ān his fædering-magum wilsumne berigean geselle his feoh to healdenne oþþæt he . x . wintra sie.	6. If a husband (ceorl) die wife and child yet living, it is right that the child follow the mother: and let that sufficient guardian be given to him [the child] from among his paternal kinsmen to keep his property [cattle ?] till he be ten winters old.

Position of the wife.

These clauses, unimportant perhaps in themselves, are useful as showing that behind the silence of the laws tribal custom still lingered on, however seldom and slightly it might be brought into evidence as fresh circumstances might suggest new clauses.

There are also some clauses which are useful as showing the continuance of the mund-byrds of king and ceorl of King Ethelbert's Laws, unchanged in amount, a century later. Mund-byrds unchanged.

By s. 11, if a man uses abusive words to another in any one's 'flet,' 'let him pay one scilling to him who owns the "flet" and six scillings to him to whom he said the words and twelve scillings to the King.' So also in s. 12, one scilling is to be paid to the owner of the 'flet,' six scillings to the person wronged, and twelve scillings to the king. The six scillings to the person insulted or wronged is the *mund* of the freeman or ceorl. Lastly, in s. 13 in case of a slaying in a drinking bout:—

Gif man wæpn abregde þær mæn drincen ⁊ þær man nan yfel ne deð scilling þan þe ꝥ flet age ⁊ cyninge xii scill.	If a man draw a weapon where men are drinking and no harm be done, then a scilling to him who owns the flet and xii scillings to the King.
Gif ꝥ flet geblodgad wyrðe forgylde þem mæn his mund-byrd ⁊ cyninge l. scill.	If the flet be stained with blood, let him pay to the man [who owns the flet] his mund-byrd and 50 scillings to the King.

Mund-byrd of the King still 50 scillings and of the ceorl 6.

Thus we have again the mund-byrds of King Ethelbert's Laws:—

Of the King 50 scillings.
Of the ceorl 6 scillings.

The crime of killing another in a drinking bout is a breach of the *mund* of the owner of the 'flet' as well as a breach of the peace of the King.

V. THE LAWS OF KING WIHTRÆD, A.D. 690–696.

One more chance remains for further information regarding Kentish wergelds, viz. in the 'Laws of King Wihtræd,' who became King of the Kentish men about A.D. 690 and, according to Bede, died A.D. 725. A century had passed since the Laws of Ethelbert were enacted, in the time of St. Augustine. Brihtwald was now Archbishop of Canterbury, and at an assembly of Church and people 'the great men decreed, with the suffrage of all, these dooms, and added them to the lawful customs of the Kentish men.' These laws are mainly ecclesiastical both in their origin and subject.

Mund-byrd of King and Church both 50 scillings, and so no change in the Kentish currency.

In the first two clauses the Church was declared to be 'free from gafols,' and the mund-byrd of the Church was declared to be the same as the King's, viz. fifty scillings—as in Ethelbert's Laws. There is therefore no marked change in the Kentish currency, though by this time it must have been almost entirely silver so far as any Kentish coinage was concerned.

Clause 5 introduces us for the first time in the Kentish laws to the distinction between the *gesithcund* and *ceorlisc* classes.

Gif þæs geweorðe gesiðcundne mannan ofer þis gemot ꝥ he unriht hæmed genime ofer cinges bebod ⁊ biscopes ⁊ boca dom se ꝥ gebete his dryhtne . c . scill. an eald reht. Gif hit ceorlisc man sie gebete . l . scill. . . .	When it happens to a gesithcundman after this gemot that he enters into unlawful marriage against the command of the King and the bishop and the book's doom, let him make bot for it to his lord with 100 scillings according to ancient law. If he be a *ceorlisc* man, let him make bot with 50 scillings. . . .

It would not do to conclude from this single allusion to gesithcund and ceorlisc men that the Kentish division of classes—eorlisc and ceorlisc—had given way before the Wessex division of classes—gesithcund and ceorlisc.

There had been no interval between this and the last set of Kentish laws long enough to have made likely any radical change in social conditions, and as the 'ancient law' alluded to was probably ecclesiastical and not especially Kentish, either in its origin or its terms, it would not be wise to build anything upon the use of the word 'gesithcund' beyond recognising the natural tendency of neighbouring peoples under the same ecclesiastical influence to approximate in phraseology especially in regard to matters of general ecclesiastical interest.

Clauses which follow regulating the penalties for work on Sundays, or neglect of baptism, or a ceorl's making offerings to devils without his wife's knowledge, or a man's giving flesh meat to his family on fast days, do not interest us in this inquiry further than as revealing lingering traces of paganism and the ecclesiastical character of these laws of Wihtræd.

There are, however, a few clauses which incidentally come within the lines of our inquiry.

The position of the freedman under Kentish custom.

Clause 8 is especially interesting as showing that when freedom was given by a lord to his man and he became folkfree, still, even though he left the district, his *inheritance*, his *wergeld*, and the *mund* of his family remained with the freedom-giver.

Gif man his mæn an wiofode freols gefe se sie folc-fry. freols-gefa age his erfe ænde wer-geld ⁊ munde þare hina sie ofer mearce þær he wille.	If any one give freedom to his man at the altar, let him be folk-free; let the freedom-giver keep the heritage and wergeld and the *mund* of his family, be he over the march wherever he will.

Here tribal custom asserts itself. The freedman, though freed at the *altar*, is to be *folkfree*, and yet, although folkfree and able to go wherever he will, he cannot *inherit*, because he is nobody's heir. He had no free parents from whom to inherit. His lord inherited what his unfree man might leave behind him. The freedman's wergeld if he were slain still

His wergeld goes to his lord.

went to his lord, for he had no free kindred to claim it. His family remained in the lord's *mund* unless they also had been set free.

These points were doubtless all incident to the position of a newly made freedman under Kentish custom, and this enactment was probably needful only to make it clear that freedom given *at the altar*, whatever churchmen might think, was not to modify the customary rules incident to freedom-giving. The evidence of the clause is, however, valuable because for one moment it accidentally lifts the veil and shows that Kentish tribal custom was in these matters much the same as we have found tribal custom elsewhere, and it is particularly valuable as direct evidence that there was a class of freedmen under Kentish custom as everywhere else.

There are also the following clauses on oaths.

Clauses on oaths of different persons.

Biscopes word ⁊ cyninges sie unlægne buton æðe.	16. A bishop's and a King's word is unimpeachable without an oath.
Mynstres aldor hine cænne in preostes canne.	17. A 'Minster's ealdor' clears himself in the same way as a priest.
Preost hine clænsie sylfæs soðe in his halgum hrægle ætforan wiofode þus cweðende 'Ueritatem dico in Xp̄o, non mentior.' Swylce diacon hine clænsie.	18. A priest clears himself by his own declaration in his holy garments before the altar, saying 'I speak the truth in Christ, I do not lie.' And so also does the deacon.
Cliroc feowra sum hine clænsie his heafod-gemacene ⁊ ane his hand on wiofode oðre ætstanden að abycgan.	19. A cleric shall clear himself as one of four of his like; with one hand on the altar, the others standing by and accompanying the oath.
Gest hine clænsie sylfes aðe on wiofode swylce cyninges þeng.	20. A stranger (gest) shall clear himself by his own oath at the altar, and in the same manner as a 'King's thane.'

Ceorlisc man hine feowra sum his heafod-gemacene on weofode ⁊ þissa ealra að sie unlegnæ. . . .	21. A ceorlisc man shall clear himself with four of his like at the altar, and the oath of all these shall be unimpeachable. . . .

These statements regarding oaths, like other laws of Wihtræd, betray their ecclesiastical origin, and following directly after the imposition of penalties for what may be called ecclesiastical sins, very difficult of proof, seem to have been inserted with special reference to them. They are interesting, however, as reminding us again that the system of oath-helpers was not absent from Kentish custom.

Under clerical influence the single oath of the stranger to be taken as good.

Section 20 of this clause is also interesting, which places the *stranger* (gest)—may we not say the 'King's guest'?—in the same position as the 'King's thane' as to the validity of his single oath. Both seem to be specially under the King's protection: in the case of the King's thane, on account of his official or military position; in the case of the stranger, probably because of the absence of his kindred. The King being in the place of kin to the stranger, his single oath is accepted.

These laws end with clauses referring to theft more or less closely resembling those so prominent in King Ine's Dooms.

Clauses as to theft like those in Ine's laws.

They state that a thief slain as a thief was to be without wergeld. If a freeman were caught in the act of thieving, the King might either kill him, or sell him over sea, or release him on payment of his wergeld. He who should seize and hold him was to be entitled to the half-wergeld, or if he were put to death to seventy scillings. A man coming from far or a foreigner, when off the public way, who should neither call aloud nor blow a horn, was to be taken to be a thief, and put to death or redeemed by a wergeld.

The last clause resembles Ine s. 20 so closely as to suggest a common origin.

(Wihtræd, 28)	(Ine, 20)
Gif feorran cumen man oþþe fræmde buton wege gange ⁊ he þonne nawðer ne hryme ne he horn blawe for ðeof he bid to profianne oþþe to sleanne oþþe to alysenne.	Gif feor cuman man oððe fremde buton wege geond wudu gonge ⁊ ne hryme ne horn blawe for ðeof he bid to profianne oððe to sleanne oððe to alysanne.

The close resemblance between these clauses confirms the suggestion that the expression 'gesithcund' in the Kentish laws of Wihtræd may have been borrowed from Wessex. Nowhere else than in these contemporary laws of Ine and Wihtræd does the term gesithcund appear, except in the fragments of Mercian law, which may thus belong to the same period.

VI. THE DIVISION OF CLASSES UNDER KENTISH CUSTOM.

We have now examined the Kentish laws especially regarding the amount of the wergelds and mund-byrds. Although we may not have arrived at absolute certainty, yet some light may have been thrown upon the important matter of the division of classes.

Mund-byrds of King, eorl, and ceorl.

So far as the amounts of the wergeld are concerned, the contrast was between the eorl and the freeman, the wergeld of the eorl being three times that of the freeman. But as regards the mund-byrd the contrast was between eorl and ceorl. The mund-byrds were :—

King . . .	50	Kentish scillings
Eorl . . .	12	,,
Ceorl . . .	6	,,

There must evidently be either identity of meaning or much overlapping in the terms freeman and ceorl. Otherwise the ceorl would be without a wergeld and the freeman without a mund-byrd.

And yet, on the other hand, there was probably some reason why the particular words used were chosen in the several clauses, and to a certain extent it may not be far to seek.

The ceorl was a man with a household and flet and so had a mund-byrd.

So far as the word *ceorl* had a special sense, it meant the married man,[1] the husband with a homestead and household, like the North-country husbandman with his husbandland. In this special sense every ceorl may have been a freeman, but every freeman may not have been a ceorl. Hence in the clauses as regards mund-byrd the contrast is between the eorl and the ceorl. Both were men with homesteads and households. Unless they had persons under their 'mund' they could not have had corresponding mund-byrds. The freeman who did not happen to be a man with a homestead and household could have no mund-byrd, because he had no precinct within which his peace could be broken, and no household under his protection. But he could have a wergeld.

So, again, in the clauses quoted relating to injuries done to servants in the Laws of Ethelbert:—

14. If a man lie with an eorl's birele, let him make bot with xii scillings.

16. If a man lie with a ceorl's birele, let him make bot with vi scillings. If with a theow of the second class, l sceatts; if with one of the third class xxx sceatts.

25. If any one slay a ceorl's hlafæta, let him pay bot with vi scillings.

[1] 'Ceorlian,' to marry a husband; 'wifian,' to marry a wife. Bosworth, *sub voce*.

The ceorl in this contrast is again a husbandman with a homestead and household and with bireles and theows and hlafætas under his roof or in his 'ham.' Wherever in the Kentish laws the word 'ceorl' is used in any other sense, I think the meaning is confined to that of the married man—the husband, as in the phrase 'husband and wife.'

So regarded, the division for purposes of mundbyrd into eorlisc and ceorlisc classes was natural, and so also, for purposes of wergeld, was the distinction between eorl and freeman. As regards the wergeld, we may consider the terms ceorl and freeman as practically interchangeable, inasmuch as every ceorl was certainly a freeman, and the unmarried freeman was probably a cadet or member of the household of some eorlisc or ceorlisc man.

Continental society included everywhere, as we have seen, such classes as the Roman liti and liberti composed of strangers and freedmen who had not so far risen in the social scale as to have fully recognised rights of inheritance and whose wergeld never was of the same amount as that of the full freeman. It is in connection with such classes that the tribal distinction of blood came in. If for the full freeman we were to substitute the word *tribesman*, with all the background of hyndens of kinsmen to fight and to swear for him involved in the term, then from the same point of view we must expect to find in Kent, as everywhere else, strangers in blood below the tribesmen, like the aillts and alltuds and taeogs of the Cymric Codes, the fuidhirs of the Brehon Laws, if not the liberti and liti of the Gallo-Romans, or, perhaps still more nearly to the point, the leysing classes of the Norse Laws.

The Kentish freedman and læt resembled the Norse leysing.

We have already found incidental mention of the Kentish freedman. He cannot after enfranchisement have been classed as an esne or a theow. There would seem to be no other class mentioned to which he could belong, unless it might be that of the læts of Ethelbert's Laws.

It is worth while, therefore, to recur to the single clause in Ethelbert's Laws already quoted respecting the læts and to examine it more closely. Within the compass of its few words there may perhaps be found evidence connecting the status of the Kentish læt with what we have learned of the status and conditions of the Norse leysing.

> 26. If a man slay a læt of the best class, let him pay 80 scillings; if one of the second class, let him pay 60 scillings; of the third, let him pay 40 scillings.

The clause does not mention to whom the payments are to be made, whether to the læt himself or, as in the case of the freedman, to his late owner or lord. But the payments are not called leodgelds as are the wergelds of freemen.

Three classes in both cases.

Looking to the payments themselves they are graduated for three classes of læts. There were also, under Norse custom, three classes of leysings gradually growing by successive steps towards a higher grade of freedom as kindreds grew up around them and became more and more nearly perfect till at last the ninth generation from the first freedman became fully free. Why may not the three grades of Kentish læts have been doing the same?

Let us compare the amounts of the payments for

the slaying of the three classes of Kentish læts with those for the three classes of Norse leysings.

We have seen over and over again that the Kentish scilling regarded as twenty sceatts was an ore or a Roman ounce of silver. Therefore the Kentish payments, stated in ounces of silver, were as follows:—

Best class of læt	80 ounces of silver
Second class	60 ,, ,,
Third class	40 ,, ,,

The Norse ore was also in wheat-grains a Roman ounce of silver. The wergelds of the three classes of leysings in the Norse laws were as under:—

Frialsgiafi or newly made freedman .	40 ores of silver
Leysing after making 'freedom ale' .	60 ,, ,,
Leysinjia-son or highest rank of leysing whose great-grandfather was a leysing[1] .	80 ,, ,,

So that the wergelds of the three classes of Kentish læts corresponded exactly in amount with those of the three classes of Norse leysings, when reckoned both in silver. And the wergelds similar.

We may further compare these payments for the Kentish læts with those for the freedman of the nearly contemporary Bavarian laws. They are stated in gold solidi of three tremisses, and the Kentish solidus was of only two tremisses. We have seen that the Bavarian freedman was paid for with forty solidi, *i.e.* sixty Kentish scillings. The payment thus corresponded with that for the Kentish læt of the second class.

These correspondences are unexpected and very significant, but the significance is made still more

[1] *Supra*, p. 239.

The grades the result of growth of kindred.

important by the clause in the Laws of Wihtræd describing the position of the newly made freedman under Kentish custom. The description of his position might almost be taken as a description of the 'frialgiafi' or newly made leysing of the Norse laws. Under Kentish law the freedman was to be folkfree, but 'the freedom-giver was to keep the heritage and wergeld and mund of his family, be he over the march wherever he will.' This was, as we have seen, almost exactly the position of the Norse leysing before he had made his freedom ale. He had as yet no kindred to swear and to fight for him. He was still under the mund and protection of his lord. His descendants could only obtain the protection of a kindred and become wholly free from the *thyrmsl* of the lord, when in the course of generations a kindred had grown up gradually around them.

So too, as we have seen, under the Bavarian laws the freedman's wergeld went to his lord.[1] Under the Frisian law the wergeld of the *litus* went to his lord.[2] Under Ripuarian law even the 'homo denarialis'—the freedman who became a Frank with a full wergeld—was recognised as having at first no kindred. If he had no children, his property went to the fisc. And it was not till the third generation that his descendants had full rights of inheritance.[3] We have already found abundant evidence of the continued force of tribal custom and tribal instincts in regard to the importance of kindred while considering the meaning and function of the hyndens in connection with the twelve-hynde and twy-hynde

---

[1] *Supra*, p. 176. [2] *Supra*, p. 199.
[3] *Supra*, p. 169.

classes of the Anglo-Saxon laws. These remarkable correspondences between the position held by the læts in Kent and that of the leysings and freedmen and liti of the Continental laws, without our making too much of them, may fairly be taken as additional evidence of the tenacity of tribal custom in these matters.[1]

VII. THE AMOUNT OF THE KENTISH WERGELDS.

Probable Kentish wergelds eorl 600, freeman 200, Kentish scillings.

Once more we return to the amount of the wergelds of the Kentish eorl and freeman.

We have seen reason to believe that the payments of 300 and 100 scillings of the laws of Hlothære and Eadric were half-wergelds, and that the full wergelds were 600 and 200 scillings.

If they may be so considered they are at once put on line with the Frankish wergelds. The threefold wergeld of the eorl becomes evidently due to his noble birth or official position. And, if the Kentish and Frankish solidi had been alike, the similarity of the wergelds would have been complete.

As in the Frankish laws.

The wergelds of the Frankish group of laws were found to be as follows :—

Lex Salica, Graphio or ingenuus in truste Regis	600 solidi	
Frank or Barbarian living under Salic law	200 „	
Lex Ripuariorum, Comes &c. in truste Regis	600 „	
Ingenuus	200 „	
Lex Angliorum et Werinorum, Adalingus	600 „	
Liber	200 „	
Lex Chamavorum, Homo Francus	600 „	
Ingenuus	200 „	

[1] In the Bavarian and Saxon laws the *litus* was paid for at one fourth the wergeld of the *liber*. The inference from this might strengthen the view that the Kentish wergeld of the ceorl could hardly be as low as 100 scillings.

In all these cases the wergeld of the Royal official or person in high rank is threefold that of the *liber* or *ingenuus*.[1]

Confirmed by comparison with the King's mundbyrd.

Confining attention now to the position of the Kentish freeman, further confirmation of the view that his wergeld was 200 Kentish scillings may be derived from a comparison of the King's mundbyrd with his wergeld, and the corresponding Continental payments *pro fredo* with the wergelds of the *liber* and *ingenuus* of the Continental laws.

The Kentish mundbyrd of 50 Kentish scillings was one fourth of the Kentish freeman's wergeld if 200 Kentish scillings.

The Mercian mundbyrd of five pounds of silver was one fourth of the Mercian wergeld of 1200 scillings of four pence, or twenty pounds.

The Wessex mundbyrd of five pounds would be one fourth of the Wessex wergeld proper if the latter might be looked upon as the same as the Mercian with the mundbyrd added.[2]

The Alamannic and Bavarian payments *pro fredo* of 40 solidi were one fourth of the Alamannic and Bavarian wergeld of 160 solidi.

And Brunner[3] and others consider that, although the payment *pro fredo* was sometimes an extra payment, the 200 solidi of the Frankish wergeld equalled 160 solidi with one fourth added *pro fredo*.

---

[1] I adhere to this view after careful consideration of the elaborate argument in the *Die Gemeinfreien der Karolingischen Volksrechte*, von Philipp Heck (Halle, 1900), in reply to the criticism by H. Brunner in the *Savigny-Stiftung für Rechtsgeschichte*, xix Band, 1899.

[2] 1200 scillings of 4*d.* with one fourth added = 1200 scillings of 5*d.*

[3] *Deutsche Rechtsgeschichte*, i. 225–6.

Now, if instead of holding the Kentish freeman's wergeld to be 200 Kentish scillings we were to take it to be the *medume* wergeld of 100 scillings, we should destroy the correspondence of the King's mundbyrd with the wergeld, and make the mundbyrd half the wergeld instead of a quarter: unlike what it was in the other laws. This hardly seems a likely supposition.

And also with payment for eye, hand, and foot.

We get still further evidence if we compare the payments for the eye, hand, and foot in the Kentish and Continental laws. We have seen that the Kentish payment was 50 scillings, *i.e.* the same as the King's mundbyrd and one fourth of the wergeld of 200 scillings. In the Alamannic and Bavarian laws and in those of the Chamavi the payment for these, like the payment *pro fredo*, was one quarter of the freeman's wergeld. In the Frankish laws it was one half. But the reason of this is, not that either the Frankish payment *pro fredo* or the wergeld is less than in other laws, but that the payment for the eye, hand, and foot is greater. The Frankish payment for the eye, hand, or foot was 100 solidi of three tremisses, *i.e.* half as much again as the Kentish freeman's wergeld would be if only 100 Kentish scillings of two tremisses; which again seems unlikely.

At first sight the Wessex payments for the eye, hand, and foot present an anomaly. The Wessex twelve-hynde wergeld of 1200 Wessex scillings of five pence at a ratio of 1 : 10 corresponds, as we have seen, with the Frankish freeman's wergeld of 200 solidi. The payment for the eye, hand, and foot in King Alfred's Laws is $66\frac{2}{3}$ Wessex scillings, *i.e.* only one eighteenth of the twelve-hynde wergeld. But the explanation no doubt is that in the Laws of King Alfred the payments for injuries are stated for the *twyhynde*-man's grade, those for the eye, hand, and foot being one third of the twyhyndeman's wergeld of 200 Wessex scillings.

Kentish freeman's wergeld most likely 200 Kentish scillings, or 4000 sceatts.

On the whole, therefore, these considerations seem to strengthen the supposition that the Kentish freeman's wergeld was 200 Kentish scillings. That the Kentish wergeld should differ from that of Mercia and Wessex need not surprise us, seeing that we started with the warning that we should find it so as regards both the *barones* and *villani*. To the writer of the so-called Laws of Henry I. the eorl was no doubt the *baro* and the freeman or ceorl the *villanus* of Norman phraseology. And we need not wonder at his confusion if he had nothing but the laws to guide him. It is necessary, however, to look at the question of the wergelds from a broader point of view than his could be.

It must not be forgotten that the Continental wergelds of the Merovingian period were all stated in gold solidi. The first emigrants into Britain must have known this perfectly well. Kentish moneyers coined gold tremisses, and when they afterwards coined silver it was in silver tremisses of the same weight, which earned the name in England of 'sceatts.'

Any exact comparison of English and Continental wergelds must obviously be dependent upon the ratio between gold and silver.

Archbishop Egbert's priest's wergeld also 4000 sceatts—*i.e.* 200 ounces of silver or *Mina Italica* of gold.

The Kentish scilling of two gold tremisses at 1 : 10 was reckoned in the Laws of Ethelbert as equal to 20 sceatts—*i.e.* to the Roman ounce—and the wergeld, if of 200 scillings, was thus, as we have seen, a wergeld in silver of 200 ounces or 4000 sceatts. We have seen also that Archbishop Egbert claimed for his priests a wergeld of 200 ounces of silver, which thus would accord exactly with the Kentish wergeld of 200 scillings. It might almost seem that he may have consulted his colleague the Archbishop of Canterbury and fixed his clerical demand in accordance with the Kentish wergeld rather than with that of Wessex or Mercia.

Nor was there anything unnatural or abnormal in the Kentish wergeld of 200 ounces of silver, inasmuch as 200 Roman ounces of silver at a ratio of 1 : 10 would equal the *Mina Italica* of twenty Roman ounces or of two ancient Roman pounds of gold.

We may therefore with confidence, but without claiming certainty, fairly state the Kentish wergelds in Kentish scillings and sceatts, thus :—

Kentish wergelds.

	Kentish scillings		Sceatts
Eorl . . .	600 (possibly 300 ?)	=	12,000
Freeman . . .	200 (possibly 100 ?)	=	4,000
Læt (1) . . .	80	=	1,600
„ (2) . . .	60	=	1,200
„ (3) . . .	40	=	800

And when put together in this way the proportion between the wergeld of the freeman and that of the læts becomes important. In the Norse laws the leysing's wergeld was one sixth that of the hauld or odalman. In the Bavarian and Saxon laws the wergeld of the *litus* was one fourth that of the freeman. Anything like these proportions in Kent would make a wergeld as low as 100 scillings for the freeman very improbable.

Lastly, perhaps it may be fair to the reader to recur once more to the question of the Kentish scilling. If any doubt should remain as to whether we are right

The sceatts could not have been farthings.

in regarding the sceatt as the silver coin of that name, twenty of which went to the Roman ounce until it was superseded by the penny of Offa and Alfred, surely that doubt must now be dispelled. For if, according to the view of Schmid and others, the sceatt were to be taken as a farthing or *quarter* of a sceatt, the correspondence of Kentish with Continental wergelds and payments *pro fredo* would be altogether destroyed. The eorl's triple wergeld at a ratio of 1 : 10 would be only one sixth (and if 300 scillings only one twelfth) of that of the Frankish noble or official, while the Kentish freeman's wergeld would be reduced to one sixth (or if 100 scillings to only one twelfth) of that of the Continental *liber* or *ingenuus*.

One perhaps must not say that such a result would be impossible. But would it be a likely one? We should have to suppose that the Jutish chieftain, perfectly familiar with the Continental wergeld of the freeman as 200 or 160 gold solidi, equated by long tradition with the round number of 100 head of cattle, upon settlement in Kent reduced the wergeld of the freeman to one sixth or one twelfth of what it was in the country he came from. From what we know of the tenacity of tribal custom everywhere, especially as regards the amount of the wergelds, it is difficult to conceive of his doing so.

VIII. RESULT OF THE KENTISH EVIDENCE.

We are now in a position to take a broader view of the wergelds, Continental, Kentish, Wessex, and Mercian.

To the incidental mention of the fact that the Kentish freeman's wergeld, if 200 Kentish scillings, equalled the gold *Mina Italica* may be added the further incident that it was equal to 100 'sweetest cows' of the Alamannic laws. Whether accidental coincidences or not, these facts bring us back to the point with which this inquiry started, viz. the wide-spread normal wergeld of 100 head of cattle and its very general traditional equation with a gold mina.

The Kentish, Wessex, and Mercian wergelds thus brought into line with the normal Continental wergeld of 200 and 160 gold solidi or 100 head of cattle.

The main facts elicited as to the amount of the wergelds in the course of this inquiry are these.

At the date of the Kentish Laws and generally during the seventh century we find three wergelds in use in England for the freeman :—

The Wessex wergeld of	6000 sceatts	at 1:10 = 600	gold	tremisses
" Mercian "	4800 "	at 1:10 = 480	"	"
		at 1:12 = 400	"	"
" Kentish "	4000 "	at 1:10 = 400	"	"

And on the Continent we find the two wergelds :—

Frankish	200 solidi	= 600 gold tremisses
The other	160 "	= 480 " "

Now, in the fairly contemporary laws of the Ripuarian Franks, and of the Burgundians, the traditional values of animals we have found to be stated as follows :—

Ox	2 solidi	= 6 gold tremisses
Cow	1 solidus	= 3 " "

And in the nearly contemporary Alamannic laws the traditional values were :—

Best ox	= 5 gold tremisses
Medium ox and sweetest cow . . .	= 4 " "

Within the range of these variations in the ratio between gold and silver, and in the local value of

The differences covered by ratio between gold and silver 1 : 10 and 1 : 12.

animals, there seems to be ample room and reason for the variations in the money values of the wergelds.

(1) 100 oxen of 6 tremisses (*i.e.* 600 tremisses) equal the Frankish wergeld of 200 gold solidi, and at 1 : 10 the Wessex wergeld of 6000 sceatts.

(2) A long hundred of 120 cows of 4 tremisses (*i.e.* 480 tremisses) would equal the wergeld of 160 gold solidi, and at 1 : 10 the Mercian wergeld of 4800 sceatts.

(3) 100 cows at 4 tremisses (*i.e.* 400 tremisses) make the Kentish wergeld of (if we are right) 200 Kentish scillings of 2 tremisses, and at 1 : 10, 4000 sceatts. If we change the ratio to 1 : 12, then a Kentish wergeld of 100 cows of 4 tremisses would in silver equal the Mercian wergeld of 4800 sceatts. In other words, the difference between the Kentish and Mercian wergeld may be explained, either as one between 100 and 120 cows, or, the number of cows remaining at 100, between the ratios of 1 : 10 and 1 : 12.

There is thus in these fairly contemporary values of Western Europe, in the seventh century, or within the Merovingian period, so obviously room for the variations in the wergelds that, whether as to origin the differences may be of historical interest or not, at any rate for our present purpose we are fairly warned by the general coincidence in the wergelds not to make too much of the differences.

Kentish freeman and the twelve-hyndeman = Continental *freeman*.

The Kentish laws, therefore, lead us with some confidence to recognise the practical identity of the wergeld of the Kentish freeman with that, not of the Wessex ceorl, but of the twelve-hyndeman.

We have been led cautiously step by step to this

result, and, whether the problem raised by it be capable of solution or not, it is important that it should be fairly stated and considered. Even if the Kentish freeman's wergeld was only 100 Kentish scillings, it would more nearly correspond with the six-hyndeman's wergeld than with that of the Wessex ceorl. On the other hand, the wergelds of the Kentish læts are very fairly on a level with that of the Wessex ceorl. Taking an average between the second and third class of læts the correspondence would be exact.[1]

Kentish læt and the twy-hyndeman = the Continental *freedman.*

If, therefore, the wergeld of the Kentish freeman may be regarded as practically equivalent to that of the Continental *liber* or *ingenuus* on the one hand, and to that of the twelve-hyndeman of the Anglo-Saxon laws on the other hand, and if that of the Kentish læt was like that of the Norse leysing and of the twy-hyndeman, then once more it becomes natural and right, and in accordance with ancient custom, that in the Compact between Alfred and Guthrum the twelve-hyndeman should be made 'equally dear' with the Norse hauld, and so with the *liber* or *ingenuus* of the Continental laws, while the twy-hyndeman should be held 'equally dear' with the Danish leysing.

[1] 60 + 40 Kentish scillings = 1200 + 800 scætts. The average 1000 sceatts = 200. Wessex scillings of 5 scætts.

CHAPTER XV.

GENERAL CONCLUSIONS.

Bearing of the results upon the division of classes and the character of holdings.

BEFORE concluding this Essay it may be well in a final chapter to consider its results in their bearing upon the conditions of early Anglo-Saxon society, and especially with regard to the division of classes and the character of the holdings.

The object has been to approach these difficult questions from the point of view of tribal custom.

The amount of wergelds the main clue.

The main clue to an understanding of the division of classes has been the amount of the wergelds.

The trouble taken to arrive at a correct knowledge of the currencies in which the wergelds were paid, tedious as it may have seemed to the reader, will not have been thrown away if it has led to the recognition of the fact that there was a very general correspondence in the amount of the wergelds tenaciously adhered to by the tribes of Western Europe, whether remaining in their old homes or settled in newly conquered countries. The amount of the wergelds was not seemingly a matter of race. Cymric and German customs were singularly similar.

The general correspondence in wergelds throughout Western Europe.

If the Irish eric fine formed an exception, Irish tribal custom nevertheless had many things in common with Cymric and German custom in other respects.

The solidarity of the kindred connected with family holdings.

It was from a study of the wergelds and the rights and liability of relatives in their receipt and payment that some idea was gained of the solidarity of the kindred under tribal custom. And this solidarity of the kindred was found to be closely connected with the family character of tribal land-holdings, of which the Cymric gwely was a typical example. Where direct evidence of this family element was wanting the liability of the kindred for the wergeld remained as an indication that it once had existed.

The normal wergeld of 200 gold solidi or 100 head of cattle.

In reviewing the evidence of these matters and attempting to bring the results to a focus, we begin with the fact that with comparatively few exceptions the normal wergeld of the full or typical freeman was everywhere so large—200 gold solidi, the heavy mina of gold, traditionally representing 100 head of cattle. This wergeld was too large by far for the individual slayer to pay, and possible only as a payment from one group of kindred to another.

The Anglo-Saxon wergelds brought with them into Britain.

We have seen reason to infer from the Kentish, Wessex, and Mercian wergelds that the Anglo-Saxon tribes shared in these traditions, and, so to speak, brought their wergelds with them into Britain. And we have found that Anglo-Saxon custom as regards the wergelds was substantially similar to that of the Continental tribes.

No feud or wergeld within the kindred.

From Beowulf we learned that, as there could be no feud within the kindred, a homicide within the kindred could not be avenged or compounded for. There was no galanas or wergeld in such a case under either Cymric or German custom, and evidence was found in the so-called Laws of Henry I. that it had been so also under Anglo-Saxon custom. Up to the time of the Norman Conquest the punishment of parricide was practically left by the laws to the spiritual jurisdiction of the Church (*supra*, p. 335).

Wergelds paid and received by paternal and maternal relations.

The principle which required both paternal and maternal relations to join in the payment and receipt of wergelds, and nearly always in the proportion of two thirds and one third, was also common to Cymric and German tribes. This principle depended upon a view of marriage likewise common to both. A blood relationship was established as regards children of a marriage, while husband and wife for many purposes remained in their own kindreds. There being no blood relationship between husband and wife, the husband's kindred alone were liable for his crimes and the wife's alone for her crimes, and neither the husband nor the wife received any portion of the other's wergeld or was liable for his or her homicides. Such was the custom under the Cymric codes and the laws of the Bretts and Scots, and Anglo-Saxon custom as described in the so-called Laws of Henry I. was similar.

The half wergeld of strangers in blood.

The tribal feeling which allowed tribesmen and strangers to live side by side under their own laws, and made the Salic and Ripuarian Franks award a full wergeld to tribesmen of allied German tribes, while it gave only a half wergeld to the Gallo-Roman possessor who was not of their blood, was, it would seem, brought with the invading tribes into Britain.

Danish and English tribesmen were allowed to live side by side under their own laws and acknowledged as 'equally dear,' with a similar wergeld, while, at all events in the cases which come under notice, complete strangers in blood were awarded only a half wergeld as in the Continental laws.

We have not attempted to settle the question how far there was a Romano-British population left in the towns, but we have found incidental traces and hints that in Northumbria, Wessex, and Mercia there were 'wilisc' men—Welsh or British—who had only a half wergeld, being treated as strangers both in this respect and also as regards the substitution of the ordeal for the oaths of kindred (p. 403).

The ordeal the alternative to the oaths of kinsmen.

The principle that a man who could not bring to his protection the oath of his kinsmen must be brought to the ordeal was one of widely extended tribal custom. And it was emphasised by the adoption of the ordeal as a Christian ceremony solemnly performed in the churches under both Frankish and Anglo-Saxon law.

The man of no kindred becomes a dependent on some one else's land.

There can be little doubt that in the solidarity of the kindred under tribal custom we have to do with the strongest instinct which everywhere moulded tribal society. So far as it had its way and was not confronted by more potent forces it must have almost necessarily ruled such matters as the division of classes, the occupation of land, and the modes of settlement.

When we inquire into the grades of society under tribal custom they seem everywhere to have their roots in the principles of blood relationship. A man who has no kindred to protect him needs and seeks the protection of a chieftain or lord. By the force of tribal gravitation he sinks into the dependent condition of living upon another's land.

Whether he be a freedman who has risen from the rank of the theow or thrall, or a free tribesman of low position, or one of a conquered race, or a stranger immigrant, and whether he be cottier or the holder of the typical yardland, until in the course of generations a kindred has grown up around him, he remains in the dependent condition. He is indeed a freeman as compared with the theow or thrall, but when Alfred and Guthrum make their compact and agree that Dane and English shall be reckoned as equally dear at the normal wergeld of the full freeman it is not of the dependent class they are thinking. They give to this class and to the Danish leysing or newly made freedman a twy-hynde instead of a twelve-hynde wergeld.

The twy-hynde class was the dependent class of gafolgeldas, with a lower wergeld.

It might at first sight be supposed that this twy-hynde condition of the dependent class in England, so far as it may have included Anglo-Saxons, must have been the result of degradation in social status between the first settlements and the time of King Alfred, but we have sought in vain for evidence of an earlier higher position in the Laws of King Ine. And, on the whole, even when regarded solely from a tribal point of view, it does not seem unlikely that strangers in blood and freedmen and dependent followers of the conquering chieftains should find themselves after conquest and settlement in the economic condition of tenants and gafolgeldas on the lands of protecting lords. Nor would it be strange that, when in a new country and under other influences this uniform dependent economic condition had once become a general fact, the whole class, in spite of variety of origins, should find itself marked by a twy-hynde wergeld.

The twy-hynde class were equated.

It does not follow, however, that because in the compact between Alfred and Guthrum the twy-hynde class were reckoned as equally dear with the Norse leysing that the Anglo-Saxon 'ceorl who sits on gafol-land' was generally in as low a social position as the Norse newly made freedman. It is enough that according to the evidence, he was a dependent tenant, let us say, under the lordship of a twelve-hynde man or if settled upon royal demesne of some gesith or official of the king.

With the Norse leysing.

Still it may be well to look once again at the position of the Norse leysing, because, after all, it is with the leysing that the Anglo-Saxon twy-hynde gafolgelda was equated in a compact made after King Alfred's victory, and so when the two chieftains seemed to be treating on equal terms. Surely King Alfred was not intending to degrade the Anglo-Saxon dependent class. Presumably he was making a good bargain for them.

The low condition of the leysing.

The early Norse laws were settled long after the date of this compact, upon the conversion of South Norway, and, as in other cases, they were framed with the express purpose of making room in the legal system for the Christian Church and so in some sense with its sanction. And yet so deep was the gulf between classes even then that a certain portion of the churchyard was set apart for leysings, and in no case were they to be buried in the portion reserved for classes above them. And if after giving his freedom-ale and so attaining the first step in freedom and independence the leysing should die leaving destitute children whose support ought not to be thrown back upon his lord, we have seen that the way out of the difficulty was to dig a grave in the churchyard into which the leysing's children were to be placed and left to starve to death, the last survivor being the only one which the lord thenceforth had to maintain.[1] This was the position of the leysing at the bottom of the ladder of freedom.

But he rose by steps as a kindred grew around him.

But we found the leysing of the Norse laws rising by steps into greater freedom and better social position. And the process throughout was founded upon the gradual growth of kindred. It was the lack of kindred to swear for them and defend them which placed them low in the social scale, and it was the gradual growth of kindred generation after generation which marked the steps of their rise into better social position with higher wergelds.

In England it was so once, but the rungs of the ladder drop out.

When we turn to the Anglo-Saxon laws we seem to detect similar tribal principles originally at work but with differences which may very probably be referred to the circumstances attendant upon conquest and settlement in Britain.

The law of tribal gravitation here as elsewhere, aided, no doubt, by other potent forces, had been at work placing the man with an imperfect kindred in a dependent position at the bottom of the social ladder.

And it is important to note that at first the middle rungs of the ladder by which a man could climb out of the dependent position seem to have been present here as in Norway. The evidence is scanty, but sufficiently important.

From the Kentish laws the presence of stepping-stones into greater freedom may be inferred in the case of the three classes of *læts* with their rising wergelds. And in a precious fragment of ancient

---

[1] *Supra*, p. 265.

custom happily rescued from oblivion we found evidence that, originally at all events, there had been a way out of the ceorl's twy-hynde condition at the fourth generation of landholding connected with payment of gafol to the king's utware and direct service to the king. But we recognised that the collector of the fragment looked longingly back to ancient custom, speaking of it in the past tense, as if it was no longer in force.[1]

It would obviously not be wise to trust solely to the negative evidence of the silence of the laws, but in this case the silence seems to confirm the evidence of the fragment. For the pathetic tone of the fragment finds an echo in the fact that all traces of the middle rungs in the ladder seem to have vanished from the later laws. There is no mention in Ine's laws or in Alfred's of there being or having been several grades of freedmen or læts. Even the half wergeld of the six-hynde stranger who has risen to the possession of five hides silently disappears after King Alfred's time. From whatever cause, so far as the evidence goes, the twy-hynde class seems to have become a homogeneous class in which, in spite of different origins, distinctions were merged in a common economic condition. Differences of origin were perhaps forgotten as the result of comradeship in the long struggle against the Danish foe.

And this kept open the gulf betwoen twy-hynde and twelve-hynde classes.

We thus seem to be driven to recognise the width and to some extent the bridgelessness, already in King Alfred's time if not in King Ine's, of the gulf between the position of the twelve-hynde landed class

[1] *Supra*, p. 367.

and that of the twy-hynde dependent class of gafol-geldas and geburs who were tenants on their land

It seems probable that, though technically and really free in the sense of not being thralls, the twy-hynde class, broadly speaking, may have found themselves very early, if not from the first, placed in an economic condition of service and servitude, including work as well as gafol, which by the ultimate disappearance of the middle rungs of the ladder might very easily slide into what is loosely called the 'serfdom' of later times.

In the meantime we realise that the abjectness of this semi-servile condition may be very easily exaggerated by modern associations with the terms 'service' and 'serfdom.'

It is when we turn from the twy-hynde class to the position of the class above them, of gesithcund and twelve-hynde men, that we learn that a part at least of the risk of misunderstanding may lie in the difference between the tribal notion of service and freedom and the more modern one.

Position and services of the twelve-hynde class.

What, then, has tribal custom to teach us as to the position and services of the twelve-hynde class?

Reverting once more to the compact between Alfred and Guthrum, Dane and English are to be equally dear at eight half-marks of gold. The Englishman, without any limiting adjective, is the twelve-hynde man. And he is put on a level with the Danish typical free landholder, the hauld or odalman of the Norse laws, whose wergeld under Norse law was that of the typical freeman everywhere—equivalent to the normal wergeld of 200 gold solidi, the mina of gold, the traditional wergeld of 100 head of

On a level with the Norse odalman.

cattle. It was six times that of the Norse leysing, just as the twelve-hyndeman's wergeld in England was six times that of the 'ceorl who sits on gafol land.'

The English twelve-hynde man is therefore put on a level with the Norse odaller or typical landholder. And so, as we have seen, the ceorl who rose by the middle rungs of the ladder into the twelve-hynde position had *inter alia* to become a landholder of 5 hides, and his family became gesithcund only after the landholding had continued to the fourth generation. His great-grandchildren then became gesithcund with a twelve-hynde wergeld.

The twelve-hyndemen were therefore landholders, surrounded, in principle at least if not always in practice, by a kindred. But what kind of a landholding was it?

Twelve-hynde men were land-holders.

Approaching the question strictly from a tribal point of view, the solidarity of the kindred involved in the payment and receipt of wergelds would certainly suggest that those who had a right to receive and the obligation to pay held a position in their kindred quite different from that of the modern individual owner of land.

Position of the first settlers.

The analogy of Welsh and Irish and Salic and Norse and Scanian tribal custom would lead us to infer that the Anglo-Saxon settlers in England must have brought with them traditions of tribal or family ownership more or less of the type of the Cymric gwely, though doubtless modified by emigration and settlement in a new country.

After all that has been said, traditions and perhaps actual examples of the individual ownership of the 'Romanus possessor,' and, still more likely, actual

Separation from their kindreds threw them on the protection of the king.

experience of the Roman type of landed estates, may have survived in Britain from the period of the Roman occupation, and the Anglo-Saxon settlers may easily have been influenced in the matter of landholding by what as conquerors they came to supplant. But they can hardly have wholly cast off their own tribal traditions and instincts. The continued payment and receipt of wergelds show that they did not. Even, to take an extreme case, if they came to Britain as single settlers having left their kinsmen behind them, still kindreds would gradually grow up around their descendants in the new country. And tribal custom left to itself would give to them landed rights, quite different from those of the individual owner. But the interval, apart from other outside influences, may well have subjected tribal custom to a strain.

From the point of view of this interval it may not be unreasonable to revert to the clauses of King Alfred's laws on 'kinless men' and the Norman precedent, that the king was to take the place of the missing maternal kindred and of advocate for a Norman if he had no other.[1]

Unless, therefore, the twelve-hynde settler was surrounded by a full kindred in the new country, he must, according to his own tribal custom, have found himself much more of an individual than he was used to be, and therefore more dependent upon the protection of his chieftain or king.

We must not, on the one hand, conceive of the twelve-hynde settler as having all at once adopted the independent position of the Roman 'possessor,' though

---

[1] *Supra*, p. 322; and Laws of Alfred, s. 27 and 38.

circumstances may have sometimes severed him as completely from his 'parentilla' as the ceremony of the Salic law. Nor can we, on the other hand, conceive of him always as a tribesman surrounded by his kindred. He may evidently, on the one hand, be released from many of the trammels involved in membership of a kindred, but, on the other hand, he is thrown more than ever under conditions of service to the king.

Service under tribal custom not degrading. But the ties of kindred involved restraint on individual action.

Let us for a moment revert to the tribal conception of these trammels and services. They did not always involve degradation of social condition. They often, as we have seen, were the mark of the attainment of a higher position.

The kindred of the aillts or strangers who settled upon a chieftain's land under Cymric custom was acknowledged in the fourth generation of continued occupation, but at the moment a kindred was acknowledged its members became *adscripti glebæ*. When the Irish fuidhir did the same his descendants of the fourth generation found themselves not only bound to the land, but also bound together by something like the rules of the Cymric gwely, so that one of them could not sell or charge his share without the consent of the others. We found the same thing in Norway, where the rules for payment of the wergelds by relations were more elaborate than anywhere else, and where the growth of kindred seems so completely to have ruled the rise from one social grade to another, till at last a man whose great-grandfather's great-grandfather was a freeborn landholder became an odaller. If at first sight we were to picture the odalman to ourselves as an individual

The Norse odalman a sharer in the odal, with duties to his kindred.

freeholder of Roman or modern type we should soon find out our mistake when we learned that if he wanted to sell his odal he must first *consult his odal-sharers.* When examined closely the fact became evident that it was the *group of kindred* that by long settlement on the land had become odal, and that the shares of individuals in the odal were subject—with, of course, many differences—to some such tribal customs as those of the Cymric gwely. The odalman was thus not a single isolated landowner. He was surrounded by kindred odal like himself, reciprocally bound to fight for one another and swear for one another, and to share in the payment or receipt of one another's wergeld. The odalman was protected by his kindred, but his freedom of individual action was restricted by it.

The Salic alod a family holding.

So also under Salic law the joint inheritors of the alod on *terra Salica*, with right of redivision between great-grandchildren *per capita*, were in the same way trammelled, and when by a solemn public form they released themselves from their obligations to their kindred they relinquished also all rights of inheritance and protection (p. 134).

Are we to consider these Continental analogies to be without relevance to Anglo-Saxon landholding?

Dr. Konrad von Maurer, in those masterly papers contributed in 1855 to the 'Kritische Ueberschau' which are still so valuable, rightly lays stress upon the power of the *kindred* as the great rival of the power of the *state* in the development of Anglo-Saxon polity. We find but little direct allusion to the kindred in the laws, it is true. But incidentally and as it were by accident we have learned from passages mentioned in their proper place that so late as the time of Athelstan there were kindreds both twelve-hynde and twy-hynde powerful enough to defy the King's peace.[1]

This is in itself a significant reminder that more or less of tribal custom remained in force behind the screen of the laws from which most of our evidence has been taken. And yet we seem to be almost forced to the conclusion that if we try to realise the position of the twelve-hynde settler we must regard him, at all events for the first few generations, as in a very different position from that of the Norse odalman in the old country. Even though as head of his family he may have brought descendants and dependents with him, he could not in the new country be at once surrounded by kinsmen and odal-sharers who with himself had hereditary rights in the land.

Anglo-Saxon twelve-hynde settler pays gafol and service direct to the king.

We thus come round again to the point that so far as he may have been separated from his kindred the first Anglo-Saxon settler must have found himself thrown upon the protection of his chief and into a position of individual service. He becomes, as we have seen according to the scanty evidence of the Laws of Ine, a king's gesith, with military and judicial and administrative duties to discharge, put into a post of service which he cannot relinquish at pleasure. Service to the king has to some extent taken the place of the restraints of kindred, and so in a sense, like the twy-hynde man, he has become a gafolgelda, but paying his gafol and services direct to the king, and *adscriptus glebæ*,

[1] *Supra*, pp. 415-416.

but tied to an estate and an official position instead of to a yardland.

This view of the position of the gesithcund and twelve-hynde class rests very much upon the incidental evidence of the Dooms of Ine, but the truth of it is confirmed by the independent evidence of the precious fragment already referred to. For its interesting evidence shows that, in addition to his holding of five hides of land, it was precisely into this position of gafol-paying and service *direct to the king* that the ceorl of ancient custom had to climb in order to earn the gesithcund status and the twelve-hynde wergeld.

Thus we arrive at a definite and practical mark distinguishing ultimately, and perhaps more or less from the first, the twelve-hynde and twy-hynde classes.

The twelve-hynde or landed class paid gafol and did service direct to the king. The twy-hynde or dependent class paid gafol and did service to the landed class, who from this point of view were middlemen between the twy-hynde gafolgelda and the king.

The holding direct from the king easily becomes a manor.

We seem, therefore, thus early to arrive at something analogous to Professor Maitland's technical definition of the Manor as the fiscal unit from which gafol is paid direct to the king, while its lord is the receiver of the payments and services of its tenants. The single landholder who is not under a manorial lord in the Domesday survey is said to hold 'as for a manor'—though he may have no tenants.

It may be worth while in this connection to allude to another general feature of the manorial estate on both sides of the Channel which if not directly of tribal origin must at least have worked in close sympathy with tribal custom.

Tribal character of the manor as a judicial unit.

The gesithcund man officially charged with the control of a district or estate easily became in a manorial sense lord of the dependent tenants upon it. And the judicial and magisterial adjunct to the lordship became a prevalent feature of the typical manor.

We have seen that the 'sac and soc' of later times may have grown from the root of the tribal principle involved in the sacredness of the precinct or area of protection of the chieftain and, in degree, of every grade of tribesman who possessed a homestead. How large a place this principle occupied is shown by the prominence of the *fredus* in Frankish law and of the *mundbyrd* in the early Anglo-Saxon laws. The manor was a complex product of many factors, and tribal custom was certainly one of them.

Was it a family holding?

Once again, what kind of a holding was that of the twelve-hyndeman? Was it a family holding, and what were the rules of succession?

Place names in favour of its being sometimes a family holding.

Unfortunately, we do not know how far the immigrants came in kindreds and families or as followers and 'gesiths' of military chieftains. But, in any case, if we may take the evidence of place-names the great number of patronymic names of places would lead to the supposition that the holdings were family holdings. The *ham* may at first have been the estate of a gesithcund man held direct of the king with gafolgeldas and geburs under him holding yardlands and doing work on his demesne. But when it becomes an *ingham* the patronymic termination points to the lordship of the manor having been held, as time went on, jointly, in somewhat the same way as the Cymric chieftainship in the gwely. His sons and grandsons and great-grandsons may really have had their rights of maintenance all along, and ultimately, if they were allowed to do so, they may have sometimes divided the inheritance instead of continuing to hold it jointly. Tribal instincts working alone would probably follow some such line as this.

But it is easy to see that the nearer the holding of the twelve-hyndeman approached to a benefice or office the stronger would be the tendency towards single succession instead of divisions among heirs.

During the century or two after the first settlement there was time, no doubt, for the growth of kindreds, and the thane in the king's service would soon become the head of a family group; but, on the other hand, many influences were at work undermining the solidarity of the kindred and strengthening the manorial element. Tribal instincts die hard. But probably there never was full opportunity for the growth upon English soil of anything like the solidarity in landholding of the Norse kindreds of odal sharers tracing back their family possession for four or five generations.

Folk-land may have devolved under tribal custom.

There is but little evidence on the rights or rules of succession to be found in the laws. And the silence is suggestive of the continuance of custom. Even the diplomatic evidence of wills and charters is so much restricted to boc-land that it perhaps throws a shadow rather than direct light upon the ordinary devolution of land which had not become the subject of the Romanised rules of ownership, conveyance and testamentary disposition.

But if Professor Vinogradoff is right in his view that folk-land was that land which was still held under ancient custom, then for anything we know, in spite of documentary silence, folk-land may still have been held more or less as family rather than individual property even in later times.

If the suggested analogy between the *terra Salica* of the Salic laws and the *folk-land* of Anglo-Saxon documents could be proved, the family character of the holdings in both cases would receive confirmation. At the same time the frequent concurrence of relatives in Anglo-Saxon dispositions of land and the common form of deprecation of future interference on their part would at least be consistent with the supposition.

But feudal principles would tend towards single succession outwardly.

That as time went on the growing force of feudal principles would demand single succession to landed estates whenever they could be regarded as benefices is what might be expected. And it is worth noting that under later feudal custom, by a kind of compromise, what was really a family holding was often artificially moulded for practical purposes into a single holding with apparent single succession.

A single holding may cover internal family divisions.

In the Domesday survey are many instances in which thanes or soldiers here and there hold manors or fractions of manors 'pariter' or 'in paragio.' And when the feudal tenancy 'in parage' is examined in its fully developed form on the Continent, it is found to present many resemblances to what under Cymric custom the family holding of a tribal chief of kindred might be if the chief alone were regarded as the landed person doing homage to the superior lord for all his kindred and if, in the next stage, when the gwely was internally divided between brothers, one of them only did homage for the rest. There were indeed in tribal custom as to the chieftainship and the constitution of the gwely traits which easily allowed themselves to be developed on feudal lines. For the present purpose, however, the point seems to be that within what looks from the outside like a single individual landholding there may have been internal family divisions which are not apparent.

Passing now from what may be regarded as the holdings of the twelve-hynde class, more or less tending to resemble manorial estates, to the yardlands of the twy-hynde class, room may perhaps be found even in their case for the exceptional continuance of the family element in spite of the apparent single succession.

Kentish family holdings.

The Kentish holdings in sulungs and yokes instead of in hides and yardlands seem to go back to the earliest Kentish records. The fact that, in spite of the difference in date between the evidence of the earliest charters and that of the Domesday survey and the surveys in the Battle Abbey records and the 'Black Book of St. Augustine,' the holdings seem to have been throughout in sulungs and yokes points to continuity. And when these sulungs and yokes in the surveys are found to be very often held by 'the *heredes* of so and so,' or 'so and so and his *pares*,' it seems fair to suggest that in these Kentish holdings there may have been a survival of family ownership.

Whether it were so or not, this later Kentish evidence shows at least that the continuance of family holdings was not necessarily inconsistent with external uniformity in the sulungs and yokes of the open-field system in Kent. And if so, why may not the same thing be true in exceptional cases of the hides and yardlands of Wessex and Mercia?

Contrary principles have a strange way in practice of finding a *modus vivendi* till one of them at last overrides the other.

Gavelkind holdings were family holdings.

It will be remembered that one of the complaints of the existence of kindreds powerful enough to defy the king's peace in King Athelstan's time came from Kent. And if these facts may be taken as evidence that the solidarity of kindreds had been better preserved in Kent than elsewhere some tribal light might perhaps be thrown upon the survival of the custom of gavelkind in Kent.

It is not a matter upon which we must dwell, but evidently the gavelkind tenure must have been something different from the prevalent tenures of other districts. The difference cannot have been the equal division of the sulungs and yokes between sons as contrasted with the single succession to the yardlands of other districts, because the sulungs and yokes were apparently not interfered with by the gavelkind division among heirs. And when the right of the youngest son under the custom of gavelkind to succeed to the parental hearth is compared with the similar right of the youngest son in the case of the Cymric gwely the inference becomes very strong that the gavelkind holdings were family holdings and the gavelkind divisions internal divisions within the family, like those of the Cymric gwely, not necessarily interfering with the permanence of the sulungs and yokes of the open-field system of which the family holdings were composed or in which the family had rights.

The surveys of Kentish manors in the records of Battle Abbey and the 'Black Book of St. Augustine' present instances sometimes of sulungs and yokes held by the *heredes* of a deceased person and sometimes of others which maintain their unity for purposes of payments and services although in the possession of several holders. The sulung in these cases seems to have continued to be the unit liable for the fixed ploughing and other services irrespective of the question who were its occupants.[1]

Once more perhaps some light may be gained from Cymric tribal custom.

Analogy of the Cymric tref-gordd.

We have learned from the Cymric evidence that a district might be divided for purposes of revenue and food rents into sub-districts, irrespective of who might be the occupants. And we have seen also how the Cymric trefgordd or unit of pastoral occupation, with its one plough and one churn and one herd of cattle under a single herdsman, could remain a permanent taxable unit paying the tunc pound in

[1] This is not the place to enter into the details of the Kentish holdings, but reference may be made by way of example to the $5\frac{1}{2}$ 'sulings' of 'Christelet' in the *Black Book of St. Augustine.* The suling is still the unit for services and payments. The '*Suling de Fayreport*' contains 300 acres (and was probably originally a suling and a half), but it is divided into 11 holdings, 8 of 25 acres each and 3 of $33\frac{1}{3}$ acres each. Six of the eleven holdings are still occupied by persons bearing the name of 'de Fayreport' or the 'heredes' of such persons, and probably the others may belong to relatives. The '*Suling de Ores*' is, on the other hand, divided into about 40 quite irregular holdings, varying from less than an acre to 44 acres. Several are still occupied by 'heredes' of persons of the family 'de Ores.' (Cottonian MSS. Faustina, A. 1, British Museum, fol. 567 *et seq.*) The manor 'de Ores' is in the list of those afterwards disgavelled: see Elton's *Tenures of Kent*, p. 400.

lieu of food rents, whoever might at the time be its occupants and have cattle in the herd. Within the lines of tribal custom itself the members of a Cymric gwely might be spread over a district and their cattle distributed among many tref-gordds, while from the chieftain's point of view the local units of taxation were uniform and regular.

But the yardlands were mostly holdings with single succession on payment of a relief to the lord.

But this must not blind our eyes to the fact that the yardlands on Anglo-Saxon estates were, so far as we can see, for the most part really individual holdings with actual single succession. However hard tribal custom may have fought for the family element, the manorial element in the end seems to have prevailed on most manors so as to secure, for the purposes of the lordship and the convenience of manorial management, single succession to the yardlands. The fact that as early as King Ine's time we see new individual holdings of geburs being made by the allotment of yardlands and homesteads to individual tenants in return for gafol and work, when taken in connection with the 'Rectitudines' brings us back to the likeness of these holdings to the holdings of the *villani* of later times. We see in the allotment of stock to the gebur, of which we trace scattered evidence, the fact on which the principle of the later villenage was based. Only when both homestead and yardland came from the lord was there to be work as well as gafol under King Ine's laws. The stock of the holding according to the 'Rectitudines' belonged in theory to the lord and upon the tenant's death returned to the lord. The continuance to another tenant on the payment of a relief involved the admission that the holding and its outfit were a loan from the lord.

The manorial element must not be lost sight of.

The fact that in exceptional cases family holdings were able to maintain their own under manorial management must not be allowed to lead us to underrate the power of the manorial element. There were in tribal custom itself as described by Tacitus elements of what we have elsewhere spoken of as the embryo manor, but this must not blind our eyes to the fact that something more was required to produce the general uniformity of holdings and single succession upon manorial estates than tribal custom working alone.

If from a tribal point of view we try to understand the growth of manorial serfdom and see how on the Continent it was seemingly the result of the combination of two leading factors, tribal custom and Roman methods of land management, it becomes hardly possible to ignore the presence of something like the same combination of two interacting factors on British or English ground.

With the manorial side of serfdom in its connection with the widely prevalent open field system we have already attempted to deal in a former volume. That there may have been some continuity and continuance of estates managed on the Roman system can hardly be denied. However far the policy of extermination of the old inhabitants was carried, it never extended over the whole area. And the whole of Britain was not conquered in the same century. Even if the continuity of estates in Britain should be considered to have been entirely broken by the Anglo-Saxon invasions (which is hardly conceivable), it must be admitted that continuity and likeness between England and the Continent as to land management was very soon restored on monastic and other ecclesiastical estates, and perhaps also upon what was Royal domain. Nor can it be doubted that herein was a force greatly strengthening the manorial element.

Tribal custom only would not meet the whole case.

If we limit our view to the tribal side only of the problem, we recognise that in Scandinavia and in the Cymric districts of our own island and in Ireland tribal principles working alone tended powerfully, without help from the Roman side, to produce a class of tenants becoming *adscripti glebæ* after four generations of occupation, but it did not produce either in Norway or in Wales or Ireland or in Celtic Scotland that general and typical form of occupation in uniform yardlands or 'huben' so prevalent in England and Germany on manorial estates with ostensibly single succession and services in so many points resembling those of the Roman colonate.

Whether the manor was the indirect or direct successor of the Roman Villa—*i.e.* whether the continuity was broken or not—the *manorial* use of the open-field system of agriculture seems to be required to produce the uniformity of holdings in yardlands and the single succession which marked what is roughly called the serfdom of the manorial estate.

The open-field system not of manorial origin.

It is hardly necessary to repeat that the open-field system itself was not of manorial origin. It was essentially an economic result and differed very greatly in its forms. Its main object seems to have been fairness and equality of occupation. Under tribal custom, in Wales, it arose out of coaration of portions of the waste or pasture by the common plough-team to which the tribesmen or the taeogs, as the case might be, contributed oxen. The strips were day-works of the plough taken in rotation by the contributors according to the place of their oxen in the plough-team for the season, and they returned into common pasture when the crop had been removed. The tribesman in the pastoral stage was the owner of oxen but not of the strips ploughed by them. They were merged again in the common pasture of the district in which he had rights of grazing for his cattle. And the cattle, and not the corn crops, were the main thing upon which the system turned.

Whatever method of distribution may have been followed, as arable farming increased and the strips became more and more permanently arable, mostly on the two-field or the three-field system, the area of unploughed land was more and more restricted and the pasture over the stubbles and fallows obviously became more and more essential. The cattle, on the one hand, required the pasture on the stubbles and fallows, and the land, before being ploughed again, required the manure arising from the pasturing of the flocks and herds upon it.

Where open-field husbandry still subsists in Western Europe, whether on this or the other side of the Channel, the owner of the strips has still no right of grazing upon his own strips till upon the appointed day when the common right begins of all the holders to graze their cattle in a common herd or flock over the whole area. This right is known in France as the 'vaine pâture,' and it is still the most important and indestructible element in the open-field husbandry. In the great open fields around Chartres a man may plant his strips with vines if he likes, but to this day, if he does so, he must let the sheep of the commune graze over them after a certain date, in exercise of the immemorial right of the *vaine pâture.*

But uniform holdings and single succession are marks of manorial lordship.

In all this no manorial element need be present, and when the manorial element is absent there is not necessarily any uniformity or single succession in the holdings. But when manorial management comes upon the top of this widely extended and all but universal system of agriculture, whether in Roman times or later, the bundle of scattered strips which under tribal custom could be ploughed by a pair of oxen whether alone or in joint ploughing is very naturally taken as the typical holding. And thus when we find in the Laws of Ine and later records gafolgeldas and geburs settled upon yardlands and doing service by week-work on the lord's demesne the natural inference must be that it is the result of manorial land management and that there has come into existence already something like a manor with something like a community in serfdom upon it, using the prevalent open-field system as the shell in which it will henceforth live so far as its agriculture is concerned.

And so it seems natural to attribute to the manorial management and the manorial requirement of fixed services and dues the uniformity of the holdings and the single succession by which the uniformity was preserved. The power which seeks and makes uniformity seems to come from above. Agricultural communities of free tribesmen who had become individual freeholders (if such could be conceived of as prevalent in King Ine's and King Alfred's time) would probably have used the open-field system in a quite different way. And we see no trace of it in the evidence.

Later evidence of free holdings may not be to the point.

When, however, we have said this we have no disposition to ignore or make light of the later evidence upon which great stress has quite rightly been laid by Professor Maitland in his remarkable work on 'The Domesday Survey and beyond,' showing that there were in some districts villages, in which the manorial element was apparently absent in the time of Edward the Confessor, though appearing as manors after the Conquest. He has suggested that in these villages not only the manor in name but also the manor as a thing was apparently non-existent. There was in these cases apparently, in King Edward's time, no demesne land upon which the services of a tenantry in villenage could be rendered, and the tenants were often sokemen who had individually put themselves under the protection of this lord or that, instead of there being one lordship over the group, as in a manor.

The Danish wars left many estates vacant, which may have been reconstructed on feudal rather than manorial lines.

These lordless villages on the eve of the Conquest as shown by the entries T. R. E. in the Domesday survey and especially in the 'Inquisitio Eliensis,' merit more careful study than has yet been given to them, and so far as they can be shown to prove the existence of free villages of *liberi homines* or *socmanni*, after the Conquest merged sometimes in the class of *villani*, I am ready to welcome the evidence. But unless they can be traced back to earlier times, their occurrence mostly in the Danish districts interspersed with other villages which were manors and had demesne land, together with the singular fact that the holders in these villages were commended to several lords, suggests that their peculiar position may date from the time of the Danish invasions, and be the result of the devastations as to the effects of which the 'Liber Eliensis' contains so much evidence. Many a manor may have lost both lord and tenants, and have been filled up again by the great lords of the district with new tenants—soldiers and servants who had served in the wars, it may be. Thus these cases, in which many features of the ordinary manor were apparently missing in the time of Edward the Confessor, may be of recent date and so, while important when viewed in relation to the Domesday survey and the changes made by the Conquest, not specially instructive as regards earlier Anglo-Saxon conditions.

The fact regarding the Danelaga still very little known.

Unfortunately, as we have seen, the laws of the Danish period, while recording existing and modified Anglo-Saxon customs on various points, leave us in the dark as to Danish custom, whether of old standing in the Danelaga or newly imported in King Cnut's time. It was, no doubt, known to the invaders, and it was enough for them to say 'as the law stands,' though we do not know what it was. The whole question of the Danelaga was purposely omitted from the scope of my former volume, and now, after twenty years, still remains a subject requiring careful examination by future inquirers.

But this cannot be done completely until the minute work which Professor Maitland and Mr. Round and Mr. Corbett are gradually doing upon the

Domesday survey itself in its local details has been further pursued, and it lies, with so many other branches of a difficult subject, beyond the limits of the inquiry made in this volume.

New feudal tenures may have had a tribal root.

Reference may, however, be incidentally made to the numerous cases in which, in order to describe the nature of the tenure of socmanni and others under what were perhaps new conditions, the fact was recorded in varying phrases whether this person or that could or could not leave or sell his land. Of some it is stated 'possunt recedere,' of others 'non possunt recedere'—of some 'possunt vendere,' of others 'non possunt vendere.' Though these tenures may have been comparatively modern and may belong to a period of advanced feudal conditions, still it may be possible that some trait of tribal custom may lurk at the root of the distinction. From the manorial point of view, it was necessary to record of the socmanni whether they had only limited rights in the land subject to the performance of services and 'consuetudines' (which, by the way, seem to have been very much like those of the villani) or whether they were permanent freeholders who could sell their holdings and leave the land when they liked.[1] The position of the tenants in this respect was probably dependent upon the tenure under which they held, *i.e.* upon whether they were tenants with only life interests, or for successive lives, or, as we should say, tenants in fee. After the devastations of war many new tenants must have been put upon desolated manors, and Professor

[1] See Mr. Round's interesting chapter, 'Sokemen and their Services.' (*Feudal England*, pp. 28–34.)

Maitland has very rightly laid stress in another connection on the traditional habit of granting leases for three lives only, so that a holding might ultimately return to the lord. He has pointed out that when Bishop Oswald (A.D. 962–992), exercising manorial rights over the great domain of the Church of Worcester made these leases to thanes on certain services for three successive lives (*i.e.* for the lives of father, son, and grandson) he did it expressly for the purpose of securing to his successor full power to renew them or not.[1] And from a tribal point of view it may be a pertinent question whether the restriction to the three generations had not some indirect connection with the tribal custom or instinct, so often alluded to, which gave to the fourth generation of uninterrupted occupation fixity of tenure and status.

St. Oswald's tenants for three successive lives.

Recurring to the scattered cases of thanes holding 'in paragio' and by no means confined to the Danish districts,[2] it was necessary to state in the Domesday records, as in the case of the socmanni, whether they had or had not power to leave or to sell, and it may be useful that we should be reminded by these cases, in which feudal custom had possibly arisen out of tribal custom, that tribal custom was not unknown to the Danish and Norman conquerors of England. The Danish immigrants came from a district in which tribal custom was still fresh and vigorous. The Normans too, as is shown by the so-called Laws of Henry I., found Anglo Saxon custom by no means altogether alien to their own instincts.

Tribal custom known to Danes and Normans.

[1] *Domesday Book and beyond*, p. 306 *et seq.*

[2] *Ibid.* pp. 204–209.

Before concluding this essay perhaps a further observation should be made.

We have learned in the course of this inquiry that it does not do to take too insular a view of Anglo-Saxon conditions. The similarity of wergelds, and indeed of tribal custom generally, has throughout become very apparent. But perhaps it is hardly more striking than the similarity in the *modifications* of tribal custom found in the laws on both sides of the Channel.

In their migrations and conquests the conquering tribes found themselves everywhere breathing a moral atmosphere in which it was difficult for the old tribal instincts to live. In such matters as the responsibility of a master for his slave's homicides and of relatives for their kinsman's crimes we have watched as it were modifications of tribal custom in the course of being made, here and there, on almost identical lines. May it not have been so also in regard to the important matter of the division of classes?

Romanising and Christian influences apart from the manor.

If we have recognised rightly the tribal principles originally at the root of the distinction between the twelve-hynde and twy-hynde classes there is no reason why we should not recognise also that besides the potent force of manorial management there may have been other influences at work widening the gulf between the two classes, and, so to speak, reducing to a level the members of each class by breaking away the rungs of the ladder between them.

It must not be overlooked that in the earliest Continental laws most nearly contemporary with those of Kent—Alamannic, Bavarian, Burgundian, and

Wisigothic—the divisions of society have a very artificial look, as though largely based upon wealth rather than the tribal principles of kindred.

Now, German writers are not agreed upon the point whether these artificial divisions found in these earliest of the laws ought to be regarded as belonging to ancient German custom or whether they may not rather be traced to Roman influences.[1]

The earliest laws most influenced by Roman traditions.

We have already seen how necessary it is in connection with these early laws to discriminate between ancient custom and the new influences which were working in them in the direction of individualism and the disintegration of the kindred. The earliest laws are, as we have seen, just those in which tribal custom had fared the worst.

Non-tribal division of classes.

In the Alamannic Pactus of the sixth century (Fragment ii. 36) the grades for wergelds were as under:—

(1) 'baro de minoflidis,'
(2) 'medianus Alamannus,'
(3) 'primus' *or* 'meliorissimus Alamannus.'

And these were subdivisions of the *ingenuus* class, for there were below them the *lidus* and the *servus*. In another clause (iii. s. 25) a similar division is applied to animals. The penalties are given for killing ordinary, 'mediana,' and 'meliorissima jumenta.'

In the Burgundian law the division of society into three grades—*optimates*, *mediocres*, and *inferiores*—

[1] Compare Brunner's chapter 32, 'Adel und Freie,' in his *Deutsche Rechtsgeschichte*, p. 247 *et seq.*, with *Das Römische Recht in den Germanischen Volksstaaten*, von Prof. Dr. Alfred von Halban (Breslau, 1899), pp. 132, 207, 262, 280, and 294. And see Dahn's chapter 'Der Adel,' p. 88 *et seq.*, in his *Die Könige der Germanen*, Band vi. (Leipzig, 1885).

is found in the *Lex Romana* and is applied to Romans and Burgundians alike. These divisions seem to supplant those of kindred, and to have no tribal principle at their root.[1]

In the Wisigothic laws the disintegration of tribal society is so far advanced that the wergelds of the *ingenuus* class are regulated, not by kindred or social position, but, as we have seen, according to the age of the individual.

It is difficult not to connect the substitution of artificial grades for those dependent on kindred with the Roman tendency to divide society into 'patrician' and 'plebs,' and the 'plebs' according to position and wealth into *honestiores* and *humiliores*.

Already in Cæsar's time we see how difficult it was from a Roman point of view to understand the relation under tribal custom of the dependent tribesmen to their chieftain. Cæsar does not seem to have recognised the link of blood-relationship between them. To his view the chieftains were *equites* and the tribesmen almost their *servi*. It was difficult otherwise to bring the two classes within some recognised category of Roman law.

So it was no doubt, in degree, at the later period in the case of the conquering German tribes, when the Romanising forces were mainly in clerical hands.

The influence of the Church also told in favour of the artificial and anti-tribal division of the people into great men and small men. Its tenets of individual responsibility favoured individualism.

---

[1] Compare the tendency to triple divisions in the Kentish Laws: *supra*, p. 465.

The anti-tribal influences of the Church in Southern Europe.

Canon XVI. of the Council of Orleans (A.D. 549) shows that the ecclesiastical mind in Gaul was familiar with the division into classes 'majorum et mediocrium personarum.'

A canon of an earlier Council (A.D. 511) shows how by taking refuge in a church a homicide received protection till composition was arranged, and how thus the question of wergelds was brought within clerical recognition. Once brought within its power the Church was not likely to let it slip from its grasp. And the collections of Formulæ of the Merovingian period show how the clergy joined with the other authorities in arranging the payment of wergelds and the prevention of private vengeance. From these formulæ it would seem that the payment and perhaps the amount of the wergeld had become to some extent a matter of mediation and arrangement through the intervention of 'boni homines' who were sometimes 'sacerdotes.'[1] And when the award was given and the payment made, it was natural that a formal charter of acknowledgment in stay of vengeance on the part of the relations of the slain should be insisted upon. Each set of formulæ contains a form for this purpose. The matter of wergelds had become a subject of Franco-Roman conveyancing.

Evidence of Merovingian formulæ as regards wergelds.

Romanising and clerical influences thus working together in connection with wergelds would naturally tend to exclude from consideration the question of

[1] Marculfe, ii. 18 and 16. *Formulæ Lindenbrogianæ*, 16. And see F. de Coulanges' useful chapter on 'Organisation judiciaire chez les Francs' in *Quelques problèmes d'histoire* (1885).

Clerical influences in England in favour of individualism, evident in the modification of custom found in the Anglo-Saxon laws.

kindred, and to make the payment of the wergeld a matter for the homicide alone.

Long before the time of King Ine these Romanising influences must have been at work in England, as elsewhere, introducing new considerations of justice and the position of classes founded on Roman law and Christian feeling, and not upon tribal custom.

We have recognised some such action as this in the nearly contemporary Canons and in the Kentish laws, as well as in the later Anglo-Saxon laws, and indeed again and again throughout this inquiry, so that while we have had to notice again and again the extent to which the Church succumbed to tribal custom when it suited its purpose to do so, it must not be forgotten how much of the modification of custom found in the laws was due to the influence of the Romanised Church.

It is not, therefore, enough to recognise only Romanised forms of land management under clerical influence. We must recognise also something of the same persistent antagonism of the Church to tribal custom which on the Continent had already in the sixth and seventh centuries sometimes succeeded in extruding considerations of kindred from the matter of wergelds, and to a great extent also from the question of the division of classes.

Last words.

With this further recognition of outside influences, this contribution towards the understanding of a difficult question must come to an end. All that can be claimed on its behalf is that a few further steps in advance may have been made good. It may seem to have resulted rather in the restatement of some of the problems than in their solution. But this is what might be expected from the attempt to approach a subject which has many sides especially with light from the tribal side only. Following the true method of working from the known to the unknown, it is not until such a problem has been approached separately from its different sides that a final solution can be reached; and this involves the fellow work of many historical students.

In the meantime, without ignoring or seeking to minimise the force of other important influences, it may, I think, safely be said that we have found the influence of tribal custom upon Anglo-Saxon polity and economic conditions as apparent, all things considered, as there could be reason to expect.

It was a factor in economic development which, among others and in due proportion, has to be reckoned with, and its study has the special value that it helps to bring the student of the Anglo-Saxon laws to regard them from the point of view of the Anglo-Saxon settlers themselves.

INDEX.

PRINTED BY
SPOTTISWOODE AND CO. LTD., NEW-STREET SQUARE
LONDON

Printed in Dunstable, United Kingdom

91238169R00318